THE NEW EUROPEAN CINEMA

*Film and Culture*

## FILM AND CULTURE

*A SERIES OF COLUMBIA UNIVERSITY PRESS*

*EDITED BY JOHN BELTON*

# THE NEW EUROPEAN CINEMA

## Redrawing the Map

*Rosalind Galt*

*Columbia University Press*
*New York*

Columbia University Press wishes to express its
appreciation for assistance given by the University
of Iowa for the publication of this book.

Columbia University Press
*Publishers Since 1893*
New York   Chichester, West Sussex

Library of Congress Cataloging-in-Publication Data
Galt, Rosalind.
   The new European cinema : redrawing the map /
Rosalind Galt.
      p. cm.—(film and culture)
   Includes bibliographical references and index.
   ISBN 0-231-13716-8 (cloth : alk. paper)
   ISBN 0-231-13717-6 (pbk. : alk. paper)
   ISBN 0-231-51032-2 (electronic)
   1. Motion pictures—Europe.  I. Title.  II. Series.
   PN1993.5.E8G35  2006
   791.43094—dc22

                           2005033601

♾

Columbia University Press books are printed  on
permanent and durable acid-free paper.
Printed in the United States of America
c 10 9 8 7 6 5 4 3 2 1
p 10 9 8 7 6 5 4 3 2 1

Acknowledgment is gratefully made for permission
to reproduce stills from *Underground* to CIBY
DA/PANDORA/1995.

# Contents

# Acknowledgments

Many people have helped shape this book. Mary Ann Doane, Philip Rosen, and John Caughie were invaluable readers during the early stages of the project, while Corey Creekmur and Sasha Waters Freyer offered detailed and insightful commentary on later versions. Nicole Rizzuto read drafts tirelessly and offered both editorial insight and intellectual inspiration. With Karl Schoonover, Kerry Herman, Rebecca Wingfield, Chris Cagle, and Kirsten Ostherr, I debated film theory, feminism, and art history. This project developed in dialogue with their work, and I hope it bears some traces of their brilliance. Friends, teachers, and colleagues who have contributed ideas, criticism, and support include Neil Lazarus, Ellen Rooney, Massimo Riva, Réda Bensmaïa, Loren Noveck, Paul Haacke, Mette Hjort, Angela dalle Vacche, Dudley Andrew, Steve Ungar, Rick Altman, Louis Schwartz, Kathleen Newman, Lisa Collins, Jessica Levin, and Evelyn So. Claudia Pümmer helped with research and formatting, and Anastasia Saverino worked on the index. Chapter 2 benefited greatly from discussions with participants at the 2001 Screen Studies Conference, and chapter 5 from the anonymous readers at *Cinema Journal* who reviewed a shorter form of the argument. Thanks also go to the readers for Columbia University Press, who offered productive suggestions for revision. Last but by no means least, this project has gained tremendously from discussions with my students over the years.

In tracking down film prints, Richard Manning at Brown University was a stellar resource and a gonzo movie god. Also helpful were the staff at the Museum of Modern Art (MoMA) Film Study Center, the New York

Public Library, the Donnell Library, and the British Film Institute. Staff at the University of Iowa's library provided technical and research assistance. Some films proved difficult to locate, and here I received help from Ellen Elias-Bursac, Radmila Gorup, and Vitaly Chernetsky. Misha Nedeljković kindly sent me tapes of some rare Yugoslav films and in addition offered readings, advice, and historical perspective. Thanks also to filmmakers Bettina Ellerkamp and Jörg Heitman, who graciously shared their work with me. Thanks also go to all at Columbia University Press, especially Irene Pavitt, Cynthia Garver, and Juree Sondker.

Parts of chapter 2 were published as "Italy's Landscapes of Loss: Historical Mourning and the Dialectical Image in *Cinema Paradiso, Mediterraneo*, and *Il Postino*," *Screen* 43, no. 2 (2002). Parts of chapter 5 were published as "Back Projection: Visualizing Past and Present Europe in Lars von Trier's *Zentropa*," *Cinema Journal* 45, no. 2 (2005).

Finally, I want to thank those closest to me for their love and support: Adrian Goycoolea, who, in addition to sharing my life, spent countless hours on this project preparing frame stills; my mother, who was my first role model as a feminist and cultural critic; and my late father. My father instilled in me a love of Italian landscape and culture, with which came a foundational narrative of leftist loss. He served in Italy in World War II and returned with our family year after year as a tourist and student of Italian. I could not have formulated my reading of the Italian political landscape without his memory.

THE NEW EUROPEAN CINEMA

# 1 Mapping European Cinema in the 1990s

In the early 1990s, Europe became, as if it had not been so before, a question of space. The fall of the Berlin Wall in 1989, the break-up of the Soviet Union, the break-down of Yugoslavia, and the unification of Germany produced radical upheavals in every aspect of European life, but most urgently, they made a collective demand on an idea of Europe as a psychic, cultural, or geopolitical location. For the first time since the end of World War II, the borders of Europe were disconcertingly unstable. Through the 1990s, this traumatic overturning of spatial categories was augmented with a more gradual, although by no means painless, redefinition: the expansion of the European Union to include members and potential members as far apart as Finland, Bulgaria, and Turkey. It is clear that as the physical and political territory of Europe altered in the post–Cold War years, so, too, did its cultural imaginary. What is less clear is how we can read these changes cinematically: how European cinema represented revisions of European space narratively, formally, and stylistically, and, indeed, how the terrain of "European cinema" itself was acted on by the forces that were reshaping the continent.

## Rethinking Post-Wall Europe

This question of Europe has grown in stature over the years since 1989, in cinema studies no less than in political philosophy. While Jacques Derrida's 1991 essay *The Other Heading* inaugurated an important philosophical discourse on the "new Europe," the British Film Institute's 1990 conference "Screening Europe" had already asserted a comparable inquiry into the new European cinema and where it might be heading. For the conference participants, as for Derrida, the possibility of European identity formed a central, and often troubling, problematic. Filmmaker Chantal Akerman claimed that there is no such thing as a European film, while critic John Caughie described the difficult process of becoming European.[1] Derrida pinpoints the difficult nature of this identity: the half-constructed European subject is caught between the devil of nationalistic dispersion and the deep blue sea of Eurocrat homogenization. Thus, "the injunction seems double and contradictory for whoever is concerned about European cultural identity: if it is necessary to make sure that a centralizing hegemony (the capital) not be reconstituted, it is also necessary, for all that, not to multiply the borders, i.e. the movements and margins. . . . Responsibility seems to consist today in renouncing neither of these two contradictory imperatives."[2] For an ethics of Europe, Derrida argues, this bind demands an impossible duty in which the European subject must respond, simultaneously, to two contradictory laws. European cinema, it seems, experiences a similar structural dilemma: how to become European—as opposed to simply continuing an older model of national cinemas—without degenerating into the filmic correlative of Brussels bureaucracy, the Europudding.

As film historian Mark Betz has noted, this debate obscures at least as much about European cinema as it illuminates. Films made in Europe have frequently been coproduced by two or more countries at least since World War II, and the idea of "pure" national film cultures is a myth.[3] According to this historical revision, "Italian" or "French" art films are always already European, and the anxieties of the cultural moment immediately after the fall of the Berlin Wall (post-Wall) miss the point or, at the very least, beg the question. Betz points to a telling moment in the British Film Institute (BFI) conference, where a question from the audience about coproduction went unanswered by the panelists, who were unable or unwilling to consider European-ness as part of a mode of production. However, although Betz is quite correct that this unanswered question is symptomatic of an inability to think about European identity, the nature of this missed point is also significant—and has consequences both for European film production in the 1990s and, more to my point, for the developing model of its critical response.

For although we cannot directly map a political anxiety about national versus supranational sovereignty onto the film community's unease around international coproduction, we can make out a discursive commonality in both cultural and political mobilizations of "Europe" in the post-Wall years. Once again, Derrida establishes the terms of the debate, when he calls for a Europe that refuses self-identity and engages rigorously with what he terms "the heading of the Other." This ethics of the Other combines the contemporary philosophical elaboration of Emmanuel Levinas with a reading of Europe as a spatial and temporal figure (the "heading"). Clearly, this is a reading of some subtlety, but, given the level of ideological struggle over the terms and conditions of the new Europe, it is perhaps not surprising that public discourse on European identity tended to take up the question in exactly the binary forms of Europe/Other that *The Other Heading* problematizes. Thus, while conservatives made national sovereignty, immigration, and ethnic minorities into social problems, film cultures evolved an opposing liberal concern with regionalism, minority representation, and transnationalism.[4]

I do not want to condemn this shift, either as a series of cinematic practices or as a critical paradigm. The manifold concerns of, say, diasporic Turkish filmmakers, *beur* film, and European film studies cannot be reduced to one ideological imperative, and insofar as we can identify common ground, this is a terrain that has been highly productive, both creatively and theoretically.[5] However, it seems to me that to focus on films that narrate the "Other" of Europe so directly, that articulate an anti-Eurocentric hybridity so transparently, is ultimately a self-exhausting critical endeavor. Derrida asks:

> Is there then a completely new "today" of Europe beyond all the exhausted programs of *Eurocentrism* and *anti-Eurocentrism*, these exhausting and yet unforgettable programs? (We cannot and must not forget them since they do not forget us.) Am I taking advantage of the "we" when I begin saying that, in knowing them now by heart, and to the point of exhaustion—since these unforgettable programs are exhausting and exhausted—we *today* no longer want either Eurocentrism or anti-Eurocentrism?[6]

I, too, would like to take advantage of the "we." If we are to take seriously the post-Wall European subject's impossible responsibility, we cannot stop with a comfortably liberal celebration of the Other. To adapt Paul Gilroy's notion of anti-anti-essentialism, any theoretical revision of European cinema needs to articulate an anti-anti-Eurocentrism.[7]

Such a position has recently been explored outside the field of film studies. Always good for a provocative line, Slavoj Žižek poses the question thus: "When one says Eurocentrism, every self-respecting postmodern leftist intellectual has as violent a reaction as Joseph Goebbels had to culture—to reach for a gun, hurling accusations of protofascist Eurocentric cultural imperialism. However, is it possible to imagine a leftist appropriation of the European political legacy?" Žižek begins to answer his own question (albeit in the form of another question) when, in a different article, he asks, "How are we to reinvent political space in today's conditions of globalization?"[8] What is crucial in this second formulation is that Žižek, like Derrida, stages the question of Europe as simultaneously a matter of space and of time. The time is punctual: Europe is a topic of today. Žižek is no less concerned than Derrida with today's conditions, but he speaks from a different location, quite literally. The European political legacy is conjured here not from Europe's headland, the cape, or capital inhabited by French philosophy but from the rapidly changing space of southeastern Europe: the recently and painfully redrawn map of the Balkans.

Why should we care from where each writer writes? Their locations matter not because their nationalities are intellectually determining but because anti-anti-Eurocentric thought intervenes in the relationship between material and discursive spaces. For Derrida, this means the wide-ranging social effects of the heading: the logic by which Europe imagines itself as a spatial and temporal advance-guard for the world. For Žižek, it demands a rethinking of political space, the space of politics, in the temporally constituted terrain of "the former Yugoslavia." We could point, also, to Etienne Balibar's work on European identity, which analyzes the meaning and constitutive power of borders.[9] Like the heading, the border is a spatial trope that is rhetorical but not merely metaphoric. In centering his discussions of European racism and transnational identity in the figure of the border, Balibar illustrates the theoretical desire to articulate material borders—politically defining spaces—with and through the idea of Europe, its discursive imaginary.

Like this work in political philosophy, I would suggest, film studies needs to form the question of Europe as a matter of space and of time. An anti-anti-Eurocentric consideration of contemporary European cinema must not speak only of coproduction, of European Union funding, and of national heritage; neither must it speak only of the diasporic, the hybrid, and the radical. Rather, it must take on the logic of cartography: a form of writing that articulates both the discursive and the referential spaces of nations (recall that both Borges and Balibar imagine the mapped border as performative, a slippery relationship of image and referent). Cartography encompasses writing and drawing, politics and aesthetics, the political and the physical; it binds spectacle to narrative, graphic space to geopolitical space. And post-Wall European cinema, I will argue, mobilizes exactly this enunciative structure. It maps the spaces of Europe "today," speaking both of and from the changing spaces of the continent. Most important, it does so as a textual work, coarticulating cinematic space and geopolitical space.

The production of cinematic space has been a recurrent area of film theoretical inquiry, where space is always, to some degree, understood in a relationship to time, temporality, or history.[10] The nature of the (temporo-spatial) relationship between profilmic space and cinematic space plays a fundamental role in theories of cinematic specificity. As such, space is a determining element of the cinematic per se. This question has of late returned to theoretical prominence—and not coincidentally. In an article on theorists of cinematic specificity, Thomas Elsaesser—another European theorist who elsewhere has been explicitly concerned with questions of Europe—glosses Siegfried Kracauer thus:

> In the often tortuous dialectic between photography and history which Kracauer was at pains to tease out all through his life, the cinema is given a redefinition which, it seems to me, is neither strictly ontological nor epistemological, and yet allocates it a place in a fundamental development of the Western mind: the systematic translation of the experience of time into spatial categories, as a necessary precondition for an instrumental control over reality, but with its equally necessary corollary, namely a narcissistic or melancholy bind of the subject to that reality as *image*, itself envisaged in the psychologically coherent but ideologically ambivalent form of loss and nostalgia, fragment and fetish.[11]

This is an astonishingly rich passage, reading cinematic space both through Kracauer's ontological insistence on the essential qualities of the cinematic image and, at a slightly greater remove, through his Marxism. By extension, Elsaesser implies, we must conceive the *historicity* of the cinematic image at once in terms of the temporality of the subject and in terms of a dialectical understanding of historical process.

Here, Elsaesser (and, indeed, Kracauer) speaks of history as such, the category of temporality that is overcome, or at least tamed, by its translation into images, into film, into space. But, of course, Elsaesser is also historicizing both Kracauer and this ideological work of cinema in the context of the "real" histories of the twentieth century. The desire for an "instrumental control over reality" leads inevitably to theories of fascism and to the particular uses of geopolitical space, and of the cinematographic image, in twentieth-century Europe. We cannot separate these theoretical discourses on cinematic space and time from the histories and places that have underwritten them; this is no less true for the history of the post-Wall continent than it is for the traumas of mid-century. As the borders of Cold War Europe crumbled, so, too, did dominant narratives of postwar history and, to some extent, the theoretical apparatuses with which history could be thought. It is for this reason, perhaps, that Elsaesser's contemporary rereading of Kracauer seems to resonate so deeply. For in the European cinema of the 1990s, the cinematic image becomes readable precisely as a troubling of space and time. Certain European films, I will demonstrate, textualize this uncomfortable encounter, and they do so exactly as Elsaesser's contemporary reading of the cinematic suggests: through a mobilization of the historical image that is inflected with those fin de siècle themes of "loss and nostalgia, fragment and fetish."

Where, then, does one start in the drawing of maps? It is tempting to essay the bird's-eye view, the imperial sweep of the world map, with which we can locate European cinema in its proper relation to international currents. To be sure, post-Wall cinema can be viewed as a part of postclassical or even postmodern cinema: it must operate in the eddying currents of global film markets, the development of new distribution and exhibition structures, and the festival-fueled circuits of international art cinema. We can chart material relationships among European art cinemas, Hollywood blockbusters, and the East Asian New Waves, or we can draw theoretical connections around the uses of spectacle, genre, or affect in these contemporary forms. For better or worse, we must do these things. "European cinema," as a cultural discourse, cannot signify without reference to at least one Other, and if Hollywood has been the dominating Other throughout most of the history of European film production and criticism, it is now necessary to consider a global dimension.

Many European films circulate in a global art film market, in which European-ness asserts specific (although not constant) levels of both cultural and economic capital. European films code internationally as both "not-American" and, in many markets, "not-Asian," "not-Latin American," and "not-Middle Eastern." In addition to these external references, films—even coproductions—function within an internal European hierarchy, where French, British, and Italian mean quite different things to audiences than do, say, Czech, Swedish, and Portuguese. These encrustations of cultural meaning are by no means new (although the range of foreign films available in many markets is), but they are mutable, and like any other historical period, the postclassical era can be characterized by specific forms. In the 1980s and 1990s, this environment produced new kinds of production (television funding, increased coproduction, mainstream/art house crossover films) and new areas of critical interest (heritage culture, postcolonial and minority representations, transnationality). However, while we must keep in mind these large-scale charts of contemporary world or European cinemas, I am not convinced that we approach the question of cartography best by means of such a map. Rather than chart the shapes of European cinema exhaustively from above, it might be more in the spirit of mapping to trace some of its disputed borders: that is, to consider the debates in and around which an analysis of European films can be located.

## Whither Heritage?

Particularly prevalent in western Europe, the heritage film is a critically and industrially contentious notion that gets to the heart of contemporary discourses on European culture, identity, and film production policy.[12] Like many such critically invented terms, the heritage film is not an easily definable category. In general terms, however, we can say that such films use high production values to fill a mise-en-scène with period detail, representing their national pasts through sumptuous costume, landscape, and adaptations of well-known literary novels. Generally costume dramas (the name is telling) rather than history films per se, and mostly dealing with romanticizable eras such as the nineteenth and early twentieth centuries, these films are most often criticized as nostalgic attempts to whitewash the national past for both reactionaries at home and the more gullible foreign markets. Critical and industrial debates here intersect, for the popularity of the heritage film has led to an emphasis on such projects among west European state funding bodies. By popularizing the historical in terms of nostalgia and mise-en-scène, the heritage film has opened up a space within European film culture, not only for increased American and domestic box office but also for a renewed circulation of national identities.

The heritage film has been widely criticized within Europe. Andrew Higson argues that British heritage films cover over political critique with pleasurable mise-en-scène, while Antoine de Baecque considers that what he terms "official" European cinema has a common polish, a homogenized prettiness that lacks genuine engagement with place. Instead of representing the genuine differences in European cultures, he claims, heritage films smooth out history and image. De Baecque contrasts this negative view of an official European cinema with what he

considers a contemporary countercinema, including films by Emir Kusturica, Lars von Trier, Alain Tanner, Pedro Almodóvar, and Otar Ios-
seliani.[13] Several of the films I will be considering fit neatly into de
Baecque's and Higson's notions of the regressive European film:
*Cinema Paradiso* (Tornatore, 1988), for instance, has been widely viewed
as an Italian iteration of the British nostalgic heritage film. Especially in
the context of international distribution, this type of film is often seen to
lose whatever edge a national narrative might involve and to appear to
foreign audiences as just another pretty European indie.

And yet, it will be apparent that my intervention is not that of de
Baecque, for while he contrasts Kusturica and von Trier as counter-
auteurs to the official discourse of Bernardo Bertolucci and *la belle image*,
I will be examining some very pretty films alongside those of Kusturica
and von Trier. For just as postclassical cinema has blurred the distinction
between art house and mainstream, so it is ultimately untenable to
maintain the mainstream/countercinema binary in the changed terrain
of contemporary European cinema. The nub of this debate is the status
of the spectacular image, which for Higson operates to distract the spectator from any political content in the narrative, and for de Baecque provides too beautiful an image of European history and culture. While this
argument makes sense when films as disparate as *La Vie de Bohème*
(Kaurismäki, 1992) and *Camille Claudel* (Nuytten, 1988) are compared,
these boundaries break down when other examples are considered.
Films like *Chocolat* and *Beau Travail* (Denis, 1988 and 2000) use a lush
mise-en-scène in the context of a complex reconsideration of French
colonial history, while filmmakers like Derek Jarman and Peter Green-

*Camille Claudel*   Camille is framed by monuments of European cultural heritage.

*Chocolat*   Landscape images stage a critique of European colonialism.

away use countercinematic forms to reimagine typical heritage topics like literary adaptation—*Prospero's Books* (Greenaway, 1991)—and artist biopics—*Caravaggio* (Jarman, 1986). Thus, rather than attempting to separate out the good and bad versions of European heritage cinema, I want to exert some pressure on the terms of debate: to take seriously *la belle image* and to pinpoint what kinds of historical and spatial engagements the heritage image enables.

Although Richard Dyer astutely points to the significance of the stately home in British heritage films,[14] the visual center of *la belle image* is landscape. Whether the Tuscan orchards in *A Room with a View* (Ivory, 1985) or the Provençal poppy fields in *Manon des sources* (Berri, 1986), the genre depends on the production of a beautiful landscape, often drawing from European traditions of Romanticism and realism in painting, in which its historical romance narratives can take place. And for Higson, de Baecque, and most other readers of the heritage genre, it is axiomatic that both the melodramatic narratives and these spectacular images preclude any progressive historical engagement. This argument, however, depends on assumptions about both melodramatic form and the cinematic image that are by no means self-evident. The substantial bodies of film theoretical work on melodrama and on the image demand that we use a more nuanced approach to read their intersection with history, nation, and spectacle. If we begin by theorizing the relationships among specific national histories, landscape images, and melodramatic narratives, it might be possible to map the heritage film differently.

The British films that first defined the heritage film tend, like *Cinema Paradiso* and *Manon des sources*, to narrate apparently apolitical histories. We will need to reconsider this commonsense attribution of "political-ness," as this is one of the points on which discourse on heritage proves weak. However, even before we problematize the notion of a political history, it is clear that some heritage films do narrate political stories and use national or landscape images as part of this process. Most obviously, there are the World War II melodramas in which a romantic story inter-sects more or less closely with the history of Nazism. Recent examples include *Aimée and Jaguar* (Färberböck, 1999) from Germany and the Spanish drama *¡Ay, Carmela!* (Saura, 1990), although this trope is not exclusively post-Wall and slightly older examples such as *La Dernier Métro* (Truffaut, 1980) are also common. Tying a melodramatic narrative closely to the idea of national space is a film like *When I Close My Eyes* (Slak, 1993), in which Slovenian history returns to haunt the present in the image of a field where the heroine's father was killed for his political activism. Landscape here is far from beautiful nature, and yet the her-itage structure of national melodrama is similar to that of the west Euro-pean films.

A more troubling example is *Land and Freedom* (Loach, 1995), a film that is usually read in the context of Ken Loach's politically committed oeuvre, and yet uses national landscapes and melodramatic narrative in a way very similar to that of the heritage film. Here, just as in *Cinema Par-adiso*, there is a young male protagonist, a beautiful southern European setting, and a narrative centered on romantic loss, framed by a present-day coda from which point the historical past can be looked back on with a certain nostalgia. In *Land and Freedom*, the historical setting is the Span-ish Civil War, and the hero is a young British man eager to fight for free-dom by joining up with the Spanish Republicans. His letters are found by his granddaughter in the 1980s, at a moment in British history when socialist solidarity was radically undermined. The political overtones of the story are overt, but melodramatic convention demands that political investment be embodied in an object of romantic desire. Thus, the death of the beautiful soldier Blanca prompts emotion, with politics and romance intersecting when the "Internationale" is played at her funeral. What is suggestive about this example is that Loach is rarely considered in terms of melodrama, much less the heritage film, and indeed he is often cited as precisely the opposite. Thinking about *Land and Freedom* in relation to the visual pleasure of the landscape image, and in terms of nostalgia for a lost past, demonstrates the porousness of the heritage/countercinema boundary and the way in which we might begin to think about issues of nostalgia and spectacle as ideologically weighted.

## Framing Popular Memory

The imbrication of history and nostalgia in art cinema predates the heritage film, with the French popular memory debates of the 1970s forming a discursive nexus in which Marxist and poststructuralist theories of historicity intersected with a French cultural reexamination of wartime collaboration and other national histories. Films like *Lacombe Lucien* (Malle, 1974) became controversial for their revisionist—and unheroic—depiction of the French Resistance and the collaboration of the French populace during World War II, and film theorists such as Marc Ferro and Michel Marie were joined by Michel Foucault and by disciplinary historians in debating the ethics and aesthetics of representing the national past.[15] In an interview with Foucault, the editors of *Cahiers du Cinéma* take a firm stand against *la mode rétro* (retro style), claiming that *Lacombe Lucien* and *The Night Porter* (Cavani, 1974) are both cynical and reactionary, fetishizing the décor of the past while ignoring real history. Foucault, for his part, glosses the rhetorical strategy of such films, claiming that a refusal of heroism is not the refusal of rightist nationalism that one might think: "But below the phrase, 'There were no heroes,' is hidden another phrase which is the real message: 'There was no struggle.'"[16] If the new style of historical film was widely read as reactionary on the Left, it was nonetheless viewed as illustrative of an important shift in historical representation: later in the same interview, Foucault asserts that there is a battle being waged over history, with the ownership of "popular memory" as its central contest.[17]

This debate responded to existing trends in west European film culture: as Pierre Sorlin argues, many history films from this period do not represent stable narratives of historical truth but are constructed as inquiries still in progress. He cites Alain Resnais's *Stavisky* (1974), and we could also point to similarly canonical instances from other national cinemas: *Die Patriotin* (Kluge, 1979), say, or *The Conformist* (Bertolucci, 1970). However, the modernist art cinema's formal destabilizing of classical historical narrative remains peripheral to the question of popular memory. *Lacombe Lucien* is structured as a fairly classical history film, and while the French historians' debate touches on formal deconstructions of historical "truth," its real concern is with the radical implications of constituting memory—individual and cultural—as a legitimate category of history writing. In cinematic terms, this impetus is readable less in films that problematize linear narrative and more in films that stage such partial cultural memories as history.

In fact, we can see this structure at work even in the more modernist texts. *The Conformist*, like *Lacombe Lucien*, stages conformity, like collaboration, as a survival strategy for a young male protagonist. In both films, the generation gap between youthful protagonist and middle-aged audience and critics enables the history represented to be read as memory: the recovered traumatic past of the sometimes less-than-heroic wartime generation. In the popular memory debate, it is exactly the status of the subject of memory that is in question. Whose memories are these, and where does facing up to the past shade into recuperating unethical national acts through nostalgic regression? Clearly, this was a central question for French public intellectuals in the 1970s, at the moment when World War II was returning as a pressing cultural question. As Germany and Italy began to look back on the fascist past, so France was able to face the history of Vichy more directly.[18] But the cinematic engagement with popular memory is not bounded by this moment in French national discourse or by attempts to interrogate wartime histories: throughout the 1980s and 1990s, narratives of memory, and particularly childhood memory, became a popular subgenre in European cinemas.

Structuring personal rather than heritage histories, these films narrate a young protagonist coming of age in a historically specific setting, with the story often framed as flashbacks or narrated *as* memory by the same character as an adult looking back at his past. Many of these films use comedy to locate national histories within "universal stories" of family drama and childhood romance: here we can point to *My Life as a Dog* (Hallström, 1985) and *Toto le héros* (Van Dormael, 1991). In others, the comedy involves a more satirical view of national history, and, given the region's histories of both black comedy and political censorship, it is perhaps not surprising that many examples of this use of the childhood comedy trope come from eastern Europe. Thus, both *When Father Was Away on Business* (Kusturica, 1985) and *Tito and Me* (Marković, 1992) poke fun at Communist Yugoslavia, while emphasizing political distance from their critiques by dint of careful location of the story in the historical past. Less ideologically contentious than the French films, these later invocations of popular memory can seem open to the same critiques as the heritage film: the problem becomes not a self-absolving version of history but yet another avoidance of the political, this time through the self-involved world of childhood.

But if the political clarity of the *Cahiers* debate was obscured in the various iterations of national popular memories, it became a defining strand of British cultural criticism from the 1970s through to the 1990s. British writers recast the question of memory in terms of class and identity, while interrogating the relationship between realism and the historical image as a matter of representational ethics. Television provided the first object of critical attention, with Ken Loach and Tony Garnett's series *Days of Hope* (1975) becoming an ongoing subject of scholarly contention in the pages of *Screen*.[19] The series looked back on British labor history, depicting a working-class family's experiences from World War I to the General Strike of 1926. While the complaints of viewers about inaccurate costuming details were cited in *Screen* as misunderstandings of the ideological valences of social realism, such public investment also demonstrates the ethical and emotional stake, for the national audience, in popular memories. The question of who remembers connects these texts to the French ones, where the claim to speak for working-class subjects produced a debate on the implications for realism of any such staging of remembered experience.

The issues of nostalgia and spectacle were added to those of class representation when, over a decade later, Caughie and others debated the ideological implications of Terence Davies's films *Distant Voices, Still*

*Distant Voices, Still Lives*   Popular memory is staged in family tableaux. (Courtesy British Film Institute)

*Lives* (1988) and *The Long Day Closes* (1992).[20] In these films, Davies frames his 1940s and 1950s families in a series of tableau-like shots, aping the look of slightly stiff family snapshots, but also foregrounding an excessive, not quite realist mise-en-scène. History here resides in the details of clothing and cosmetics, the faded colors of old floral dresses, and the romantic popular songs sung with gusto by the women and viewed with melancholy irony by the present-day spectator. Like the films of the Merchant Ivory team, and even Martin Scorsese's *The Age of Innocence* (1993), Davies's emphasis on the material details of the historical mise-en-scène is criticized by Caughie and others as fetishistic.[21] However, the films' emphasis on working-class families, and particularly on the lives of working-class women, enables a countering argument in which the detritus of popular memory, and its tendencies toward nostalgia and melancholy, is precisely the point.

Davies, like his contemporary Derek Jarman, is readable in terms of queer authorship: both directors are/were openly gay, and while Jarman's films are often more radical in textualizing queer subjectivity, Davies mobilizes a subtler tessellation of autobiography, memory, and a politics of representation. The protagonist of *Distant Voices* is nowhere coded as gay, although extratextual discourses situate the film as partly autobiographical. More to the point, the fetishistic rendering of the historical mise-en-scène locates the film's enunciation in the feminine spaces of memory-work, where the women of the family—and the protagonist who looks back—stitch together identity out of the harsh stuff of life. Reading the image this way, we can see the excessive elements of mise-en-scène as projecting a fantasmatic space for the gay (or female) subject in an oppressively macho historical scene. Nostalgia here, like Jarman's entirely nonrealist queer histories, is inevitably overwritten with pain, refusing the contemporary discourse of an apolitical and frictionless nostalgia, in favor of a difficult return that is closer to the term's original meaning.[22] Thus, in *Distant Voices* the nostalgic appeal of the women's camaraderie is offset by the men's casual brutality and emotional impotence. The family tableaux, which structure nostalgic memory in their faded colors and in their "old photograph" compositions, demand a doubled reading. On the one hand, the scenes are affective, staging the past through melancholic loss. On the other hand, the fragile nature of this nostalgia—the fact that it can exist only through the feminized labor of old snapshots and remembered songs—reminds us simultaneously that the "real history" is one of violence and poverty. The psychic urge to mourn that which we are glad to lose underwrites the apparently simple nostalgia of the image.

## Contesting Spectacle

There is a recurring element in all these debates, an element that can best be defined as the status of cinematic spectacle. As we have seen, both the heritage film and more art-cinematic examples like the films of Terence Davies have been criticized for employing the beautiful image at the expense of genuine engagement with the past. This suspicion of the spectacular image is not limited to the history film but is perhaps concentrated there, since in the historical film issues of realism and representation are most visibly at stake. This connection between ethics and aesthetics fueled the debate around Holocaust dramas that in the United States focused on the somewhat visually pretty *Schindler's List* (Spielberg, 1993) and in Europe resurfaced around the highly unrealistic *Life Is Beautiful* (Benigni, 1997).[23] While some critics felt that Steven Spielberg's black-and-white cinematography and Roberto Benigni's stylized concentration camp debased the Shoah, others argued that realism was an impossible and undesirable goal in representing such unthinkable events. Even without such emotive topics, though, the 1980s and 1990s have been characterized by a critical opposition to visual excess that maps both a theoretical refusal of "postmodern style" and a specifically European backlash against the glossy, expensive Hollywood blockbuster with which local film cultures can never realistically compete.

Michel Chion crystallizes the European critique of postmodern spectacle in a historical taxonomy of the image that moves from the gaudy to the anti-gaudy and, finally, the neo-gaudy. Using the French *cinéma du look* as his prime culprit, he argues that whereas early color film emphasized color because of its novelty and a perception that it more closely depicted reality, and whereas classical film toned down color to heighten realism and to spare its use for occasional dramatic effect, postclassical neo-gaudy film returns to bright colors, now used indiscriminately and reflexively, without depth or realism.[24] As the example of *cinéma du look* suggests, European films of the 1980s and 1990s did engage with visually rich styles, using mise-en-scène and cinematography in ways that were self-reflexive, mannered, or at the very least striking. We can trace this impetus in visually dense films such as *Delicatessen* (Jeunet and Caro, 1991), which uses a comic-book aesthetic to create a fantastic diegesis; in the bright colors and excessive scenarios of Almodóvar's films, such as *What Have I Done to Deserve This?* (1984); and again in the narrative abstraction and digital manipulation of the image in *The Pillow Book* (Greenaway, 1996). However, it is clear from these examples that there can be no simple attribution of mainstream versus countercine-

*What Have I Done to Deserve This?*    Neo-gaudy images are filled with excessive color and detail.

matic or, indeed, of classical depth versus postclassical surface. *Delicatessen* apes the faded color palette of 1940s nostalgia, repositioned in a fantastic future in which Paris is populated by cannibals and underground-dwelling vegetarian guerrillas. Pedro Almodóvar multiplies locations of excess in the service of queer explorations of gender and Spanish national identity. And Peter Greenaway patiently deconstructs the sacred cows of British bourgeois culture, with a proliferation of significatory systems that defies any notion of the spectacular image as empty. We could even attribute a neo-gaudy style to Jean-Luc Godard's films of the period, such as *Passion* (1982), or to Krzysztof Kieślowski's *Three Colors* series (*Blue*, 1993; *White* and *Red*, 1994). Neo-gaudy spectacle is widely visible, but it is neither politically nor aesthetically unitary.

At the same time, there is a countervailing refusal of exactly these trends. Of course, European cinemas have always been largely low-budget and hence have a practical investment in what we might call an aesthetics of almost-poverty. Nonetheless, countering spectacle is not simply a matter of gritty realism: with Dogme '95, anti-spectacular cinema became arguably the most influential European film movement of the 1990s.[25] The signatories of the Dogme Vow of Chastity promised not to use special effects, to periodize, or to make genre pictures but only to shoot on location with available props and natural lighting. The manifesto states: "Today a technological storm is raging of which the result is the elevation of cosmetics to God. By using new technology anyone at any time can wash the last grains of truth away in the deadly embrace of sensation. The illusions are everything the movie can hide behind."[26] Although not entirely serious, and not entirely hewed to by its members, this manifesto demonstrates both the centrality of spectacle in any efforts to rethink European cinema and the way in which historicity has become closely connected to spectacle, even—or perhaps especially—for those who seek to oppose them both. For the members of Dogme, historicity is as much a problem for realism as spectacle, a position that makes no sense in relation to, say, classical Hollywood history films but, rather, is logical only in response to the spectacular histories of the European heritage film. While the grainy digital video (DV) of Thomas Vinterberg's *Festen* (1998) produces its own visual beauty, its low-light and low-life immediacy clearly stands in a dialogic, if antagonistic, relationship with the aesthetics of *la belle image*.

While this cinematic and critical debate around the status of the image is grounded in European histories of representation, neither the broad critique of the spectacular image nor the notion of a return to the spectacular is limited to Europe. The question of spectacle as a style was discussed explicitly in the 1980s as part of the largely American debate on postmodernity, while a more film-historical approach has dominated recent discussions of postclassical cinema. I will return periodically to some of the conflicts arising from the postmodern debates, but for now it is sufficient to note that the Jamesonian critique of the spectacular image as empty, superficial, and affectless has been widely criticized and yet even more widely assimilated into mainstream critical discourse on the cinematic image, including that in Europe. In terms of film history, the notion of the postclassical is also originally American but has taken on a global range. What Miriam Hansen has characterized as a new cinema of attractions is evidenced in Hollywood special effects blockbusters but also, more relevantly for this project, in the visually arresting mise-en-scènes of the 1990s Asian New Waves.[27] Can we draw a map of European cinema that runs through Hong Kong?

The colonial relationship has long been articulated in European cinemas (especially those among the United Kingdom, France, India, and Africa), with colonized space functioning as exotic backdrop for Western romance, adventure, and psychodrama. Spectacle, in these texts, is not empty but produces meaning in a system of visual and narrative power that is both gendered and raced.[28] As Homi Bhabha suggests, however, even in these colonial narratives we can trace the structure of liminality: a staging of cultural difference that foregrounds borders, fissures, and hybrid spaces.[29] The radicality of this cultural difference must be opposed to any ideologically bland notion of cultural diversity or plurality, and in this territorial and temporal instability, the writing of post-colonial identities can take place. To be sure, we can link Hong Kong cinema to Britain through their opposing perspectives on the colonial relationship, but such a move would no doubt prove problematic. We cannot once again annex Hong Kong for Europe. More productive is to reread Western theories of postclassical spectacle (the postmodern, the cinema of attractions) through the spaces and images—what Bhabha calls, in another context, the "territorial paranoia"—of colonial space.

In the same moment as post-Wall cinema, Hong Kong culture was also experiencing a uniquely punctual relationship to space and history. Ackbar Abbas claims that Hong Kong cinema in the years leading to the 1997 handover to China visually condenses the territory's anxieties about its own disappearance. Reading not only film but also architecture and fiction, Abbas argues that Hong Kong is characterized by a "space of disappearance."[30] He claims that since Hong Kong is almost without history, and its colonial past was about to be erased, history is to be found fleetingly, in spatial relationships and missed encounters. This situation was the exact opposite of that in Europe of the 1990s, where spectacle and historical representation were easily conflated. How, then, does postclassical spectacle intersect with (colonial) histories or aesthetics with ideology?

One film that seems to address these questions is Wong Kar-wai's *In the Mood for Love* (2000), in which the vanished Hong Kong of the early

*In the Mood for Love*    The grass-covered hole is a material signifier of loss.

1960s is captured just at its final moment.[31] The film uses aesthetically beautiful images, slow motion, excessive mise-en-scène, costumes, and lighting to construct a spectacular and nonrealist past that nonetheless stages the painful disappearance of a material place and time. The narrative is structured around romantic loss, where an ambiguous relationship develops between a man and a woman whose respective spouses are having an affair, and the ending cements this melodramatic trope of what might have been. The hero travels to Angkor Wat and whispers his secrets (presumably his pain at never having spoken his love) into a small hole in the wall of the temple. He covers it with mud, to hold in the secret, in a narrative twist that follows the "too late" structure by which Franco Moretti has characterized the affective moment in melodrama.[32] Finally he speaks, after a whole narrative in which the lovers cannot take that risk. But his speech is not heard. There is a close-up of the hole, after he has left, and the image of the blades of bright green grass, still attached to the bit of earth he has stuck in the hole, brings together spectacular and narrative affect in a moment of pure loss. The temporal and spatial specificity of these blades of grass—in the wrong country, and years after the affair—bears the weight not just of this romantic loss but the loss of the Hong Kong of the 1960s and the politics of disappearance in the 1990s.

Abbas does not talk about *In the Mood for Love*, whose release postdates that of his book by several years, but Wong's film enables us to connect the "space of disappearance" to the postclassical structuring of the spectacular image. For Bhabha, such crises in national representation provide spaces of productive instability: using the Derridean supplement to describe the space in which "the nation's totality is confronted with, and crossed by, a supplementary movement of writing," he argues that "it is in this supplementary space of doubling—not plurality—where the image is presence and proxy, where the sign supplements and empties nature, that the disjunctive times of Fanon and Kristeva can be turned into the discourses of emergent cultural identities, within a nonpluralistic politics of difference."[33] *In the Mood for Love* suggests that we can also read this supplementary doubling cinematically. Where the spectacular image is both presence and proxy, both a signifier of and a replacement for the disappearing colonial territory, then we may be able to read spectacle also in terms of temporal disjuncture and emergent cultural identities. And this, as it turns out, it also a necessary move for Europe. Bhabha insists, following Frantz Fanon, that a postcolonial reading of textual strategies not only forms an Other space from which to read anticolonial work but also demands a reconceptualization of Western theories and of European spaces. He trenchantly asks: "Does the language of culture's 'occult instability' have a relevance outside the situation of anti-colonial struggle? Does the incommensurable act of living—so often dismissed as ethical or empirical—have its own ambivalent narrative, its own history of theory? Can it change the way we identify the symbolic structure of the Western nation?"[34] Repositioning postclassical spectacle through contemporary Hong Kong film suggests that the cinematic destabilizing of colonial space may also destabilize European theories of political space, history, and the spectacular image.

## Historical Loss

Several of the films I have discussed—including *In the Mood for Love*; *Distant Voices, Still Lives*; and *Land and Freedom*—share another discursive pattern: a narrative of loss forms their primary mode of engagement with the historical past. As Elsaesser argues, loss and nostalgia can be considered constitutive of cinematic temporality, but the *longue durée* of modern subjectivity is nonetheless subject to locally specific articulations. For Hong Kong, the disappearance of colonial identity and the return to China provoke anxiety, while in Europe in the 1990s, we find other sorts of disappearance, other ghostly returns. For historian Mark Mazower, late-twentieth-century Europe is characterized by a "sense of fin de siècle disorientation," a problem that "reflects the specific historical experience of Europe this century, and the carnage that followed its once-fervent faith in utopias."[35] This formulation implies a European subjectivity confused by history, disenchanted—a Europe at a loss perhaps, but far from suffering from nostalgia for carnage. Mazower is correct in his assessment—it is apparent that we must situate the post-Wall continent in relation to the violent histories of Nazism and Communism—and yet there is an experience of loss to be found within this process of disenchantment.

We can locate the emergence of this discourse of loss first in the immediate crisis that the fall of the Wall prompted for the European Left, in which the triumphalism of the West German Right in 1989 (and the rightist Christian Democratic Party's victory in the East in 1990) seemed to presage an inevitable obsolescence of European socialism. In Germany, the reunification debate produced a broad range of opinion, from the East German dissident socialists' desire to create democratic socialism in a reimagined German Democratic Republic (GDR) to the conservative—and ultimately victorious—view that the GDR should be assimilated into the Federal Republic of Germany (FRG) with as little ceremony as possible. From many leftist writers, though, came the fear, articulated by Peter Schneider, that the Right was right after all.[36] Celebrations of the democratic revolution entailed a trickier positioning for those who did not want to subscribe either to a telos of capitalist triumph or to straight-forward apologism. The problems of the German intellectuals and leftist politicians (East and West) quickly became the problems of progressive European discourse in general. Žižek's question—"Is it possible to imag-ine a leftist appropriation of the European political legacy?"—defines the dilemma of the European Left not simply as a matter of politics but fun-damentally as a question of how to read history.

As European identities were thrown into flux in 1989, it became pressing to consider the histories that had led to this point. In precisely this moment it became possible, and indeed imperative, for European cultures to look back at the history of the postwar system and for the Left to stage that look in terms of loss. The history at stake in this narrative of loss and disenchantment, I will argue, centers on the immediate post-war years in Europe, from 1945 to 1948. Whereas the art cinema of the 1960s and 1970s began to reexamine the war years (most significantly in Germany, Italy, and France) in the wake of 1989, the period immedi-ately following the war came under reconsideration. The political crisis caused by the sudden reintegration of East and West was also a moment of potential for change: to reimagine both national and supranational identities. And the desire to move on from the Cold War era and to imag-ine the end of this historical period was played out cinematically in a need to rethink the history of its beginnings.

For the Left, the question of 1945 to 1948 was: What went wrong? This question is formed differently across the continent, for things went wrong in a multitude of ways. The most significant difference, of course, is that of Western and Eastern Europe, in which the West experienced a rapid return to a conservative hegemony, while the East wrestled with supposed socialist states that rapidly repressed their populations and marginalized those who fought for democratic socialism. And while these two sets of dissidence frequently seemed to have little to say to each other, the situation in Germany in 1989 proved their positions closer than one might have thought during the years of partition. In the brief period of optimism before and after the fall of the Berlin Wall, socialists on both sides imagined the "Third Way," which would take the best from both systems. The rapidity with which this vision collapsed under the weight of East German desire for freedom and West German economic pressure found both Lefts together again, once more plucking defeat from the jaws of victory.

Thus, for history films in the early 1990s what is important is not so much the reconsideration of a historical moment in and for itself but the implications of that history for the present. While New German Cinema forced a public acknowledgement of Nazism that was, one could argue, long overdue, the films I will be analyzing are more concerned with the relationship *between* 1945 and 1989. In Italy, for example, 1945 was a moment of optimism, in which a leftist coalition was on the point of creating a new Italian republic. Then, in the 1990s, the collapse of the First Republic demanded a reevaluation of its inception. For the former Communist countries, 1945 was, of course, the moment before the institution of the Soviet bloc and, correspondingly, the last point at which a discourse of European-ness was possible. This is why Žižek wants to rehabilitate some version of Eurocentrism for the new Europe, insofar as this notion of continental identity is exactly what had not been possible for the fifty years of partition. For the cinema of the early 1990s, it therefore becomes crucial to assert a new set of relationships to the national and European past. Not all these films should necessarily be thought of as leftist texts per se, but all are engaged with these ideological shifts, their implications for various European spaces, and the question of how this present can be related to the postwar past.

The chapters that follow do not attempt an overview of contemporary historical films; rather, they consist of a series of detailed case studies, focusing on one film or a group of related films in a particular country. There are various reasons for this approach: first, far too many films were made across Europe in the 1990s for any kind of overview to make critical sense; second, since this project is not analyzing a preexisting genre or national cinema, the idea of a coherent and numerically significant body of related texts is less central than a concern for the specific work of each film; third, and perhaps most important, the arguments that I will be making require a depth and breadth of textual analysis that can occur only in the context of such lengthy case studies. Both methodologically and theoretically, I will be making a claim for the place of textual analysis in film theory and history. In order to discuss adequately the complex interrelations of history, loss, and the cinematic image, close attention must be paid to textual elaborations of space, time, and spectacle. Only by analyzing formal discourses of mise-en-scène, editing, and narrative structure can we tease out the stakes of an anti-anti-Eurocentric textuality.

The films do share certain crucial elements, however. All were made in the late 1980s to the mid-1990s, and all narrate European histories in or from the mid-1940s. History films of a sort, these texts nonetheless circulated not as generically historical but more as art cinema. Most obviously, what these films have in common is their doubled historical locations, for all were made around 1989, and all tell stories about the end of World War II and the beginning of the divided Europe. And, although formally diverse, these films share a mode of textualizing these histories by elaborating connections between cinematic and geopolitical spaces and between past and present temporalities. This process of textualization is central to our discussion, for the status of the film text is not merely that of historical or theoretical example. My aim is to coarticulate film theory with history, and in doing this the role of textual analysis is of central importance. In these contemporary European films, the staging of history and space is enabled by particular mobilizations of the cinematic image, most readily summed up in the (nonetheless ambiguous) idea of spectacle.

The point of bringing together these films is not so much to outline a new genre as to tease out a moment, a way in which film intervenes in the production of historical and political meaning. The histories at stake are primarily political, but, like Elsaesser, I am just as interested in film histories or, rather, the histories of cinema. The historical moments in which the films were made, and those represented textually, correspond to worldwide shifts in modes of production, as well as to changes in various European cinematic forms. Thus, any investigation of the textual staging of history has to take into account both the history of Europe and the cinematic history within which the films are made. These, however, are not so separate and cannot be neatly categorized as antinomies of text and context. Rather, the film histories of both the postwar moment in which the films are set and the post–Cold War moment of their production become a part of the films' elaboration of historical space.

Chapter 2 considers a group of Italian films that were made in the years immediately before and after the dramatic fall of the Italian First Republic in 1991. Fitting relatively smoothly into the category of heritage film, *Cinema Paradiso, Mediterraneo* (Salvatores, 1991), and *Il Postino* (Radford, 1994) form a series: all romantic melodramas, all focusing on the lives of young men, and all narrativizing the years immediately after World War II in Italy. These films would appear to fit into the notion of *la belle image*, centered as they are on beautiful landscapes within which their historical romances take place. However, I argue that both the national image and the melodramatic narratives of these films subtend a politically potent engagement with a specific national history. This chapter examines the uses of the beautiful landscape image in relation to theories of mourning, melodrama, and historical loss. It also considers questions that will prove recurrent around the heritage film, nostalgia, and indexicality; it reads the spectacular image through theories of cinematic specificity but also through Walter Benjamin's concept of the dialectical image.

Chapter 3 begins to shift the critical terrain to that of the continent as a whole, considering the effects of 1989 on political and cultural definitions of Europe. It discusses the cartography of the new Europe, examining how films from several countries produce cinematic maps. Beginning with an analysis of how visual theories have taken up a discourse of cartography, this chapter explores filmic tropes of geopolitical space from the city and the nation to more difficult in-between spaces such as the border. In parts of Europe like the Balkans and Germany, the space engendered is not beautiful but complex, limited, or impossible. In addition, this chapter moves from heritage films to art cinema (by no means a clear generic leap) and outlines the contemporaneous debates around post-Wall art film.

Chapter 4 analyzes *Underground* (Kusturica, 1995), locating this controversial film within theoretical debates on Balkanism, in which Western representations of the Balkans are situated within an epistemological structure similar to that of Edward Said's notion of Orientalism. Kusturica has frequently been attacked for presenting stereotypical images of Serbian, Croatian, and Bosnian characters, but this analysis focuses less on ethnic "images of" criticism and more on questions of enunciation and address. It asks: Can a Balkan film speak? and How can we read the iteration of Balkanist tropes in a Balkan film? While Yugoslav and post-Yugoslav film is usually read within a straightforward, if highly charged, ideological discourse, this chapter articulates national space with a textual logic of melancholia and with a film history of Yugoslav neorealism. The question of representing the 1940s, I suggest, is also thinkable in terms of cinematic histories of the nation. In this chapter, the spaces under consideration are not the beautiful landscapes of the Italian films but the mise-en-scène of the cellar and the impossible space of Europe, as seen from the abjected and denationalized space of Yugoslavia.

Chapter 5 focuses on *Zentropa* (von Trier, 1991), a film that addresses postwar German space, looking back to the zoned postwar Germany, but that also demands an international perspective in extratextual terms. *Zentropa* is not simply a coproduction but a coproduction that narrates a history of another country. While Germany is one of the film's coproduction partners, the film is also French, Danish, and Swedish and is most often considered in relation to its Danish director. Moreover, *Zentropa* reflexively repeats a history of international representation on the German ruins: this chapter situates *Zentropa* in terms of the history of the *Trümmerfilm* (ruin film), as well as in the context of German and international cinema's response to Germany's place in the postwar European order. *Zentropa* is an unusual text—a film about nation that is almost impossible to categorize in national terms. Eschewing conventional discourses of national cinema, my analysis interrogates the film's construction of cinematic space through a generic history of monstrosity, femininity, and dark European spaces, articulating its referentiality through questions of film noir, horror, and the feminine, European monster. It also relates this cultural history of German/European monstrosity to the film's formal technique of back projection, considering how projection becomes a mode of articulating—and disarticulating—political spaces.

In each of these case studies, cinematic form provides the basis for an analysis that seeks to think both historically and theoretically about the staging of history and demands that the relationship between spectacle and ideology in contemporary cinema be closely examined. If we are to attend to the subtle vocalities of post-Wall European cultures, to read outside overtly political narrative interventions or supranational film policy, it becomes necessary to reestablish the centrality of the film text. This is not a formalist position—quite the opposite. Rather, if European cinema studies is to move beyond a bland historicality, close attention to textual work is the best way to reconcile the demands of poststructural theory and film history. If an anti-anti-Eurocentrist cinema is possible, we must map its borders, its contradictions, and its appearances in the European film text.

# 2  The Dialectic of Landscape in Italian Popular Melodrama

In his book on landscape painting, *Political Landscape*, Martin Warnke briefly discusses the derivation of his title, a term that he assumed had a long history.[1] Instead, he discovered that the phrase was coined only in 1849, and then in relation to a landscape painting that quite literally described a political, rather than a pastoral, landscape. Its first use as a description of the terrain of a national politics was by Joseph Goebbels, who criticized a film for not being fascist enough for the German political landscape. This discovery alarms Warnke, and he rapidly returns to the painting, using this earlier and safer version to justify his book's title. But these two origins are more suggestive of the relationship between politics and visual representations of landscape than Warnke's brief discussion would imply.

There is, first of all, an unremarked connection between these deployments of the term: in each case, what is being discussed is not any actual political situation but a visual text—first a painting and then a film. Landscape, after all, is a visual concept. But there is equally a difference in their deployments insofar as there is a switch in the levels of metaphor between the two uses of the phrase. In 1849 the landscape has a material existence, and politics is the metaphor employed to explain the image; by the 1940s real politics are at stake, and landscape is the metaphor evoked to explain them. This latter meaning has become the dominant one: has become, perhaps, a figurative cliché by which politics as a field is conjured rhetorically. It is telling, therefore, that Warnke would be determined simultaneously to retain his title and to disavow its more substantive origin. It is understandable, of course, to want to avoid using a Nazi turn of phrase, but the origin of the term in Nazi Germany, and its close connection to images, underwrites a nexus of meanings around landscapes, representation, and politics that is both potent in postwar European culture and inevitably tinged with suspicion.

The spatializing rhetoric of the "political landscape" condenses what Walter Benjamin called the aestheticization of politics in fascism[2] at the same time as it hints at landscape as nationally charged space, with all the overtones that the materiality of European land implied during World War II. And yet despite, or perhaps because of, this rhetoric, landscape has figured frequently in postwar visual culture in Europe, especially in cinema, and often with a quite different political valence. We could point to Italian neorealism as a key countering discourse, where images of landscape such as those in Roberto Rossellini's *Paisà* (1946) are deployed precisely as an anti-fascist strategy, making a claim for landscape's contribution to a progressive politics, resignifying European space. By the 1990s, however, the perceived spectacularization of politics in the mass media formed part of a renewed anxiety around the politics of the spectacular image, an anxiety manifested in relation to cinema with the Marxist critique of a postmodern culture of surface and image. Because landscape images form an important part of contemporary European cinema's emphasis on mise-en-scène and visual pleasure, they have become central to this critique (think of the critical response to the widescreen vistas of *The English Patient* [Minghella, 1996]).[3]

In the context of post-Wall European cinema, however, when the physical space of Europe was once again politically central, it becomes crucial to interrogate the geographical, historical, and ideological stakes of any claim to visualize national landscapes. These images tap into a powerful nexus of ideas about European identities and cannot simply be dismissed as postmodern eye candy. In fact, I would suggest that landscape images in film are uniquely able to investigate this relationship of politics, representation, and history because landscape as a mode of spectacle provokes questions of national identity, the material space of the profilmic, and the historicity of the image. By examining a group of Italian films that narrativize postwar national histories in the context of spectacular and visually pleasurable locations, I want to think about the specificity of landscape images in cinematic terms: to read mise-en-scène as an ideological articulation of space and as a political landscape that invokes a particularly European formulation of history.

## Italian Heritage

*Cinema Paradiso, Mediterraneo,* and *Il Postino* appear to be readily categorizable as a group of related films, a strand within a historically specific cinematic practice. All three are set from near the end of World War II to the early 1950s; or, rather, they are principally set at this time, for all three also have a narrative coda at a later date, usually in the present. All three have as protagonists young Italian men or boys growing to manhood in the postwar Italian context, and all are structured by a melodramatic romance narrative. *Cinema Paradiso* tells the story of Totò, from his movie-obsessed childhood in Sicily, through a doomed first love affair, to a present-day career as a film director in Rome. In the lengthy first section of the film, Totò forms a bond with Alfredo, the projectionist at his local cinema, and the film's melodrama deals with both this friendship and his romantic relationship with Elena. Similarly, *Il Postino* narrates hero Mario's relationship with the poet Pablo Neruda, as well as his romance with Beatrice. Mario is the postman who brings Neruda's mail during his exile in Italy, and the poet teaches Mario lessons in political awareness as well as in seduction. *Mediterraneo* takes place on a Greek island, where a group of Italian soldiers spend the war largely untouched by battle. The protagonist, Farina, falls in love with local prostitute Vassilissa and decides to stay in Greece when the war is over. Farina's captain, like Pablo Neruda and Totò, ends the movie looking back on the postwar years from the present day.

In addition to these narrative similarities, all three films became immensely successful in the global market, most strikingly in the United States, where all were nominated for Oscars and were in the 1990s in the top ten foreign-language films in terms of box office grosses. In addition, all three films did well in Italy itself (although *Cinema Paradiso* was not popular immediately) and can be seen as key texts in an early 1990s renaissance in domestic film consumption that was in part jump-started by *Cinema Paradiso*'s success at the Cannes Film Festival (where the film won the Special Grand Jury Prize) and in the United States (where it won the Academy Award for Best Foreign Language Film). And in the context of contemporary European film production, all three can be typed as heritage cinema, a genre characterized in part by elements of melodrama, historical narrative, and international distribution alongside a mise-en-scène of national nostalgia.[4] As such, these films form a useful case study for looking at the workings of the heritage film in terms of its historicity and spectacle. However, the films are also fine examples of the problems inherent in using the "heritage"

tag, for the heritage film is very much a generic mix—a complex amal-
gam of various genres, forms, and industrial factors. The apparent obviousness of the European heritage film, to both popular critics and aca-
demics, has prevented the kind of close analysis of individual films that
is necessary for a more nuanced theorization of the category. The vague-
ness of the heritage category certainly produces as many problems as it
solves for placing these Italian films.

Andrew Higson describes the genre as a middle-class product,
"somewhere between the art house and the mainstream,"[5] and thus far
at least, his definition is applicable. Indeed, this formulation points to
the historical specificity of such films, coming as they do at the moment
in which such a blurring of the boundary between art cinema and mainstream cinema is not only possible but, for the beleaguered European
film industries, economically necessary. European coproductions, and
the rise of television funding for feature films in the 1980s through
channels like Channel 4 in the United Kingdom, France Télévision 1
(TF1) in France, and Zweiten Deutschen Fernsehen (ZDF) in Germany,
helped sustain a more commercial European mode of film production
and exhibition, but they did so in a way that produced a redefinition of
"art house" or art cinema, a shift toward films that could remain con-
ceptually distinct from American higher-budget genre films but would
have the potential for a wider distribution than an earlier form of modernist European art film. *Cinema Paradiso* and its successors fit into this
rubric exactly, certainly in terms of their structures of production, distribution, and exhibition. *Cinema Paradiso* was coproduced by, among
others, Radiotelevisione Italiana (RAI), the Italian state television network, and the production arm of the French channel TF1, while *Il
Postino* was produced by a combination of Italian film production companies and Le Studio Canal Plus in France. To categorize the films
through this mode of production is useful to the extent that many foreign films are circulated predominantly through this kind of branding
process. All three films were released in the United States by Miramax
and, at least in the United States, are recognizable as what has become
known popularly as a "Miramax" kind of film: culturally respectable,
while not overly demanding; more widely distributed than is common
for foreign films; and often nominated for major awards.

While there may be significant overlap between the kinds of film production enabled by the new European coproduction bodies and what
Higson means by heritage film, they are not quite coterminous. Higson
describes heritage films as "quality costume drama,"[6] a definition that
makes perfect sense in regard to his examples of Merchant Ivory films

set in Edwardian England or colonial India but sits uneasily with Italian films set in 1945 or later. Can a film set after World War II really count as a costume drama? This question perhaps shows up the uncomfortable fit between these Italian films and the heritage category, but it reveals further the difficulty of fitting this kind of historical film into any single genre. They feature narratives set in the past but are certainly not history films in the usual sense of relating historically significant stories of famous events or personalities. And while they have melodramatic elements, they are set rather too recently to include many of the pleasures that Sue Harper talks about with reference to costume drama and its historical mise-en-scène.[7] They could be placed as period dramas, perhaps, although while this category is too vague to exclude any film with a historical setting, it connotes a more distant, more exotic, period of representation. Nor are they films in any other established genre that allows for narratives set in the past—they are not, for example, historically located gangster films such as *Miller's Crossing* (Coen, 1990) and *The Krays* (Medak, 1990).

Outside their historical settings, we could consider them in terms of more broad cinematic genres, but again the films turn out to be hybrids. Certainly, the narratives include many melodramatic elements; I will discuss the effects of these structures in more detail later, but for now it is enough to note the films' concentration on romance plots and their concern with affect. In all cases, the narrative operates to produce tears in the spectator. And yet, despite being based on narratives that are characteristic of women's films, or perhaps their contemporary equivalent, "chick flicks," they do not revolve around female protagonists, but young men, and tend to produce a wholly masculine subject position. Even generically, the melodramatic plot is undercut somewhat: in *Mediterraneo*, for example, the love story is embedded in both a war setting and a comedy. In addition, the "between art house and mainstream" structure that Higson points out clearly involves some elements of art cinema; the films are slow moving on occasion and more concerned with mise-en-scène and the pleasures of spectacle than is conventional in Hollywood melodrama. Characterization often takes precedence over narrative, and discourses of quality attend the historical and national cultural elements of narrative.

Higson himself discusses the difficulty of using heritage film as a genre, certainly as a coherent one, pointing out that because the category was largely invented by critics rather than either producers or audiences, and intended frequently as a negative criticism, it becomes something of a self-fulfilling prophecy. Only the bourgeois and conservative historical films are called heritage films, and so the category comes to seem defined by this critique. He suggests expanding the genre to include films set in the recent past and featuring working-class characters—such as *Backbeat* (Softley, 1994) and *Distant Voices, Still Lives*—and to include many European and, indeed, world examples. I am interested in his attempt to expand the genre insofar as it enables more room to rethink the terms of the heritage debate, which, certainly in reference to British films, had become somewhat stale. And it is certainly productive to compare, say, *Cinema Paradiso* with the films of Terence Davies, with which it has substantially more in common than with more conventional heritage films like *A Room with a View*. But what seems more productive than the addition of some less conservative films is to open out the terms of those critiques to inspection, to consider how and why we criticize heritage films, and to use these issues to approach the Italian films.

The first set of words commonly employed to critique heritage films are "sentiment," "melodrama," and "nostalgia." When *Cinema Paradiso* topped a British newspaper poll of the best films of the 1980s, reviewers expressed surprise that such a sentimental film should be so popular with British audiences. One reviewer argued: "It seems that the golden-hued air of dreamy nostalgia placed in a Mediterranean setting, complete with shouting peasants, doe-eyed bambini, funny fascists, village idiots and the Araldite bonding of traditional family life, avoids all the baggage which a more explicitly British treatment inevitably brings on board—Victorian repression, twilight-of-Empire anguish, class struggle and greyness."[8] A similar review of *Il Postino* called the film a "lazily predictable tale of Mediterranean backwardness, stocked with cliché characters—local fisherman, smouldering dark beauty . . . black-clad widow, seedy politician, anti-Communist local priest . . . and helped along with sentimental detail."[9] And, again, with *Mediterraneo*: "It rests too comfortably for its own good on a string of clichés: loveable, incompetent Italian soldiers . . . thieving Turks . . . a buxom whore with a heart, and any amount of balmy evenings of hard drinking and soft landings."[10] The complaints of clichéd character types and sentimentality imply a melodramatic rather than a realist historical narrative, and reviews in other countries reiterated the same terms of description.[11] The recurring complaints, then, are of sentiment, nostalgia, sloppy or whitewashed history, a touristic view of the region, and a reactionary political slant—all the same criticisms, more or less, that are made by academic critics of heritage films.[12]

One particularly pointed example of a related scholarly critique is Susannah Radstone's discussion of *Cinema Paradiso*,[13] which is useful in this context not only because these films have rarely been analyzed in any theoretical depth but also because she addresses several issues that will become of central importance to my argument. Like the journalistic critics, Radstone argues that the film is nostalgic and hence has no genuine engagement with history. Using Fredric Jameson's concept of "history/nostalgia,"[14] part of his discussion of postmodern history films and the retro mode, she accuses the film of rejecting any social critique or historical friction in favor of the easier pleasures of an airbrushed myth of a collective memory, a pastiche of history. For Radstone, the film is neither personal nor social but, rather, exemplifies a structurally regressive strategy that is characteristic of the patriarchal and ahistorical tendencies in postmodernity—what she calls "turning everything into an exhibit."[15]

Her analytical focus here is on the films shown within the film, the many clips seen by Totò at the Paradiso, which come to define both his cultural memory and that of the nostalgic spectator. For Radstone, these sequences give the lie to the film's claims of representing an individual memory, as they are recognizable and conventional clips from a canonical history of film—examples include *La terra trema* (Visconti, 1948) and *The Lower Depths* (Renoir, 1936). In their sameness and connection to a meditated narrative of history, they conflate the personal with the social in a way that is reactionary.[16] I will return to the question of the films within the film, but what is particularly suggestive for us here is Radstone's reading of this historicity through both Jameson's argument on postmodern nostalgia and Benjamin's concept of *Erfahrung*. For Radstone, these nostalgic film clips are the opposite of Benjamin's theory of experience, and in falling into the less radical *Erlebnis* can be read not only as postmodern nostalgia but as a metadiscursive *histoire*, lacking the connective power of storytelling.[17] Thus, Radstone extends the debate around nostalgia and historical memory, connecting these questions both to Benjamin's theorizations of experience and to a historically specific debate around contemporary film form.

The second critique of this kind of historical text is inherent in the debate over heritage film itself, for, Higson's self-awareness notwithstanding, the concept is defined almost purely through the deployment of a negative defining move.[18] This move involves several levels of critical attack: at the level of extratextual history, at the level of narrative, and, most important, at the level of the image. The extratextual and narrative criticisms are linked, in an argument that the films fail to engage with contemporary politics and use historical settings as a way to avoid pressing issues of representation. Higson thus claims that the heritage film grew in the 1980s alongside more multicultural societies in Europe and so allowed the predominantly middle-class white audience to reenter a disappearing world of unchallenged white privilege.[19] As a corollary to this historical case is the narrative argument that the films fail to engage with current social issues within their diegeses; they ignore marginal groups and do not offer, as more political films might, realist engagements with social realities.[20]

Most problematic for Higson, though, is the ideological effect of the image in heritage films, which he argues deploys an excessively pictorial and decorated mise-en-scène in a way that undercuts any political promise that the narratives might otherwise have contained: "Even those films that develop an ironic narrative of the past end up celebrating and legitimating the spectacle of one class and one cultural tradition and identity at the expense of others through the discourse of authenticity and the obsession with the visual splendours of period detail."[21] For example, in *Howards End* (Ivory, 1992), the narrative may valorize the newly created bourgeoisie or the bohemian Schlegel family, but the lengthy shots of plush interiors cannot help but privilege the aristocracy. A large part of this impulse, of course, is specific to British heritage films and to the mise-en-scènes of a class system based on property and land ownership. Richard Dyer implies as much in his discussion of heritage films in terms of a museum aesthetic and as heritage attractions.[22] The attractions he is referring to are country houses, themselves on display in reality as a part of the tourist industry. But Higson's argument, although it derives from the British films in which this critique has a specific object, is wider than Dyer's and attempts to problematize mise-en-scène in heritage films in general. Thus, "the image of the past in heritage films has become so naturalised that, paradoxically, it stands removed from history: the evocation of pastness is accomplished by a look, a style, the loving recreation of period details—not by any critical historical perspective. . . . They render history as spectacle, as separate from the viewer in the present."[23] Or, more succinctly: "The pleasures of pictorialism thus block the radical intentions of the narrative."[24]

This key critique makes explicit what is implicit in many of the other arguments against heritage history films: the sense of anxiety around the image and around the spectacular image as historical. This anxiety surfaces across theories of the heritage film, as well as in Radstone's connection of heritage to retro postmodernism. I will return to this anxiety and will take issue with Higson's ideological reading of the image and with Radstone's use of Jameson and, more particularly, of Benjamin. However, I will begin with the question of narrative and consider in more detail how *Il Postino*, *Mediterraneo*, and *Cinema Paradiso* can be read as nostalgic and melodramatic. Rather than stopping with these terms as epithets of self-evident critique, it is necessary to examine both the films and their historical context in some depth in order to interrogate the significance of these narrative structures.

## Italy Postwar: What Went Wrong?

Earlier, I quoted a magazine review in which *Cinema Paradiso* is criticized for showing "funny fascists"[25]—in other words, for failing to represent the seriousness of fascism. In light of discussions around such films as *Life Is Beautiful*, such a complaint is perhaps timely, but I bring it up again not for this ethical debate but to point out that it is, simply, historically wrong. There are no fascists in *Cinema Paradiso*, funny or otherwise, because the narrative takes place after World War II is over, or, at the very earliest, it begins in the closing months of the conflict in 1945. And, as the film is set in Sicily, which was liberated in 1943, this slight uncertainty is irrelevant as far as a fascist presence goes. It need hardly be said that my reason for uncovering this mistake is neither to discredit the reviewer nor to spot the kind of nit-picking historical glitches that spectators of historical films are traditionally fond of discovering. Failure to notice the end of World War II does seem to be somewhat more than a glitch, but the significance of this slip is not limited to the accuracy of the review. Instead, I would like to suggest that this blunder is symptomatic of a larger problem with the way these films are read: with a lack of attention to Italian political and cinematic history, which, in turn, facilitates claims of historical emptiness such as Radstone's and enables critics to dispose of the films as apolitical. It becomes easier to dismiss a text as historically empty when the history at stake is misread or ignored. This is not an empiricist claim on historical knowledge or textual accuracy but a methodological question with a direct influence on how we can theorize the operation of historicity in these texts.

The misreading is a simple one and is contained both in Peter Aspden's ignorance of the Italian postwar situation and in his presumption that the site of historical engagement (and its potential problems) must be fascism. There is a sense that for Italy only a discussion of the years of fascism or war can count as truly facing up to the past and that a choice of subject that postdates fascism by such a short period is, inevitably, evading the issue.[26] This sense is compounded by a comparison with Italian art films of the 1960s and 1970s, when representations

of fascism were a common topic, taken on by many of the most internationally lauded auteurs. Examples include *The Conformist, Amarcord*
(Fellini, 1973), and *Christ Stopped at Eboli* (Rosi, 1979). Thus, just as
1980s and 1990s films are disadvantageously compared with the art
house films of the decades before in terms of aesthetics, so they are easily considered at best less serious and at worst reactionary in their politics. If a history film is apolitical, then the symptom of this will be a lack
of fascists (or only "funny" ones), and a lack of fascists can correspondingly signify only a lack of political engagement.

Such an interpretation fails to consider the political significance of
the years immediately following the end of World War II in Italy, where
from 1945 to 1948 a struggle took place over how Italian national identity would be remade, concluding with the formation of the First Republic and the installation of a party system that remained in power for fifty
years. The breakup of the unified anti-Fascist Resistance (CNL), the
defeat of the Italian Communist Party (PCI), and the victory of the rightist Christian Democrats (DC) speak of a moment that is far from safe
historical territory for Italians, but is in fact more fraught than a reiteration of a fascism that all can agree on condemning. And while fascism
may have been a crucial topic in the 1960s and 1970s, when the war was
first being reconsidered in European culture at large, the years 1945 to
1948 became an equally compelling topic in the early 1990s, when the
postwar republic came under increasing pressure and finally, in 1992,
collapsed altogether.

For the Italian Left, the key historical question of the 1990s was not
How did we allow fascism to happen? but What went wrong after the
war? The long partition of Italy between 1943 and 1945 produced a
strong partisan coalition that, by the end of the war, was already part of
a national debate on the future government of the country. And when
the Communist leader Palmiro Togliatti returned to Italy from exile in
the Soviet Union with a new plan for the transformation of the PCI into
a democratic socialist party, that debate was directed toward a wholesale
rethinking of the role of the Left in the new order.[27] Of course, the country was in a precarious condition, and the legacy of fascism was hardly
dismissed, but nonetheless, as Elizabeth Wiskemann puts it, "there was
a tremendous feeling of national exhilaration. This had been a second
Risorgimento, the Italians felt, a more real one in which all classes had
participated."[28] As the new constitution was drawn up in 1946, there
was a moment of unique possibility, in which political parties were
being created anew, and to speak of an entirely new nation appeared to
be no exaggeration. This exhilaration was most evident in the Left,

which, as the mainstay of the Resistance, had pushed successfully for a Left-leaning coalition government in 1945. This CNL-based government instituted a leftist policy program: the redistribution of wealth, introduction of a progressive income tax, economic reconstruction, and swift purging of Fascists from positions of power.[29]

But, as both historians and contemporary commentators have attested, this spirit of optimism was short-lived. As early as 1945, former partisan commander Ferrucio Parri was replaced as prime minister by Alcide de Gasperi, a rightist Christian Democrat, who effectively blocked most of the left-wing proposals. In Spencer Di Scala's words:

> Many Italians who fought in the Resistance believed it would be the starting point of a social revolution. Probably this hope was doomed from the start because Allied armies dominated the country, a reality the Communists rushed to recognise. Indirect Allied support allowed the conservatives to postpone indefinitely the economic provisions of the Parri government, end the purge of former Fascists and regular administrative officials tainted by Fascism, and replace CNL-nominated local authorities by traditional officials. Whether or not a revolutionary situation—or even the conditions for radical reforms—ever existed, it ended with Parri's fall, which "marked the comeback of all the old conservative forces in Italian society."[30]

As well as refusing to institute any of the Parri government's more radical plans, the DC failed to effect the fundamental shift of power necessary to open up the state to real change. Former Fascists remained in their posts, and the structures of local and regional government were allowed to continue with little interference. And as Di Scala makes clear, Italy's wartime allies exerted a good deal of influence at the crucial juncture. In 1947, de Gasperi made a trip to the United States, shortly after which he sacked all the leftists in his government: U.S. financial aid to Italy came on condition of a stable and rightist government, and de Gasperi was evidently taking no chances. Pier Paolo Pasolini summed up the viewpoint of the Left in claiming that "the events of 1945 were not the radical reformation of the Italian government that the Christian Democrats would claim them to have been. Rather they were superficial changes . . . made to ensure the continuity of power by Italian capitalists working together with the Catholic church, the politicians of the Right, and the U.S. State Department."[31] By 1948, the PCI was facing bad publicity not just from the powerful forces of the DC and its American backers but from a stream of newsreels showing Soviet troops invading East

European countries and enforcing Communist regimes. The elections of that year were fought in what one critic has called an "atmosphere of anti-Communist hysteria,"[32] and in April the DC won a landslide victory. It was to remain in power, almost without interruption, for the next forty-five years.

To a certain extent, the political impact of these years is explicitly present in the films, readable at the edges of the mise-en-scène and in the peripheries of the narratives. In *Il Postino*, an election campaign is being fought, mostly in the background of the main plot. But the stakes of this election are made visible in one sequence in which Mario tells the DC candidate Di Cosimo that he is voting PCI, only to have Di Cosimo denounce Mario and his hero Pablo Neruda, claiming that the Fascist Gabriele D'Annunzio is his poet. The right wing's fear of the PCI is made clear in one shot of the village in which a DC election poster is visible toward the left edge of the screen, its image a hammer and sickle, with the slogan "because this isn't your flag." And when Di Cosimo is elected and immediately pulls out of a promised building deal, leaving Mario's bar without its promised business, the rapid disillusionment with the DC government becomes briefly central to the narrative.

*Mediterraneo* does not deal with this period of disillusion, breaking off (except for its final sequence) in 1944. However, it does include the feeling of optimism about the chance to rebuild Italy among the characterizations of its rescued soldiers, verbalizing this concept quite directly

*Il Postino*   "Because this isn't your flag."

through the characters of La Rosa and Lo Russo. Thus, when La Rosa arrives by plane and tells the soldiers the news of Mussolini's fall, Italy's division, and joining forces with the Allies, he adds: "There is much to do, we can't remain outside of it, there are big ideals at stake." And even more directly expressing PCI sentiments, Lo Russo tries to persuade Farina to return to Italy with him by telling him that Italy "needs rebuilding from the ground up . . . we'll build a great nation, I promise you." Similar sequences could be isolated in *Cinema Paradiso*, such as the scene from the other side of the political divide in which a family is forced to leave town, unable to get any work because the father is known to be a Communist.

My contention is that the relation of these films to the political events of 1945 to 1948 is not primarily contained in these few direct references but is structured through a projection of politics onto romance. In each film, the moment of political possibility can be thought directly only as a moment of romantic possibility, embedded in melodramatic and nostalgic narrative of loss. In *Cinema Paradiso*, Totò is a young aspiring filmmaker who falls in love with Elena, the unreachable daughter of a local banker. His affair with her is brief, but he never forgets or entirely gets over her. The moment of political potential is thus rewritten in terms of his youthful belief in romance, while the scenes of his present-day cynicism construct that originary loss as determining all that comes after. *Mediterraneo* makes the narrative connection between the briefly textualized political excitement of La Rosa's arrival and romance clear: in the sequence immediately after La Rosa's patriotic speech, Farina announces his love for Vassilissa; in the following scene, the couple get married. Political potential is immediately translated into romantic potential, with the thought of Italy displaced directly onto the image of Vassilissa.

In *Il Postino* the imbrication of the two is even more explicit, as the film's displacement of politics onto romance is enacted as the tension between Mario and his Communist boss over the meaning of Pablo Neruda. Whereas Mario is infatuated with the idea of Neruda as a Romantic artist, the "poet loved by women," his boss insists that he is the poet "loved by the people." This binary functions throughout the film to negotiate the spectator's relationship to the narrative, in which our knowledge of Neruda's political and historical reasons for being in Italy (and our knowledge that Mario's boss is therefore at least partially correct) can come to function only through Mario's textual need for poetic lessons in romance in order to woo his love, Beatrice. The text circles around this double bind of what is historically known versus what is narratively necessary. Thus, using the real historical personage of Neruda invokes extratextual knowledge: that Neruda came to Italy while in exile from Chile, and that political tensions within Italy almost had him expelled again. As Neruda's biographer says: "He comes to Italy in search of a refuge and an amorous hideout, but even here he runs smack into the Cold War."[33] The tranquility of the island is undermined by historical tensions but is also still structured as an "amorous hideout." What becomes central in the narrative is Neruda's ability to coach Mario in writing poetry to seduce Beatrice, to help Mario become the "poet loved by women."

This deflection of politics onto romance enables the films to represent the political mood of 1945, but they do so from a historically specific viewpoint: that of the time the films were made, which for the sake of brevity I will refer to as the early 1990s, although the films' release dates span the years 1988 to 1995.[34] That all three films should be made within a few years of one another, and that they should all deploy narratives of romantic loss to imagine the postwar years, is symptomatic not so much of the continuing influence of the postwar period in Italian cultural memory but of a more precise shift in the relationship between this particular history and the films' present. This shift, which made a reimagining of the postwar years newly compelling and newly painful, included the events leading to the collapse in 1992 of the Italian First Republic.

## The End of the First Republic

If the events of the early 1990s in Italy seem less well known than many of the other seismic shifts that composed the end of the Cold War in Europe, perhaps this is because there is still a debate over how much the end of the First Republic can be connected to international geopolitics and how much it was grounded in the Italian national system. For the purposes of this discussion, it is not possible to consider these questions in great detail, but it is important to understand how each element structured the postwar republic and how that system came apart when it did. The landslide victory of the DC in 1948, with its anti-Communist panic and promise of much-needed American aid, ushered in a system unique in Europe: a constitutional democracy in which, despite free elections, there was no real change of government in almost fifty years.[35] As Sarah Waters has argued, Italy operated in a permanent and curiously stable state of crisis in which coalition governments rose and fell with startling frequency but remained composed of all the same politicians. The system worked principally to keep the PCI out of office, and it did so successfully by ensuring that the other two main parties, the DC and Italian Socialist Party (PSI), constantly entered into subtly changing coalitions. Cold War rhetoric and the fear of Communism, then, partly structured this oligopoly,[36] but it was also composed of a vast and increasingly corrupt corporatist bureaucracy through which all elements of Italian society, from major industries to the most everyday transactions, eventually had to pass. The fact that power never changed into opposition hands enabled this system to grow unchecked, and by the 1980s the *partitocrazia*, or rule of the parties, was taken for granted as the definition of the Italian state.[37]

What precipitated the end of this system was the huge scandal that began to come to light in February 1992, when a Milanese city official was caught taking bribes.[38] He named names, and those named named more names, and soon many of the country's politicians and industrialists were implicated in what was known as Tangentopoli.[39] The speed and scale of the scandal's escalation spoke of a breakdown waiting to happen, and soon Operation Clean Hands (*mani pulite*) was threatening, in the words of Alexander Stille, "to overturn the party dominated system that has run the country since World War II."[40] The discoveries made by the judges were all-encompassing: from routine kickbacks in local government to the implication of top Fiat executives in bribery[41] and of major politicians in Mafia deals. One-fifth of the sitting members of parliament (MPs) were put under investigation, and three former prime ministers were forced to resign, including Bettino Craxi, prime minister until the scandal broke, and Giulio Andreotti, arguably Italy's most important postwar leader.[42] Craxi fled the country to escape trial, while Andreotti stayed and was charged with advising the Mafia.[43] The effect of the investigations is hard to overestimate; as one commentator put it: "Operation Clean Hands has hit Italian politics like a cyclone . . . after this, nothing will ever be the same."[44]

A cyclone indeed. In less than two years, the entire party system imploded, as new parties such as the regionally based Northern League and media tycoon Silvio Berlusconi's Forza Italia appeared and won immediate support. The old parties collapsed, unable to reform themselves sufficiently to escape a total loss of public confidence. The PCI, which had split in 1991 into the moderate Party of the Democratic Left (PDS) and the hard-line Communist Rifondazione, was the only pre-1992 party still in existence by 1994.[45] In April 1993, Italians voted overwhelmingly in a referendum for a change in their voting system, away from the proportional representation that had allowed for a succession of coalitions and in favor of a system closer to the "winner-take-all" or relative majority system used in the United Kingdom.[46] The result of this constitutional, political, and popular upheaval was, as reported in *Macleans*, "what senior politicians are calling a peaceful revolution—one that promises to sweep away the web of political and financial power that has enmeshed Italy since the Second World War."[47]

The collapse of the party system was sudden, but the pressures that caused it had been building up through the 1980s and had certainly reached a crisis point by the early 1990s. The conventional historical explanation for the sudden crisis is the fall of Communism in Eastern Europe: during the Cold War and thus for the entire duration of the First Republic, fear of the PCI had kept the DC in power. No matter how aware the population may have been of corruption, the status quo was successfully pitched as the lesser of two evils. When the Soviet Union broke up, there was no longer a threat greater than a corrupt regime, and so the scandals could be uncovered.[48] Many historians have recently argued for a more complex explanation, not rejecting the influence of the events of 1989 but adding causes internal to Italy. Martin Bull and Martin Rhodes, for example, argue that the growing disjuncture between a successful private-sector economy and the failing state apparatus showed that the expropriation of public funds had gone as far as it could go before the whole system fell apart.[49] In addition, the move toward greater European cooperation, and especially the promise of the single market in 1992, had produced a desire to become more European, in terms of both economics and culture. In this context, the Italian system seemed like a liability. In any case, it is clear that even before the final collapse of the party system, a climate was growing in which Italian public culture had to reexamine its own basic assumptions.

For Italy, such a national self-examination had to reconsider the institution of the First Republic, for only in this way could the system be viewed as historically contingent and open to change. As Stille says, "Italians are rebelling against a system they had regarded as eternal and inevitable,"[50] the point being that the party system was so entrenched that political change required a change in the nature of the state. For Umberto Eco, the comparison is again to revolution: "We are living through our own 14th of July 1789."[51] Thus, the crisis forced not just a political shakeup but a reconsideration of national identity. In an article in an American magazine, Federico Fellini wrote that "all of us must reflect on what the Italian identity really means."[52] *Cinema Paradiso*, *Mediterraneo*, and *Il Postino* are made in this climate, and placed in context their look back to the immediate postwar years takes on a different valence. The national anxiety attending the end of the First Republic forces a return to the moment of its inception, and the leftist question What went wrong? is able to be articulated for the first time as a question of national significance.

It is for this reason that these films about the postwar years appear when they do, but this crisis of national identity also offers an explanation of why they take the form that they do. From the standpoint of the late 1980s and early 1990s, and certainly from a leftist position, 1945 signifies that moment of possibility that fails. Thus, for films to reimagine those years does entail a certain nostalgia, a yearning for the moment when a different outcome was still possible. But, contrary to the criticisms that accuse the films of using nostalgia to produce a stable and hence reactionary relation to history, the combination of 1945 and 1992 sets up a dynamic relation between past and present, in which nostalgia subtends a historical and political critique. This is why both *Mediterraneo* and *Cinema Paradiso* include sequences set in the present, in which their postwar romances are nostalgically revisited from a place of present-day loss. For example, Totò in *Cinema Paradiso* watches his old 8-mm films of his first love, Elena, knowing that he has never again recaptured such happiness. This loss is articulated as directly political in *Mediterraneo*, where the Communist Lo Russo has returned to the Greek island, decades after promising to build a new Italy. He tells Farina: "Life wasn't so good in Italy. They didn't let us change anything. So I told them: You win but don't consider me an accomplice." This moment acts as a coda to the character's earlier optimism, but the weight of the relationship between these historical spaces cannot be borne by such direct references. Instead, such nostalgia for the moment of possibility, combined with knowledge of its inevitable failure, can be represented only in a form able to structure history in terms of loss and mourning, knowledge and desire: in other words, as melodrama.

## Mourning and Melodrama

There is a substantial body of work in film theory on the ways in which melodrama has operated as a genre to psychologize ideological problems and to render them legible within a domestic or romantic frame.[53] Thomas Elsaesser's influential essay "Tales of Sound and Fury: Observations on the Family Melodrama" argues that the formal elements of mise-en-scène, alongside the claustrophobic familial narratives of classical melodrama, crystallize a particular historical and ideological structure: "This is why the melodrama, at its most accomplished, seems capable of reproducing more directly than other genres the patterns of domination and exploitation existing in a given society, especially the relation between psychology, morality and class-consciousness, by emphasising so clearly an emotional dynamic whose social correlative is a network of external forces directed oppressingly inwards, and with which the characters themselves unwittingly collude to become their agents."[54] This symptomatic reading precisely delineates a relationship among an individualized emotional narrative, a spectacular or excessive mise-en-scène, and a larger social structure, and it is within this nexus that we can begin to locate the Italian films' staging of history.

One article that is particularly suggestive in the context of these films is Steve Neale's "Melodrama and Tears,"[55] in which Neale rereads a much-cited piece by Franco Moretti[56] from a psychoanalytic and film-specific point of view. This article is useful with respect to the romance narratives of these films because it offers a way to focus on analyzing narrative structures and affect. For Moretti, the production of affect— the moment at which the reader cries—is achieved when the protagonist's point of view is suddenly brought back into line with the reader's, after a period in which the reader knows more than the characters. And, he argues, "what makes it produce a 'moving' effect is not the play of points of view in itself but rather the moment at which it occurs. Agnition is a 'moving' device when it comes too late."[57] Clearly, this narrative move depends on temporality, deriving its emotional effect on the reader from her realization of the irreversibility of time and the futility of any desire to make it take a different route. The Italian melodramas harness this structure of temporality and attach it to the look back on an irreversible history. Neale adds to Moretti's outline the structure of "if only,"[58] in which the moment of agnition comes with a wish that things could have been different; this wish structures the films' look back from the present, and, in Elsaesser's terms, translates Lo Russo's sentiment of "if only we could have built a better country" into the protagonists' sentiments in the domestic realm.

The final segment of *Cinema Paradiso*, in which a middle-aged Totò returns to his childhood home for his old friend Alfredo's funeral, first refracts the painful look back across all the elements of his life and then condenses them by means of the film that Alfredo has left him. Here, the narrative of romantic loss operates as part of a much wider loss: that of his youth, his family whom he never sees, his best friend, his formative experiences of cinema spectatorship, and the isolated village culture

*Cinema Paradiso*   Totò sees Alfredo's cinematic "letter," provoking the film's moving moment.

that has now become modernized. These elements are invoked in turn as Totò meets his mother and sister, watches his film of Elena, revisits the now-modern square, attends Alfredo's funeral, and returns to the Paradiso cinema for the last time before it is demolished. However, only when he goes back to Rome and views the reel of film that Alfredo left for him does the moving effect occur. The film consists of all the kissing scenes that Alfredo had been obliged to edit out of films for the Paradiso at the behest of the censoring local priest and that Alfredo had repeatedly refused to give to the young Totò.

Neale discusses Moretti's concept of point of view in filmic terms, arguing that the moving moment in film melodrama necessitates a shift of both optical and narrative points of view, although the two may not always coincide.[59] This is such a moment, where the impossibility of optical points of view meeting produces tears in the spectator. In viewing this film, Totò finds out what the spectator knew all along: that Alfredo did love him and that sending him away was painful for him, done only so that Totò could succeed unhampered by his past. However, not only is Alfredo dead, but he was blind also, so Totò can see only that which Alfredo could not or, rather, that which Alfredo could have seen only in the distant past, in the postwar years of Totò's youth. Thus a connection is made, but one structured through temporal distance and the lack of the loved object. Like *Letter from an Unknown Woman* (Ophüls, 1948), one of the films considered by Neale, there is a kind of letter from the dead to spark remembrance, but here the "letter" is a visual text in itself. And it is a text not of narrative but of symbolic meaning. It is not a direct message from Alfredo but consists of a performative statement: what was once unable to be seen (censored) is now visible, and Totò's belated understanding of his own past provokes the historically located spectator to tears.

In *Il Postino*, the spectator does not witness the protagonist's moment of agnition but discovers it at a remove; the realization is itself temporally displaced, too late. We discover when Neruda returns to the island some years after the events of the narrative that Mario was killed taking part in a leftist demonstration at which he was to read a poem. As Moretti says: "To express the senses of being 'too late,' the easiest course is obviously to prime the agnition for the moment when the character is on the point of dying."[60] And hence the moving moment occurs not because Mario has died but because of where and how he has died. Up until this point, the writing of Mario's poetry has reflected the narrative's displacement of politics onto romance: the poet loved by the people versus the poet loved by women. A further binary is set up between saying and doing, and in this structure the opposition between politics and romance is repeated. In its first version, Beatrice's mother is convinced that Mario must have done something to Beatrice, not believing that he could have invented the intimate endearments of his poem. What he said, for her, is just as dangerous as what he did. In the final sequences of the film, this structure is reprised as we learn of Mario's death. Mario never gets to read onstage, and instead we see shots of chaotic crowds and one of his poems, a piece of paper lying on the ground. What he said is once again conflated with what he did, as the "saying" of reading a poem becomes the "doing" of political action and martyrdom. But this time around, Mario's action involves a realization of what the spectator, along with Neruda, has known all along: that politics is, after all, necessary to poetry and that speech can also constitute political action. His realization comes too late, however, and the terms are once again conflated as the political loss of the demonstration's suppression becomes legible in the romantic loss of Mario's death.

There is also a sequence in *Il Postino* that corresponds to Totò's playing of Alfredo's film reel and sets up another moment of communication that comes too late. Early in the film, Neruda asks Mario to describe something of the beauty of his island into a Dictaphone, for Neruda to send home to Chile. Besotted with Beatrice and unable to appreciate his surroundings, Mario can only repeat her name. Later, when Neruda has left, Mario uses the Dictaphone once more, now to attempt to record what he realizes is the true natural beauty of the island. He tries to capture the island with this inadequate technology, "recording" the color of the sky and the movement of waves. As with Alfredo's film, Neruda does not receive this gift until Mario is dead, and hence there is no direct communication between the characters. These instances of technically mediated communication correspond to what Peter Brooks calls the "text of muteness,"[61] in which melodrama is characterized by the points at which communication breaks down and only gestures are possible, not words. The mediated nature of these communications makes them something of a variation on this mute text. Mario does speak to Neruda in a way, but the speech is recorded and so, like Alfredo's film, comes from the past. It cannot hear, and the hearer cannot reply; like film itself, the enunciation is determined through an apparatus of absence.

In this temporal displacement, the melodramatic structure reproduces the pain of historical loss; through the affective gap in the code of signification, the films condense not only the finality of the characters' deaths but also the unbreachable space between the past moment of potential and its painful consequences in the present. Thus, temporality in these narratives works to regulate a nexus of knowledge, loss, and desire for a past state that Neale characterizes in psychoanalytic terms as the mark of failure of the fantasy of union, the falling away from the dyadic relationship of "effortless communication and mutual understanding"[62] in which the subject must repeatedly mourn this originary loss. In this reading, the temporality of melodramatic affect is inevitably structured by fantasy, and, therefore, the films' historicity also would have to be understood not simply in terms of a projection onto romantic themes but as bound up, as an affective experience, in psychoanalytic structures.

It is in this addition of a fantasy element to Moretti's more straightforward narrative analysis that Neale's argument offers its most productive avenue of investigation, for while these films do contain the "too late" structure of the moving text, they do so as part of a temporality that synthesizes narratives of subjective and historical loss and so involves both psychic and social mechanisms. Neale claims that crying does not occur when all conflict has ceased, as Moretti argues, but occurs as a function of an unresolved desire (the wish that things in the past could have been different), and he argues that this formulation enables a more open and more complex relation of temporality to desire. For Moretti, tears indicate a closing down of possibilities and, hence, a reactionary narrative effect. But for Neale, "an unhappy ending can function as a means of postponing rather than destroying the possibility of fulfillment of a wish. An 'unhappy' ending may function as a means of satisfying a wish to have the wish unfulfilled—in order that it can be preserved and re-stated rather than abandoned altogether."[63] Here, the focus shifts from the decisive point of resolution to the more ambiguous relationship *between* tension and resolution.

The Italian films respond to this more open-ended view of tears, whereby the "unhappy ending" performs a temporally doubled work. Within the historical narrative, the affective resolution could be said to produce tears of resignation. Alfredo and Mario are dead, and in political terms the optimism of the postwar years is definitively over. But by returning, in the present, to that history of failure, the films recontextualize the lost past in relation to an equally emotive political present that *is* open to change. If the past cannot be changed, its relationship to the present can be, and here the films engage with a temporality of possibility. Returning to the failed moment of the past enables a holding open of the wish and, hence, of possibility for the future. In this doubling, the films narrativize the moment of national crisis: the melodramatic production of affect does not close off movement but reenacts the historical closure of the 1940s in order to redefine, not abandon, the political stakes of the 1990s.

This notion of a doubled temporality changes our reading of nostalgia in these films, as the affective look back can no longer be thought of as simply an elision of history. If anything, the films suggest that it was the time between 1945 and 1992 that elided history and did so at the instigation of the foundational myths of the postwar nation. Thus, in *Cinema Paradiso*, Alfredo's message to Totò that he must never come back, that it would be crippling and depressing, is readable as the state of Italy before it is forced to go back, as it were. The bribery scandals forced the country to reexamine its political system from the beginning, a process that required a nostalgia for lost leftist hopes and, as a corollary, the desire for change that needed to be rediscovered. If nostalgia is understood in this way, then Radstone's critique of a Jamesonian emptiness is considerably weakened. She argues that "the endings of both *Cinema Paradiso* and *The Long Day Closes* therefore condense nostalgia for lost ideals with a pathos that suggests a wish that things might be different. Though undoubtedly 'in question,' phallic masculinity remains in place and History shores itself up against the incoming tide of memory."[64] But as Higson points out, the relationship between past and present in nostalgia is not always a reassuring one:

> Nostalgia is always in effect a critique of the present, which is seen as lacking something desirable situated out of reach in the past. Nostalgia always implies that there is something wrong with the present, but it does not necessarily speak from the point of view of right wing conservatism. It can of course be used to flee from the troubled present into the imaginary stability and grandeur of the past. But it can also be used to comment on the inadequacies of the present from a more radical perspective.[65]

This is precisely the point on which Radstone's reading of the films' nostalgia breaks down, for while, as she says, the narratives do not end with any radical change, the impetus to critique the present vis-à-vis the specific past of the postwar years condenses exactly the historical tensions that would be instrumental in producing radical change in Italy only a few years later.

Radstone's argument also has points of strength, and it is indeed possible to read these films' referencing of well-known movies as mythifying a false, sentimental version of Italian-ness. Certainly, they are often referential, deriving narrative incidents and locations from films and other artifacts of Italian cultural memory. For example, Sicilian novelist Leonardo Sciascia describes his own youth at the cinema: "The showroom was an old theatre and we always went out on the balcony. From there, we spent hours spitting at the stalls; the voices of the victims burst out."[66] *Cinema Paradiso* contains a minor character who throughout the film does exactly this. However, just as the *Sight and Sound* reviewer quoted earlier felt that a British film could not represent the heritage past without the baggage of the British Empire, the nostalgic mythification of these scenes cannot help but revive the historical failure of the myth at the same time as it cites its pleasures. The generation of 1948 ultimately gave birth to Tangentopoli, and it is impossible to see images of those years without the baggage of this historical knowledge.

Nostalgia, in this context, has more in common with the psychic structures of mourning than with the regressive pleasures suggested by Radstone's pathos or Higson's search for "an imaginary historical plenitude."[67] Freud describes mourning as "the reaction to the loss of a loved person, or to the loss of some abstraction which has taken the place of one, such as one's country, liberty, an ideal, and so on,"[68] and it is significant that at the heart of this definition is a process of displacement. Mourning is the "normal" version of the more pathological condition of melancholia, but even within mourning, there is a complication or a perversion the process when abstractions "take the place" of a loved person as the focus of the object loss. This is the case with the films, where the loss is of a particular idea of nation, and a historical moment stands in for a lost object. In a sense, the historical film must always invoke the process of mourning, for mourning is precisely about creating a representation of that which no longer exists. For Freud, the subject does not want to abandon his libidinal attachment to the lost object and, hence, turns away from reality to produce a fantasy in which the object can be kept alive.

But while all historical films may produce a libidinal attachment to an object that, by dint of its historicality, no longer exists, what is striking in these films is the binding together of this filmic structure both to a specific historical lost object and to a further displacement within which mourning can be narrated. Thus, in the process of mourning work, "each single one of the memories and expectations in which the libido is bound to the object is brought up and hyper-cathected, and detachment of the libido is accomplished in respect of it."[69] In these films, the memories and expectations of the postwar years are revisited through direct representation of that period but are also transfigured into romantic objects and narratives, and in this way they are hypercathected through the discourses of melodrama and affect. The plots around Farina and Vassilissa, Mario and Beatrice, and Totò and Elena[70] provide a place in which mourning can occur. The films can thus be read as enacting an abstracted mourning process for the spectator, replacing an abstract object loss with the loss of a loved person at the level of narrative.

Hypercathexis is what binds mourning to melodrama: the tears that come from the object located in the past, its remembrance from the present, and the "too late" trope by which the past is made to speak more significantly in and to the present than it could in its own time. The temporality of Neale's understanding of melodramatic affect is contiguous in these texts to the temporality of mourning: the return to the past in order to redefine the subject's relation to the object world in the present. And in the films, both of these forms of temporal organization are imbricated with historicity—a relation to a past understood as historically determining, not merely temporally previous.

It is this nexus of relationships that readings such as Radstone's, which take melodramatic affect as evidence for a lack of historical engagement, are unable to account for. Indicative of this problem is her placing of *Cinema Paradiso* as melancholic and hence as narcissistic rather than social, as "history/nostalgia" rather than truly historical. For Freud, melancholia is indeed both narcissistic and regressive, the outcome when the lost love object is removed from the other and returned to the self so that "an object-loss [is] transformed into an ego-loss."[71] Melancholia is a mourning gone awry, in which the lost object has too little resistance and the subject either does not know what she has lost or does not know what is lost in that thing. It is tempting to transpose this template onto many heritage films, to read plots that do not deal with politics or History (in either a classical or a countercinematic way) as a withdrawal from historical consciousness, and to read melodramatic structures as narcissistic, allowing the spectator only the pleasures of overidentification and empty emotion.

However, historical loss is not subsumed by ego loss in these films. Only by ignoring the specificity of Italian history would it be possible to read their postwar settings and contemporary codas as exhibiting a lack of historical friction. And while the films narrate this historical loss through individual romantic losses, this is a strategy of displacement, not replacement. The distinction becomes clear at the moments of agnition, where personal loss enables the expression of historical loss, rather than veiling or curtailing it. In *Cinema Paradiso*, to take Radstone's own example, while Totò remains central to the narrative of loss, his eldest embodiment remains something of a cypher, impossible to identify fully as the child and adolescent of the majority of the film, too different an actor. And so, in the final scene, spectatorial identification is limited, and Totò functions primarily as a conduit for the spectator's tears, tears that are provoked not by his loss but by the film reel's signifiers of historicality, of a difference that is not contained by his character but encompasses the political and psychic gulf between that past and this present.

## The Female Figure in the Landscape

What this reading of narrative in terms of nostalgia and melodrama elides is the question of gender. There is a fairly obvious feminist critique to be made here, for the films require that woman functions as a mere figure, a trope that always and only refers to something else. In locating the lost object of history within romance plots, the films map political desire onto sexual desire. The female protagonists of the romances are thus semiotically simple figures, anchoring this system of historical signification through the conventionally patriarchal codes of classical representation. All three are spectacularized and fetishized, their narrative significance defined by their excessive visibility and hence desirability in the mise-en-scène. Beatrice in *Il Postino*, in particular, tends to be figured in fetishistic close up, including several outstandingly extraneous shots of her cleavage. Elena in *Cinema Paradiso* is a cypher: first seen from the point of view of Totò's 8-mm camera, she remains at a distance, and her disappearance from the narrative is self-consciously unexplained, a function of feminine mysteriousness. Beginning in Totò's frame, she ultimately disappears out of the film's frame. That both women function primarily as a shorthand of desire is clear from their names: Beatrice and Elena (Italian for Helen), both famous literary figures of beauty and loss. And while Vassilissa in *Mediterraneo* performs a more substantial narrative function, she embodies another kind of cultural shorthand, the stereotypical hooker with a heart of gold.

The displacement of meaning from narrative to mise-en-scène is familiar in feminist film theory, and much criticism of melodrama involves a consideration of the genre's gendered tensions between narrative and image.[72] Of course, theorists of melodrama such as Mary Ann Doane and Linda Williams[73] focus on films that produce a less ideologically stable gendered image than these films do, and in which the social position of women is central. While the historical drama or heritage film is a somewhat feminized genre, these films are not women's pictures per se, and the instrumental function of the female characters makes clear their peripheral status. It would certainly be possible to conceive of the films as male melodramas, given the passive protagonists who cannot find a place in traditional masculine domains of war or work.[74] How-

*Cinema Paradiso*    Elena is a cypher, seen in Totò's 8-mm films.

ever, although such an avenue of investigation could prove productive, I bring up the question of gender not so much to offer another take on the films' narratives but to point out a theoretical lack in the consideration of the heritage film's image.

As I argued earlier, there is an anxiety around the image in criticism of these films, a fear of the spectacular historical image that implicitly looks to a formal realism to secure historical authenticity. Mise-en-scène does have a role within this discourse of grounding the narrative image accurately, but anything excessive to narrative necessity casts doubt on the seriousness of the enterprise. (Within this discourse, for example, a film like *Saving Private Ryan* [Spielberg, 1998] could deploy a visually excessive and affective mise-en-scène of broken and mutilated bodies, for the images were justified rhetorically as more realistic than those in any previous war film.) Thus, for Radstone or Jameson, the nostalgic image is too beautiful to be true, and for Higson the so-called heritage shots of aesthetically pleasurable views or buildings "fall out" of the narrative.[75] Each claim about historicity is based on a splitting of the functions of narrative and image, a binary structure in which visual pleasure works only to undermine—or, better, to halt—the possibly radical signification of historical narrative.

What is striking is the extent to which this discourse is predicated on the structures of feminist film theory and yet deradicalizes its conception of the image. For clearly Higson's spectacular heritage shots that "fall out" of the narrative owe a debt to Laura Mulvey,[76] but in a simplified rhetoric in which these moments of spectacular freezing can indicate only a blockage of meaning. To be sure, the context of psychoanalytic theory is lost, but in shifting the terrain from patriarchal images to historical representation, the ideological complexity of spectacle is also left behind. For Mulvey, neither spectacle nor narrative is negative simply by refusing meaning; rather, both operate as part of an intensely productive ideological system. And in much psychoanalytic feminist theory following Mulvey, the image is a privileged site of contestation, the place where hegemonic meanings can start to break down. Thus, while questions of gender may be peripheral to the narratives of these films, I would argue that feminist film theory is crucial to theorizing the relation they propose between historical narrative and spectacular mise-en-scène. Against Higson's logic, it is crucial to theorize as productive the pleasures of spectacular historical images.

The chief locus of spectacle in these three films is landscape: an Italian rural landscape in *Cinema Paradiso* and *Il Postino* and a Greek island in *Mediterraneo*. Each film was shot on location, and the narratives take

*Il Postino*    Pablo Neruda views the Mediterranean seascape.

place within spaces coded as spectacular, from the sequences in which Mario and Neruda talk on the beach in *Il Postino* to Totò's walks with the priest along a country road that overlooks a dramatic shoreline in *Cinema Paradiso*. In addition to these narratively motivated locations, there are many instances of shots and sequences that are not motivated, that function directly as visually pleasurable spectacles: landscape images that indeed "fall out" of the narrative. *Mediterraneo*, for example, begins by setting up suspense around its thus far largely unseen narrative space. The soldiers disembark from their boat to find an apparently deserted island and some graffiti that threatens "Greece is the tomb of Italians." But soon this threat is dissipated as the inhabitants reveal themselves to be friendly, and montage sequences of the various spaces of the island, now unconnected from any narrative tension, reveal direct spectatorial engagement with the landscape to be one of the chief pleasures of the film. Such moments can readily be compared with the "heritage shots" in British heritage films, although the content of the images is naturally quite different. Rather than showing country houses or gardens, the Italian films focus on uncultivated spaces: mountains, bays, and seascapes; and pre-modern, peasant villages or small towns. These rural spaces work to connote historicality, for in addition to avoiding more up-to-date locations like cities, the unchanging nature of landscapes works alongside representations of traditional practices such as fishing to produce a sense of distance from the modern world.

*Mediterraneo*   The soldiers are integrated into the local landscape.

This connection of landscape to pastness, or to a rural lifestyle that
appears historically rather than merely geographically distant, certainly
has a long history in forms such as naturalism in literature and pastoral
landscape painting of the kind that Warnke discusses. But as cinematic
images, these mountainscapes and seascapes need to be considered in
relation to landscape photography, for it was in photography that landscape took on the discursive baggage that helps form the critical response
to these films as spectacle. Rosalind Krauss argues that not only does
landscape photography have to be understood in a different context from
painting, but there are (at least) two very different discursive contexts for
landscape images within photography and photographic texts tend to be
misread when these get conflated.[77]

Krauss discusses the reception of a series of nineteenth-century photographs that were generally read within the dominant modernist art
photography discourse as graphic images in which the surface of the photograph, its framing, and its composition are primary and the aesthetics
of representation takes precedence over the realistic qualities of the
image. She contrasts this interpretation with the photographs' original
context, a scientific mapping of geographic space. She connects this form
to the introduction of "views" within Victorian mass culture and thus to

a popular discourse of landscape as a form of scientific-touristic knowledge. Now, clearly, film is not the same thing as photography, and it is as important not to conflate the two as it is to avoid conflating nineteenth-century views with modernist art photographs. Still, Krauss's discussion sets up the terms for the ways in which contemporary film landscapes are still read and, by extension, suggests how similar interpretative strategies in the context of cinema might produce new readings. For Krauss, the problem is that photographs that should be read within the epistemological context of the view are instead misunderstood as modernist art images. But in contemporary cinema, an ambivalent version of both these discourses is at work, producing an epistemology specific to contemporary film landscapes.

First, there remains a broadly modernist aestheticizing discourse that reads landscape graphically as surface. This mode is often valorized in the context of art cinema where a nonrealist mise-en-scène is part of a claim to radicality. And in postclassical film, art-cinematic visual strategies are sometimes central to the location of certain popular films as quality products, as in the epic vistas and self-consciously aesthetic cinematography of *The English Patient*. But this example demonstrates the ease with which the valorizing impulse can slip into a fear of pictorialism, producing a criticism of "all style, no depth." This fear of mise-en-scène, in which landscape becomes readable as a screen blocking a perceived narrative depth, is peculiar to cinema, and especially to a postclassical cinema in which visual excess has become closely linked to claims of a process of "dumbing down"—of deteriorating content.[78] Not identical to Higson's critique of the heritage image, this ambivalence nonetheless imbues his reading of the pictorial.

Krauss's second discursive context—the nonauthored, scientific, or popular view—is also part of contemporary cinema, and although as a mode of perception it has been less aesthetically dominant than modernism, recent work on the visual history of tourism and the touristic image has traced recurrent patterns from such nineteenth-century views to picture postcards and cinematic practices.[79] Once again, what is substantially a positive rereading in Krauss applies mostly as critique in the context of film, where claims of a touristic view imply either a scholarly argument around colonialism and the gaze or a critical accusation like those leveled at *Cinema Paradiso* and *Mediterraneo* that the film is clichéd and stereotypical. Although the former claim is more relevant to an example like *The English Patient*, the problem is not with this argument in itself but with its indiscriminate application to all landscape images. For while Krauss is able to structure these two contexts as alternatives for interpreting photographs, in the field of contemporary cinema the two work together to form a lose–lose structure. On the one hand, the films are too artistic, posing landscape as graphic composition and favoring aesthetics as form over meaning. On the other hand, they are too popular, replicating a touristic gaze typical of bourgeois pop culture in which the landscape image can signify only distraction and a lack of geographic or historical friction. In either case, the image is once again the site of a lack, a falling away from meaning.

The difficulty, then, is to think landscape outside this epistemological bind: to read it not as a sliding surface, an aporia of meaning, but as a specific form of spectacular image that produces meanings and spectatorial relations as complex and ambiguous as those produced in other types of spectacle. To begin to rethink landscape in this way, it is necessary both to bring back to the surface the feminist work that offers a film-specific understanding of the structures of the image and to analyze what happens differently when the image is not tied to a gendered body. If the female characters in the films can, in classical terms, be seen as images standing for desire, what can landscape as spectacle stand for?

One way to address this issue is through the discursive context of another body of Italian films in which landscape became a privileged site of meaning: neorealism. Made mainly between 1945 and 1948, neorealist films are concurrent with the moment of political optimism that the 1990s films mourn, and neorealism represents many of the same geographic spaces. Furthermore, in neorealism, landscape is often claimed to be central to the films' project of reclaiming Italy for an anti-Fascist identity. Thus, *Paisà* represents Italian resistance and liberation through a series of narratives, each set in a different geographic location, while *La terra trema* focuses on exploited workers in a rural Sicilian fishing village. On the films of Giuseppe De Santis (and particularly *Tragic Hunt* [1947]), Mira Liehm says that they work to create a "dramatically presented landscape, which was not permitted on the screen during the fascist regime."[80] There is an inkling here of the political historicity of landscape that I will address in more detail, but I want to concentrate for now on De Santis's own valuation of his landscape imagery, which he outlines in an article entitled "Per un paesaggio italiano."[81]

Identifying neorealism with landscape images, De Santis argues that "if we consider that a great number of films among those most valued belong to a genre in which a landscape has a primordial importance— *White Shadows in the South Seas, Tabu, Que Viva Mexico, Storm over Asia*— then it is clear that the cinema has an even greater need to use the same element of landscape that communicates almost immediately with the spectators who above all want to 'see.'"[82] This formulation is telling, for it implies the next question: What is it that these spectators above all want to see, and what it is that landscape shows them? The obvious answer is that landscape works as part of neorealism's discourse of authenticity: that along with nonprofessional actors, real locations show the unmediated truth of Italy. However, even without critiquing the ideological basis of this version of realism,[83] it is clear that within De Santis's own discourse, landscape does not show what the spectators want to see but, rather, operates similarly to the fetish. For what the spectators of neorealism above all want to see is the truth of humanity or the truth of exploitation (depending on their ideological positioning), not, in any case, the truth of geography. What landscape does show is its own visibility: as a scene or a vista, it exists to be looked at, and in its own transparency, it stands in for a truth that cannot be so easily represented.

It is perhaps not irrelevant that this claim defining landscape's role as fulfilling a desire to see should come from De Santis, a director whose most famous film is *Riso amaro* (1949), in which what is seen is not so much the truth of Italy as the breasts and legs of actress Silvana Mangano. A double slippage takes place here, both from landscape to the body and

*Riso amaro*    Silvana Mangano's legs and thighs are emphasized by her costume for work in the rice paddies.

from realism to spectacle, and while De Santis writes about the national importance of representing landscape, the film was criticized as too spectacular, was banned in Italy, and became something of a cult object in Europe and the United States. In this instance, the fetish quality of what the audience wants to see is quite clear, and the image of Mangano standing in the rice paddies combines bodily and landscape "truths." The spectacular body that stands in for the truth itself is again a structure analyzed in feminist theory, reminiscent of Linda Williams's argument about pornography: that the excessive visibility of the body is itself a fetish, standing in for an impossible truth of pleasure.[84] The metonymic link from landscape to the female body is a standard patriarchal one, and *Riso amaro* exploits this connection of women to nature. But if we can read it in the other direction—that is, read the Italian landscape as fetishized in a way similar to that of the female body—then this might open up a useful way of getting at landscape's function. We can say that woman is connected to place and this is not original, but to say that place is readable within the same structures as woman might enable us to analyze place more theoretically. Landscape, like woman, is imagined to be immediate, to communicate directly to those who above all want to see.

We can see this connection most clearly by returning to the female characters in the 1990s films: where Vassilissa, Elena, and Beatrice form the locus of historical mourning within the romance narratives, they are, in turn, linked visually to those spectacular landscapes that signify historicity within the mise-en-scène. In *Mediterraneo*, Farina is first figured as an orphan without connections, either to place or to people. Shortly after the men arrive on the island, a sequence begins with a picturesque long shot of the mountains and the bay, and then tracks left to Farina sitting beside the lieutenant, who is drawing the landscape. The lieutenant has already forged a connection to the place, not only by drawing, but also through his knowledge of ancient Greek culture. He quizzes Farina, who confesses to having no wife or family and to knowing no Greek. The lieutenant gives him a book of Greek pastoral poetry, which he reads that night while another soldier reads a love letter for his wife. Here, landscape, culture, and sexual/familial relationships form a nexus of meaning, defining a sense of historical location. Vassilissa will function to give Farina this necessary connection, not just through their romance but by her connection with place. Unlike the lieutenant, her link to Greece is through not literary traditions but sexual ones: as she explains, she is a whore, her mother was a whore, and her grandmother was a whore. Their relationship short-circuits the need for historical knowledge of Greek culture, providing Farina with a direct connection to place.

The connection operates even more directly in the scenes involving the Munaron brothers, who opt to keep watch on the mountains that remind them of their native Savoy. Between the scenes of the lieutenant giving Farina the poetry book and his reading it that night, there is a shot of the brothers watching the sun set over the water, an image easily readable within pictorial conventions of the picturesque and the beautiful. While Farina meets Vassilissa, the brothers meet a shepherdess who lives in the mountains, and their romances proceed in parallel. The shepherdess is figured as particularly close to nature, never leaving the space of the mountain but enjoying a rural idyll as she swims naked and has sex with the brothers. As all three are linked to the landscape, so they are linked, "naturally," to one another. And the pictorial shots of the mountain views they inhabit structure the same visual pleasures as their naked bodies within the landscape.

If landscape functions alongside the female characters to produce the pleasures of romantic nostalgia, then it also works to structure the sense of mourning and loss that the historical look backward of these narratives involves. Thus, to continue with the example of *Mediterraneo*, when the lieutenant returns to the island in the 1990s, he visits Vassilissa's

*Mediterraneo*   The shepherdess is closely linked to the mountains.

grave, first seen in a wide shot, with the grave in the foreground and a view of the mountains and bay in the background. The gravestone itself contains a photograph of Vassilissa as a young woman, to which we cut in a close up. Thus, the look back is figured first through a double image of the woman and of the landscape, in which the placing of Vassilissa's image inside the space of a gravestone forms an internal frame signifying loss, constructing both her image and the larger frame of the landscape view as temporally removed. Although the landscape is, unlike Vassilissa, present, the framing places both images as objects of mourning, signifiers of the romantic moment that is now lost. The hypercathexis of the lost object encompasses both, not only because the lieutenant has not seen either Vassilissa or the island in the intervening years but also because both are, for the spectator, privileged sites of historical difference.

I have been arguing that landscape functions in the image similarly to the way in which the romance plots do at the level of narrative: that is, to construct a subject position of politically inflected mourning and loss around the temporal relationship between 1945 and 1992. But this func-

*Mediterraneo*   Vassilissa's gravestone, with her photograph in the center of the cross, forms an internal frame.

tion is not limited to the moments at which landscape is connected metonymically to those romances. Rather, the visual structuring of the landscape image itself produces meaning, similarly to the way in which the spectacular bodily image has been understood in feminist theory. In "falling out" of the narrative, the spectacular landscape forms a distinct semiotic register in which visual pleasure and affect produce meaning differently than does the narrative discourse. In psychoanalytic feminist theory, this distinction is important because while both spectacle and narrative form a patriarchal regime of viewing, the tension between them offers a space for counterreadings. And the spectacular image has formed the primary focus of many feminist interventions, where the textual power of the image of the woman proves ideologically ambiguous, unsettling the patriarchal work of classical narrative.

The situation in these films is not identical, and my aim is not to transplant a very specific theoretical elaboration onto another object. However, if feminist film theory is to be understood not simply as an analysis of a certain type of film but as a methodology, then it becomes crucial to extend its theorization of spectacle, to deploy its explanatory power, even when the image in question is not directly gendered.[85] In fact, this is already being done: as I have argued, Higson's reading of spectacle and narrative implicitly draws on Mulvey's model, and his understanding of the image is refracted in much criticism of postclassical cinema. The problem is that once separated from an explicit discourse on gender, the patriarchal valorization of narrative (temporal, clear, linear, masculine) over spectacle (spatial, excessive, emotional, feminine) abandons the stake in theorizing the image as productive and reinstates a gendered logic by default. My aim is to resituate a film-specific feminist epistemology in taking seriously the ideological work of the spectacular image. More specifically, I want to examine how the landscape image in these films signifies as spectacle, and how its visual pleasures encode an ideologically complex relationship to narrative. In doing so, as we have seen, it is necessary to reframe somewhat, to consider the cinematic history and visual specificity of the landscape image, but it is also necessary to retain a feminist understanding of how spectacle works. Thus, the discourse of visibility and immediacy that structures the landscape spectacle as a kind of fetish must be examined more closely in order to theorize how it also produces an affective rhetoric, and how this rhetoric can be imbricated with structures of mourning and historicity. The next section will analyze the ways in which the landscape image itself becomes the key site for this ideological work.

## "A Strange Weave of Space and Time":
## Landscape, Index, and Aura

If spectacular landscape signifies an aporia that, in its sheer visibility, seems to speak only of itself, then it is possible to locate this discourse not only within theories of ideology and the image but also as central to accounts of the cinematic index. From Louis and Auguste Lumière's rustling leaves to André Bazin's reading of neorealism,[86] landscape images have been privileged signifiers of cinema's capacity to touch on the real. This discourse underwrites De Santis's call for a *paesaggio italiano*, for landscape, more than any other subject, appears to testify to the unmediated presence of the profilmic. Of course, this claim on the real can be disputed in a number of ways, and I want to keep in mind my reading of De Santis: that the "truth" of landscape operates as a fetish, standing as a figure for a desire that is hidden in plain sight. To understand how these films structure a relation to history through this mode of apparent immediacy, it is important to account for the affective power of the landscape image, and I argue that this power is grounded in the ability of these cinematic images to short-circuit representation.

While writing on the photographic image often considers the question of what it is that breaks through or stands outside representation,[87] theorists of cinematic specificity have tended to concentrate on the indexical nature of the apparatus rather than on the real as an exceptional moment within individual texts. Roland Barthes's notion of the punctum posits instances of the real that evade the representational strategies of the photograph, but he is adamant that these moments of affect are possible only with the contemplation of a still image.[88] Similarly, Hal Foster's Lacanian reading of Andy Warhol's *White Burning Car III* and *Ambulance Disaster* (both 1963) depends on the detail, the obscene tear that defaces the surface of the photographic print, and so enables a momentary connection of the spectator to the traumatic Real.[89] But again, this effect is possible only in a still image, and one that is viewed within the context of an art, and so becomes the object of a temporally sustained gaze. By contrast, Bazin's discussion of film and ontology[90] is based on the chemical process of registration of images, and at some level applies to all films, regardless of their content, as does Siegfried Kracauer's theory of film as the recording of physical reality.[91] Even where Bazin distinguishes opposing tendencies, the differences occur between films, not within the image itself. However, the privileging of the landscape image implies a concern, even within theories of medium specificity, for how the operation of certain images within this apparatus can be particularly charged.

In *Theory of Film*, Kracauer gives an example in which an actual landscape offers an experience of the cinematic that no studio copy could produce. He cites approvingly Blaise Cendrars's "hypothetical experiment,"
imagining "two film scenes which are completely identical except for the
fact that one has been shot on the Mont Blanc . . . while the other was
staged in the studio. His contention is that the former has a quality not
found in the latter. There are on the mountain, says he, certain 'emana-
tions, luminous or otherwise, which have worked on the film and given
it a soul.'"[92] Here, by preserving the integrity of profilmic space, the
mountain operates fundamentally not as mise-en-scène but as a guarantor of the medium's ontological status. In common with Bazin and,
indeed, with Barthes, this conception of realism is tied to the temporal
nature of the medium, in which the affect—or the "soul"—of the image
derives from its ability to preserve that which was there, the materiality
of an object in time.

But if the temporal relation to the real is what connects these theories
of indexicality and medium specificity, Kracauer's argument is particularly suggestive when it discusses what happens to the landscape image
in a historical film; and here we can see a correlation in film theory to
Barthes's punctum, to the real that breaks the structure of representation. For Kracauer, historical narratives are by their nature uncinematic,
for they refuse the impression of endlessness by which film refers to a
larger reality outside any given text. Thus, he claims, "whenever a film
maker turns the spotlight on a historical subject or ventures into the
realm of fantasy, he runs the risk of defying the basic properties of his
medium. Roughly speaking, he seems no longer concerned with physical reality but bent on incorporating worlds which to all appearances lie
outside the orbit of actuality."[93] To claim that historical films are uncinematic is an interesting twist on the more common complaint that they
are unhistorical, but what I want to concentrate on is what happens
when landscape images are used within historical narratives.

Here, Kracauer argues, there is a conflict between the realistic and
formative tendencies of cinema, in which the indexical landscape image
undercuts the historicity of the narrative, breaking the spectator's belief
in the diegetic world. His example is Carl Theodor Dreyer's *Day of Wrath*
(1943), which contains a "problematic mixture of real trees and period
costumes." Thus, "the trees form part of endless reality which the camera might picture on and on, while the lovers belong to the orbit of an
intrinsically artificial universe. No sooner do the lovers leave it and col-
lide with nature in the raw than the presence of the trees retransforms
them into costumed actors."[94] In this moment of splitting, the indexical

reality of the trees short-circuits the representational meanings of the narrative space and, in doing so, momentarily replaces historicity with temporality, the time of filming instead of the time of the narrative. I will argue that this structure informs the Italian films, where the excessively spectacular landscape vistas are readable as indices, pulling against the historical codes of the mise-en-scène.

As Kracauer points out, this effect is at its strongest with a distant history, so it does not produce shock in the Italian films whose histories are more recent. The potential for conflict is also reduced in heritage films, as they are often set in rural landscapes that we perversely consider to be historical, even though we know they are not. Therefore, instead of producing the kind of "irrevocable staginess"[95] that Kracauer clearly identifies as a problem, the effect of splitting in the Italian films is refracted across the surface of the text, producing a friction rather than a shock. (An exemplary moment would be the scene in *Cinema Paradiso* where Totò and Elena try to hitch a lift, the pastness of their car momentarily undercut by the effect of the wide shot of a mountain range behind them.) Nonetheless, this idea of a conflict within the frame opens up a productive space within these texts. As Miriam Hansen says in her introduction to Kracauer: "The same indexicality that allows photographic film to record and figure the world also inscribes the image with moments of

*Cinema Paradiso*    Totò and Elena's car breaks down, confronting period production design with timeless scenery.

temporality and contingency that disfigure the representation."[96] In the Italian films, this disfiguration describes a tension within the landscape image between its narrative and indexical properties.

To understand how this tension constitutes an experience of historical mourning in tune with that of the films' melodramatic narratives, we must coarticulate Kracauer's indexical tension with a quite different theorization of temporality and the real: Benjamin's concept of the aura.[97] To analyze the historical landscapes of these films in terms of the aura is not an obvious move, for in his most celebrated discussion of the aura, in "The Work of Art in the Age of Mechanical Reproduction," Benjamin not only claims that cinema destroys the auratic nature of authentic works of art but further condemns both historical films and filmed landscapes. On Abel Gance's plan to film the lives of artists such as Rembrandt and Beethoven, Benjamin speaks of a "far-reaching liquidation" of history,[98] and when he critiques the reproducibility in which the work of art's presence is depreciated, he adds that "this holds not only for the art work but also, for instance, for a landscape which passes in review before the spectator in a movie."[99] On the basis of this argument, it would seem that the images I have been discussing are actively anti-auratic. However, as Hansen points out, the aura is a slippery concept in Benjamin's writings, an idea that he repeatedly redefines and toward which his attitude is both ambiguous and changing.[100] For Hansen, the negative assessment of the decline of the aura in the Artwork essay is uncharacteristic, and she notes that in much of his later work, Benjamin "tries to redeem an auratic mode of experience for a historical and materialist practice."[101] Rather than opposing the auratic to mechanical reproduction *tout court*, Benjamin looks for the auratic within the modern, as part of his attempt to theorize history outside the idea of progress.

In "A Small History of Photography," for instance, Benjamin suggests that the aura is, after all, possible within modernity and, moreover, within the photographic image.[102] We can pinpoint the draw of the photographic for Benjamin in his description of the "magical value" of an early photograph: "No matter how artful the photographer, no matter how carefully posed his subject, the beholder feels an irresistible urge to search such a picture for the tiny spark of contingency, of the Here and Now, with which reality has so to speak seared the subject, to find the inconspicuous spot where in the immediacy of that long-forgotten moment the future subsists so eloquently that we, looking back, may rediscover it."[103]

He goes on to analyze this effect as auratic, a question not of the photographic process per se but of a spectatorial relationship to a certain kind of image. Here, the aura does not derive, as it does in a painting, from the authenticity of the original object but forms an experience unique to photography, in which the temporal distance and material reality of the subject are what compel the viewer.

The image produces a momentary effect of the real, an effect that is similar to what happens when Kracauer's trees force a realization of indexicality. In the spark of contingency that is felt despite the artfulness of the photographer, there is a comparable sense of disfiguration, of the affective power of the real cutting across the intended structure of meaning. And what the example of the early photograph makes explicit is the importance of temporality to this effect. While Benjamin defines the aura first in terms of presence (the physical presence of stage actor and audience in the same space), he consistently amends this approach by transposing the auratic effect onto an inanimate object, so that there can be no return of the gaze. In the photograph, we see the temporal component of this missed encounter, in which subject and viewer approach reality from different—and distant—historical moments. The irruption of the past within the present (and the future within the past) offers a break with linear history, a break in which other meanings become possible. While Benjamin's aura is not reducible to the index, its confluence of time and space suggests the aura as a useful tool for thinking about the cinematic image, particularly with regard to temporality and historicity.

Before considering the historical implications of this effect, however, I want to turn to the most striking element of the auratic in the context of my own reading, which is that Benjamin repeatedly defines it through the image of a landscape. His definition in the Artwork essay more or less repeats the earlier terms of that in "A Small History of Photography," where he asks: "What is aura, actually? A strange weave of space and time: the unique appearance or semblance of distance, no matter how close the object may be. While resting on a summer's noon, to trace a range of mountains on the horizon, or a branch that throws its shadow on the observer, until the moment or the hour become part of their appearance—that is what it means to breathe the aura of those mountains, that branch."[104] As in *Cinema Paradiso*, *Il Postino*, and *Mediterraneo*, the privileged signifier of an affective relationship to the past is imagined as a long shot, a distanced view of a natural landscape. Of course, for Benjamin, this particular landscape is defined by its presence, like the stage actors whose gaze can be returned. And yet it is never simply a "real" landscape: the auratic, for Benjamin, is a social and historical object, and yet one that he repeatedly conjures by means of a natural figure.

Hansen addresses the seeming disparity between Benjamin's initial definition of the aura in terms of the reciprocity of the gaze and his example that is not human but inanimate. She asks what the element is in the auratic experience that allows us to apply it to nature. Her answer is "that forgotten human element . . . is nothing but the material origin—and finality—that humans share with non-human nature."[105] In other words, the mountain and the branch remind us of materiality, temporality, and thus ultimately of death. The experience of the aura through landscape offers a sense of history in the abstract, of the pure sense of time, its passing and its inexorability, the shiver of absence that such seeming presence implies. And while for Benjamin this experience depends on the presence of the physical space of the landscape, I would contend that it is present in these films, working as the indexical spark of contingency that erupts in photography or as the trees that disfigure the historical representation for Kracauer. Rather than defining the spectator's relationship to the apparatus, as in the bourgeois art object, the aura here has become an internal textual effect, whereby the landscape image diffuses across the surface of the films an experience of historical and temporal loss. This abstracted loss grounds the affective structure of the films' mise-en-scène: the landscape of the mountain, the branch, and the tree continually breaks out of representation, reminding the spectator that the historical moment of the narratives has passed and can be looked back on only belatedly, from the present.

If the aura operates to abstract the relationship of the subject to temporality, however, that relationship is nevertheless always in fact social and its abstraction is necessarily a deflection. As Benjamin succinctly puts it in "Central Park": "Derivation of the aura as a projection of a social experience of people onto nature: the gaze is returned."[106] The landscape image must not be seen as some kind of immanence but, rather, is able to signify as an abstraction only when it is, already, part of a concrete history. The example of the mountain and the branch is embedded in analyses of the social, historical, and, above all, political significance of cinema and photography, and it is to these questions that the auratic landscape ultimately speaks. Similarly, the landscape image in film is not inherently or universally auratic but can function in this way only as part of such a social structure of deflection. Thus, the landscapes of the Italian films could not produce an effect of auratic loss if this abstracted structure of temporality did not also, and at the same time, involve a projected experience of an actual historical loss. The same historical structure that is projected onto the romance narratives is also refracted across the landscaped mise-en-scène, and the spectacular images that could be perceived as merely touristic or beautiful are, rather, imbricated with the social logic of Italian political loss and thus interpellate the spectator not as a tourist but as a subject in mourning.

This effect is perhaps most visible in the final shots of *Mediterraneo* and *Il Postino*, both of which cut or track from a scene of characters in mourning to long shots of the landscape. These shots underline the connection of landscape to the romance narratives, tying the abstract auratic effect of temporality in the landscapes to the specific experience of historical loss expressed by the characters in the preceding sequences. Thus, in *Mediterraneo*, the final scene includes Lo Russo's repudiation of political will, completing the shift from his desire to build a great country to his admission of defeat, and comes directly after the lieutenant's discovery of Vassilissa's death. The camera tracks left from the now old men to reframe on the mountains, where the auratic break is immediately readable in terms of this narrative mourning. *Il Postino* ends with a similar move toward a pure landscape image, and a few scenes earlier there is an even more explicit binding of affective landscape to mourning work, where Neruda finally hears the Dictaphone tape that Mario had made for him before his death. The tape contains Mario's attempt to record the island, to capture in sound that which can only be an image: the sea, the cliffs, the sky. These images are visible to Neruda and to the spectator only in the knowledge of Mario's death, and hence their technological presence (doubled by recording) is tied to the irrevocable pastness of their production.

Theodor Adorno critiques the displaced nature of this relation to the social in Benjamin, claiming that Benjamin's location of the aura in the mountain and the branch replicates the alienating work of capitalism by making a fetish out of nature.[107] Benjamin's response is that the natural objects he discusses are not the product of labor, and so the aura could not be reduced to the commodity fetish. This exchange is relevant to a reading of the aura in film not only because it brings up the structure of the fetish but because, in citing the commodity fetish, it sheds light on the critique by Higson and others of the heritage image. For Adorno, the image of nature serves only to veil the structure of capitalism, and it is in this spirit that Higson critiques the beautiful mise-en-scène of heritage films, claiming that these images allow films to reify the history they represent by keeping the spectator in thrall to the fetishistic pleasures of spectacle rather than engaging with the potentially critical narrative. However, the relation of the auratic image to the social does not express the logic of either/or, in which the image prevents an understanding of the social, but rather operates as a both/and structure, a cir-cling relation that is more akin to the Freudian than the Marxist fetish.

Here, the binding of the natural and the social, of narrative and spec-tacular meanings, enables us to pick apart the films' deflection of politi-cal engagement onto a remembered past. The temporal structure of the aura in these films intersects both with the logic of mourning and with a broader understanding of Benjamin's theories of history. In the latter, the necessary political stake in rethinking history demands that the past cannot remain merely in the past, but must always have a determining effect on the present and on social change. And yet, the relationship between past and future is never direct or progressive: the intertwining of utopian and restorative strains in messianism works to deflect any conception of the future onto a lost past and, of course, vice versa, so that any conceptualization of political change must always at the same time involve a painful excavation of history. Thus, in the films, the look back precedes any potential look forward, so that the social need for change in the future can be imagined only through a mournful return to the changes of the past. This political desire is deflected further onto the auratic landscape image, so that its temporality (the shiver of death and absence) can be made cinematically meaningful in terms of mourning and the concrete losses of the postwar generation. These deflections nei-ther evade engagement with the present nor replace narrative with visual meaning but, rather, place the landscape image as the pivot around which past and future, politics and affect, narrative and specta-cle are centered.

This recursive temporality can be seen in these films where the future as such is never textualized and where a political relation to historical change can be imagined only through the mourning of the past. In terms of their narratives, there is little sense of stake in the future, which is one of the reasons the films have been dismissed as reactionary. Thus, there is no implication by the end of the films that the characters have embarked on a new phase of their lives. In *Cinema Paradiso*, there are at least unresolved questions: Can Totò break free of his life of casual rela-tionships and find a more genuine happiness? But in *Il Postino*, Mario is dead, and Beatrice and Pablito are not characters the spectator has ever been called on to identify with. Pablo Neruda has a future, to be sure, but in the public domain of "real" history, not in the film. And in *Mediter-raneo*, the main characters have given up on the future as a social or political project: old men, they have escaped to a Greek island in order to return to nature, rejecting change and progress as a lost cause.

Instead, the future is deflected onto past time: the future that must already be mourned as lost. In the postwar setting of each film, the future is exactly what is at stake, the burning question of the day. And inexorable temporality, the signifiers of mortality, inhere in the closing off of this question, the having-been-decided of that future from the point of view of the present. Structurally as well as thematically, the future has declined, aged, or even died. What dies of this future narratively is Mario in *Il Postino* and, in the other films, the youthful promise and optimism of the protagonists. What produces affect, though, is not these signs of change in themselves but the doubling of narrative historicity and indexical presence that oscillates in the visual sameness of the landscape. To return to the scene in *Mediterraneo* of Vassilissa's grave, it is the similarity of both framed images to their historically earlier versions that makes the lieutenant's look back affective. Both her photograph and the landscape look the same, yet the time in which both Vassilissa and the landscape existed together is gone. The photograph of one whom we know is going to die is reminiscent of Barthes's photographic temporality, but in the cinematic landscape image the inscription of temporality is different. The mountains and the bay look the same partly because they are the same, and as Kracauer's "real trees" they break out of the historical fiction. But this disjuncture between diegesis and landscape is most forcibly apparent retrospectively, in the contemporary segment of the narrative where the auratic experience of the past's distance rejoins the narrative of mourning even as it disfigures its surface.

This disfiguration of the present is also visible in other aspects of the mise-en-scène in the present-day codas of both *Mediterraneo* and *Cinema Paradiso*. When Totò returns to Giancaldo for Alfredo's funeral, the village square is recognizably the same place, but modernized, with cars, advertising billboards, and a new gas station. Similarly, in *Mediterraneo*, the lieutenant returns to the island on a tourist ferry filled with crowds of people. In both cases, the contemporary space is characterized by additions: more people and objects that function as a surplus, added onto and veiling what was there before. A surplus is also visible in the aging of the actors, who are made up to look like old men. Inevitably disruptive, this addition to their faces and bodies operates similarly to the new cars and crowds as a disfiguration, whereby the present is readable only in terms of its difference from the past. And in *Cinema Paradiso*, these changes are narratively linked to mourning, as the spectator must scan the frame to find recognizable spaces and characters during the funeral scene. The chief difference between the past and the now is a

*Mediterraneo*    Makeup to age them is a surplus on the faces of the actors.

death, but it is as a disfiguration rather than a disappearance that historical change must be visualized.

Here, the doubled temporality of the auratic image returns the experience of history and memory to the terms of mourning, whereby the routing of the future through the past contains the structure of hypercathexis. Contrary to Radstone's assessment of *Cinema Paradiso* as exemplary of *Erlebnis*, I would argue that this imbrication of spectacular and narrative historicities produces an experience of the past that is not containable within the rubric of Benjamin's traditional form of history. It is at the moment when the landscape images short-circuit the conscious historical representation of narrative that they are at their most affective and also their most historical. For the textual memories evoked by the aura are precisely those of Italian political loss, displaced onto the image and cathected in the affective landscape. Mourning work, here, is akin to *Erfahrung* as an experience of history that is both subjective and socially determined.

It is also significant that this experience of temporality is contained in an image and is thus spatialized. For not only does the auratic effect of the landscape depend on an arrangement of space and time, but both

Benjamin's and Kracauer's theorizations of historicity and of temporality depend on a process of spatialization. Benjamin famously invokes a spatial image, Paul Klee's *Angelus Novus*, to imagine the process of history.[108] Kracauer's work on film focuses less insistently on history (although his earlier work treats history much more so than does the later *Theory of Film*), but his concern for the materiality of the image nonetheless continually interrogates the categories of space and time. As Elsaesser argues of Kracauer's work as a whole: "The metaphor that predominates is that of travel, the traversal of space in the medium of time, to which correspond—quite ambiguously—the role of the subject as observer, flaneur, tourist, since for Kracauer, time and temporal extension are always at crucial moments frozen into the snapshot, the vista, and thus are most intensely experienced as space."[109] In this stopping of time in the space of landscape, history in these films is most felt.

And not only felt: for in the construction of a temporal relation through a spatial one, and in the both/and logic by which the mise-en-scène signifies simultaneously as immediate and as referential, the landscape in these films forms what Benjamin terms a dialectical image. For Benjamin, the dialectical image is crucial to a theory of history outside narratives of progress, and the concept brings together his interpretation of Marxism and his use of messianic time in the idea of past and present in constellation. In *The Arcades Project*, he insists on the necessity of thinking history in this way:

> It is not that what is past casts its light on what is present, or what is present its light on what is past; rather, image is that wherein what has been comes together in a flash with the now to form a constellation. In other words: image is dialectics at a standstill. For while the relation of the present to the past is purely temporal, the relation of what-has-been to the now is dialectical: not temporal in nature but figural. Only dialectical images are genuinely historical . . . images . . . and the place where one encounters them is language.[110]

The relationship between past and present here is not developmental, but it is also not completable; history is never that which happened in the past. Rather, it is conceptualized as a political and experiential moment in time, a space in which past and present can be brought into conjunction, to form a dialectical relationship in which a particular historical constellation can be imagined anew. And as a linguistic form, the image is certainly thinkable in terms of film.[111] My claim for these films is that landscape functions as such a dialectical image, forming a critical reading of the Italian postwar history of 1945 and 1992 by setting up a productive stasis between two opposing operations of mise-en-scène, which are brought together textually and narratively in a tension that cannot be resolved.

The first element of this structure is precisely the auratic: the force with which the landscape image ruptures or short-circuits representation and, hence, produces an affect of pure temporal distance, of materiality and its loss. Thinkable as a crossroads of the aura, the indexical, and Kracauer's trees that break belief in a historical narrative, this mode evokes the real insofar as the landscape image offers to stand in for the experiential truth of the thing itself. The affective power of this mode is predicated on its ability to break out of signification and to produce an emotional effect not from any specific materiality but from its displacement onto abstract space and time. At the moment of this representational break, however, the landscape image also moves in exactly the opposite direction, for this image of temporal loss necessarily recalls that which it has deflected: the social narrative of an actual history and its material losses, the time of 1945 as felt in 1992. This history connects the landscape mise-en-scène to the films' narratives, where both produce a spectatorial position that repeats the emotionally charged cathexis of mourning. The "real" history of the failure of the Italian Left both entails and is entailed by the auratic "real" of the image, their contradictory formal operations binding a historical narrative and temporal experience into dialectical tension.

The main result of the dialectical image for Benjamin is the possibility of a radicalized relationship to history, in which the present as much as the past can be reimagined, reexperienced, and critiqued. In Konvolut N of *The Arcades Project*, where he discusses history and the dialectic, Benjamin claims that "the materialist presentation of history leads the past to place the present in a critical condition,"[112] and in Konvolut K he considers the idea of awakening as "an attempt to become aware of the dialectical . . . turn of remembrance."[113] What remembrance enables in the films is a relationship to the past that is both critical and emotional, distanced and immediate, and indeed cannot be one without the other. Furthermore, the relationship to history must come from a point in the present, for both the distance of the past and the closeness of the present are necessary components of remembrance. In enabling a reexperiencing of the loss of leftist hopes in the 1940s, the films produce an awakening to the situation in the early 1990s. At the moment preceding the *mani pulite* scandals, Italian political culture was indeed in a critical condition, and only by reawakening critiques from the beginning of the republic could its end be imagined at all. In the final section of this chapter, I will return to the historical and political specificity of the Italian landscape to interrogate how this dialectical image works textually and ideologically.

## Landscape and Neorealism

If the spectacular landscape promises in its visibility to show the truth of Italy, the corollary of asking what meanings this truth stands in for is to ask why this fetish, this particular kind of image, should be able to carry such significatory weight. In other words, what is specific to these landscapes that enables this dialectical structure? To answer this question, it is necessary to circle back to De Santis and the stake of Italian neorealism in representing a national-political space in the 1940s. It would be possible to produce a fairly straightforward historical reading of the importance of landscape in Italian culture in general and neorealism in particular: many of the standard works on Italian cinema cite the influence of novelists such as Giovanni Verga and Ignazio Silone on neorealism's focus on rural life.[114] Liehm goes further, arguing that "beginning in the early Renaissance, with Petrarch, Boccaccio and Ariosto and followed later by Goldoni and others, Italian artists had sought to render the flow of life rather than indulge in the kind of meditative creation, typical, for example, of German literature. Fascination with the landscape, a perspective that was the most treasured heritage of the neorealists, was inherent in this tradition."[115] And if landscape was historically central to Italian cultural production, De Santis connects its use in cinema to the politics of the wartime Left, claiming that the rural setting of many neorealist films made a crucial space in which to represent the peasants and workers who had formed the first mass resistance to fascism.[116]

Just as the standard histories of Italian film discuss neorealism's concern for a politically inflected national landscape, they also produce a dominant narrative of Italian cinema based on the influence of neorealism on all subsequent film movements. Exemplary here is Millicent Marcus's account of neorealism as a *via maestra* (master road) with regard to which all subsequent films must position themselves.[117] This version of a national or perhaps nationalistic film history should not be accepted without pause, not least because it repeats the kind of linear progressive narrative that the idea of the dialectical image works to refute. Nevertheless, it seems fair to say that by the 1980s at least, neorealism had become sufficiently canonical that references to its forms or specific texts are a commonplace in Italian culture.[118] When many films of the 1980s and 1990s cite neorealism, the centrality of landscape images to its political aesthetic makes such a mise-en-scène an obvious point of citation.

*Mediterraneo, Cinema Paradiso,* and *Il Postino* contain numerous references to some of the key texts of neorealism, setting up a connection to this moment in Italian cinema when landscape was marked as politically and aesthetically significant. Some of these citations center on the landscape itself: the opening shots of the bay in *Il Postino,* in which fishing boats are seen at sunrise in a picturesque long shot, directly reference *La terra trema.* Other references are more diffuse, ranging from the job advertisement in *Il Postino* that recalls *The Bicycle Thief* (De Sica, 1948) in its demand for a man with a bike, to the sentimentality of *Cinema Paradiso*'s version of childhood that again cites De Sica. Indeed, even Totò's name is self-consciously referential, for Totò is the name of the protagonist in *Miracle in Milan* (De Sica, 1951) and was the name of a popular film and stage comedian of the postwar era, as well as that of his character in Pasolini's *Hawks and Sparrows* (1966). And, of course, the historical moment of neorealism, from the end of the war until the late 1940s, was also the time in which the films' narratives are set and the time of leftist optimism that they mourn.

These references construct a historical logic whereby landscape sets off a metonymic chain, linking the historical narratives of the films to both a cinematic and a political history and, further, to a national-cultural history of landscape to which neorealism itself laid claim. But while this intertextual logic explains why landscape might offer a privileged mise-en-scène of postwar history for Italian cinema, it is not the whole story, for the historical space between the neorealist landscape and its reiteration in the 1990s is also part of the dialectical image, forming another both/and circuit. To reference neorealism is to make a certain truth claim for the image, and especially the landscape image, within the dominant critical logic whereby neorealism's representation of landscape promised to show directly the truth of Italy. However, by citing this image fifty years after the fact, neorealism has become itself historicized, and a gap is opened up so that the image can no longer stand directly for truth but, instead, connotes a certain history of truth-telling. Once again, ontology doubles back onto epistemology as the past is experienced from the distance of the present.

Neorealism is based on a claim of authenticity that applies to the social but derives in large part from the status of the image. Bazin describes it in terms of presence and immediacy, claiming that neorealism "knows only immanence. Only from the aspect, from the pure appearance of peo-

*La terra trema*    The film opens on the bay of Trezza, its central social space.

ple and the world does it intend to deduce, a posteriori, the lessons they conceal. It is a phenomenology."[119] This claim of transparency invokes indexicality but links it to specific modes of representation and specific mises-en-scènes—in particular, the natural and the timeless. Thus, the bay of Trezza in *La terra trema* is readable in terms of Krauss's aestheticizing discourse, which at this point is still able to operate positively in film criticism. The presence of the natural features of the bay authenticates the drama of the fishermen, underpinning the film's claim to reality status and enabling a reading in which the enduring quality of the landscape underwrites the timelessness and humanity of the characters, outside the modernized world of the spectator. But when *Il Postino* references this landscape, its claim on a similar truth discourse is necessarily disjunctive, for the nostalgic distance between the two texts precludes a pure sense of indexical presence and replaces it with an absence. The landscape viewed is not, historically, present at all, and to reference it is also to reference this loss.[120]

Contained in this disjuncture is the shift from texts structured by representing the present to those representing the past, for while *Il Postino*, *Mediterraneo*, and *Cinema Paradiso* are all historical films, almost all of the neorealist films they refer to deal with the present, telling stories about the immediate problems of Italy. Angela Dalle Vacche describes the project of neorealism as to "shoot in the present tense,"[121] and this

*Il Postino*    The framing of the bay closely copies that in *La terra trema*.

attention to the historical moment defines the political power of a film like Rossellini's *Paisà*. Dalle Vacche quotes Gian Piero Brunetta's reading of the film, in which "history passes over the body of these characters and even today . . . we are struck by the perfect congruence of all elements and by the perception of a profound change in an apparently immobile landscape and body politic."[122] Dalle Vacche is interested in the discourses of embodiment produced by nonprofessional actors, but what is important in terms of landscape is that for Brunetta the film provides an exact match between narrative and mise-en-scène in which the authenticity of the form produces a real connection with the immediacy of the historical moment. This matching can be placed in opposition to Kracauer's disconnection of actor and landscape in the historical film, and while any nonhistorical film would resolve this problem for Kracauer, neorealism's immediacy and location shooting are traditionally held to provide the closest possible connection between profilmic reality and narrative space. It is significant, then, that the recent films cite this moment of greatest conjunction between narrative and place, while, in their historical perspective, forcing a disjuncture on exactly that score. In citing a discourse of seamlessness, they break it open.

The temporal immediacy of neorealism is part of its claim to represent the political and national truth of Italy—for example, in *Rome, Open City* (Rossellini, 1945), where the war-damaged space of Rome authenticates the narrative of partisan opposition to fascism. Roland Schneider exemplifies a common reading of this aesthetics, arguing that "as for the image of the people, the filmmakers, powerless, had no other recourse but that of direct, mute witnessing."[123] Witnessing, as a political strategy, depends on historical presence, on the indexicality of the photographic image, and on location shooting. It is also a strategy that focuses on critiquing present conditions in order to force some kind of change, and, as such, neorealism has been called "the repository of partisan hopes for social justice in the postwar Italian state."[124] As such, it is also a chronicle of the failure of those hopes, and for contemporary films to reference its politics is inevitably to take on the difference of this historical perspective. *Cinema Paradiso* includes a scene nearly identical to one in *La terra trema*, in which a group of men wait for casual work, but the Communist is stigmatized and fails to get a job. Whereas in the earlier film, this injustice could be read as a call to action, in *Cinema Paradiso* the inevitable failure of such action is already known, the historical process located in the past tense. This doubled relationship to political and filmic history is part of the dialectical image and not merely an ironized rejection of the political "truth" of neorealism. The ideological and cinematic codes of the 1940s are still the basis of Italian leftist identity and yet were as false then as they are now. The films cannot *not* refer to neorealism, yet must cite its impossibility at the same time as its necessity.

A reiteration of the neorealist landscape forces a consideration of the distance between 1945 and 1992, but it also frames the relationship as one of national identity, in the very concrete terms of the geographic space of Italy: its political landscape. We can approach this spatialization of the concept of the nation thematically, for neorealism is also commonly read as an attempt to reconstruct a national identity out of the ashes of fascism.[125] *Paisà*, for example, is often interpreted in this vein, where its movement from Sicily to the Pò Valley reenvisions the physical space of Italy for the partisans and Allied soldiers. This thematization of the nation is repeated at a historical remove in the more recent films, where such a sense of *patrie* has become the object of cynical humor. In *Mediterraneo*, for example, the password for the soldiers on guard duty is "Queen Margherita," but this patriotic signifier of national identity is misremembered in a debased form by one of the men as "Pizza Margherita." This thematic shift from direct denotation to ironic doubling is, in turn, symptomatic of the historical one from optimism to pessimism. However, such thematization of national identity is of less significance than the material specificity of location, for the dialectic within which landscape signifies both indexical truth and a metonymic chain of specific historical meanings also includes a geopolitical logic. Just as the structure of temporal loss in the aura displaces a locatable social loss, so the form of the tree and the branch also implicates a specific content: a locatable place with social and textual legibility.

## North and South

The location of all three films can be broadly defined as the South. *Cinema Paradiso* is quite geographically specific, describing Giancaldo as a village on the southern coast of Sicily; in *Il Postino*, the island is a fictionalized version of Capri, here a smaller island off the coast of Naples; and in *Mediterraneo*, the location is not Italy at all but a Greek island, placing the Italian characters farther south still than any part of their home country. These locations can be read as more references to neorealism, for many key neorealist films are set in the South—including *La terra trema, Anni difficili* (Zampa, 1948), and *In the Name of the Law* (Germi, 1949)—and take as their main theme the poverty and oppression of the Southern peasants. But this reference is only part of a complex web of meanings within which the image of the South operates in Italian politics and culture, and through which concepts of a singular national identity are problematized. In these films, the trope of the South

*Cinema Paradiso*   The barren landscape and modern viaduct form a typical Sicilian view.

connects history and landscape to both the internal and external shapes of the nation—that is, to the relationship between the internal politics of Italy and the wider geopolitics of Europe and the world. During the crucial period of 1945 to 1948, Italy was in an ambiguous position within Europe, ideologically definable as neither East nor West. Its transition from fascism left it with no clear history of alliance, and while it had economic reasons to court the United States, its strong Communist Party had links to Eastern Europe. At an international level, Italy's East/West status was of disproportionate strategic value, but internally this problem was displaced onto a North/South divide, with the economic and political results of partition adding to an already entrenched understanding of the South as a peripheral space within the Italian state. Within the logic of the mise-en-scène, the Southernness of the landscape image is a structural part of its affect, presenting the history of the Italian Left as a geographic problem, one of North and South, and of East and West.

The political, economic, and cultural split between the north of Italy and the south did not begin with World War II, but in the war years it developed a structuring influence on national identity and political debate.[126] While the country was partitioned, the South enjoyed a relatively secure period with no fighting and under a pre-Fascist-style government that, along with the Allies, returned the king briefly to power. As a result, Southerners were more inclined to support a new version of the status quo after the war than to institute radical change, and the region was not just more inclined to conservatism but less in favor of broad coalitions. The North, by contrast, saw heavy fighting, and many Italians were involved in the partisan movement, which represented not only Communists but also Socialists, Liberals, and Christian Democrats. As many political shades rallied round the anti-Fascist CNL partisans, a spirit of coalition was built that gave the Left much more support than it had gained in the South. This political divide remained after the war, with the PCI finding much of its support in the North, and the South becoming the bastion of the DC. In addition to this party political geography, the postwar years saw a massive divide develop in terms of wealth, as industrialization rapidly changed the North, leaving much of the South rural and impoverished. The subsequent magnification of the differences between the regions means that even in the postwar years, and certainly by the 1990s, any representation of a southern location implies not only a rural landscape but a poor and, from a leftist point of view, politically distant one.

The perceived distance of the South, its peripheral status in postwar Italy, has also conventionally been thought of within a discourse of primitivism: the racist cliché of Northern Italians is "after Rome, Africa." This idea is not limited to folk wisdom but recurs in historical and political analyses in which the South is considered to be less "European" than the rest of Italy. A typical example from the 1950s is Bernard Wall's book on the cultural geography of postwar Italy, in which he claims:

> The Deep South is almost as unknown to Northern Italians as it is to foreigners. In Italy Northerners often talk about Calabria as they talk about Eritrea or Tripolitania: as a kind of colonial land in which European standards no longer exist and whose inhabitants are dirty and barbarous. And there is a certain economic truth on what they say. Calabrians and Lucanians . . . are as illiterate as Arabs, and their way of life, which has hardly changed since Roman times, or changed for the worse materially owing to over-population, has in some ways more in common with the Eastern Mediterranean than with the bicycle and cinema civilisation of Milan.[127]

This description condenses the "civilized" abjection of the South as fundamentally different and the anxiety as inherent in the process of rapid modernization: that the failure of a historical shift (from pre-modern to modern) could result in a geographic shift (out of the Northern space of "Europe" and into the Southern one of "barbarism"). As recently as the 1980s, DC party secretary Aldo Forlani could oppose a presidential system by arguing, "We don't want to become like Africa or South America."[128] Given that the more obvious examples of a presidential system to emulate might be France or the United States, Forlani's rhetoric appeals to a fear of Italy becoming more "Southern" and less European. In this way, Italy's internal division has historically been projected onto anxieties about its international identity in Europe.

The idea of the South, then, becomes the nub of many problems of Italian national identity, and the films' locations in the "South" play on this imbrication of internal and external geographies and of geographical with historical categories. To the extent that the films construct a heritage image of picturesque rural life, they could be read as taking part in the discourse of primitivism, albeit in a contemporary touristic, rather than overtly racist, register. Certainly, the signifiers of Southernness in the landscape are those of the rural and the pre-modern, focusing in both *Cinema Paradiso* and *Il Postino* on barren countryside, scrubby hills, and small villages. Also emphasized is the sea, from the opening shot of *Cinema Paradiso* through a window looking onto the ocean to the many seascapes of *Mediterraneo* or the beach that Mario walks along in

*Il Postino*. These repeated images of the Mediterranean suggest the physical distance of the islands in each film from the mainland, a distance that again connotes the cultural difference as well as the physical distance of the South. The rhetorical distance of this particular kind of rural landscape is emphasized in *Mediterraneo*, where the location is not Italy but a fantasy South, a Greek island where the signifiers of Southernness can be exaggerated, forming a kind of Mediterranean *typage* within which all the characters are enabled to "find their roots."

As with the question of landscape in heritage cinema, however, what could be misread as touristic spectacle is, in these films, part of the construction of historical mourning, where the specificity of the southern locations is tied to the nostalgic and melodramatic narratives. Both *Il Postino* and *Cinema Paradiso* include scenes in which their island locations are authenticated internally, with the protagonists watching their own region represented in the cinema. In *Il Postino*, the scene comes early in the film, in a newsreel describing Pablo Neruda's arrival in Rome and exile to a "beautiful island." As the screen images show the village and its inhabitants, the locals watch their own space reflected back at them and shout, "that's me!" at the screen. In *Cinema Paradiso*, recognizable news and film clips in a cinema scene connect location to historicity and nostalgia. The sequence begins with a newsreel, this time describing a Resistance rally, and so fixing the scene as shortly after the war has ended. The film that follows is *La terra trema*, and the onscreen credit explains that the film was acted by Sicilian fishermen. The audience in Giancaldo is, mainly, Sicilian fishermen, so once again the film is reflecting its own audience's geographical and historical location back to them. However, in this case the sequence is not about a communal experience but a subjective one, where Totò, bored with the newsreel, turns away from the screen to look toward the projection booth. The next shot is an optical point of view of the lion's head that surrounds the projection space, and in Totò's fantasy the lion roars as the camera zooms rapidly toward it. As a memory embedded in a flashback structure, this sequence encapsulates Totò's cinephilia, but it also binds that cinematic nostalgia to the political landscape of the postwar years and to the material landscape of Sicily. The displacement from the screen to the apparatus mimics that of politics onto romance, and, like this, it produces a historical point of view predicated on desire as well as loss. Imagined among Sicily, Resistance, neorealism, and fantasy, the roaring lion establishes the essentially imaginary, yet historically powerful, nature of political nostalgia.

The connection of this historical point of view to the South is not simply a matter of geographic recognition but is cut through with the prob-

lematic nature of regional meanings. In *Cinema Paradiso*, the South becomes part of the affective narrative of historical loss—for example, in a
scene immediately following Totò's discovery that his father has died in
the war. Alfredo has told Totò that his father looked like Clark Gable, and
as the boy and his mother walk past bombed-out buildings, Totò sees on
a wall the remains of a movie poster advertising *Gone with the Wind*
(Fleming, 1939). The poster serves as a reminder of his father to Totò, but
it also invokes for the spectator another narrative of North and South,
locating the father's death both in the context of civil war and in a melodramatic story. The comedy of the film derives from Totò's desire to live
in a movie, but its melodramatization of the South is also legible in cinematic terms.

In addition to the temporal distance produced in these nostalgic and
melodramatic sequences, the ancient nature of the landscape allows the
South to connote the national past in a way that contrasts with the cos-
mopolitan modernity of mainland Italy. Physical distance collapses onto
temporal distance—for example, in *Cinema Paradiso*, where Totò's
return to Giancaldo from Rome seems almost like time travel to an older
Italy. The unchanging space of the village connotes a heritage past that
precedes the modernity of the city, just as the neorealist references to
Sicily precede historically the reminders of *La dolce vita* (Fellini, 1960)
in the scenes of Totò's rootlessness in Rome. This division is also gendered, with the South of Totò's family home connoting femininity as
well as the rural, primitive past, and the North standing for the masculine urban spaces of the modernized present.

In this way, while this "distant" or exotic South can be conceptualized
as such only from the position of the North, the unmarked "European"
part of Italy, the North can mourn its historical loss only by projecting it
onto its primitive other. The space of the South becomes the only place
that Italian national history can be envisioned, for only in the South can
it be located as fantasmatically distant and already lost. It is thus possible to argue that, as with its auratic projection of history, the geography
of the southern landscape enables an affective engagement with the past
that would be impossible in a different kind of physical location. The distance of the South that enables it to stand in for a nostalgic past also
enables it to function as a privileged signifier of the time before the First
Republic, the moment of possibility for the Left. The time of DC hegemony becomes coextensive with the modernization and rapid social and
economic change that produced Italy's economic miracle in and for the
North. Thus, the discourse within which the South is seen as being outside modernization enables the southern landscape image to stand, in a

geographical and historical slippage, for the pre-modernized past of a socialist utopia manqué.

But, of course, this projection, like that of neorealism, doubles back on itself, and if the exotic primitivism of the South allows it to stand for a space of historical desire, its regional history forces a split on exactly those terms. First, the very distance invoked by the southern landscape, its connotation of backwardness, makes an uncomfortable fit with a left-ist position concerned with Italian nationhood. The specificity of the location fights against any simple expression of national loss, forcing the question of whose loss is being narrated. Furthermore, while the South provides a space for the fantasy of political potential, it simulta-neously offers a reminder of why and how the historical moment of 1945 went awry for the Left. While the North would have offered the possibil-ity of more heroic narratives, based on clear-cut Communist or anti-Fascist politics, the South returned to political in-fighting and reaction before the war ended and, as is depicted in *Il Postino* and *Cinema Pa-radiso*, offered little promise for Communists. Thus, the southern loca-tion of the films reiterates the structure of the dialectical image: its pris-tine beauty connotes at once the time before the political changes of the DC years and the inevitability of those changes. Nostalgia can be visual-ized only at a remove, but it is displaced onto the precise place that his-torically refused radical political change.

The structure of the dialectic prompts the question of what relation-ship this displacement of East and West onto North and South has to the 1990s; in other words, from where does this historical problematic sig-nify? As I have argued, the auratic landscape involves an oscillation of distance and closeness in which the temporality of the subject in mourn-ing is as important as that of the historical lost object. We can take the same perspective here, and we again find that the period leading to the collapse of the Italian First Republic is crucial. At this moment, national political discourse invokes the question of North and South and of East and West, forming a constellation in which, in Benjamin's terms, remembrance of a specific past is necessary to the process of awakening.

While the North/South divide was an ongoing political and cultural issue during the intervening years, historians such as Donald Sassoon make the claim that the economics of corporatism exacerbated the effect of the divide by skimming too much from the prosperous North.[129] By the late 1980s, the economy had reached crisis point, and feeling in the North was that the region was contributing disproportionately to prop up the poorer South.[130] Certainly, there was a familiar prejudice at work here, with the market-driven North condemning the rural South as lazy, but this discourse could become so powerful only in the context of systemic corruption that did indeed filter capital from the Northern cities. In the wake of the *mani pulite* scandals, this resentment was given an explicit voice, with the rise of the Northern League, a new political party that sought to speak for a submerged regionalism. The party gained substantial support, but this was not the North of the partisans: rather, it can be considered in terms of the new radical rightist parties that grew across Europe in the 1980s, and, like some of them, its appeal was implicitly and sometimes explicitly racist. At the moment when the films are looking back to the inception of the modern North/South dynamic, this dynamic again contributes to Italy's national crisis. Just as the North/South split took on increased weight at the beginning of the Cold War, so its ideological power was renewed in the wake of the Cold War's end. In order to reimagine the nation, it would be pressing to rethink the history of the split. There was a significant shift in the relative meanings of those terms, for while in 1945 the South constituted a problem for the Left, by the 1990s it had become the only space untouched by the post–Cold War rightward swing of the urban voters who embraced Berlusconi's free-market rhetoric and the Northern League's racism. For this reason, perhaps, it is the South, and not the North, that becomes the desirable object of a leftist nostalgic gaze in the 1990s.

The relation of the internal mapping of Italian identity to its wider international positioning also recurred in the early 1990s, not in regard to the Cold War structure of East and West but in terms of Europe itself, and the moves from the late 1980s on toward European integration. Here, again, Italy was in an uncertain position, as its weakened economy led, in 1991, to fears that the country would be unable to meet European currency convergence requirements.[131] The daily newspaper *La Repubblica* expressed what had become a major public anxiety, announcing that "Enterprise Italy, overwhelmed by debt, will miss the European train."[132] The impetus to become more European appears on a social as well as a purely economic level, where the panic about Italy's ability to join the European Single Market can be read as part of the structuring national anxiety that identifies Europe as a question of North and South. What it means for Italy to be more European is to be less Southern, less "backward" in the rhetoric of Southern primitivism from which the North can never fully escape. And while European cooperation was a popular policy, there is a contradictory desire at work here that speaks to the affective power of the southern landscape in the films: as long as Northern Italy considers itself to be always already European, the South is able to stand in for that which is more truly Italian. This is the fetishistic process of abjection and recuperation that underwrites the mise-en-scène of the South, in which the material distance of the landscape defines both the space where the nation becomes a problem and the space in which national specificity inheres. Thus overdetermined, the southern landscape becomes the privileged site of fantasy.

To raise the question of Italian identity, and the relationship of the national to the international, is also to evoke the heritage film, in which national landscapes or, indeed, stereotypes operate as brand images that enable European films to circulate in the global market. The anxiety around Italy's place in Europe that the films work on textually is part of the same historical problematic that produces the heritage film as a leading European mode in the 1980s and 1990s. Films such as *Jean de Florette* (Berri, 1986) and *Enchanted April* (Newell, 1992) negotiate the requirement to produce a national cultural discourse for audiences and producers at home, and the sometimes contradictory need for that discourse to be legible—and, indeed, pleasurable—for a less knowledgeable global audience. Of course, such tensions between national and international reception are not new, and neorealism is a key example of their interaction. Many neorealist films were not popular on their initial Italian releases, and the DC government opposed their international distribution on the grounds that films like *Umberto D.* (De Sica, 1952) gave a bad impression of Italy to the rest of the world.[133] It was only after they were lauded abroad that they came to prominence within Italy.[134] One of the points of similarity between the films of the early 1990s and those of the 1940s is their repetition of this distribution and reception history, for *Cinema Paradiso* was also regarded as something of a failure within Italy until after it won international recognition, and it was in the wake of this success that *Il Postino* and *Mediterraneo* were given wide release in Italy.

The recurring question is how to constitute the Italian nation in relation to the rest of the world, and in both periods this becomes part of the textual work of the films and an issue of reception. By the 1990s, however, the relation of Italy to Europe and the world was both a political crisis and a determining factor in film production. As Stille points out, the system of corruption and *partitocrazia* could work only in a closed market, and in order to enter the new Europe and the rapidly globalizing economy Italy had to rethink its national past and present.[135] At the same time, film production across Europe was more dependent than ever on international coproductions, and the impossibility of competing directly with Hollywood had produced, in the 1980s, the response of the nationally specific heritage film. The economic need to articulate the national with the international applied across the European film industries, but it was only in Italy that this imperative coalesced with both a wider political consideration of the nation and a cultural imperative to rethink the national history that had led to the crisis. *Cinema Paradiso, Mediterraneo,* and *Il Postino,* then, do not so much subvert or undercut the conventions of the heritage film as render textually material and politically productive its structuring tensions. Readable in terms of melodrama, romance, and spectacle, they are—not despite but through these functions—also structured by a logic of mourning that demands a nationally and ideologically directed subject position. In the constellation of historical and visual signifiers of 1945 and 1992, the spectacle of landscape functions as the linchpin that binds critical distance with affective closeness, temporality with historicity, and the period of optimism with that of crisis. In this dialectical image, the desire for a point of origin for a historical failure opens up the potential for what Benjamin would call an awakening, in which the reimagining of the past prompts a critical reexperiencing of the present.

# 3   A Conspiracy of Cartographers?

For Tom Stoppard's paranoid Rosencrantz (*Rosencrantz and Guilderstern Are Dead* [Stoppard, 1990]), space is purely a matter of representation and, in true postmodern style, he has lost faith in the authority of the map:

> *Guildenstern*: What a shambles! We're just not getting anywhere.
> *Rosencrantz*: Not even England. I don't believe in it anyway.
> *Guildenstern*: What?
> *Rosencrantz*: England.
> *Guildenstern*: Just a conspiracy of cartographers, you mean?

As the cannier Guildenstern's sarcastic comment implies, however, we cannot read cartography simply as conspiracy. The existence of England, after all, is not in doubt. What is at stake is the production of cartographic authority: who draws the maps, and what relationship is articulated between image and reality. This question emerges forcibly in Europe in 1989, when events began to produce new territories and indeed new mapmakers. Less publicly, though, 1989 also saw the beginnings of a new critical challenge to cartographic authority. In this year, the geographer J. B. Harley published "Deconstructing the Map," an article that, in reading maps in relation to poststructuralist theories of textuality and power, essentially initiated the area of critical cartography.[1] The coincidence of these dates is felicitous, suggesting a historical linkage of political and intellectual change; the breakdown of the Cold War geopolitical order not only entails the well-known crisis of Marxism but also involves a theoretical shift in how we think about the representation of space.

For European cinema post-Wall, new works of mapping were necessary in order to inscribe new kinds of space—as Eastern and Western Europe gave way to more complex political landscapes, cinematic space became a key territory in which change could be imagined. Thus, while the previous chapter took literally the concept of a "political landscape," this chapter is more concerned with the spirit than with the letter of that phrase, turning to films that rethink the political, rather than the physical, map of Europe. Of course, the distinction between physical and political mapping is always to some extent a fiction, for, as we have seen, even an image of nature is implicated in a structure of historical and social meanings. Nonetheless, there is a difference in cinematic terms between the landscape image and the more conceptual landscape of national and international space. These kinds of spaces are never directly visible, but, as with Harley's critique of cartographic textuality, they must be carefully read. In what follows, I trace both a filmic and a critical path, considering how theories of space and spatial representation, as well as art cinemas, provide forms of textuality in which we can engage the changing map of Europe.

## Questioning the Map

Rosencrantz and Guildenstern's witty exchange has more than a rhetorical connection to these issues, for the film version of *Rosencrantz and Guildenstern Are Dead* is an early example of post-Wall and postmodern European art film. The film traces the trajectories of two minor characters from *Hamlet* in the interstices of known history. Located somewhere between the heritage literary adaptation and the self-referential art film about art (similar to the later *Shakespeare in Love* [Madden, 1998], coscripted by Stoppard), *Rosencrantz and Guildenstern* narrates the unsuccessful attempts by Shakespeare's minor characters to figure out what their purpose is and who is pulling their strings. The film opens with the two men trying unsuccessfully to remember anything before being summoned that morning to see the king. Upon arrival, their movements weave in and out of the better-known events at Elsinore. Behind the scenes, as it were, they try to make sense of what little information they have been given. As it turns out, paranoia is not an unreasonable response to events, since, as the knowledgable spectator already knows, our heroes will be sent to England with a sealed letter requesting that the king execute them. As the traveling Player tells them: "The bad die unhappily, the good unluckily: that is what Tragedy means."

*Rosencrantz and Guildenstern* can provide a useful bridge between the popular forms of the heritage history film and a more specialized art cinema. The film draws from the conventions of the British literary adaptation, which is closely related to the heritage film. (The adjacence of these forms in British cinema occurs both because the canon of English literature is commonly adduced to the category of "British heritage" and because many defining texts of the heritage genre are themselves literary adaptations. See, for instance, *A Passage to India* [Lean, 1984], *Maurice* [Ivory, 1987], and *Howards End*, all from E. M. Forster novels.) Thus, *Rosencrantz*'s Shakespearian language, historical setting, and supporting cast of respected theatrical actors are easily readable in a heritage framework. The world of *Hamlet*'s narrative resembles a nonexistent Shakespeare adaptation, perhaps directed by Kenneth Branagh. But, just as the play's characters move uncertainly around the edges of *Hamlet*, the film's leads, Tim Roth and Gary Oldman, are film actors, thrust into a theatrical world, lost in the diegesis of heritage. By bracketing the world of Hamlet as incomprehensible to the protagonists, the film constructs a self-reflexive and art-cinematic play on the heritage genre.[2]

In fact, the film's art-cinematic form focuses on this self-reflexive play with representation. Its structuring joke is that, as fictional characters, Rosencrantz and Guildenstern have only the few lines of *Hamlet* that mention them from which to draw their identities and knowledge of the world. Before they were awakened by the king's messenger, they literally did not exist. This premise enables a complex staging of fictional space, in which the spectator's knowledge of *Hamlet* is constantly refracted in a proliferation of narrative forms. Most simply, the spectator frequently knows more than do the characters, as when they try, unsuccessfully as usual, to figure out what is wrong with Hamlet. And throughout the film, reflexivity is foregrounded, as when the players mime the plot of *Hamlet* for the castle's servants, or when the play within the play includes within it yet another play, this time a puppet show. Fictional spaces multiply, and within this prison house of representation, the real place of England becomes an uncertain abstraction.

Rosencrantz and Guildenstern's existential dilemma irresistibly invokes contemporaneous work on postmodernity. We may be reminded, for instance, of Jean Baudrillard's well-known reading of Jorge Luis Borges's story "On Exactitude in Science," in which an empire creates a map the same size as its territory, only to abandon the map and let it rot across the far corners of the nation.[3] For Baudrillard, even this decay of representational truth does not go as far as the postmodern condition of simulation, in which there is no longer a referential ground for the image. The simulacrum precedes and, indeed, replaces real space. However, while there is no outside to *Rosencrantz and Guildenstern*'s fictional Denmark, the film does not, like Baudrillard, reject any notion of reference. More significant here than the theory of simulation is the place that cartography holds within theories of representation. In conjuring the postmodern condition, and even though he immediately claims that the allegory is false, Baudrillard is compelled to begin with the image of a map.

A more suggestive contemporary account is Fredric Jameson's discussion of cognitive mapping, in another of the canonical texts of postmodernity.[4] Jameson also uses cartography as a way to imagine a postmodern relationship to spaces, but in citing Kevin Lynch's term, he stresses the political implications of mapmaking. Beginning with the shift from subject-centered itineraries and sea charts to modern star maps that enable a relationship to totality, Jameson suggests that the postmodern subject is, like the pre-modern one, faced with a space that cannot easily be totalized. Thus, he claims, "the conception of space that has been developed here suggests that a model of political culture appropriate to our own situation will necessarily have to raise spatial issues as its fundamental organising concern."[5] He goes on to suggest that this new cultural form could be defined as an "aesthetic of cognitive mapping," a form that attempts to give shape to new structures of complex totality. This idea, that a textual aesthetic of mapping might be required in order to reimagine social space, offers one way to connect theories of postmodernity to the cultural spaces of post-Wall Europe.

In the case of *Rosencrantz and Guildenstern*, the terrain being mapped is in the first instance textual: the film reimagines the fictional space of *Hamlet* rather than any actual location. Just as Jameson's subject makes mental maps in order to navigate the postmodern city spaces of Los Angeles, so Rosencrantz and Guildenstern struggle to find a way through the text of *Hamlet*, unable to see from the bird's-eye vantage point of the spectator, who knows where this is going. But if Rosencrantz does not believe in England, the film does, for it is the social space of *Hamlet*, Shakespeare, and the British heritage film that is being redrawn here.[6] Moreover, while Stoppard's original play, written in the 1960s, stages a vertiginous hall-of-mirrors discourse on *theatrical* space, the film version, like Siegfried Kracauer's real trees, prompts an intrusion of material reality. Unlike Kracauer's examples, *Rosencrantz* plays on this juxtaposition of actual and fictive spaces: in keeping with Rosencrantz's skepticism, we never see England. And in a refusal of heritage logic, the film was not shot in either Britain or Denmark but in Slovenia, Croatia, and Yugoslavia. This geographic replacement is visible in the architectural style of Elsinore, in the central European aesthetic of the puppets, and in the ethnic appearance of the Balkan actors who play the players. With this eruption—in northern Europe—of these signifiers of southeastern Europe, the film's real spaces complicate its fictional discourse on cultural power and national identity.

This kind of second-order mapping, in which it is not a country or region that is reimagined but an image of national culture, becomes particularly important in British cinema, where the canon of literary history has been central to competing discourses of national identity. Here, Stoppard can be placed alongside Derek Jarman, whose *Edward II* (1991) reimagines Christopher Marlowe's play from a queer perspective, or Peter Greenaway, who deconstructs the heritage image in *Prospero's Books*, a complex digital transformation of Shakespeare's last work. In all these films, the language of the source text is left almost untouched, while the image track constructs new and often radically different meanings. In *Rosencrantz and Guildenstern*, line readings of *Hamlet's* text throw identity into doubt, with intonations that imply that nobody has any idea which character is which. Thus, the literary texts form a ground, a national landscape that cannot be remade but can be reenvisioned, made to speak otherwise.

In its self-conscious play with space, *Rosencrantz and Guildenstern* exemplifies the beginning of a process of textual mapping that we can trace across European cinemas in the 1990s. Much like the film's hapless philosophers, post-Wall art cinema has two structuring problems: the ontological and the epistemological. Simply put: What is Europe, and how can we understand it? While there is clearly no singular response to these questions—European art cinema is as diverse as ideas of Europe—we can borrow Jameson's claims about cognitive mapping in order to clarify the ideological stakes of posing the questions. For Jameson, mapping "allows us to rethink these specialised geographical and cartographic issues in terms of social space—in terms, for example, of social class and national or international context, in terms of the ways in which we all necessarily also cognitively map our individual social relationship to local, national, and international class realities."[7] The sections that follow consider how post-Wall art cinema maps several kinds of socially determined spaces: city and national spaces, spectacular space, international space, and borders. What connects ontology with epistemology for Rosencrantz and Guildenstern is, in the inexorable logic of literary history, death. As we shall see, in post-Wall art cinema, too, the redrawing of space and time often juxtaposes textual play with historical finality.

## Reading Space

In the twentieth century, space emerges as a central term in theorizing modernity and, later, postmodernity. While the field of spatial inquiry is too vast and too multidisciplinary in nature to attempt to cover here, it is useful to chart some of the routes by which space becomes such an important category to contemporary cultural studies. As we have seen in the previous chapter's discussion of Walter Benjamin, the work of the Frankfurt School is central in articulating the relations among space, time, cinema, and modernity. However, Anthony Vidler maintains that, until recently, the importance of space to the Frankfurt School was often downplayed: "On one level, of course, it is already a commonplace of intellectual history to note the fundamental role of spatial form in the cultural analyses of social critics like Theodor Adorno, Siegfried Kracauer and Walter Benjamin. . . . And yet it is true that the central position of these spatial paradigms in the development of critical theory has more often than not been obscured by the equal and sometimes opposite role of temporality, of these theorists' concern with historical dialectics."[8]

What prompts a return to the theorists of space in modernity is, at least partly, the renewed importance of space as a defining feature of postmodernity. We have already considered Jameson's claim that cognitive mapping is the only means to produce a politically engaged postmodern culture, as well as Baudrillard's use of the ruined map as a metaphor for the loss of reference. In addition to these texts, many areas of postmodern criticism, philosophy, and social theory emerged in the latter half of the twentieth century, often influenced by Henri Lefebvre's seminal work, *The Production of Space*. Lefebvre argues that space must be understood as socially produced, and it is particularly in the area of critical geography that this approach helped define new paradigms of thinking space. David Harvey, to take one example, proposes that the condition of postmodernity is defined by a new emphasis on space over time, while Edward Soja and Charles Jencks theorize urban spaces and architectural style, respectively.[9]

What makes these social theories useful for considering filmic space—beyond their broad claims to describe the spatial experiences of modern life—are the ways in which contemporary critical theory has begun to articulate connections between globalized postmodern space and various material fields of spatial production: art, architecture, cinema. An early example of this kind of work is Jameson's reading of postmodern culture, but as the debate has matured, more medium-specific analyses have emerged, most significantly in art history. This critical terrain develops the debates on modernity into the contemporary era and has two signal advantages for cinema: first, it offers ways to think about cultural texts in relation to evolving geopolitical spaces, and, second, it simultaneously mounts critiques of those geopolitical and geographical systems with which it must engage.

For example, Victor Burgin argues in *In/different Spaces* that the social scientific versions of postmodern geography—Soja, Mike Davis—fail to consider the work of fantasy in the social production of space, or, in Lefebvre's terms, that they consider only spatial practice, not representational space. In thinking artworks spatially, he maintains, we must add back the psychic investments that geography strips from the experience of place: subjectivity, desire, identification. In a similar vein, Rosalyn Deutsche criticizes David Harvey's account of postmodernity as masculinist and totalizing, ignoring the crucial influence of feminism in developing postmodern culture and theory. Her examples include feminist artists such as Cindy Sherman and Barbara Kruger, but she is equally concerned with the ways in which feminist theories demand a more situated and political perspective on the contested interfaces of public art and urban space.[10]

These art historical readings of the geographic suggest, if not a model for approaching cinema, then certainly a significant area of disciplinary overlap. As Irit Rogoff argues, "We must recognize geography to be as much of an epistemic category as gender or race, and that all three are indelibly linked at every stage."[11] In her study of mapping in contemporary art, *Terra Infirma: Geography's Visual Culture*, she argues persuasively that cartography—the visual rendition of geographic spaces—is not simply a metaphor or theme but, rather, a central category of understanding subjectivity, history, and representation. Rogoff, like Harley, points to the place of maps in condensing power: their ability to name, write, and organize social spaces and their history in colonialism and the narration of the nation-state. Analyzing the political work of artists such as Mona Hatoum, Hans Haacke, and Joshua Neustein, Rogoff reads artistic remapping as a kind of countercartography, a disturbing of identity and hegemonic power. Understood this way, cultural texts that foreground geographic representations might offer a productive way to interrogate the politics of contemporary space.

While this kind of political remapping has become a major strand of contemporary art, it is less dominant in cinema. However, Rogoff's argument is suggestive for cinema studies, particularly in its refusal to use any positivist notions of geography. Echoing Jacques Derrida in *The Other Heading*, she links geography to ethics, stating that "it seems imperative to shift from a moralizing discourse of geography and location, in which we are told what ought to be, who has the right to be where, and how it ought to be so, to a contingent ethics of geographical emplacement in which we might jointly puzzle out the perils of the fantasms of belonging as well as of the tragedies of not belonging."[12] Thus, it is not the case that cartography suggests a new and improved cinematic map of Europe, but that we might find a new ethics of mapmaking, a countercartography of European identity.

## Hara-kiri in Berlin

One film that engages with this task is *Berlin.killer.doc* (Ellerkamp and Heitman, 1999), which works (and plays) on the spaces of Berlin in "the interim." The film is constructed a little like an experimental reality-TV show *avant la lettre*: a group of real characters sign up for a citywide game of "killer," the children's game in which each player is contracted to "kill" another one. The protagonists then make film or video diaries, recording their experiences as both murderer and victim as they traverse the spaces of the transforming city. The film's narrative immediately proposes a work of remapping, as the opening sequence introduces not only the characters but also the building sites of Berlin's Mitte. The interim describes the time in which post-Wall Berlin is being remade politically, culturally, and architecturally, and the film superimposes on this public remapping a more subjective and marginal cartography.

This subjective relationship to space underpins the film's cartographic logic, for we quickly leave behind the grand architectural projects mushrooming across the Mitte in order to focus on small-scale, deliberately inconsequential actions. Each killer must follow his or her victim, and thus we accumulate sequences shot by players walking in streets, conducting surveillance in bars, and idly watching apartment buildings. The defining modern figure of the flaneur is updated and imbued with both boredom and threat.

Characters undertake tedious stakeouts of each other, and in a climactic scene, two stuffed rabbits belonging to a Japanese woman named

*Berlin.killer.doc*   Berlin's urban spaces are framed in the process of transformation.
(Courtesy Bettina Ellerkamp and Jörg Heitman)

Akiko are kidnapped. To save her bunnies, Akiko must agree to commit
hara-kiri in a kitschy midnight ceremony. In this storyline, the *kawaii*
subculture of Japanese cute aesthetics trumps the monumental scale of
Berlin's urban spaces.

The film creates several alternative cartographies. Most direct is the
encounter with in-between spaces, where the game prompts interactions between players and semiotically loaded city spaces. One character
films himself sitting in waste ground, talking about the huge empty
spaces to be found in Berlin, what Andreas Huyssen has called its
"voids."[13] Others describe Berlin's provincial character and their fears
that it will be lost among the featureless global architecture that is pro-
liferating. In one scene, a victim goes to hear a reading in the Jewish
cemetery, held in response to racist attacks on the site. The murderer
spies on his victim through a hole in the wall, and we cut between shots
of the hole and the victim. The scene follows on from another player's
discussion of Berlin as a city that contains all of twentieth-century history compressed in one space. Along with the political weight of the
reading, this conjunction implies for the image of the hole a historical
significance, another "void" of Berlin. It is also, of course, a returned

*Berlin.killer.doc*    Akiko commits hara-kiri to save her bunnies. (Courtesy Bettina Ellerkamp and Jörg Heitman)

gaze. We know that the killer is looking through the hole, that there is now a subject for this historical void.

The structuring logic of the "killer" game also produces an alternative method of mapping: the trope introduces a fundamental element of chance into the film's representations. Any character may be killed at any time, and both the locations and actions of the film are improvised by the actors. Berlin becomes a city organized solely by the artificial and aleatory system of the game. Thus, *Berlin.killer* has intimations of automatic writing and Berlin's Dada history, but it also suggests the immaturity of the new city, as with a child using games to explore identity and transgression. Of course, the element of chance is also an element of crime—the film's Berlin is subject to sudden and inexplicable violence. With car bombs and letter bombs, many of the "murders" evoke Germany's recent history of domestic terrorism, as well as broader specters of global violence. But framed by the fictional game, these references become reflective rather than visceral. As a place in flux, Berlin reverberates with echoes of the crimes of elsewheres and elsewhens.

Finally, the film's formal structure raises the question of the document: How is it possible to record Berlin's fragmented and rapidly changing present? How does one document identity in flux? The answer is twofold: a self-referential accretion of documentary forms, and a representational play of fiction and reality. The documentary forms derive from the diaries of the players, as well as from the third-person narration of the film. They include super-8 film, video, and still photography, as well as other types of document, such as the digital file that names the film, the game's Web site, and the time, date, and place stamp that recurs on the image. The spectator cannot take any of these "documents" as direct accounts of reality, since each is seen to be partial and mediated. Furthermore, each document is partly documentary and partly fictional, since the game narrative mixes social actors with a highly fictional murder narrative. This contradictory relationship to the real is condensed in the murder scenes, where moments of pure fiction intrude into the documentary narrative. In one such scene, a car explodes; in another, a staged car crash depicts fake blood. Instead of the fictional films with moments of indexicality (as discussed in chapter 2), here we have a nonfiction film with arresting, disjunctive fictive images.

*Berlin.killer* creates a countermap of Berlin space, at the level of both content and form. Out of the self-styled center of the new Europe, the film conjures a place of unbelonging as much as identity: players come from England, Japan, and the United States, as well as from the city's former West and East. And once part of the game, characters must contemplate not just the journeys across the city that their diaries will describe but their ontological status. What is the new Berlin becoming, and how does one exist here? Thus, as one character draws a route in thick black pen across her map of Berlin, she considers her *killer-Dasein* (killer-being), questioning how one can define oneself in relation to both the Other and the city.[14] In Deutsche's and Rogoff's terms, this cartographic strategy replaces masculinist totality with a feminist-influenced emphasis on the partial view. Moreover, the film extends this critique in film-specific ways, setting in motion a narrative that weaves itself out of trajectories of power and vision. The film creates a map based on the place of looking relations in any organization of social space.

## Cinematic Cities and Nations

Although the influence of spatial theories has been felt more in the field of art history than in film, there is a substantial critical discourse on cinematic representations of the city. From Weimar cinema on, the city has been a central figure in modernist art cinema, as well as a common location for popular European films. And the centrality to cultural studies of theories of modernity has ensured that concepts like the flaneur, the metropolis, and the street have recurred in European film theories and histories. Giuliana Bruno, who has written widely on the topic, cites a history of city films and modernity, from early panoramic views through Dziga Vertov, F. W. Murnau, and Pier Paolo Pasolini.[15] Similarly, in an overview of the cinematic city, Stephen Barber describes a trajectory of urban displacement and alienation related to changes in city planning in postwar Europe. He narrates a history from neorealism through revolution and instability in the 1970s to contemporary postcolonial malaise.[16]

Barber suggests that the cinematic city has recently addressed the events of 1989, with Leos Carax's *Les Amants du Pont-Neuf* (1991) using the ebullient street celebrations of France's bicentennial to figure the fall of the Wall. Certainly, not every film set in a city can be read this way. But neither is *Berlin.killer.doc* an isolated example of the cinematic connection between the city and contemporary Europe. In a more traditionally Marxist vein, *The Town Is Quiet* (Guédiguian, 2001) analyzes the race and class fractions of postcolonial France by means of a cross section of life in Marseilles. The characters represent social types—we have the yuppie wife, the black kids who rap, the prostitute, and so on—but Marseilles stands as the film's central figure, connoting a dispossessed working-class, immigrant population and France's messy, South-facing aspect. Repeated lengthy pans across the city's harbor locate the various social groupings within the same profilmic space, if not the same social universe. And, perhaps in a nod to *The Conformist*, repeated renditions of the "Internationale" by various characters link the narratives to a melancholically lost leftist past.

In their tones of euphoria and melancholia, both *Les Amants du Pont-Neuf* and *The Town Is Quiet* point to the role of emotion in post-Wall cinematic spaces. Unlike the more stoic texts of the European New Waves, contemporary art films often play with melodrama and affect. This question of emotional landscapes has been examined by Giuliana Bruno in the evocatively titled *Atlas of Emotion*. Bruno is one of the most prominent film theorists to write specifically on space, and, as one might imagine, she locates film geographies alongside artistic ones. She shares with art historians like Rogoff an interest in alternative maps, pointing to both paintings and films as modes of writing in which counterhegemonic journeys might be undertaken. However, Bruno is specifically concerned with relationships among films, social spaces, and the body—architectures of emotion that she names "intimate geographies."[17] Her readings range from domestic architecture to international journeys, but, like Burgin, Bruno demands throughout that we think of textual journeys in terms of desire.

We can trace these political and yet intimate geographies in films that map the nation, as well as those centered on cities. *Bhaji on the Beach*, a popular example of new British filmmaking, reimagines the traditionally white seaside resort of Blackpool as a multicultural space through a day trip taken by a South Asian women's group. Positioned as a feel-good comedy, the film's title sets up a comic juxtaposition between Indian and British traditions. And, although its narrative touches on social issues such as interracial romance, intergenerational conflict, and white racism, the film constructs identities as much through a mobilization of cinematic spaces as through these narrative conflicts. In several sequences, an Asian woman named Asha is romanced by a white man in parodies of Hindi film styles. Some of these sequences refer to classic Indian films, while other, more comic scenes show the white suitor in "Indian" make-up, enacting a Bollywood-esque musical number. While these sequences represent Asha's Hindi film fantasies, her paramour typifies a fading northern English tradition of seaside theater. Declaring that Blackpool looks "just like Bombay," the film quite overtly globalizes British national space, playing with the perils and pleasures of national identity.[18]

*Bhaji on the Beach*    Blackpool's kitschy seafront is compared with Bombay.

Other national examples of remapping abound, often connected, as with *Bhaji*, to the conventions of the road movie. Narratives that traverse national spaces enable a discourse on the shape and nature of the nation. An example from France is *The Adventures of Felix* (Ducastel and Martineau, 2000), in which Felix, a young French North African man, decides to hitchhike from Brittany to Marseilles to find the father he never knew. Like *Bhaji*, the film fits easily into a liberal multicultural discourse: besides being North African, Felix is gay, and en route he encounters racism and homophobia, as well as more life-enhancing examples of the French rural public. Away from the road movie genre, the films of J. J. Bigas Luna have been argued by Paul Julian Smith and others to articulate Catalan national identity.[19] While films such as *Jamón, jamón* (1992), *Golden Balls* (1993), and *The Tit and the Moon* (1994) are often viewed as typical Spanish sex comedies, Smith points to their parodic mobilization of landscapes and stereotypes as a politically acute vision of contemporary Catalonia. In all these examples, sexuality works to negotiate between the body and political space, producing intimate maps of the contemporary nation.

Of course, not all geographies can be understood in the self-contained modern spaces of the city and the nation. Burgin points to the importance of fragmented spaces in postmodernity and connects this to recent theorizations of the exile, the foreigner, and the Other.[20] And, in his *Atlas of the European Novel*, Franco Moretti makes maps of the urban, trans-European, and colonial routes through which the modern novel passes.[21] These issues have become increasingly important in European cultures, as the growth in the number of films about immigration, postcoloniality, and minority communities demonstrates. More important than simple representation, though, are the ways in which films figure complex relationships to spaces of belonging. Irit Rogoff asks: "Can terrains and topographies and landscapes have a double consciousness, a mutual inhabitation?"[22] Her examples are African-American art, but we could as easily think about Black British film or the double nomenclature of "Eastern Europe" as opposed to "Europe."

One film-based study that takes up this kind of "uncanny geography" is Hamid Naficy's *An Accented Cinema*, which uses language as a metonym of exile, diaspora, and immigration.[23] For Naficy, the stylistic accent marks the trace of double consciousness in diasporic cinemas. A European example of this structure is Turkish German film. Here, feminized space is crucial, echoing Deutsche's claim that we must think postmodern spaces through gender. Naficy points out how many Turkish German films focus on the ways in which Turkish women are trapped within domestic spaces, reading interior locations and constricted framing as a condensation of both the women's limitations within traditional Turkish cultures and their limitations within Germany (refusal of citizenship, prejudice against Muslims, demand for assimilation). Both *Berlin.killer.doc* and Turkish German films point to the transnational elements of the national film, especially in post-Wall Germany. However, to address Europe as a supranational space, it is necessary to think beyond the nation and to consider the category of the international in European film production.

## Inter-, Supra-, and Transnational Space

The mapping of spaces larger than the nation raises the issue of international coproduction, a structure that enables an institutional, as well as a textual, production of space. Coproduction is neither new nor uniquely European. Moves toward greater cooperation in film production among European countries began in the 1940s, and by the early 1950s the Western European Union, one of the precursors to the European Union (EU), funded noncommercial films made by more than one member state.[24] Today, coproduction is common across the world, with American, European, and Asian countries, for example, joining forces to gain wider funding and distribution for projects with a culturally diverse appeal.[25]

What often links these various examples of coproduction is a principle of cultural value, in which coproduction is supposed to support film projects that might not otherwise be commercially viable or to enable national cultures to be more fully represented in film. Although they are inherently international, coproductions have historically been encouraged by national governments in Europe, which regarded supranational funding and production bodies as part of what Steve Neale calls "the promotion and development of national Art Cinemas under the aegis of liberal-democratic and social democratic government."[26] Thus, coproduction is industrially and ideologically linked to the concept of art cinema, and from the beginning it brought the international nature of the medium into a tension with discourses of national cultural identity.

As art cinema changed in the 1980s, so did coproduction. With an economic squeeze on many domestic industries, and political moves toward increased European cooperation, coproduction grew rapidly. John Hill cites an estimate "that while only 24 (out of 781) films made in

Western Europe in 1975 were international co-productions this figure had risen to 203 (out of 552) by 1991."[27] And Angus Finney confirms the continuation of this growth through the 1990s, reporting that coproduction accounted for 12 percent of total European production in 1987 but that this figure rose to 37 percent by 1993.[28] This shift brought a change not only in the national origin of funding but also in the nature of its sources: as Terry Illot points out, most of the new sources were television stations and European subsidies. Thus, in 1994, 65 percent of all European films in production had some kind of subsidy money, and 51 percent had television funds.[29] New European initiatives include MEDIA, a plan from the European Union to stimulate production with loans and subsidies for scripting, production, distribution, and promotion, and the Eurimages fund, which is part of the Council of Europe and funds films made by three or more member states.

The expansion of these kinds of programs is clearly linked to the increasing interconnection of European countries and the rise in the years approaching 1992 of a liberal discourse on the European project. While EU membership was limited in the 1990s to west European nations, cinema and television organizations worked more rapidly toward a broader idea of European identity. Thus, Eurimages included east and south European countries such as Poland and Turkey, and the European Broadcasting Union's membership stretched from Iceland to Morocco.[30] Seen in this context, the rise of coproduction in the late 1980s derives both from a new discourse of European filmmaking as a cultural project (as distinct from previous concerns for national filmmaking in Europe) and from the necessity of partnerships to gain funding. Thus, we can read coproduction as both a financial and a cultural imperative, inherently related to questions of European identity, audience, and textual address.

The idea of a specifically European film has had many detractors, however. Both leftist and conservative critics have dismissed what they see as a bourgeois and bureaucratic vision, in which the coproduction is understood as filmmaking by committee. The leftist critique is exemplified by *Cahiers du Cinéma* critic Antoine de Baecque, who views the problems with European film as overlapping with that of the contemporary art film; it has become safe, characterized by a homogenous beauty without distinguishing features. He identifies this retreat from radicality as another problem of heritage culture, arguing that the new European film is too smooth, domesticated by the beautiful image.[31] The fear is thus not of European cinematic identities per se but of a false identity, in which all films look the same and national or cultural differences get ironed out in a homogeneous bourgeois aesthetic. The name given to this (perhaps chimaeric) bad European film is the Europudding.[32]

For Serge Toubiana, also writing in *Cahiers*, this problem is symptomatic of a shift away from the European art cinema of auteurs. He argues that only politicians, funding groups, television companies, and technocrats have a stake in an idea of Europe, while filmmakers tend to be more interested in the specificity of time and place. They speak of the local and the singular, while films that attempt to produce a European vision after the politicians' desires become overcooked Europuddings.[33] Thus, the discourses of European cinema follow those of the contemporary art film, but in this case, the critique of the image is linked to the problematic nature of European-ness, not just to aesthetic and political reaction. Toubiana is correct in his assertion that many recent European films do not construct themselves *as* European; coproduction notwithstanding, they work to represent a singular national culture. Sally Potter's *Orlando* (1992), for example, is a British, Russian, French, Italian, and Dutch coproduction. But with a British director and star, and a narrative that adapts a British novel about British history, the film scarcely offers a broadly European perspective. Or, to take another auteurist example, *Ulysses' Gaze* (Angelopolous, 1995) was cofunded by Greece, France, and Italy, but despite its international cast and crew, the film's focus on the Balkan landscape and identity grounds it in Greek director Theo Angelopolous's nationally or regionally specific concerns.

Chantal Akerman articulates this position directly: "I don't think there is such a thing as European identity. The reasons why this question has arisen are, on the one hand, the increasing global dominance of Hollywood, and on the other, the existence of the European Community and its ability to put money into European co-production."[34] On the one hand, this is a commonsense truth, as, of course, there is no such thing as a singular European identity, objectively existing and available to all European spectators. On the other hand, this very fact provides a potentially more interesting insight into the problem of coproduction than Akerman's practical attitude suggests. European-ness in the 1990s is at once a much desired mode of identification and an impossible one. Unlike national identities, which became increasingly naturalized in this period while often criticized, supranational identities are lauded in the public sphere but less popularly available.[35] And art film, with its historical project of representing national cultures, alongside its new situation of international production, is central to this paradox. Caught among highly national markets and international funding, the European ideal and fear of the Europudding, coproduction has a unique relationship to European identity.

In his discussion of the concept of national cinema, Philip Rosen points out that many of the more rigorous studies of national cinemas have had a diachronic element, not claiming that all films made in a country are national but, rather, that at particular historical moments the national emerges more forcibly.[36] If we can extend this formula to include a supranational space, then the 1990s were such a moment for the idea of European cinema, even if the nature of this new discourse on the European is precisely defined by its difficulty or even its impossibility. Only once coproduction had become such a dominant part of European filmmaking practice, and only once the end of the Cold War and the expansion of the EU had made the idea of Europe once again culturally and politically central, could a cinematic discourse of Europeanness emerge. In this new cultural context, European identity becomes a structural problem for the coproduction.

What happens increasingly is a textualization of this problem. A key example of this change is *Zentropa*, a German, Danish, Swedish, and French coproduction that uses a web of intertextual references to textualize its hybridity. (In chapter 5, I discuss this film in more detail.) Such references are often dismissed as postmodern window dressing,[37] but I would suggest that referentiality here indicates the way in which art cinema can no longer take for granted its part in a European culture. In the context of both the new Europe and the postcolonial critique of Eurocentrism, Europe is no longer able to function as the unmarked center for an art cinema that pretends to universality. *Zentropa*, therefore, constantly recapitulates its cinematic heritage, marking its European origins in a way too excessive to be naturalized. It refers to a pantheon of European art film stars in its casting: the film is narrated by Max von Sydow; its femme fatale is played by Barbara Sukowa, frequent collaborator with Werner Rainer Fassbinder; and the American general is Eddie Constantine, best known for his role in *Alphaville, a Strange Adventure of Lemmy Caution* (Godard, 1965).

This homage extends to the crew also, as the cinematographer, Henning Bendtsen, worked with Carl Theodor Dreyer, for whom he shot *Ordet* (1955) and *Gertrud* (1964). In addition, the film is full of textual references, particularly to films made in the late 1940s, the time that the narrative is set. Examples include *Germany Year Zero* (Rossellini, 1948) and *The Third Man* (Reed, 1949), from which the film takes the narrative of denazification and the innocent American hero in a zoned city, respectively. This obsessive marking of historical origins even extends beyond the period of the narrative, where the film's noirish mise-en-scène cites German Expressionism—the hypnotist character, for example, reminding us of *The Cabinet of Doctor Caligari* (Weine, 1920).[38] And, of course, such markers can be read geographically too, citing Swedish, German, French, Danish, Italian, and British cinemas. These references no longer function as signs of art cinema in general but are reinserted into a geographically and historically specific system.

Even films that are not such mixed coproductions textualize European transnational space. *Lovers of the Arctic Circle* (Medem, 1998), for example, is a Spanish and French coproduction, but it charts an itinerary from Spain to Finland, in which its lovers traverse the continent without meeting. Journeys across Europe are central: one protagonist, Otto, becomes a pilot so he can more easily cross European spaces, while for Ana, the Arctic Circle is a fantasmatic space, a projection of fantasy identification from the Mediterranean to the frozen north. This imaginary space is specifically European, for the emigration of Ana's mother to Australia is dismissed as "too far." The film is concerned with charting the psychic territory of Europe: Finland and Spain are as far apart as it is possible to be within Europe, but not the "too far" of another continent. With the lovers journeying to the ends of the continent to find each other, this, to be sure, is an intimate geography.

European spaces both contemporary and historical take on a quality of fantasy, as locations in which the lovers' narratives intersect. The film structures both a temporal and a spatial axis of causality: the historical

*Lovers of the Arctic Circle*    The Arctic Circle runs through the middle of Ana's cabin.

narrative connects a German and a Spaniard who met during the Spanish Civil War with their respective grandchildren, while the spatial axis traces the main characters' journeys from Spain to the Arctic Circle. The encounter in the 1930s works out better than expected, as the young Spanish man saves a German soldier, who responds to this kindness by deserting and marrying a Spanish woman. The apparently easier contemporary relationships are thwarted, however, as childhood sweethearts Ana and Otto cannot find each other and are framed together only when we see the reflection of Otto in Ana's dead eyes. Despite the apparent ease of modern travel, creating a European union proves more difficult than it was during wartime.

A romance like *Lovers of the Arctic Circle* may seem distant from more politically engaged art-cinematic texts like *Berlin.killer.doc*. But the transnational is always connected to the local, and fantasmatic spaces are no less implicated in politics. We might consider, for instance, that Julio Medem, the director of *Lovers*, also directed *The Basque Ball: Skin Against Stone* (2003), a controversial documentary on the Basque separatist movement. Across these texts, relationships among local, national, and European identities can be traced, and the idea of Europe as a spatial-historical object, the literal and figurative image of Europe, begins to be worked on in cinematic terms, as a question of image and narrative, space and time.

## Spectacular Politics

In considering the cartographies of European art cinema, the question of spectacle becomes politically central. As we have seen, spectacle is a significant issue in the largely pessimistic body of work on contemporary art cinema. Whereas Neale cites as characteristic of 1960s art film "an engagement with the look in terms of a marked individual point of view rather than in terms of institutionalized spectacle,"[39] most of the critics of 1980s and 1990s film specify a turn toward the spectacular as the defining shift in the post–*Star Wars* art film or in contemporary film tout court. Thomas Elsaesser argues that instead of resolving around metaphysical themes, the contemporary art film turns inward: "Authority and authenticity lie nowadays in the way film-makers use the cinema's resources, which is to say in their command of the generic, the expressive, the excessive, the visual and the visceral."[40] Michel Chion has coined the term "neo-gaudy" to critique the "formulaic aesthetic" of recent European art film.[41] As with heritage films, contemporary art films are often negatively compared with the allegedly more radical films of a generation earlier.

This critical move is part of a larger theoretical problem around spectacle, and we have seen an example of its operation with regard to the critical reactions to the Italian heritage films, in which the beautiful image was argued to "fall out" of the narrative, blocking any political meaning the film might otherwise have contained.[42] However, this tendency to separate form from content, spectacle from meaning, takes on a more overtly political valence with regard to art cinema, and especially art films that thematize historical change. Thus, films that address Cold War history directly are frequently judged according to how they mobilize the spectacular image. An illuminating case study of this question is Emir Kusturica's *Underground*. (In chapter 4, I discuss this film in more detail.) No doubt because the film was perceived precisely as "serious" and "historical" art cinema, criticism of its spectacularity focused not on the question of cliché or the touristic but on the politics of its representations. And because of the continuing violence of the wars in Bosnia, the film found itself in the middle of an international controversy, debated by philosophers and public intellectuals from all over Europe.

The debate began in the wake of *Underground*'s winning the Palme d'Or at Cannes in 1995, which was perceived by some to be a sympathy vote for a film from the war-torn former Yugoslavia. However, Montenegrin critic Stanko Cerović denounced the film and Kusturica's public actions and statements as partisan, exhibiting Serb nationalist tendencies, bias against Croats and Slovenes, and implicit support for Slobodan Milošević's war in Bosnia.[43] He further contended that the west European film community was too ignorant about the former Yugoslavia to notice this ethnic stereotyping[44] and had gotten its praise politically wrong. This argument was taken up by some French philosophers, most notably Alain Finkelkraut and Bernard-Henri Lévy. In response to their very public attacks on the film, various west European writers, including Hans Magnus Enzenberger and Serge Regourd, rushed to defend the film.[45]

What is striking about this debate is that it did not resolve into two competing ideological readings of the film but opposed those who read the film only as an encoded political statement to those who defended the aesthetic freedom of the artist. The film's defenders for the most part did not refute any of the political claims of Cerović and Finkielkraut but instead stood as fellow artists defending free speech and an "art for art's sake" formalism. Regourd, for example, lauds the film for the aesthetic inventiveness of its shots and images and describes his admiration of "a rare artistic creation, an exceptional cinematic work that gives full meaning to the famous notion of 'cultural exception.'"[46] The film's attackers, for their part, took the antispectacular separation of form and content to something of an extreme, reading the film as propaganda, in which the visual operates as a veil to hide a political message.

Dina Iordanova makes a claim to a balanced approach, and her history of the film and its impact is undoubtedly one of the most informed on the subject of Balkan history and politics. However, her account of the debate repeats symptomatically the methodology of most of the film's critics, as when she summarizes: "*Underground* . . . came under ardent critical fire from people who claimed to be able to penetrate beyond the staggering imagery and to decipher the arcane historical and political propositions upon which the film was built."[47] Here, she clearly articulates the idea of spectacle as something to be broken through so that the hidden political meaning beneath can be seen. The image in itself becomes meaningless, forming at best a surplus and at worst the veil of a kind of cinematic false consciousness. In her own assessment, she adds the issue of history, stating that "if one leaves aside the visual particularities, *Underground* is a historical film which offers a clear perspective for interpreting the current violent state of affairs in the Balkans."[48] Here, historical interpretation must be separated from the visual, and thus the visual itself is defined as ahistorical. This argument combines the question of spectacle with a fairly conservative approach to historical films in which a film is read only for the historical position that can be extrapolated. It is seen not so much as a cinematic text but as a perspective for interpreting events—an argument in hieroglyphic form.

Slavoj Žižek's ideological critique of the film is part of a larger argument about the relationship between ethnicities and capitalism, but his reading nonetheless rests on spectacle as a site of attack. He maintains that "the political meaning of this film does not reside primarily in its overt tendentiousness, in the way it takes sides in the post-Yugoslav conflict—heroic Serbs versus the treacherous, pro-Nazi Slovenes and Croats—but, rather, in its very 'depoliticized' aestheticist attitude."[49] I will return in more detail to the substance of Žižek and others' ideological claims, to the important question of if and how *Underground* "takes sides" in the post-Yugoslav conflict. But for now I want to focus on the rhetoric of spectacle, in which there is a slippage where the political criticism is hitched to a formal strategy to which it has no necessary connection. The first part of this slippage is "guilt by association," whereby aestheticism seems to lead directly from a prejudice against Croats and

Slovenes. Whether or not this accusation of ethnic bias is tenable, it operates entirely apart from the question of spectacle: the same style could
just as easily privilege another group, and, indeed, the film has been
defended as not at all pro-Serb.

The second and trickier part of the slippage is between the concept of
depoliticization and that of an "aestheticist attitude." Žižek's broad point
is to attack the trend toward what he calls depoliticization, an ideological shift in which multinational capital thinks itself depoliticized, and
thus ideology itself becomes the discourse excluded from the dominant
ideology. Whereas ideology in the past operated to exclude some given
ideological position *as* ideological, and therefore outside the realm of the
supposedly neutral hegemony, now the claim is of an end to the era of
ideologies, with any claim at all on politics being excluded from the discourse of power. For Žižek, this repression of politics only leads to the
return of extremist ideologies of racism and fundamentalism, an argument that he uses to conclude that it is this Western logic of multicultural capitalism that caused the Balkan conflict, rather than ancient
Balkan differences. This ideological reading is compelling, and its
claims on the relationship between the West and the Balkans will
become important to my argument in the following chapter. However,
the theory of depoliticization is not at all connected to the idea of aestheticism, either by definition or in Žižek's argument.

As with the question of direct political bias, the logic of depoliticization, if we can even claim it to be directly deployed in film, could be
structured by a variety of formal and narrative strategies; Žižek gives no
reason why an "aestheticist attitude" should be the privileged or necessary correlative for such an ideology. Furthermore, he does not expand
on what he means by an aestheticist attitude, nor does he argue for its
political valence in filmic terms. While we can infer that he means by the
term a discourse of spectacle, of beautiful mise-en-scène, and of excess
in the image, he offers no clear definition, and nowhere does he provide
evidence for the claim that such an aesthetic entails the political point he
derives, in fact, from narrative. His conclusion is therefore weak, based
partly on an assumption that spectacle is self-evidently reactionary and
partly on an analogy that cinematic excess represents, and is ultimately
the same as, the excess of ethnic cleansing and slaughter in Bosnia.[50] As
rhetoric, this is excessive itself and does little justice to the political complexity of the cinematic image.

If Žižek's reading is embedded in a sophisticated assessment of global
capital in the 1990s, Finkielkraut takes up a more polemical version of
the Jamesonian position in which spectacular cinematic historicity is a

signifier of duplicity and ideological reaction.[51] In *Le Monde*, he contends that "in awarding [the Palme d'Or] to *Underground*, the Cannes jury believed that they were singling out an artist of abundant imagination. In fact, they honored a servile and flashy illustrator of criminal clichés; they praised to the skies the rock, postmodern, messed up, trendy, American-ized, and shot-in-Belgrade version of the most nonsensical and menda-cious Serb propaganda. The devil himself could not have come up with such a cruel outrage to Bosnia or as grotesque an epilogue to Western frivolity and incompetence."[52] Here, the rhetorical extremity of the propaganda argument becomes apparent, as Finkielkraut constructs a metonymic chain that connects postmodernity and Americanism—shorthand for spectacle in this context—with not only the irrelevant specter of "rock," and its acolytes trendiness and mess, but also the poli-tics of Serbian nationalism and Western ignorance. Although this listing of clichéd bogeymen could seem unconvincing when taken out of context, the rhetoric was powerful: Finkielkraut's verdict on *Underground* gained ground, despite his confession that he had actually never seen the film.

Not having seen the film does not appear to have been as much of a handicap as one might expect, for the debate as a whole was character-ized by an absence of textual analysis. Instead, the criticism focused mainly on Kusturica himself, with the film's provenance as art cinema enabling an auteurist discourse in which the director's intentions could be inferred from his personal statements and actions. This is the basis for Cerović's scathing critique, in which he accuses Kusturica of making statements supportive of Milošević and of collaborating with institutions linked to the war. He goes on to argue that "such moral collapse could not fail to be reflected in his aesthetic meanderings, and his latest film shows real impotence masked by a firework display of noise, colour and mean-ingless scenes."[53] His logic is thus that Kusturica's personal failings must, even passively, come to define his films and that the text itself is only a reflection of its ideologically compromised auteur. Spectacle is still a veil, but a veil covering not textual politics but authorial immorality.

Iordanova takes up this approach, criticizing Kusturica for having chosen to live in Belgrade rather than Sarajevo and condemning the film's politics on the basis of an interview with the director in *Cahiers du Cinéma*.[54] Her point—that comparing the conflict to an earthquake is problematic, as it turns planned political events into an inexplicable nat-ural disaster—is well taken, and based on this source, Kusturica's own opinion of the Bosnian war does not sound very politically nuanced. (Of course, it is just as easy to find a quotation to suggest exactly the oppo-site: in an interview in *Libération*, Kusturica asks, "How can we defend the idea of a multi-ethnic Bosnia if we have destroyed the idea of a multi-ethnic Yugoslavia?")[55] However, just as it is important not to read form as a veil for a hidden ideological content, so it is crucial not to let an auteurist approach prevent analysis of the film itself. This is why it is necessary to theorize *Underground*'s politics through the specificity of the image rather than by bypassing its form altogether.

I have spent some time detailing the debate around *Underground* to illustrate the imbrication of theories of spectacle in recent cinema with the historical topics and institutional forms of the films and to show how this relationship can have high political stakes. I have concentrated on the position of those attacking the film, for it is this position that most clearly takes up the film and cultural theory critique of spectacle, using it to produce what seems to me to be an inadequate and limiting political intervention. However, the defenders of the film offer no stronger method, and just as the attacks on *Underground* are theoretically inadequate, so are the defenses that ignore substantive issues of ideology and form in favor of an equally auteurist and politically vapid championing of the freedom of the artist. I return to the political logic of *Underground* in chapter 4, but for now I am concerned more with the limitations of the debate on the politics of spectacle. Thus it is necessary to escape from the confines of this circular logic and to think in a film-specific way about how post-Wall films deploy spectacle in relation to history, ideology, and European space.

## The Borders of Europe

While Ackbar Abbas suggests that Hong Kong experienced in the 1980s and 1990s a sense of imminent disappearance, a disturbed relationship with its own location in space and time,[56] the problem for Europe in the 1990s was not a disappearance but a reappearance of what had been there before: as the map of the continent was redrawn in the early 1990s, it came increasingly to resemble that of a historically earlier moment. It became commonplace to point out that while atlases published only a few years earlier were now substantially inaccurate, those from the beginning of the century were once again close to representing Europe, with their unified Germany, absent Soviet Union, and ethnonations in the Balkans. Thus, temporal moves forward were partially experienced as historical and spatial moves backward, and discussions around "the end of history" and the "New World Order" troped geopolitical changes in historical terms.[57] This doubling back of a geographi-

**Europe 1937**

International boundaries derived from
Department of State Map Division
Map No. 10400, April 1947

**Not labeled:** Andorra, Liechtenstein,
Monaco, San Marino, and Vatican City.

Names and boundary representation
are not necessarily authoritative.

**Abbreviations**

ALB.    Albania
BELG.   Belgium
CZECH.  Czechoslovakia
LUX.    Luxembourg
NETH.   Netherlands
SWITZ.  Switzerland
U.K.    United Kingdom

The boundaries are shown for Europe in 1937. (Geographical Notes 2/3, 1992. Courtesy United States Department of State, Bureau of Intelligence and Research)

cal onto a historiographical logic also describes a temporal disturbance, and one, like Abbas's claims about Hong Kong, that is legible in cultural terms.

Many of the films discussed earlier can be read in relation to this cultural logic; *Lovers of the Arctic Circle* looks back from contemporary Spain to the anti-Franco struggle, while *Berlin.killer.doc* traces the historical palimpsest of the new Berlin. Across Europe, 1990s films addressed the new order. In affluent northwestern Europe, themes of immigration and multiculturalism dominated, while in eastern and east-central Europe, contemporary stories about life under capitalism jostled with revisionist histories of the twentieth century. Filmmakers from various countries took on the war in Bosnia, although conditions made indigenous filmmaking a challenging enterprise for much of the 1990s. However,

The boundaries are shown for Europe in 1989. (Geographical Notes 2/3, 1992. Courtesy United States Department of State, Bureau of Intelligence and Research)

nowhere were these events experienced more acutely than in the countries that formed the fault lines of the old Eastern and Western Europe—countries such as Germany, the Czech Republic (Czechoslovakia), and the successor states of the former Yugoslavia—and it is in these countries' films that we find the most acute responses to Europe's changes.

Films made in nations along the border of Eastern and Western Europe often render visible the difficulties and desires of this new cartography. While these countries have varied film industries and traditions, we can discern across these borders a recurrent interest in European Otherness, a desire to chart new itineraries and to see identity otherwise. An early instance of this impetus is the German documentary *Videograms of a Revolution* (1992), directed by Harun Farocki and Andrei Ujica, in which the filmmakers compile footage shot by many Romanian groups and individuals in an attempt to document the

The boundaries are shown for Europe in 1992. (Geographical Notes 2/3, 1992. Courtesy United States Department of State, Bureau of Intelligence and Research)

uniquely mediatic nature of the Romanian revolution. This strategy is both alienating and affective: the spectator becomes highly aware of the position of the camera and sometimes of the danger that the cameraperson is in. At the same time that the film questions the objectivity of the politically contested video image, it commands authority in its capturing of a complex profilmic now. Like Bazin's description of a whale attack in *Kon-Tiki* (Heyerdahl, 1950), filming the overthrow of Nicolae Ceauçescu attests to the experience of revolution in its temporality as much as in the content of its images.[58]

In addition, as a German film about East European events, *Videograms* forces an awareness of the border whose partial dismantling it narrates: the insider/outsider split between its (East) European participants and its (West) European directors. (In fact, there is another internal border here, because while Ujica lives in Germany, he was born in Romania. In

*Videograms of a Revolution*   Those witnessing the Romanian revolution were in a
dangerous position.

Naficy's terms, his filmmaking practice is exilic, accented.) In its attempt
to engage visually with an Other, Farocki and Ujica's film can be compared with feminist films such as Trinh T. Minh-ha's *Reassemblage*
(1982), in which Trinh speaks as a Vietnamese interlocutor of Senegal,
and Chantal Akerman's *D'Est* (1993), in which Akerman travels to the
former Soviet Union. Here, though, a feminist and postcolonialist deconstruction of the documentary voice is mobilized to trouble the dominant
binary of postwar Europe.

A film that makes even clearer the importance of itineraries, of charting subjective transnational routes, is *Chico* (Fekete, 2002), a German,
Hungarian, Croatian, and Chilean coproduction. The protagonist is a
national and ethnic mongrel, part Jewish, part Christian, with a heady
mix of European and South American roots. Beginning in the 1960s, he
takes part in political upheavals in Bolivia and Chile; travels to Europe;
works as a spy, a soldier, and a journalist; and ends up in the 1990s fighting for Croatia in the Yugoslav wars. Chico's narrative forms a pica-
resque itinerary, weaving through many wars and revolutions, but amid
the chaos there is a persistent questioning of the relationships among

spatial identities (nationality, ethnicity, language), histories (war, revolution, coup), and ideologies (from South American socialisms to European post-Communism). *Chico* points out that the changes in post-Wall Europe cannot be understood in a vacuum and that the ideological crisis of the Left touched on quite disparate geopolitical constituencies.

Czech art cinema is typically less engaged with the European Other: perhaps because of its strong national cinematic tradition, post-Wall Czech films have largely mobilized historical rather than transnational narratives as the space within which to imagine political change. Many of these films fit comfortably within the heritage genre, including *Dark Blue World* (Sverák, 2001) and *Divided We Fall* (Hrebejk, 2000). Distributed internationally as accessible and melodramatic Holocaust dramas, these films recount national histories in the wake of a political process of reimagining national identities, historical responsibilities, and ethics. A more ambiguous text is *Buttoners* (Zelenka, 1997), a portmanteau film that includes contemporary narratives, as well as a key story set during World War II. Unlike most heritage war narratives, however, this one takes place in a foreign country, Japan, and narrates the lucky escape of Kokura, slated as the target for the atomic bomb that was diverted to Hiroshima because of bad weather. The rest of the film consists of several small stories, interconnected in unexpected ways. The Japanese narrative returns when a group of girls at a séance raises the ghost of one of the American pilots, who wants to apologize for his actions in 1945.

Director Petr Zelenka is known for his absurdist style, and *Buttoners* can be read within a Czech aesthetic history of surrealism. The film's coincidences of time, space, and characters suggest that geopolitics, like love, is arbitrarily determined. But, as with a previous generation of Czech surrealist films that includes Jan Svankmejer's uncanny animations, the fantastical events in *Buttoners* entail a political logic.[59] While arbitrary cruelties often refer obliquely in Czech cinema to the absurdities of life under state Communism, *Buttoners* suggests a new state of affairs: a lack of any social or ideological fixity, seen, for instance, in bizarrely humorous sexual perversity (the title characters remove upholstery buttons with false teeth). An integral part of this incoherent system is the haunting presence of the history of World War II. Here, the apparently arbitrary itinerary slips from Hiroshima to Prague and from sexuality to technology. The Other is not western Europe as much as Japan, America, and the altered place of Czechoslovakian history in the world system.

For northern Europe, the borders of East and West appear less pressing, but their effects are no less real. In Lukas Moodysson's *Lilya 4-ever*

*Lilya 4-ever*   In an abandoned factory, postindustrial rubble frames Soviet history.

(2002), made more than a decade after the end of the Soviet Union, new issues supersede the immediate fall-out of state Communism. Here, trafficking in women is the "social issue" addressed by the narrative. The film makes clear the connections among post-Soviet wild capitalism, west European economic dominance, and the exploitation of young women. Lilya is a teenager abandoned by her mother, when the mother runs off to the United States with her new boyfriend. Tempted by an offer to start a new life in Sweden, Lilya is kidnapped and forced into prostitution. On one level, the film operates a fairly direct extended metaphor in which Lilya is equally rejected by her mother and her motherland (a nameless post-Soviet republic), whose unregulated capitalism has left her father's former workplace empty and its young generation kicking around in soulless housing projects. More important than this nameless state is Europe, and particularly the still-significant border of East and West, which Lilya traverses as an unwitting captive. It is the invisibility of this East/West border—its official nonexistence in the new Europe—that begets the invisible lives of women like Lilya.

*Lilya* forms an intriguing case study of the different regional itineraries that post-Wall cinema can map. Like many contemporary Nordic films, it is concerned with transnational identities. But unlike the pan-Nordic space constructed by the various national funding bodies, *Lilya* emphasizes an exploitive rather than a cooperative north. Stylistically, too, the film makes awkward connections. Its working-class characters and relentless pessimism draw from British histories of social realism, while from Dogme it takes a digital video (DV) aesthetic and melodramatic narrative of an abused woman. But the film also includes religious

fantasy sequences that sit less easily with these Western versions of realism. The difficulty with this itinerary can be seen in the problems that
occurred when Sweden wanted to select the film as its Academy Award
submission: since the film was mostly in a "foreign" language, it was
originally judged ineligible. Russian-speaking Lilya could not represent
Sweden. The academy relented, but this small controversy illustrates the
film's awkward location: in staging northern Europe's implication in the
European border, the film opens up new spaces of political and fantasmatic exchange.

## Impossible Spaces

We may consider these border films as a point of emergence of
the new Europe: as texts that can make clear the stakes in any developing politics and aesthetics of European-ness. Within this structure,
arguably, the countries most radically transformed by these upheavals
were Germany and the former Yugoslavia. While both *Zentropa* and
*Underground* take as their primary historical object and location a single
country—*Zentropa* is set in zoned Germany in 1945 and *Underground*
mainly in Yugoslavia from 1941 to 1992—they do not work as the Italian romances do to tie nationally coded images to political histories but,
instead, appear to visualize the space of the continent. And while these
films are textually quite different, what connects them is a shared difficulty in conceptualizing spatial identities, both in terms of the nation
and in terms of that nation's relationship to Europe as a whole. Before
addressing each film within its national context, then, it might be productive to consider what these locations have in common and why they
provide such rich and troubling ground for a spatial and historical
analysis.

The relationship of nation to Europe is a particular problem for any
discursive figuration of Yugoslavia or Germany. Since the end of World
War II, these countries[60] have occupied unique places in regard to the
Cold War geopolitical settlement: very different from each other, but
comparable in that neither of them was fully locatable within the dominant taxonomy of Eastern and Western Europe. Germany was split into
the German Democratic Republic and the Federal Republic of Germany,
while Yugoslavia, by contrast, became a single, federal nation after the
war, but in splitting from the Cominform in 1948 was removed from the
Soviet sphere of influence and could no longer be considered simply a
part of the Eastern bloc. Thus, both (all three) countries can be seen as

signifying problems or limits for the logic of Eastern and Western Europe, and, indeed, *Underground*'s director, Kusturica, has said of his own European identity that "I was born at this extremely painful border between the East and the West."[61] The idea of the painful border is one shared by both Yugoslavia and Germany, and with the dissolution of these borders in 1989 to 1992 some of the most significant events in the formation of the new Europe were precipitated.

In Germany, the Wall became a new metonym of European change, this time indicating the collapse of Communism in its televised opening and rapid destruction. In 1990, reunification took place, and the nature of the new Germany's inevitable strategic and economic dominance in Europe became a central subject of debate for the European Community, while within Germany the persistent cultural and economic gap between the former East and West rewrote Cold War geography as a new political problem. In Yugoslavia, the pressure on the spatial logic of the Cold War did not result in a unification but in a breaking apart. The secession of Slovenia from the Yugoslav federation in 1990 was the first step in what looked like a transition to Western-style democracy but proved to be a more complicated series of civil wars, in which the right-wing nationalism and territorial expansionism of Slobodan Milošević caused the bloody and drawn-out contestation of Serbia's borders and thus of Yugoslavia's various national spaces.[62] In both cases, a spatial politics of borders and nationalisms is significant in the 1990s and in recent national histories.

These moments correspond to the time in which *Zentropa* and *Underground* were made—that of German reunification and of the wars in the former Yugoslavia—and to the historical moment in which the narratives begin. In other words, for both films, national and European spaces are both a historical and an ideological issue. *Zentropa*'s narrative takes place in 1945, suspended between the legacy of Nazism and the separation of Germany into East and West. While Nazism was an ideology predicated on the control and transformation of European space,[63] the postwar structure installed by the Allies began with zoning and led directly to a de facto splitting of Germany's national space into competing ideological blocs.[64] Thus, both the Nazi guerrillas and the Allied occupiers depicted in the film are making explicit, and ideologically weighty, claims on European space.

Space plays no less a part in Yugoslav histories, and *Underground* begins in 1941, at the moment of inception of the national liberation struggle, when the prewar state was partitioned by the Nazis. However, even this moment is readable as "national" mainly from the point of view of Tito's Communists and is contested by nationalisms in play in Serbia and Croatia during the 1940s, as well as the 1990s. As John B. Allcock points out, "No international frontier between the former Yugoslav federation and any of its neighbours is older than the end of the Balkan Wars (1911–13)."[65] Allcock concludes that the problems of Yugoslavia "have to do in very large measure with the difficulty (perhaps one should say in relation to the Balkans, the impossibility) of mapping nationality onto territory."[66] The spatial problems of an extremely ethnically mixed population were crucial to the region well before World War II, but in both the 1940s and the 1990s their political implications became particularly acute.

That this spatial conflict should become legible in historical terms can be seen in the way the verb "to balkanize" has entered the English language, meaning "to divide an area into overly small states." This linguistic example reveals the way in which history itself is a discursive problem for Yugoslavia. The negative tenor of the term "to balkanize" indicates the extent to which, at least in English-speaking countries, historical disposition has become the standard explanation for all events in the Balkans. The idea of balkanization is that the region can stand as exemplary of a kind of spatial logic consisting of pre-modern tribal hatreds, susceptible to endless belligerence and incapable of forming a modern multiethnic nation state. In this way, far-distant history is invoked to contextualize events: this happened during the 1990s war in Bosnia, which was frequently "explained" as a natural resurgence of ancient enmities. (This idea of a territory still caught up in its ancient feuds is similar to the discourse of the rural pre-modern south in Italy, although here it is used to more politically direct ends.) For this reason, any kind of history film on the subject of Yugoslavia will be overdetermined, as historical discourse itself is always already implicated in this primitivizing rhetoric.

History is a very different problem for a film about Germany, but it is also a problem of overdetermination. In this case, the issue is not one of an overly distant history, medieval and complex (exactly Byzantine), whose use in the present is problematic, but of a history that is too recent, too well known, whose relevance is constantly politicized. To make a history film about Nazism and German postwar history risks cliché, following as it does an ideological path already marked out by New German Cinema, as well as the Holocaust industry. The terms of historical debate are well worn in this case, and particularly with regard to art cinema, and yet the framework within which German national identity and its corresponding history can be imagined has been radically altered by reunification.

I am suggesting that both Germany and Yugoslavia were defined in the 1990s by a unique troubling of space and time, in which the reappearance of a historically earlier mapping of their national borders demands a cinematic reconnection of the histories that began and ended their postwar spaces. Of all the itineraries mapped by new European films, those from Germany and Yugoslavia contain perhaps the most difficult relationship to European space and history. Because of their contested political landscapes, defined by national borders that are always an expression of a historical and ideological process, history in these "national" cinemas is necessarily addressed as a problem of space. In chapters 4 and 5, I address these national cinemas individually, examining how each articulates space as a function of historicity and assessing how film texts work over these problems in terms of the image.

# 4   Yugoslavia's Impossible Spaces

If the historical film inherently consists of a work of mourning, producing a representation of that which no longer exists, then Emir Kusturica's *Underground* troubles this structure from the beginning. The film opens in medias res, with the Nazi bombing of Belgrade in 1941. Communists Marko and Blacky are wanted for subversive activities, and they escape with their families to the cellar of a relative's house. While the relatives stay underground, Marko and Blacky continue to fight the Germans. When the courageous Blacky is injured, Marko sends him back to the cellar, steals his girlfriend, and manages to convince all those underground that the war is continuing for the next fifty years. Exploiting them as munitions manufacturers, Marko becomes an important figure in Tito's government and carves a reputation for himself as a war hero. Decades later, after an explosion, Blacky and his son Jovan escape from the cellar, and, coming upon the Balkan wars of the 1990s, Blacky believes that they are still fighting World War II. Meanwhile, Marko's brother Ivan has turned up in Berlin and discovers a network of tunnels that appear to connect all of Europe underground. Through these, he returns to Yugoslavia, where he kills the duplicitous Marko and commits suicide. In the end, only Blacky survives, and he rejoins his dead family and friends in a fantastical scene of celebration.

In this narrative of exploitation and destruction, what we never see is a time before war or a national space to be mourned. Whereas *Cinema Paradiso*, *Mediterraneo*, and *Il Postino* use the beautiful landscape image to create a representation of the Italian past, *Underground* consistently refuses any direct visualization of a landscape that could be inferred as national. There are few exterior long shots in the film, despite its epic narrative, duration, and overtly national-political subject matter. There are some exterior scenes in wartime Belgrade, a couple in the city interspersed through the Cold War years, one in 1990s Berlin, and, at the very end of the film, three sequences set in the Yugoslav countryside. Aside from these important exceptions, almost the entire film takes place indoors and in nonrealist spaces that work to refuse any naturalization of mise-en-scène as historical space. There is no direct image of loss, no desirable historical landscape in which mourning can take place. Instead, *Underground* uses a spatial metaphor to articulate its historical narrative: that of the border between aboveground and underground space—the city and the cellar.

## Underground Nation

As its title suggests, the underground cellar is the film's central trope, an underworld in which Blacky and his extended family are condemned by Marko to spend fifty years. This dark and enclosed space, which is also domestic and urban, is the polar opposite of the beautiful landscape, as it prevents any engagement with the natural and political world outside. Blacky and his family are kept out of history, not knowing what has happened to their country. What immediately distinguishes the film is the extent to which both its historical and spatial structures are foregrounded: not only is the trope of the underground cellar central to the film's narrative, but this narrative is historicized as a directly political question. The intertitles that section the narrative make plain its historical structure, beginning with "The War," moving on to "The Cold War," and, in the final section, returning to "The War." The space of the cellar is coincident with the time of Communism, and Belgrade is seen as a city constantly in conflict. In *Underground*, history is not only legible at the margins of the narrative but forms its central thematic.

As a version of national space, the fantastical underground setting practically demands to be interpreted metaphorically. There is no shortage of this type of reading, which sees the film as an allegory in which Communism imprisons the innocent population in the darkness of the cellar. In this interpretation, the underground population represents the true national spirit, bravely surviving Communist oppression. Indeed, the film itself voices this interpretation when the German doctor who treats Ivan tells a colleague that "Communism was one big cellar." The very banality of this expression, however, in the mouth of the well-meaning but ignorant Western doctor, sounds a warning that the relationship of politics to space is not as simple as it appears to the outsider. The underground/aboveground binary raises questions about the location of national space and what exactly is being repressed or hidden. Historians Joseph Rothschild and Nancy Wingfield exemplify a quite different version of the national cellar. They also invoke an underground metaphor in their reading of postwar history, claiming that Communism in Yugoslavia did not solve ethnonational problems "but drove these conflicts underground, where they festered."[1] Here, Communism is also seen in terms of a repression of national traits that would surface in the 1990s, but in opposition to the apparent logic of the film, what is below the surface is the festering, negative effects of nationalism rather than a popular stoicism.

We could read the underground space differently again by connecting it to a history of World War II films. *Underground* borrows the wartime rhetoric of the "underground" resistance movement. It is for this reason that Blacky escapes the Nazis through tunnels and that both Blacky and Marko begin the film as Communist partisans. Here, the logic of underground/aboveground is mapped onto the political space of Left and Right, in a way that echoes both partisan resistance dramas and prisoner-of-war films. Unlike that in the nationalistic war film, though, the political mapping in *Underground* becomes less and less clear as the film progresses through history. Blacky is not part of the underground movement that he thinks he is, and it becomes less and less certain what such a movement could represent. Once they are no longer tied to a wartime politics, the meanings of the two national spaces become increasingly ambiguous. These few examples do not exhaust the possible interpretations of the cellar as metaphor. What they do make clear is that for all its boldness, the underground/aboveground structure offers no simple answers to Yugoslav history.

## The Emergence of Yugoslavia

To unpick the mise-en-scène of the cellar without falling into the trap of an allegorical reading, we must examine the aboveground space and historical events that bookend the film. Like the Italian films, *Underground*'s narrative begins with World War II and ends with the early 1990s, and, once again, an affective image of national history can be read in the relationship between these two historical moments. In this case, Blacky sees only the surface of the Yugoslav landscape in 1941 and again in 1992: first in Belgrade on the day that the Nazis bomb the city, and then during the Bosnian war, again in Belgrade and, finally, in a razed village. The comparison drawn between war in 1941 and war in 1992 implies a national-political reading of postwar history, but what is striking here is the impossibility of a structure of mourning.

First, the film offers no time of "before" with which to contrast its narrative of war and loss. While *Cinema Paradiso*, for example, depicts the moment of historical possibility immediately before the decisive victory of the Christian Democrats in 1948, *Underground* begins in medias res, with the Nazi invasion of the Yugoslav state. In the early years of the war, the country had come under increasing pressure as Hungary, Romania, and Bulgaria all joined Hitler's Tripartite Pact. Surrounded by hostile powers, the Yugoslav monarch, Prince Paul, was forced into accepting Hitler's terms for surrender. However, this move was hugely unpopular, especially in Serbia, and within days of this capitulation a Serbian-led coup deposed Paul. The Nazis responded by immediately overrunning and partitioning the country, beginning with air attacks on Belgrade.[2] The film opens at precisely this historical moment, on April 6, 1941.

In the opening sequence, Blacky has just returned from joining the Communist Party and is celebrating with his friend Marko. In the next sequence, set a few hours later, the Belgrade zoo is bombed and Marko's brother Ivan manages to save a chimp from the carnage. As the terrified animals run through the city, Blacky's house also comes under fire, and he leaves to rejoin his comrade. The zoo sequence is visually spectacu-

*Underground*    The film opens in medias res, as the Belgrade zoo is bombed. (Courtesy New Yorker Films)

lar, and the disjunctive sight of elephants and zebras roaming the city streets combines the violence of air attacks with an image of confusion and the overthrow of social order. (The zoo itself presents an ambiguous image of the nation. Like the museum, the zoo is an institutional signifier of national culture, and one in which native and foreign species are brought together in a transnational space. However, it also isolates incompatible animals, which, when the bombing liberates them, soon confront each other in violent scenes such as the fight we witness between a duck and a tiger.) In beginning here, the film provides no image of what came before the chaotic historical narrative of war and national destruction.

Furthermore, just as 1948 can be argued to form the determining moment for postwar Italy, so 1941 forms a corresponding turning point for Yugoslavia. Unlike most European countries, Yugoslavia did not undergo a period of constitutional uncertainty in 1945, for the foundations of its unique form of Communism had been laid during the Nazi occupation. Axis leadership both in the puppet state of Croatia and in occupied Serbia was particularly brutal, and it successfully encouraged ethnic massacres among Yugoslav peoples. As a result, resistance was rapid and popular, and by 1943 the partisans, led by Tito, were a serious problem for the Nazis. Tito had a three-point plan: liberation from the Germans, ethnic reconciliation, and Communist revolution. In 1942, the Anti-Fascist Council of National Liberation (AVNOJ) met in Bihaj and began organizing a new government for the country. The partisans gained the support of the majority of the population through their policy of protecting all of Yugoslavia's ethnic groups as much as for their Communism. As the Germans were forced out of an area, the partisans moved in, setting up new civilian administrations gradually across the country. Thus, as Phyllis Auty puts it: "There was no new political revolution at the end of the war; it had already been taking place gradually and effectively from 1942 onwards."[3] By 1945, Tito's Yugoslav state was a fait accompli. For this reason, *Underground* begins in 1941, during the invasion that was unintentionally to enable the postwar order and, therefore, at the precise moment to which postwar Yugoslavia could be dated. In contrast to the Italian films, then, *Underground* allows no space in which to imagine what came before this decisive moment.

Because *Underground* offers no image of a historical "before" to its narrative of chaos and political violence, it is difficult to locate a loss that could form the object of mourning. As Freud makes clear, mourning requires a fully conscious imagining of a loss, and during the process of hypercathexis, "all the time the existence of the lost object is continued in the mind."[4] Instead of visualizing some time when history could have been different, the film's narrative opens with the point at which the present becomes inevitable, with the idea of a different image of the nation always one step out of reach. (The interwar period would, in any case, be a dubious argument for a national utopia, being characterized by widespread poverty and, in the words of Ivo Banac, a "conflict of opposing national ideologies.")[5] The prewar period passed over by the opening scene is conjured during this same sequence in voice-over as the fairy-tale location of "Once upon a time there was a country . . ." This sentence performs exactly the psychic move of imagining the lost object of history: once upon a time is necessarily in the past, and the fairy-tale genre connotes both a romanticized version of the nation and, for the listener, the nostalgically remembered world of childhood. However, the image implied by this sentence is *not there*, and what we see, instead, is the war that comes after, when that idea of nation is already lost. There is an attempt here to visualize the lost object, but the work of mourning gets stuck in the impossibility of forming an image of any time before loss.

The replacement of a historical image with a fantasy or fairy tale returns in the film's final scene, which is also readable as an attempt to envisage a "before" to the history of war. After the deaths of Ivan and Marko, Blacky escapes the horrors of the 1990s by jumping into a well (another kind of tunnel) and, in this ambiguous suicide, rediscovers his lost family. He washes up on the banks of the river by a verdant pastoral

*Underground*    The impossible national landscape floats away from the mainland. (Courtesy New Yorker Films)

scene. There are cows swimming to shore, and in a long shot we see a flat, green meadow on which all the dead characters are once again alive, taking part in a joyous banquet. After Blacky joins the party, the land on which they are sitting breaks away from the mainland and slowly drifts into the water. This truncated landscape (shaped vaguely like Tito's Yugoslavia) is for the first time in the film readable as an affective space of national nostalgia, yet its location can only be fantasmatic: outside the narrative's historical trajectory, it can make no claim on the real. And even as fantasy, the scene's meaning remains ambiguous. Is this utopian space to be read as a past wholeness before historical loss or as a potential future to be regained? In either case, wholeness remains outside the historical narrative and is contingent on a geographic splitting that, in the context of a war predicated on the violent separation process of "ethnic cleansing," can hardly be viewed without anxiety.

## Melancholia and Cryptic Space

This failed attempt to visualize a loss is reminiscent of Freud's description of melancholia, in which "one feels justified in concluding that a loss . . . has been experienced, but *one cannot see clearly what has been lost*, and may the more readily suppose that the patient too cannot consciously perceive what it is he has lost. This, indeed, might be so even when the patient was aware of the loss giving rise to the melancholia, that is, when he knows whom he has lost but not *what it is he has lost* in them."[6] In contrast to the mode of mourning, in which the lost object is, if anything, excessively visible, the melancholic subject knows that he has experienced a loss but cannot see exactly what it is that has been lost, and thus he turns the object loss into an ego loss, re-creating the object as subjective fantasy. In readings such as Susannah Radstone's, this shift from mourning to melancholia signifies a falling away from history, a narcissism that precludes any relationship to the social.[7] I would suggest that in *Underground*, however, melancholia implies a distinct—but no less social—relationship to national identity and loss, in which the problem of history is worked over as a problem of the image.

The image of the beautiful landscape floating away from the mainland articulates the conscious experience of a loss: once upon a time there was a country. However, alongside this repeated avowal of a lost nation is the inability of the film to visualize what was lost as anything but a fantasmatic space. The film knows that a country has been lost but does not know what that country looked like and, hence, does not fully know what has been lost in it. The Yugoslavia that *Underground* proposes existed before the time of war forms a missing point of origin that constantly reiterates the problem of loss. The film is thus predicated on an impossible time, as well as an impossible space. There is no time at which Yugoslavia, or any of its various states, existed as a coherent and boundaried space. Not only is there no Yugoslavia now, but there never was an uncontested Yugoslav identity. Thus, to be nostalgic for a point of "once upon a time there was a country" is to set up a nostalgia for an impossibility.[8] There was no such fairy-tale time, and it is this impossibility that the film circles. At once, it is crucial for the national subject to construct such a narrative of historical identity, but yet there is no place in which this narrative can cohere. Melancholia is thus a symptom of stuckness, where the fantasmatic landscape demonstrates, in Nicholas Abraham and Maria Torok's terms, a loss that has been incorporated into the self, and must be constantly restated but is never fully understood.[9]

In their study of Freud's Wolf Man case, Abraham and Torok suggest the theory of encryption as an elaboration of mourning and melancholia. They argue that while mourning is a work of introjection, in which the process of hypercathexis gradually turns the painful image of the lost object into subjectively realized memories, encryption occurs when this process fails. Thus, when the subject refuses to mourn, or cannot mourn, the image of loss is incorporated, taken whole into the subject, where it remains untouched as a more or less inaccessible crypt. In this way, separation from the lost object is prevented, but so, also, is a resolution of the state of loss. In his reading of Abraham and Torok, Jacques Derrida glosses this process: "The crypt is always an internalization, an inclusion intended as a compromise, but since it is a parasitic inclusion, an inside heterogeneous to the inside of the Self, an outcast in the domain of general introjection within which it violently takes its place, the cryptic safe can only maintain in a state of repetition the mortal conflict it is impotent to resolve."[10] Here we can see the crypt as an enclosed space in which loss is at once repeated and disavowed.

Derrida goes on to make plain the work of desire in this structure: "With the real loss of the object having been rejected and the desire having been maintained but at the same time excluded from introjection (simultaneous conservation and suppression, between which no synthesis is possible), incorporation is a kind of theft to reappropriate the pleasure object. But that reappropriation is simultaneously rejected: which leads to the paradox of a foreign body preserved as foreign but by the same token excluded from a self that thenceforth deals not with the other, but only with itself."[11] This understanding of the crypt seems to coincide with Radstone's reading of melancholy, in which a melancholic relationship to history is ideologically reactionary because it replaces an object loss with an ego loss. This nexus of narcissism and nostalgia produces, for her, an inevitably false image of the past, in which the drive to retain the pleasurable object produces a convenient history that bypasses complexity and merely mirrors the spectator's desires. However, the concept of encryption demands a more complicated and, indeed, contradictory definition of melancholia, in which the social or historical element of the lost object remains and, in fact, is more painful for its imprisonment in the cryptic image.

We can see the crypt in the final landscape of *Underground*, which precisely matches Derrida's description of incorporation: "For Maria Torok, 'incorporation, properly speaking,' in its 'rightful semantic specificity,' intervenes at the limits of introjection itself, when introjection, for some reason, fails. Faced with the impotence of the process of introjection (gradual, slow, laborious, mediated, effective), incorporation is the only choice: fantasmatic, unmediated, instantaneous, magical, sometimes hallucinatory."[12] These are indeed the features that mark the historicity of the island and its uncertain pleasures: the image is fantasmatic and yet sudden, suggesting a hallucination for its protagonists as much as for the spectator. And yet this unrealistic space does not operate simply as a misrepresentation of history—for what history does it depict?—or as a rejection of history, for the image of the miniature country incorporates whole the narrative pain of war and death, recapitulating its affect while suppressing its material appearance.

While the Italian films mapped a historical relation that was fully visible, returning to the painful history of the 1940s at the moment that it became possible to mourn its losses, *Underground* returns to a moment that it cannot imagine and that therefore remains a spiky, impossible collocation within the present. The impossibility of visualizing the time or the nation that came before the history of war produces a text of encryption, making visible the loss in the only way possible. Melancholia is mapped visually across the body of the text, and thus the problem of history is constructed as a problem of space, with enclosure and exclusion, inside and outside forming the logic of mise-en-scène, as well as that of geopolitical change. The logic of the crypt refracts into the tunnels and the cellar, into every space that displays itself as a self-enclosed but unreadable sign in which the losses of history are legible in a displaced and contradictory fashion. The cellar is a cryptic image that speaks of only the missing scene of the nation and yet still refuses to show it. If the subterranean spaces of the narrative reiterate visually the

*Underground*   The claustrophobic space of the cellar is shown by filling the frame with objects. (Courtesy New Yorker Films)

structure of the crypt, the image of the island forms its historical foundation. Derrida says that "the cryptic enclave produces a cleft in space,"[13] and the image of the island floating away from the shore materializes exactly this painful gap. It is at once the image of its own psychic split, narrativizing the suppression of a history that is too painful to see and forming an enclave within the body of the film, separate from the temporal and spatial diegesis of the text, and yet incontrovertibly the missing source of its historical losses.

This uncertain collocation of past and present also determines the film's narrative of war. As a rationale for keeping Blacky and his family in the cellar, Marko tells them that World War II is still continuing; thus, when Blacky resurfaces in the 1990s, he interprets the Bosnian war as the same war that he last saw. Thus, even more directly than the melodramatic narratives of the Italian films, *Underground* sets up an explicit relationship between the history of the 1940s and that of the 1990s. This comparison is enabled also by a compression of historical time, whereby none of the characters age substantially in fifty years, and Blacky as an irregular soldier in 1992 does not look any different from Blacky as a partisan in 1942. For Iordanova, such diversions from realism function only as historical mendacity; she complains that "while exposing the Communist tampering with history [in the film within the film], Kusturica himself grossly abuses historical time. Take, for example, the over 30 year long jump between the second and third part of *Underground* (from 1961 to 1995), itself a fairly frivolous approach to historicisation."[14] However, instead of seeing this nonrealist historicity as an abuse of "real" historical time, we can counter that in this breaking of linearity, politicization becomes possible.

The implication of the film's narrative structure is that the origins of contemporary ethnic violence can be found in World War II, and not in the oft-cited "ancient tribal hatreds" or in the legacy of Communism. As Mark Wheeler suggests, "Yugoslavs may be re-fighting the Second World War."[15] For Wheeler, this is a radical claim, reinserting the Bosnian wars into a wider European history rather than placing them as an "inconceivably messy" Balkan problem. *Underground* produces this logic at both points of history, forcing the spectator to read the 1990s in terms of the 1940s, and vice versa. Thus, one of the early scenes in war-torn Belgrade includes a series of shaky 8-mm shots of ruined buildings and injured civilians, a bombed-out hospital, and soldiers moving through the streets. These shots are ambiguous: while they purport to represent the aftermath of the Allied bombing of 1944, it is impossible to see such damage and injury without being reminded of the more recent wars. Moreover, the content of the images is sufficiently ambiguous that the film could equally well have been shot in the 1940s or the 1990s. This visual condensation of time forces a connection between the European war and the more recent Balkan conflicts. And when, in the final scenes, Blacky thinks he is a partisan commander saving villages from Ustase and Chetniks, the connection reverses, and the spectator is compelled to think of the civil war in terms of world war.

Of course, this historical ambivalence also invites a possible critique, and compelling as the scene of destruction may be, it remains politically and narratively ambiguous. Blacky is still a partisan fighter; but without a nation to fight for, his allegiances are open to question. His troops claim to have captured "Ustase, Chetniks, U.N. troops, and war profiteers," a group that again brings together World War II and civil war foes. David A. Norris has read this grouping as merely chaotic, a symbol of the absurdity of war.[16] In the context of a melancholic relation to a national identity, however, this group is historically disjunctive but not politically random. Chetniks were extreme Serbian nationalist guerrillas, Ustase their state-sanctioned Croat equivalents, and both worked with the Axis powers against Tito and a federal Yugoslavia. Both, then, were enemies of the partisans. With the contemporary prisoners, both can be read as anti-Yugoslav and anti-Communist, working for the introduction of a free-market state. From Blacky's limited and confused perspective, then, all are legitimate targets—a debatable logic, but not purely chaotic or absurd.

What is melancholic in this historical conflation is its confusion of times and spaces, whereby the relation of temporal loss is clear, but what exactly the loss consists of becomes hard to distinguish. Thus, Blacky's confusion crystallizes the film's historical sticking point: while it is politically imperative to relate these two histories, it is clearly not a good thing that Blacky does not know which war he is fighting, and the confusion of the final scenes figures this conflation explicitly as a problem. The melancholic reiteration of a loss that cannot be understood produces not the "too late" structure of melodramatic affect but, rather, an ironic effect. The irony here consists not only in the spectator's greater historical and narrative knowledge than Blacky's, but also in his or her realization that this knowledge cannot, nonetheless, translate into political resolution.

To suggest that the film constructs an ironic relation to history is not to claim a flippant disregard for fact, or what might be characterized as a postmodern cynicism, although both are at the least implied in Dina Iordanova's and Slavoj Žižek's readings.[17] Rather, irony operates as a doubling in the film's relation to history, whereby the circuit of knowledge and belief must critique, and yet at the same moment reiterate, the problematic history of Balkan space. We have seen how this doubling both enables and derails direct historical comparisons and how it complicates melancholia, where an articulation of loss turns into the avowal of a fantasmatic national identity. And yet the conflicting nature of these claims of history and fantasy is precisely the knowledge with which the spectator, as opposed to the characters, must engage. How this doubling is produced in relation to political space—the mise-en-scène of the cellar and the film's relentless work of mapping—can be used to analyze how the problematics of east European space are figured in terms of historical and spectacular images. But before we get to this work of mapping, it is first necessary to locate the contextual rhetoric of Yugoslavia's historical-political spaces.

## Balkanism

Contemporary historical accounts argue that the postwar binary of Eastern and Western Europe worked to exclude the East from what became the conceptual space of "Europe."[18] As Timothy Garton Ash describes it: "The post-Yalta order dictated a strict and single dichotomy. Western Europe implicitly accepted this dichotomy by subsuming under the label Eastern Europe all those parts of historic Central, East Central, and Southeastern Europe that after 1945 came under Soviet domination. The EEC completed the semantic trick by arrogating to itself the unqualified title Europe."[19] Thus, after 1948, the key division was not Europe against the primitive South but West European civilization in opposition to the not-quite-so-European East. The eastern part of Europe was thus excluded so that the West could continue to view itself as definitional of civilization, and in the 1990s, Yugoslavia became exemplary of un-European Eastern barbarism.

The discourse that was mobilized to describe the breakup of Yugoslavia is more specific than that around eastern Europe in general and can be described as a logic of Balkanism. Central to this logic is the idea that the Balkans are inherently primitive and violent: this is what enabled the wars in Bosnia, Croatia, and Kosovo to be described not in terms of political aggression but, in the words of the *New York Times*, as the work of "irreconcilable warring tribes."[20] This notion of the Balkans as an undifferentiated mess, incomprehensible to the civilized world, is also what produced the unclear debate on *Underground* discussed in chapter 3. Commentators such as Stanko Cerović were seen as one more crazy partisan Balkan, and Western critics regarded both his accusations and the politics of the film as equally opaque. As Iordanova rather bitterly says, the shift in focus onto the debate of French and German intellectuals "meant a diversion of attention from issues of culture and politics that were not part of the West. The Balkans . . . could not possibly be of interest; they were somehow too primitive, heavy-handed or unsophisticated. The *Underground* controversy was looked upon as representative of the whole Balkan conflict, incomprehensible and annoying."[21] If the debate on the film suffered from a lack of filmic specificity, it was also diminished by Western ignorance of Balkan specificity. This ignorance was not just a background problem, for Balkanism is the discourse through and against which *Underground*'s mise-en-scène is formed, and we must understand the concept in order to read the film politically.

Balkanism has been theorized as a discourse comparable to Edward Said's concept of Orientalism,[22] in which, in Žižek's words, the Balkans come to signify "as the timeless space onto which the West projects its phantasmatic content."[23] Like Orientalism, Balkanism is a form of colonial discourse, in which the peoples of the Hapsburg and, more so, Ottoman Empires were historically viewed as savages from a west European point of view. Norris points out that in the nineteenth century, the British identified more closely with the Turkish rulers of the Balkans than with their colonized subjects and that, although these subjects were European, they were readily thinkable as primitive people, alongside

British colonial subjects in Africa or India.[24] This discourse may derive from colonial relations, but for Milica Bakić-Hayden and Robert M. Hayden it retains its rhetorical power. They argue that "in the post-colonial world, the language of orientalism still maintains its rhetorical force as a powerful set of categories with which to stigmatize societies that are not 'western-style democracies.'"[25] This argument is borne out by the late-twentieth-century use of the term "balkanization," which, Maria Todorova demonstrates, "not only had come to denote the parcelization of large and viable political units but also had become a synonym for a reversion to the tribal, the backward, the primitive, the barbarian."[26]

However, Todorova also argues that "Balkanism is not simply a sub-species of orientalism. . . . The absence of a colonial legacy (despite the often exploited analogy) is not the only, not even the main difference."[27] To understand the specificity of Balkanism, then, we must consider the geopolitical location of the Balkans, which has historically complicated the binary of West and East, Europe and Asia. While the southern parts of the peninsula were once part of the Eastern Ottoman Empire, the dominant religion is still Christianity. Orthodox Serbs may be contrasted with the Protestants of northern Europe, yet they are not Orientals like Turks or Ottomans. Norris traces the discursive confusion to 1453, when "the collapse of Constantinople and the arrival of the Turks caused a major shift in the way Europeans imagined their continent. . . . The Balkans have variously been described as the place where East meets West, not belonging fully to either world. It is Eurasia, the ambivalent lands between what is properly East and what is properly West, a bastard borderland."[28]

For Todorova, this mongrelized space was, in the twentieth century, subject to a "theoretical rationalization: the inhabitants of the Balkans as 'crossbreeds' are racially and culturally inferior, not only to the western Europeans but also to the oriental other."[29] She traces the term "to balkanize" to World War I and the idea of innate Balkan violence to interwar racialist theories. This history is telling: the exact form of early-twentieth-century racism that was so thoroughly disavowed by the West in relation to the victims of Nazism has remained acceptable as part of the west European rhetoric of the Balkans. As Todorova implies, the continuation of this discourse derives from its political convenience, distracting attention from western Europe's role in the region's ethnic problems. As Robert Bideleux puts it, "Inasmuch as the Western powers unwittingly compounded Eastern Europe's ethnic minority problems by enunciating and instituting the principle of national self-determination as the linch-pin of the post-1918 East European states system, they should not try to wash their hands of responsibility for the baleful outcome."[30] Or, as Wheeler says more succinctly, the claim of "ancient ethnic hatreds [is] an oxymoron and a lie."[31] Here, then, the modern specificity of Balkanism emerges, defining in ethnic terms the political consequences of Western foreign policy and inextricably linking a racialist rhetoric of primitivism to the expedient production of what in the 1990s became an impossible European space.

This rhetoric, as we have seen, overlaid the Western critical response to *Underground* as much as it determined political analysis of the civil wars that the film depicts. But this response cannot be understood only as a Western perversion of a Balkan text, for Balkanism is also central to the internal politics of the former Yugoslav states. Like Italy, Yugoslavia was structured in the postwar era by a north/south split, in which the southern regions tended to be impoverished and rural, while the north became increasingly industrialized and wealthy. Croats and Slovenes resented having to subsidize Serbs and Macedonians, and, even more so than in Italy, this economic split intensified existing racisms. As Rothschild and Wingfield argue:

> That the gap between the two halves should not widen further and should ultimately be closed for the sake of the federation's integrity and even viability was agreed in the 1960s, but selecting a rational and equitable strategy to achieve this goal proved profoundly conflictive, replete with ethnically loaded charges of exploitation, neglect, parasitism, colonialism, shackling, and extortion; in Yugoslavia, interregional discrepancies are inevitably experienced as interethnic tensions.[32]

This imbrication of economic and ethnic politics has had a complex history throughout the postwar years, but it is in the wake of the breakup of Yugoslavia that its Balkanist aspect becomes important in the context of *Underground*.

Bakić-Hayden and Hayden trace the rise in the 1990s of an internal Balkanism, in which there is an "increasing use by politicians and writers from the northwestern parts of the country of an orientalist rhetoric that relies for its force on an ontological and epistemological distinction between (north)west and (south)east."[33] Their claim is that "the orientalist paradigm has gained prominence in political rhetoric from the northwestern republics as the old socialist paradigms have faded."[34] While socialist Yugoslavia emphasized commonality and worked to promote equality among all federal languages and cultures, they claim that this rhetoric of brotherhood was genuinely felt by only the partisan generation, who had fought together in the war against a common enemy. By the 1980s, a new generation of politicians and intellectuals was emphasizing conflict and ethnic difference. Once again, the period from partisan struggle to the fall of Communism forms a decisive political era, but in this case the ending of the era prompts a different kind of national reconsideration from that prompted in Italy: not a new discourse on national identity but a rhetoric of absolute difference.

The rhetoric is familiar, claiming the newly independent northern states as civilized and European, while the southern regions are seen as primitive. Thus, Bakić-Hayden and Hayden cite a Slovenian writer's claim that "we Slovenes have difficulty identifying ourselves with the pro-Asian or pro-African Yugoslavia. . . . It is more important that we embodied the way of life that was created in central-western Europe."[35] This association of southern Yugoslavia with the South and the East was taken up by the Croatian Democratic Union, which called for inclusion in central Europe, as opposed to a Yugoslav state that has "consistently subordinated the Croatian state to an asiatic form of government."[36] Even more extremely, the Slovenian minister of science in 1991 described Serbia and Montenegro in terms of "a typical and violent crooked oriental-bizantine [sic] heritage."[37] And lest we think that only extremists (more crazy Balkans) would partake in this form of Balkanist racism, Todorova cites Václav Havel arguing that only Slovenia should be considered for NATO membership, as those countries to its south are not part of "the western sphere of European civilization," with its "values" and "traditions" but, rather, are "traditionally agitated," unstable and non-Western.[38]

## Underground: Balkanist Text?

Two of the theorists who describe this discourse of Balkanism also use the term to critique Underground. Both Iordanova and Žižek move from defining Balkanism as a social and political structure to citing thematic examples of it within the film. Thus, Iordanova claims that the film blames the war not on Communism but on the "impaired moral standards innate in the Balkan social character, an approach which is nothing else but a refined version of the primordialist argument according to which primal passions are being played out in the Balkan conflict."[39] The issue for her, then, is not particularly cinema specific but is the apparent political point of view of plot and/or characters. She locates Balkanism in characters like Blacky and Marko, who illustrate Balkan stereotypes, and through an attribution of whom the narrative seems to blame for the war. She suggests that it may try to blame Communism for the strife of the 1990s, but in beginning with a scene of amoral and wild behavior *before* the Communist takeover, the film reveals its true colors and places Balkan immorality as a foundation of the culture of ethnic hatred.

Žižek also takes up this thematic reading, citing Blacky as an embodiment of the "Serbian myth of the true man."[40] He adds an ideological critique, calling the film, alongside *Before the Rain* (Manchevski, 1994), "the ultimate ideological product of Western liberal multiculturalism: what these two films offer to the Western liberal gaze is precisely what this gaze wants to see in the Balkan war—the spectacle of a timeless, incomprehensible, mythical cycle of passions, in contrast to decadent and anaemic Western life."[41] Here, Žižek broadens his description of Balkanism to include the film's spectacular mise-en-scène and extravagant narrative. More nuanced than Iordanova's method of merely finding examples of Balkanist rhetoric in the film's characters, this approach nonetheless maps visual and narrative forms too directly onto ideology. The argument returns us to Žižek's opposition to spectacle, for he turns to spectacle as the embodiment of Balkanism in filmic terms. The spectacular mise-en-scène and nonrealist historicity of the cellar operates for him as a veil, obscuring political realities and creating a Balkanist myth of timelessness and irrationality. He reads the excesses of the narrative in an even more bluntly ideological fashion, claiming (as discussed in chapter 3) that these excesses encode the logic of ethnic cleansing. Just as spectacle reflects a primitivist gaze for Žižek, so does narrative excess explain genocide.

Žižek and Iordanova are right in connecting *Underground* to the concept of Balkanism, for this ideological structure is central to any radical reading of the history represented by the film, and it is indeed a key part of the film's visual and narrative structure. However, there might be a more film-theoretically nuanced way of thinking about *Underground* in relation to Balkanism, where the film would not merely stand as a repository in which to find thematic examples or formal reflections of a preexisting political discourse. *Underground* does not simply repeat the politics of Balkanism, and there is something more complex at work in the way the film mobilizes the discourse.

What might it mean for a film to mobilize Balkanism textually? If, as Žižek suggests, there is something in *Underground*'s excess and spectacularity that connotes a specifically Balkanist logic, then we must first examine how this discourse is deployed in cinematic forms and how, exactly, the spectacular image produces meaning in relation to this politics. Moreover, we need to coarticulate the politics of Balkan history not with a direct reading of the film's "point of view" but with its construction of space and time, for it is in the relationship between the space of the cellar and the time of melancholic historicity that *Underground*'s reading of Balkanism inheres. In addition, I would like to excavate what Žižek and Iordanova pass over in their thematic application of Balkanism: the extent to which the discourse is able to delineate the relationship between West and East as a relationship as much of fantasy and desire as of history and geography.

Žižek's connection of spectacle to Balkanism is too quick, relying, as I have suggested, on an antispectacular position unrelated to the specificity of Balkan politics or cinema. The spectacular image in *Underground does* produce a Balkanist discourse, but one that begins rather than ends with the idea of excess. The concept of excess has a film-specific meaning, as well as the more general one used by Žižek, and in tracing the relationship between spectacle and Balkanism, this overlap becomes significant. There are many sequences in which the mise-en-scène is potentially excessive in terms both of conjuring the Balkanist myth and of signification in the theoretical sense; one typical scene is Jovan's underground wedding. As the inhabitants of the cellar form a large, crowded party, the bride arrives strapped into a strange contraption that allows her to "fly" above the long tables, moving over all the guests in turn. In this sequence, there is excess in the number of people and

*Underground*   Constrictive framing emphasizes the horizontal space of the cellar.
(Courtesy New Yorker Films)

objects that crowd the frame, as well as in the Rube Goldbergian machine that enables the bride's flight. Her horizontal movement emphasizes the film's widescreen framing, as well as the narrowness of the cellar space, so that instead of producing a coherent narrative space, the scene has a frontal, tableau-like quality. The overall effect is of an illogical movement through a cramped space—a movement that, in the context of the cellar, reads as too much.

In fact, many of the moments of visual and narrative excess in the film are similarly spatial, combining the narrow and limited with the extravagant and complex. There are other moments of excess within the frame, such as the tank that the underground families manage to build inside the cellar and the other fabulous machines created from junk. There is also excess in the kinds of narrative space produced, the most telling example being the tunnels that run beneath all of Europe. At once claustrophobic and expansive, this network typifies the logic of excessive space that is nonetheless constantly limited and logically impossible. This effect is most visible in the shot in which Ivan climbs down a vertical tunnel beneath Berlin. The view is a lateral projection, so the tunnel splits the frame in two, with Ivan centered, but most of the frame on each side is the blank space of underground rock. The emptiness of this space focuses the spectator's attention first on the surprising fact of the tunnel, a new and expansive space where none was expected. However, the weight of those dark blocks of rock on either side of Ivan, and, by exten-

*Underground*   Excessive space is at once claustrophobic and expansive. (Courtesy New Yorker Films)

sion, in the place of the camera, remind us of the constriction of this space, as well as its logical impossibility.

A similar structure determines the film's production of temporal excess, the best example being the trope of the families living underground for fifty years but yet not changing physically at all. Whereas time elapsed is written as a surplus, a disfiguration, on the made-up faces of the actors in *Cinema Paradiso* and *Mediterraneo*, in *Underground* realism is abandoned and there is no visible difference. The same actors play characters from 1941 through to the 1990s, with their lack of aging emphasized in the relative similarity, also, of their clothes and hairstyles. Natalija and Marko may listen to modern music as the decades pass aboveground, but their physical presence is not updated. Such an impossible expansion of youth, unremarked on in the narrative, produces an excess of time but also a contraction. Where nothing and no one changes, history cannot be easily represented as loss, for the characters appear to be living still in the moment at which the narrative began. But history does intervene, as the central segment of the narrative traces the rise and fall of Tito and the beginning of the end of a federal Yugoslavia. These events never produce the distance of loss because the protagonists remain consistently young, with each historical moment appearing to be the same narrative present. Thus, the excess of time becomes constrictive, an unending present from which the protagonists cannot escape. While history continues, the protagonists cannot reach it, and the lives of Marko and Natalija, as much as those of Blacky and the others underground, become narrowed into a continuous war, love affair, and subterfuge.

If these modes of excess visually embody the Balkanist myth, they also place a contradiction at its center. As much as the mise-en-scène produces spectacles of plenitude, it also connotes restriction, and as much as the narrative insists on its historicity, the characters remain visually stuck in a temporal vacuum. Thus, every excess is also and simultaneously experienced as a restriction, so that too much also becomes too little. In this way, these examples perform the double-edged-sword structure of Balkanism, in which the "larger than life" cliché goes hand in hand with the "less than human" subtext of primitivism. That these contradictions play out predominantly in terms of space and historicity is significant, for what complicates *Underground*'s use of Balkanism is the text's enunciation of its own national position. Both Orientalism (as outlined by Said) and Balkanism (in the work of Todorova and others) are defined almost entirely in terms of a Western subject's discourse about the Oriental other. From eighteenth-century British travel writing to

American commentary on the war in Bosnia, it is always the gaze of the outsider that projects Balkan space as a screen for a Western fantasy. Even Todorova's discussion of internal Balkanism in post-Yugoslav politics is based on the northern and western republics presenting themselves as not-Balkan and, hence, as able to criticize the southern, Balkan states from the outside. *Underground*, though, is a Balkan film, speaking from the indisputably southern space of Belgrade and therefore making a claim on Balkanism from within, from the place of the primitive object of the discourse rather than its Western subject.

How does this switch in enunciative position alter the meaning of Balkanist discourse? This is a question that Žižek and Iordanova do not address, preferring to discuss the film *as though it were* a Western view of the Balkans. Of course, it would be possible to argue, extending Said, that Balkanism is simply internalized by its objects, who come to experience and represent themselves in terms of the dominant discourse. Said briefly discusses the effects of American consumerism, in which "cultural images of the Orient [are] supplied by American mass media and consumed unthinkingly by the mass television audience. The paradox of an Arab regarding himself as an 'Arab' of the sort put out by Hollywood is but the simplest result of what I am referring to."[42] This is an arguable theory of media reception, but even aside from this issue, the question of internalization must be teased out a little more in relation to Balkanism, where the difficulty of hypothesizing how Balkan cultures react to Western representations of them is compounded by the impossibility of making clear-cut distinctions. This is not Arabs and far-off Americans creating stereotypes, but European versions of other Europeans. In the "mongrel" space of Yugoslavia, any internalization of Western discourse is necessarily contradictory. Further, *Underground* cannot be viewed simply in terms of the Balkan *reception* of Western stereotypes, for the iterative production of Balkanism by a Balkan text suggests a splitting or doubling in the film's enunciation. Thus, *Underground* speaks as a somewhat disingenuous text, located in the East but constructing the image of Western Balkanist discourse, and therefore positioned both inside and outside its own enunciative space. This doubled relation produces spatial and temporal contradiction.

This is the context in which it becomes possible to reread the mise-en-scène of the cellar, for underground space here stands as the linchpin of the film's enunciation, the only place from which the Balkan text can speak. The cellar is not an allegory of any Yugoslav nation but visually structures the film's ideological double bind. Underground space is precisely not national space—it can make no claim to represent indexically the truth of Yugoslavia. Nor is it readable as European space, for, again, it has no direct relationship to any international political landscape. Within the logic of realism, it has no ground. But there is nonetheless a claim to be made on nation and on European-ness, in the family cellar and in its shadow, the network of tunnels that connect all of the continent below the ground. The cellar *is* a political landscape, but one that articulates its own impossibility from the point of view of European—which is to say, Western and Balkanist—discourse. If the Balkans are abjected by the West, seen as not fully European, then *Underground*'s response to this history is neither to refute its power by making defensive claims to civilization nor to displace abjection someplace farther south (as do the Slovenian and Croatian politicians) but, instead, to investigate the problematic structure of Balkanism by articulating its own abjection.

## Europe's Abject

In discussing the splitting of Eastern from Western Europe, the term "abjection" is often used in its more general sense—to denote a vehement rejection or exclusion—but if we turn to Julia Kristeva's psychoanalytic investigation of the abject, we again find a question of space.[43] Like the geopolitical abject, Kristeva's also is a question of borders, in which the subject demands a proper boundary between self and other, living and dead, pure and impure. It might seem a stretch to compare this kind of subjective border with the material—if also psychic—border between East and West on which Yugoslavia has historically hovered. But, as Irit Rogoff's and Giuliana Bruno's intimate cartographies demonstrate,[44] borders are always psychic as well as material. In textualizing the experience of a difficult history, *Underground* negotiates the relation of the psychoanalytic to the social through its articulation of cinematic space and of the position of the spectator. While the social space of the Balkans is abjected, the cellar and the tunnel materialize this logic visually, folding the borders of inside and outside, East and West.

In this analogy, Europe takes on the "borderline" status of Kristeva's deject, the entity by which the abject exists. This deject is defined not in terms of subjectivity but in terms of location: "Instead of sounding himself as to his 'being,' he does so concerning his place: '*Where* am I?' instead of '*Who* am I?' For the space that engrosses the deject, the excluded, is never *one*, nor *homogenous*, nor *totalizable*, but essentially divisible, foldable and catastrophic. A deviser of territories, languages, works, the *deject* never stops demarcating his universe."[45] This work of mapping and remapping could seem appropriate for the hypothetical subject of "Europe," for which the East must constantly be enclosed and yet excluded, repudiated as other. Thus, the spectacle of the cellar does not so much offer a point of identification for a Yugoslav national subject as generate an uncomfortable voyeurism. The tunnels offer a recognizable image of a dark and sinister Balkan culture, making a claim for identity only in the space of abjection. But the abject's exclusion from Europe is also a double-edged claim on European-ness. Only from inside Europe can the Balkans be abjected, as placing of primitive violence safely on the other side of a boundary re-forms "Europe" as a once-more civilized space. Europe exists by the abject, and this process inevitably rebounds, defining the continent as a whole in terms of that which it seeks to disavow. The cellar that is not after all a singular space, outside history, but that leads, eventually, to the West, structures exactly this work of psychic mapping: I am not in Europe / I am in Europe.

As with melancholic historicity, this logic is ironic, emplacing a double-voiced relationship to Balkanism. *Underground* at once speaks from and lays bare the discourse that defines the Balkans as less than modern and not-quite-European. Thus the pervasive darkness and horizontality that spreads across the mise-en-scène, constantly returning to the trope of Belgrade as a subterranean, pre-modern city. One example is the sequence in which Ivan finally finds himself below his home after searching through the European tunnel system. After wandering through brick-and stone-walled tunnels with signs to Athens and Berlin, he sees a wall

*Underground*   Mapping European space: Ivan encounters the secret tunnel from Berlin to Athens. (Courtesy New Yorker Films)

that is not constructed like the others but made from rough-cut rocks. A medium close-up of Ivan standing by the wall shows it to be blood-stained, and, when he stretches his hand out, blood drips onto him. The badly made walls and blood of course imply Yugoslavia as both primitive and violent, but the very excess of this visualization announces its ideological status. Primitivism is not naturalized, as it might be, for example, in a more realist film like Before the Rain, but falls out of the narrative to stand explicitly as a spectacle, restating the Western fantasy precisely as fantasy.

Similarly, the location of the film in Belgrade and not, say, in Sarajevo or one of the independent northern republics forces a confrontation with the object of Balkanism.[46] While it would be easy to make an argument of ideological progressivity from the point of view of Bosnia, the claim would rest on good will for the recent victims of Milošević's aggression. And while such sympathy goes without saying politically, it is not enough. As Žižek himself has argued in relation to global multi-culturalism, such a position can allow an unchallenging liberalism in which any film from a "marginal" nation is championed, and the structures of Western racism that underwrote the rise of Serb right-wing nationalism in the first place would go unquestioned.[47] Underground troubles this system by locating its narrative in Serbia, the center of the Balkanist myth. In its excessive mise-en-scène and exaggeration of primitivist stereotypes, the film does not speak about the myth of the Balkans but stages its problems. In reflecting back an exaggerated image of primitive, Eastern space, both the catastrophic space above the ground and the bloodied underground roads traveled by NATO troops prompt the question of exactly whose fantasy this might be.

If the tunnel maps a contradictory relationship to European identity, it also produces this effect for a spectator whose place is similarly split. The place of the sujet de l'énonciation is not, or not principally, that of a hypothetical Yugoslav spectator who can recognize her own national position in the narrative. Unlike the Italian films, Underground does not work to reinscribe a national history for a primarily national audience. As a coproduction and an international art film, Underground may have been unable to presume this kind of audience, but, more significant, the history that it proposes is essentially an international one. The abject exists only in relation to a subject who demands boundaries, and the myth of the crazy Yugoslav exists only in relation to the Western onlooker. What the nonrealist spectacle of the cellar refuses, then, is the conventional Western image of the Balkans, which in the context of the 1990s was that of journalistic naturalism. What realist images of war in the Balkans would invoke at this moment in time could only be more incomprehension on the part of the west European spectator— a horror certainly, but as much a distancing, a reinscription, of the faraway Western onlooker at the nightmare of Eastern excess.[48] This journalistic mode has fanned the flames of Balkanism, and it is this that *Underground*'s nonrealist spaces resist. The structural articulation of abjection, rather than the affective sight of ruins and bodies, prevents the position of the Western spectator from becoming that of the privileged onlooker who has history explained to him by classical or televisual realism. Instead of offering the international spectator an ideologically reassuring distance, this positioning within the underground space of the deject forces an uncomfortable complicity.

Refocusing like this on the structure of the cellar moves the debate away from questions of the film's explicit "message" or from what Kusturica may or may not think. Instead, more ideologically revealing is how *Underground*'s spectacular spaces structure within the text the very desires for, accusations at, and misunderstandings of Europe that the film's reception went on to rehearse. *Underground* constructs itself as a European film, its formal and narrative strategies typical of contemporary art cinema, and its funding drawn from several European countries. Furthermore, the exaggerated display of national clichés is one of the key strategies of the heritage film, and one that can, in fact, be politically progressive, as I have argued in relation to Italian films. But, as the controversy demonstrated, the film was not easily readable as a European film because art cinema and Balkan discourse were set up as oppositional. The textual impossibility of emplacing Balkan space within European space preempted only too successfully the film's own troubled reception.

Thus, the film's failure to produce a coherent European space— either within the image or as a spectatorial position—is most eloquent. The difference between how east and west Europeans view their continent is a chasm that becomes clear in the extratextual controversy, and the self-abjecting display of Balkanism within the frame restates Western ignorance even while attempting to problematize it. Thus the film demonstrates both internally and extratextually the self-defeating nature of the fantasy of a united Europe: just as the tunnels operate only to bring troops to Yugoslavia, so criticism once again played out the dominance of Western prejudice. As much as *Underground* works to connect its national space to that of the continent as a whole, the Balkans remain readable only in relation to—and as different from—the idea of Europe. Every critique of Yugoslavia's place in Europe can only restage its difference. And yet the textualization of this process is potentially productive: more than simply a film about impossible space, *Underground* becomes an impossible film.

## Images of History

As much as Balkanism is a question of space, it is also, in the logic of modernity, a question of time. The idea that Yugoslavia is distant, primitive, and tribal contains within it an assumption that is also pre-modern and historically less advanced than the West. And, whereas the West is seen as standing for progress and the march of historical time, the Balkans are viewed as timeless, operating in a cyclical and essentially unchanging fashion. Todorova touches on this argument, describing Balkanism as "a discourse utilizing the construct [Balkans] as a powerful symbol conveniently located outside historical time."[49] And Žižek adds this claim to his charge against both *Underground* and *Before the Rain*.[50] But *Underground* cannot simply promulgate this myth of timelessness, for at its most basic level it is a historical film. A film like *Before the Rain*, by dint of its single temporal location, may enable spectacular excess to connote nothing but mythical primitivism, but in *Underground* time and history cannot be totally suspended. War, Communism, and post-Communist conflict are all clearly marked as a historical process. The cellar suspends and warps the passage of time for its inhabitants but not for the spectator: the film is quite clear in its historical representation and seems to take historical confusion as its fantastic subject rather than to promote it. Blacky may not be able to understand his own historical place, but the spectator always can. But how does the film's spatial structure produce a historicity? For if the myth of the Balkans is timeless, *Underground* is constituted by history.

As the excessive mise-en-scène of the cellar suggests, the historical image in *Underground* is spectacular. As with the Italian films, historicity is produced not through the conventions of historical realism and authenticity but through a claim on an overtly cinematic language. Here, the similarities appear to end. *Underground* is not a heritage film, and its spectacle is not based on a nationally slanted version of the picturesque or the beautiful view. It makes little claim on an indexical real based on a vision of national landscape, and none on what I have described as an auratic relationship to the temporality of loss. There is no direct representation of an affective landscape, and we can trace this difference in the production of a melancholic relation to historical loss.

Instead of the clearly experienced "too late" structure of melodrama, the film confuses its historical loss, refusing any straightforward represen-tation of what has been lost or of where we could locate a national-historical image. The structure of the crypt precludes any direct repre-sentation of a historical truth. The first task, then, is to trace the contours of this spectacle, to consider where, other than the cellar, historicity is imagined. And in doing so, we may also think *Underground*'s historicity in relation to the dialectical image: to theorize how the spectacular spaces of Balkanism work to connect past and present, to read the film's spatial and temporal mapping ideologically, and to consider how the structure of art-cinematic spectacle produces, like the political land-scapes of Italy, an experience of the real.

If *Underground* refuses to provide a singular image of a national land-scape that could be mourned, it also refuses a unitary version of the past. What Iordanova complains is a distortion of historical time is more pro-ductively considered as part of a structure of layering. The narrative begins in a self-consciously conventional fashion, with the voice-over, "Once upon a time . . . ," but, as I have argued, immediately undercuts the representational value of the statement with the accompanying images of chaos. Similarly, the moment that she sees as misrepresent-ing history is an equally reflexive joke: from an intertitle claiming that "Marko Dren's disappearance coincided with the loss of the secret for-mula of Tito's Yugoslavia," the film jumps forward twenty years to news-reel footage of Tito's funeral. Clearly, the film is not making any serious claim on historical causality here, but what I think this moment does demonstrate is the primacy of the visual register over the temporality of narrative. The shift from the collapse of the building that houses the cel-lar to footage of Tito's funeral makes no sense narratively, but it does bring into focus a process of mapping, in which various registers of his-torical image are invoked throughout the film. The diegetic spectacle of the building's collapse exists alongside the indexical image of recogniz-able world leaders approaching Tito's coffin. What could be read as a metaphoric image of the building imploding is immediately turned into an ironic metonym of a wider political downfall. This layering of differ-ent visual registers is at play throughout the film, mapping historicity as a spectacular rather than a narrative logic.

We have already seen some elements of this logic: the nonrealist spaces of the underground cellar that locate Balkan history in terms of abjection, and the fantasmatic island at the end of the film, where national landscape can exist only outside historical time. To these we can add the register of historical actuality footage, in which scenes like Tito's funeral suture together documentary and fictional spaces. The opening sequence of *Underground* already begins to intersperse these layers. When the Nazis bomb the zoo, there is a series of cuts from the injured animals, to Ivan in the ruined zoo, to newsreel footage of planes dropping bombs, and then to an aerial view of a landscape. The last two shots are actual wartime footage, and are manifestly so, standing out by dint of the material aging of the film and the entirely different quality of grain from the aesthetically marked 35 mm of the zoo shots. However, they are edited into the sequence in a realist fashion, separated only at the visual level and not in terms of narrative logic. This addition not only adds factual to fictional footage, and historical to modern, but, with the aerial shot, includes a specific wartime mapping of space. The shots of the fields and city from the bird's-eye perspective of the plane add the register of landscape as strategic knowledge and as target to the cinematic convention of the establishing shot. Filmic space and military space are thus momentarily conflated.

The use of archival footage continues in the montage sequence representing the Nazi invasion. Separated by explanatory intertitles, we see newsreel shots of various towns welcoming the German army: Maribor in Slovenia, Zagreb in Croatia, and, finally, but this time with empty streets, Belgrade.[51] The massive crowds in these scenes are typical of propagandist newsreels seeking to show the popularity of the Nazis, but their sheer scale also serves the function in this context of ensuring that

*Underground*    Archival footage depicts crowds welcoming Nazi occupiers during World War II. (Courtesy New Yorker Films)

the shots are recognizably historical, even to a spectator unconcerned with the quality of the image. Crowds this big could not possibly be composed of extras (or of special effects in a European film of the period), and the image of the mass signifies historicity. Obviously "real" footage is also used later in the film, when documentary shots of Tito's coffin traveling the country form another punctuating montage. Once again, crowds are central, as this sequence shows the train with the coffin moving through the landscape and then, sometimes from aerial shots, scenes of various train stations filled with mourners eager to catch a final glimpse of the leader.

In the context of Balkanized space, it is telling that the larger spaces of the country—the political landscape of invasion and national mourning, as well as the physical one of town and countryside—are represented only in these documentary shots. On the one hand, these moments have a claim on the real that exceeds the rest of the film, insofar as their status as historical artifacts, indexically present during the history of war and death, outstrips their placement within the narrative. On the other hand, this difference also forces a distance, in which the views of the country are always readable *as* views and, hence, as partial, possibly propagandistic, unreliable images. It is important that these are all long shots, and, in fact, some are also aerial shots, taken from far above. The exemplary shot is that of the city, from the perspective of the plane dropping the bombs. This distance enables the view to encompass an entire landscape, but it also provokes the disfiguring question of origin: the aerial view does not speak from the national position of the mourner or the victim of invasion but is possible only from the point of view of the other. That this other is unreliable is evidenced also in the invasion images, which functioned historically as Nazi propaganda, and the funeral ones, which are Communist Party newsreels.

All these "real" images stand out as such, marked formally by documentary conventions and materially by different color balancing and by lines and scratches that signify the age of the film. However, the film complicates this relationship of historical actuality to fictional narrative, adding further registers of the image. In the montage sequence of Marko's rise in the Communist Party, he and Natalija are inserted into archival footage, creating a seamless effect similar to that of *Zelig* (Allen, 1983) and, most famously, *Forrest Gump* (Zemeckis, 1994). Marko stands behind Tito, makes a speech surrounded by party officials, and dances past various historical figures, while a smiling Natalija is visible fleetingly in a newsreel of marching soldiers. In these scenes, it is less visually clear which footage is documentary, and the spectator must read quickly to spot Natalija among the soldiers and decide whether the whole shot is a contemporary re-creation or whether her insertion is a digital effect. In most cases, though, the visual trickery of this effect is apparent because of the historical nature of the footage: where Marko stands beside Tito, the spectator knows that the film is a special effect. But whereas a film like *Forrest Gump* enabled at once the extratextual appreciation of state-of-the-art effects and the suturing of Gump into a stable realist narrative, *Underground* disrupts both of these pleasurable elements.[52]

First, the effects in *Underground* are not always pleasurably seamless. In one of the sequences with archival footage, Marko shakes hands with Tito. But instead of inserting Marko into the historical image along with the marshal, the effect is produced by editing: from an archival image of Tito in a wide shot with a row of soldiers, there is a cut to what would be Tito's point of view, a medium close-up of Marko extending his hand toward the camera, and then a cut back to Tito once more, turning to walk on down the line. The contemporary shot is clearly marked as brighter 35-mm film with a different quality of light than the newsreel. This cut is disjunctive, drawing attention to the temporal difference between these figures and producing historical narrative as a kind of creative geography. Evidently, the film could have inserted Marko more seamlessly into historical space, as happens earlier in the same sequence, and this unnecessary disjuncture precludes any smooth investment in the joining of present and past images. It is telling, in this context, that the places where the joins show relate to Marko and Natalija, who are consummate fakers and whose successes come both from lying to the party bosses about the source of their wealth and from the Communist Party itself, which was infamous for the faking of historical photographic images. Thus, at the same time that the film undercuts its own spectacular pleasures, it thematizes the ideological stakes in the status of the image.

Second, the film does not work toward the kind of structural coherence in which archival footage coexists with classical realism. In a film like *Forrest Gump*, this is achieved through what seems like a contradiction: it is usually evident which bits of film are historical and, hence, where the special effects are, yet the text demands a singular reading of its diegesis, with no uncertainty as to when the narrative is located. Archival footage *from* a period works alongside a fictional representation *of* the same period, such that while there must necessarily be moments of extratextual recognition of the spectacular effects, these moments ultimately can only bolster the reality effect of the realist historical narrative. In *Underground* the opposite is true; it is *not* always clear where the

*Underground*    Contemporary ruins are visible in faked newsreel footage. (Courtesy New Yorker Films)

effects are, and so (rather like Oliver Stone's also controversial *JFK* [1991]) the narrative does not produce a stable historicity but, rather, an uneasy awareness of the various levels of the image and its historical relations.

This instability can be glimpsed in the image of Natalija with the soldiers, where because there are no famous historical figures in the frame, and because the shot is brief, there is a moment of uncertainty as to whether she has been inserted into an archival shot or whether the image is a new one, made to look old. In this instance, the image is a doctored archival shot, but there are scenes in which contemporary film is artificially aged, made to look like old newsreel. As part of the sequence of the Nazi bombing of Belgrade in 1941, there are some shots of ruined city streets. The film is lined and jumpy and looks like old 16-mm newsreel footage. However, Blacky walks across the frame and, unlike Natalija, appears to be part of profilmic space. Here, then, we have faked historical footage, and the supposed material historicity of the film first guarantees and then undermines the realism of the narrative. The film directs our awareness of effects not toward supporting a historical realism but toward a conflation of the time of the filming and the time of the film. The two become completely intertwined at the level of the image, as the historical moments, like the images, are hard to separate.

The reason that the faked newsreel is momentarily convincing has less to do with its successful replication of the appearance of deteriorating film stock and more to do with the content of the image. Like the crowd shots of the Nazi invasion, these shots involve wartime images presumably too expensive to be a set—in this instance, bombed-out and ruined streets. This footage is colorized and grainy, and it comes directly after the archival shots of the invasion, but the reason it convinces as an index of war is the extent of the physical destruction on display. And even though it is new, it is documentary footage. Filmed in the aftermath of the bombing of Belgrade in the early 1990s,[53] the ruined buildings and dead bodies are real. This documentary displacement destabilizes historical representation, so there can be no simple binary of the "real" history of the historical actuality versus the representational history of the present-day fiction. This sequence signifies historical and contemporary spaces simultaneously, and it does so through an affective jolt of real destruction. When both present and past actuality films stand in for history, and when the signs of material aging of film are part of the spectacle of historical reconstruction, then there can be no univocal image of historical truth: the film's faith in the guarantees of realism, no less than in the authenticity of the indexical image, is called into question.

*Underground* also narrativizes this additive construction of a historical diegesis, constantly thematizing the problems of knowledge involved in mapping and in reconstructing historical spaces. When Ivan is in a German mental asylum, he shows the doctors a map depicting the tunnel system of Europe. But rather than a conventional political or physical map, he seems to have an old-fashioned treasure map, the kind in which X marks the spot. Finding Yugoslavia, this implies, is not a matter of geography but of fairy tale, of fiction, and of desire. Or, to take another example, when Blacky and Jovan escape from the cellar, they find themselves not in the reality of contemporary Belgrade but on a movie set in which the official party film producers are reenacting the history of Marko's heroic actions during the Nazi occupation. And, of course, this film is a complete work of fiction, casting Marko and Natalija as heroes of the revolution. Socialist realist revisionism becomes another unstable layer of historical image, here poking fun at the unreality of this mythical past.[54]

As these spatial elaborations imply, there is no single historical diegesis in which a linear national history could be stabilized. Instead, there is a kaleidoscopic array of views in which the film's historical coordinates are excessively imagined and multiplied, but history as such is never clearly visible. The images of Yasir Arafat and Margaret Thatcher at the funeral become merely one more layer of historical image and do not suggest any greater access to historical reality than do the spectacles

of the zoo or the tunnels. This explosion of narrative spaces, in combination with a refusal of realist narration, places historical truth as that
which is always out of reach or, rather, always slightly outside the frame.

## The Monster in the Labyrinth

In this multiplication of historical spaces, narrative begins to
signify differently. Instead of a clear causal chain, it takes on the structuring principle of the labyrinth. Pascal Bonitzer has discussed the
labyrinth in terms of the logic of the thriller, where off-screen space produces suspense around the unseen monster or the identity of the killer.[55]
Not only the disposition of the frame but also the shape of the narrative
construct this maze: as the protagonist maps the space of the diegesis,
his movement is centripetal, turning inward toward the center of the
labyrinth. Finally, at what Bonitzer terms the "desired meeting,"[56] all
blind space is revealed, and the face of the monster is seen within the
frame, along with the spatial organization of the narrative as a whole,
which was previously available only in partial view. This model of the
labyrinthine narrative can be adapted to the art-cinematic historical epic,
with the illogical space of the maze constructing a potentially radical
relation to historical knowledge. Historicity here becomes about the possibility or impossibility of mapping a coherent narrative space, where
the identity of the "monster" in the shape of a historical origin is not necessarily knowable.

To take as an example a text in which the monster does appear, the
Russian film *Khrustalyov, My Car!* (Gherman, 1999) produces a confusing and excessive mise-en-scène around the Soviet political landscape of
1953. The narrative centers on a village doctor who receives a mysterious
summons, but although there is a certain chain of causality, history is
not shown through the linear narrative of what happens when but in the
chaotic and repetitive structure by which narrative—and political—
space is gradually uncovered. Unlike *Underground*, space does not consist of different levels of filmic representation (newsreel, found footage,
maps, location shots, and fictional space) but is produced through a rich
black-and-white cinematography that renders a snow-covered Soviet
landscape at once beautiful and uncanny. Beginning with a local park,
which has hidden spaces where the KGB imprisons dissenters, the
mise-en-scène spreads out gradually, multiplying seen and unseen
spaces, from empty roads and fields to chaotic hospitals and disguised
prison vans. The beautiful image is rarely what it seems, and the empty

forests as much as the overcrowded sanitorium begin to connote dread. This epic spectacle of labyrinthine space maps the paranoid historical logic of late Stalinism, and the moment of revelation comes when, near the end of the film, the doctor is shown what he has been summoned to see: the dying body of Stalin himself.

Stalin's body is the center of the labyrinth: it explains the mystery of the doctor's summons, but it also structures the logic of the film's historicity and its production of cinematic space. Stalinism is described here through what can or cannot be seen, by the paranoia of disappearance, and the figure of Stalin himself grounds this duplicitous system. What needs to be seen, therefore, is Stalin's death, and in this precise bodily moment when the blind space is revealed, the grotesquerie of the system is also embodied, fully visible to itself. For Bonitzer, the center of the labyrinth is also the historical wound, the trauma that can motivate and explain the preceding narrative. In the detective film, it is often the identity of the killer or the family secret that motives the action. In terms of the historical epic, it is the originary cause to which history can be traced. But while *Khrustalyov*'s labyrinth has a very clear center in the physicality of Stalin as monster, *Underground* is less able to envision a singular historical cause.

In *Underground*'s labyrinth of historical spaces, there is no single monster to be blamed. Rather, what is unable to be seen is a national landscape: the fetishistic truth of the nation and its foundational myths. While the film multiplies historical views, the refraction of history into archives and historical documents still cannot provide a direct image of national history. As national space cannot be imagined directly, it becomes involuted. What is traumatic in this labyrinth, then, is the impossibility of finding a center, of naming and revealing the face of the monster. Norris defends *Underground* on similar grounds by claiming that its refusal to make a strong statement against the Yugoslav government is, in fact, a refusal to simplify. The film, he says, does not name one guilty party but suggests that many parties are guilty.[57] Thus, the blame cannot be neatly placed on a single figure, as it is in *Khrustalyov*, and what is significant is the absence of such a cause. If we articulate this refusal to name the monster as a question not only of political interpretation but also of the interstice of melancholia and the labyrinth, we can see the structure of this ambiguity. The film as a melancholic text cannot see what is lost and so cannot entirely solve the mystery of its own labyrinth. Thus, the truth that Blacky discovers in the final scene is a landscape, but a fantasmatic one. Blind space remains only partially visible, as what is revealed is the impossibility of a space around which the text's historical system could cohere. However, something *is* revealed in this gesture, and the fact that a landscape holds this place suggests a move toward a naming.

It might be useful here to turn to another example of narrative blind space used by Bonitzer: that of Jorge Luis Borges's story "The House of Asterion." In this story, the protagonist lives in a labyrinthine mansion and does not realize until the final line that he himself is the minotaur. This placing of the self in the space of monstrosity strikes a chord with *Underground*'s discourse of abjection. As its obsessive mapping of Europe resolves into a pristine national landscape, the film reluctantly locates its own national myth at the center of the horror it narrates. Like the unfortunate Asterion, the film cannot help but speak from the place of the monster. This is why the ending produces a mixed and uncertain emotional reaction in the spectator, and not the cathartic clarity of tears.

## A Dialectic of Failure

In this impossible and disturbing landscape image, we find the defining principle of *Underground*'s historicity. Here, 1941 and 1995 are joined in a space of desire, but this space is radically ambivalent. Its emotional impact includes both desire and horror. It encapsulates the nation but also cuts it off. Its image of the nation is both fantastical and monstrous. The subject of this history is what cannot, structurally, come into view. *Underground* forms a visual and historical knot that can, perhaps counterintuitively, be understood in terms of the dialectical image. Walter Benjamin's concept is a central plank in his attempt to theorize history outside both traditional historiography and modernist narratives of progress. But it is also a historically located theory, derived at least in part from the histories of nineteenth- and early-twentieth-century Europe with which Benjamin's analyses consistently engaged. And this location in the arcades and the ruins of modern European space suggests both a material and an analogical relation to the historical work of *Underground*. The violent legacy of Balkanism in the 1990s is one of the results of the same European history whose progress Benjamin feared; and what the remnants of the nineteenth century offered to him by way of an alternative reading of the past, so the chaotic detritus of the postwar years proposes in *Underground*. The wreckage that piles up in front of Paul Klee's *Angelus Novus* in the "Theses on the Philosophy of History"[58] is not unrelated to Europe's mid-century bloodbath or to the excessive accumulation of images and objects in the mise-en-scène of *Underground*.

In *The Arcades Project*, Benjamin describes his rejection of progressive history: "This work—comparable, in method, to the process of splitting the atom—liberates the enormous energies of history that are bound up in the 'once upon a time' of classical historiography. The history that showed things 'as they really were' was the strongest narcotic of the century."[59] More than the melodramatic Italian films, *Underground*'s art-cinematic form makes a clear break with classical historical narrative. It precisely refuses to show things as they really were, and, indeed, this shattering of the causal chain of realist historiography provokes critiques like Iordanova's. In its layering of different registers of the image, and in its spectacular and nonrealist spaces, *Underground* refuses the kind of realism that is implicated in the historical narrative of Balkan abjection and European violence. By refusing the past this narcotic stability, the film prevents the Western spectator from remaining within the comfortable space of liberal distance and, in so doing, opens up a space for a dialectical image in the conjunction of 1941 and 1995.

Benjamin defines the appearance of the dialectical image, arguing that "to thinking belongs the movement as well as the arrest of thoughts. Where thinking comes to a standstill in a constellation saturated with tensions—there the dialectical image appears. It is the caesura in the movement of thought. Its position is naturally not an arbitrary one. It is to be found, in a word, where the tension between dialectical opposites is greatest."[60] This idea of the constellation saturated with tensions locates the ideological stake in *Underground*'s layering of images: the wartime inception of the modern nation and its post–Cold War breakup form either end of a national myth that can be neither avowed nor rejected. The tensions inherent in the position of abjection coalesce in an impetus that pulls in two directions. The first is to demand that the past be read in terms of the present and that the bloody spaces of the Balkans be seen for the Western creation that they are. But this radical gesture to expose the past through the present includes its opposite: the desire to imagine a different past (and perhaps, therefore, a different future) outside the discourse of the West and therefore in the terms of some national historical space. The critique of the experience of Communism cannot locate a more genuine national identity prior to Tito's victory, and so the film's spatial logic sticks between the abjected position of the cellar and the impossibility of imagining an alternative.

The dialectical image thus functions somewhat differently in *Underground* than in the Italian films. Whereas they bring past and present into a conjunction that enables the hypercathexis of mourning, *Underground* produces the frustrated desire for mourning that is the melancholic outcome of the crypt. (As Abraham and Torok put it: "All incorporation has introjection as its nostalgic vocation.")[61] And while the Italian films invoke an experience of spectacle and the real, politics and affect, within the same image, *Underground* refracts these tensions across the body of the film. There is no single space in which the dialectic resolves but, rather, a constant interplay of partial, even conflicting, views. As a result, the dialectical image does not illuminate the solution to a historical problem but operates to bring into relief the terms of the problem itself. That there is no place from which an enunciation of the truth of Yugoslavia is possible and that any claim on national identity is inevitably coopted into the ideology it attempts to displace: this is the historical constellation that the film crystallizes. Given the uncertain and politically unstable position of the former Yugoslav nations in the 1990s, it is perhaps understandable that imagining the end of the postwar period should be harder than the corresponding textual work in Italy. Nonetheless, the conclusion remains that *Underground*'s spectacular historicity is most ideologically interesting for what it fails to do. It is in the tensions that it cannot resolve and in the images that it cannot show that *Underground* most forcibly embodies the double bind of the Yugoslav experience of history and nation.

## Impossible Images

In chapter 2, I discussed the dialectical image as a circuit of two apparently opposed cinematic elaborations of reality: the real that cuts across representation in a moment of indexical or auratic affect, and the real as representation, the production of historically specific meanings. *Underground* also deploys this oscillation between indexicality and historical signification, but in this instance the elements circle each other without ever cohering, articulating the impossible nature of this historical relation in their inability to provide a singular affective encounter with the real. To render more concrete a claim that depends on the textually and intertextually diffuse, I focus here on two images that have become archetypes of the postwar political landscape and are also typical of the work of cinematic mapping. The first image is from the film: the "documentary" shot of the city in ruins, displaced narratively from 1995 to 1941. The second, in keeping with the spirit of melancholia and the labyrinth, is the image that is not there, or that may be there but we cannot see: the political landscape of the Yugoslav past.

Both of these images condense the quality of being-in-excess-of-realism that I have argued is necessary to produce the dialectical image in film. Instead of showing the past as it really was, both imply moments that fall out of narrative, through either their spectacular excess or their indexical authenticity, or, of course, both at once. More important, perhaps, is that both images invoke the historical and material specificity of European space in the 1940s. The ruined city and the national landscape are the images par excellence of the period, the pictures that both documentary and fiction films constantly repeated in constructing the postwar moment. On the one hand, there is the image of destruction, testifying to the horror of war, to the falling away from civilization, and to the reality of the profilmic as a historically significant index; on the other hand, there is the image of the landscape, as seen in neorealism, standing as the signifier of nationhood, of what survived, of leftist aspirations for popular change, and of the determination to "build a great country." *Underground*'s dialectical image crystallizes the difficult relationship of Yugoslavia to this postwar visual history, and in its mobilization of these two images, the tensions of this relationship become most clear.

## The City in Ruins

The image of the city in ruins appears twice in the first section of the film, representing first Nazi and then Allied bombings. Located within the montage of wartime invasion, and preceding a sequence of archival images of the arrival of Nazi troops, the first ruin scene comprises four shots of destroyed Belgrade streets and offers only a glimpse of profilmic destruction. But the shots are important, as they were filmed in the 1990s, and only in these brief moments does *Underground* engage with indexical evidence of the ongoing war in the former Yugoslavia. Whereas the rest of the narrative displaces the history of war into the cellar and other fantastic spaces, preventing any direct view of contemporary events, these shots turn to the specificity of location and to the affective spectacle of the indexical image. However, in their narrative context, the shots are also historical, and just as they produce an affective sight of the present, they simultaneously construct a narrative of the past. The two moments of destruction are overlaid, and this temporal conjunction becomes particularly weighted by the choice of the ruin as the subject of the connecting image. By examining the historicity of this image, we can tease out these strands of meaning and find, too, the reason for its momentary nature.

The ruined cityscape is a key image of the immediate postwar years. Familiar from countless newsreels, it also became a common establishing shot for location-shot fiction films in the late 1940s. Most well known are the films shot in Germany, such as *Murderers Among Us* (Staudte, 1946), *A Foreign Affair* (Wilder, 1948), and *Germany Year Zero*. As Charles Najman argues, "The wars of the twentieth century took the city as their defining target and it is in their ruins and debris, in the 'vanquished' nations, that the post-war cinema found a natural setting to stage its stories."[62] The extreme devastation in the defeated countries, and particularly in Berlin, provided an obvious backdrop for narratives focusing on the legacy of war and the beginning of national and international reconstruction. However, it was not only in the defeated countries that massive destruction of cities had been experienced for the first time, and Yugoslavia suffered particularly heavy bombardment. Daniel J. Goulding points out that while feature film production was still in its infancy in Yugoslavia in the late 1940s, a huge number of documentaries and newsreels were made, "which frequently provided a searing, firsthand account of war-torn villages, cities and countryside of Yugoslavia and documented the early efforts to rebuild the shattered country."[63] Here, as much as anywhere, images of ruined buildings became a newly potent symbol in the postwar visual imagination.

For *Underground*, this image of the destroyed city signifies an originary moment, with the ruin as the wound that marks the end of the unseen time before war. In contrast to the Italian films' reliance on beautiful space, *Underground* derives its historical effects from impossible space. And the space of destroyed buildings forms an instance of impossibility, not in the structure of mise-en-scène but materially. Just as the real location of the Italian countryside underpins the mourning work of *Cinema Paradiso*, so the indexical status of the shots of rubble ground *Underground*'s discourse of national loss. In both cases, of course, the landscape was filmed in the present, and only within the narrative can it stand in for the lost space of the past. But it is unusual to have at hand ruined cities that can replicate convincingly the terrible destruction of World War II, and so this particular location's authenticity is precisely what is jarring. The landscape is not the same because it is timeless but because it is temporally acute—only at these exact historical moments do the spaces look the same. That the image of 1995 can stand in for that of 1941 is disturbing, and this momentary flash of similarity upsets realist historical narrative.[64] The image of the ruin is what positions the connection of 1995 and 1941 not as either end of a historical progression but as two moments blasted out of history in the manner of Benjamin's constellation.

In Konvolut N of *The Arcades Project*, Benjamin describes this process in terms of historical narrative. "Historical materialism," he argues, "must renounce the epic element in history. It blasts the epoch out of the reified 'continuity of history.' But it also explodes the homogeneity of the epoch, interspersing it with ruins—that is, with the present."[65] This passage encapsulates Benjamin's critique of traditional modes of conceiving history, offering a concise annotation to *Underground*'s undermining of epic narrative. The film plays with the idea of the epic and involves a narrative based on an epic scale, covering fifty years; yet it refuses a progressive, explanatory structure. The shattering of historical homogeneity is what happens with the mixing of past and present: the actors who do not age, the intertitles that return repeatedly to war, and, most of all, the ruins that conjure two different moments of destruction. Here, more literally than Benjamin could have meant, the present is composed of ruins. And these ruins enter into the past, exploding the pastness of the previous war and commenting implicitly on its distant results. What happened in the 1990s becomes part of the history of World War II as the ruins of the present haunt the image of the past. No less than the beautiful image, the spectacle of ruin falls out of narrative, provoking an affective experience of immediacy at the same time as it disturbs the narrative of the past.

But if the image of the ruin provides such a powerful conjunction of past and present, why, then, does it appear so briefly? The answer lies again in *Underground*'s inability to speak from a position of national identity and national mourning. In the films and newsreels of the 1940s, the image of the ruin stood for an overtly national loss and for the need to rebuild what it was hoped would become a better nation. But *Underground* has no access to this optimism, either in the past or in the present. As far as the present goes, there was no sign of a postwar order for what remained in 1995 of Yugoslavia.[66] The very idea of "postwar" that the ruin implies is a precarious position in relation to the breakup of Yugoslavia. Just as the film begins after the beginning of war, so it ends before the end of war. If "before the war" means before 1991 in the former Yugoslavia, "after the war" was a phrase without clear referent, at least to Serbs. And in terms of the optimism of the past, the desire to rebuild that 1940s films took as axiomatic, the film professes no faith, not even through nostalgia, for the national discourse of Communism that such a return would imply.

Thus, the image of the ruin can be entertained only as a displacement, a momentary glimpse of the present written over by Blacky's walk across the frame as an effect of the past. The body of the actor literally performs a fictionalization of the image as he crosses the frame, covering over the flash of the now with the ironic and critical content of historical narration. His movement enacts a reversal whereby instead of his presence coding as a disruption of the indexical image, the reality of ruins and bodies becomes in an instant the thing that deforms the historical image. The ruin can only appear as such a deformity—in Miriam Hansen's words, the disfiguration of representation[67]—because there is no textual position from which to experience the image as national signifier. The look back on ruins cannot be nostalgic, but it could locate a place of national identification, a reiteration in mourning of the optimism of the 1940s. The rejection of this position and of the political history it entails explains why the image of the ruin is so rapidly written over, displaced, and rejected. But yet the ruin is visible and does assert an affective claim on a national loss (the loss of nation). The ironic collocation of destruction now and destruction then suggests an irresistible recurrence, however brief, of the image of the ruin as a melancholic attachment to the image of the nation.

## The Rise and Fall of the National Landscape

The image of the landscape, no less than that of the ruin, is central to the cinematic construction of national space in immediate postwar Europe. We have already examined the most famous example of neorealism, but in Yugoslavia, too, the films of the late 1940s relied on discourses of landscape to produce a national cinema. What is striking about the few feature films produced in Yugoslavia in the years after World War II is how central the landscape image becomes to the articulation of a national identity for the new state. The Slovenian production Na svoji zemlji [On Their Own Ground] (Štiglić, 1948), the Croatian feature Življeće ovaj narod [This People Must Live] (Popović, 1947), and, most significantly, the Serb film Slavica (Afrić, 1947) all use recognizable and beautiful rural landscapes to ground their patriotic narratives of partisan national resistance. Virtually all the films made in the five years after the war deal with the recent history of resistance and the contemporary task of reconstruction, and almost all of them locate their narratives in rural settings.[68] Slavica is set on the Dalmatian coast and features local fisherman and partisans fighting against the Nazis over this distinctive and strategically important section of coastline. On Their Own Ground tells a similar tale of partisan heroes, but the setting is the alpine region of Slovenia. Again, picturesque images—in this instance, of mountains and hill villages—work to authenticate the national basis of the partisan struggle.

In 1946, the director of the federal committee for cinematography, Aleksander Vučo, stipulated that "our film art cannot and must not allow itself to have any other interests than the interests of our national authority, no other tasks than the task of educating the wide mass of viewers in the spirit of our national and cultural revolution."[69] Goulding glosses this in terms of the official aesthetics of the Communist Party, claiming that in the period 1945 to 1950, "films were conceived of as serving heuristic and propagandistic purposes and reflected the aesthetic principles of *nationalist-realism*—Yugoslavia's moderate variant of the Stalinist-Zhdanov narrowly conceived socialist realism dogma."[70] Of course, the mode of production in Yugoslavia at this time was markedly different from that in Western Europe, and it will be important to consider the ramifications, from the point of view of the present, of film production at this time being essentially a branch of government. However, while it is necessary to situate Yugoslav postwar films within the history of socialist realism, I want for the moment to consider their deployment of landscape images in relation to a wider European context of cinema and nation.

If Vučo's prescriptions for a "national realist" cinema derive in part from Zhdanovism, they also echo the rejection by many in West European film cultures of what was perceived as Hollywood's institutional and aesthetic dominance. The concern to lay the foundations for a national cinema, in terms of industrial production, formal realism, and culturally specific content, resonates with the liberal discourse of national art cinemas—found, for example, in Britain and France—and with the ideological concerns of neorealism. Vučo's claim, for example, that "truth" is more important than technical prowess or American-style high production values[71] could be lifted directly from Roberto Rossellini. And, indeed, many of Goulding's critiques of the films made in Yugoslavia under Vučo's offices could be just as easily applied to Italian films of the same period. Thus, Goulding complains of two-dimensional characters, simple morality, and melodramatic narratives—exactly the critiques that have been leveled against neorealism. Images of heroic partisan soldiers and decadent Nazis, or emotional narratives of doomed romance, are as structural to *Rome, Open City*, as they are to the products of Yugoslavia's nascent feature industry. (And while the dominant genres may be somewhat different, postwar British films that represented brave Tommies and cowardly Germans thematized the war equally jingoistically.) In fact, postwar Yugoslav films have a lot in common textually with neorealism, not least in the construction of narratives of national identity through the supposedly direct means of a landscape that shows the truth of the country.

Both of the main historical studies of Yugoslav cinema—those of Goulding and of Mira Liehm and Antonin J. Liehm—are largely dismissive of these films, designating them as propagandistic and cinematically primitive. To a certain extent this reading is accurate, for there are formal elements in the texts that accord with the tenets of socialist realism. The most apparent and, to the contemporary spectator, perhaps the most disjunctive is the use of character typing. In *Slavica*, for example, the Yugoslavs who collaborate with the occupying Italian army are identified as physical buffoons, and a broadly comedic acting style is emphasized by close-ups that make them look even more grotesque. The Italians are consistently shown in decadent pursuits such as dancing to Western music and are placed in an opulent mise-en-scène. And, like the collaborators, the actors who play the invaders contrast unfavorably with the handsome partisans. Insofar as these modes of acting and shot structure contrast with both naturalism and an ideologically critical modernism, they are able to code for the Liehms and Goulding as cinematically naïve and politically clumsy.

The Yugoslav films are certainly quite different from neorealism in terms of these formal elements, and they do not include any of the long takes or detailed social observation for which neorealism is often lauded. However, they do share the contemporaneous discourse of postwar space in which landscape images form the locus of cinematic constructions of nation, ideology, and the real. Even within the conventional film historical narratives, what invariably stands out for both critics is the discourse of authenticity based on the indexical qualities of the rural location. Thus, Liehm and Liehm praise *On Their Own Ground* for its "effort to combine the story with a real environment,"[72] and Goulding attributes to it a "greater verisimilitude of settings"[73] than is found in other films of the time. For the Liehms and Goulding, such authenticity seems to be merely a by-product of local production or, at best, evidence of how Yugoslavia's national realism began by taking a slightly looser path than Soviet socialist realism. But the narrative of *On Their Own Ground* demonstrates how regional authenticity functions beyond the realm of local color, structuring the heroism of the partisans. When captured, the partisans remove their shoes in order to die with the feeling of their own land beneath their feet. Authenticity is narrativized, further authorizing the logic of the film's mise-en-scène, in which the image of "their own land" verifies the ideological truth of the text.

The authenticity of the landscape is even more important in what is arguably the most influential film of the immediate postwar years:

Vjekoslav Afrić's *Slavica*. In this, the first Yugoslav feature after the war, the narrative of romance and partisan struggle takes place largely along the Croatian coast, and exterior shots of the Dalmatian shore and countryside connect a recognizable profilmic reality to a discourse of patriotism and national regeneration. Goulding and the Liehms once more read realism of setting as the only redeeming feature of the film: Goulding allows that it "does capture well the Dalmatian coastal setting and the dialects and authentic culture of the region,"[74] and Liehm and Liehm claim that "the authenticity of the Dalmatian surroundings balances, at least in part, the melodramatic story and the theatrical acting."[75] But as these criticisms themselves implicitly make clear, the landscape image in *Slavica* is doing work similar to that of *Paisà* and *Rome, Open City*. The melodramatic story of the couple separated by war is not an unrealistic element that the authentic setting can partly compensate for but, rather, is the corollary within the narrative to the visual logic of landscape truth.

This relationship is crystallized in one sequence of the partisans in their mountain camp. As the men sing a song entitled "Slavica," we cut from the heroine, Slavica, to a series of picturesque long shots of the surrounding landscape: the first of the far-off alpine mountains; the second

*Slavica*   The eponymous heroine exemplifies national pride. (Courtesy Misha Nedeljković)

framing a small stream in the foreground, with the same mountains in the background; and the third of rocks and hills. We then return to Slavica talking to the partisan commander, and the sequence ends with another brief crosscut between Slavica and the landscape images. This sequence produces a tight knot of meanings connecting the visual pleasures of the self-consciously aesthetic landscape vistas, those of the body of the heroine, and the idea of *patrie* contained in the partisan struggle. Once again, the indexical immediacy of the rural landscape produces a truth that is displaced onto the fetishized body of the actress—in this instance, playing a character who is overdetermined as national. Slavica, as her name suggests, is the embodiment of Slav patriotism, and this is also the name given to the boat with which the partisans defeat the Germans. Slavica the character dies attempting to save the sinking vessel, and the truth of her romantic sacrifice in the narrative is guaranteed by the equally affective spectacle of the newly national Yugoslav landscape.[76]

This connection of landscape to a melodrama of political loss is also strikingly demonstrated in a shot of a partisan grave: the simple cross topped with a Communist star is framed among trees, with the hero, Marin, looking on in the foreground and the omnipresent mountains

*Slavica*    She is also closely associated with this regional landscape. (Courtesy Misha Nedeljković)

behind. As with Slavica's death, melodrama operates in tandem with the landscape real, and just as Slavica, as a fetishistic spectacle of femininity, is able to stand in for the truth of the nation, so, too, is the beautiful landscape. Goulding points out that "*Slavica* is built on a structural model which was to be emulated by most of the other early Partisan films of this period. It is a pattern which begins by affirming Partisan-led local initiatives in specific locales, involving the distinctive nationalities of the region, and builds organically to an affirmation of the epic all-Yugoslav character of its leadership and heroes . . . which becomes the essential guarantor of ultimate victory in war, as well as the basis upon which to build a completely new Yugoslavia."[77] Thus, we have a structure in which regional specificity—the mountain and coastal views, the traditional peasant dress worn by Marin and Slavica in the celebration scene, and the sea battles that characterized this region's wartime experience—guarantees national authenticity, understood as the larger and more abstract idea of a federal Yugoslavia. Similarly to a film like *Paisà*, the image of the regional landscape underwrites a move toward a new national politics, and a narrative of wartime loss (the partisan grave or the romantic loss of Slavica) figures a call for postwar reconstruction. Naturalism, and the deployment of locations to produce a sense of indexical truth, enables a discourse of cinematic and political nationalism.

This comparison of *Slavica* with neorealism suggests that *Underground*'s relationship to a national film history is not as different from that of the Italian films as it might at first appear. Both Italian and Yugoslav postwar national identities were constructed cinematically through landscape discourses, and both national cinemas constantly return to this moment. The partisan drama has been a recurring feature of Yugoslav film, from the heroic films of the late 1940s and early 1950s, to some more critical examinations of the war in the mid- to late 1950s. Significant examples of the latter include *Daleko je sunce* [*The Sun Is Far Away*] (Novaković, 1953), *Alone* (Pogačić, 1959), and *Partisan Stories* (Janković, 1960). Or again, in the 1960s, there was a resurgence of popular and traditionalist partisan and war films, including *Kozara* (Bulijić, 1963) and *When You Hear the Bells* (Vrdoljak, 1969), as well as the critically lauded film of reconstruction *Prekobrojna* [*The Superfluous Girl*] (Bauer, 1962). Even in the New Film, which mostly attempted to deal with contemporary issues and rejected the commonplaces of national film culture, there are a few films that returned to the partisan period and questioned the "truth" of the national landscape. The most famous of these films are *Three* (Petrović, 1965) and *The Morning* (Đorđević, 1967). The postwar national landscape, then, is as central to Yugoslav film history as its equivalent is in Italy, and in *Slavica*'s long shots of the Croatian mountains and shoreline, we find its originary moment. These shots, with their affective immediacy and self-consciously indexical claim on a political "truth," are precisely the image of the national landscape that is missing from *Underground*.

The reasons for this absence are historical and can be found in the politics of postwar cinema, as well as in those of the new Yugoslav state. One of the key distinctions between neorealism and the Yugoslav postwar films is that while neorealism was opposed by the government after 1948 and did not represent an aesthetic hegemony at the time, the Yugoslav films were at the least indirectly government produced and were certainly a part of a nascent Titoist cultural policy. As Vučo makes plain, the structures of postwar cinema, including in large measure the deployment of landscape, realism, and codes of regional authenticity, were to be linked to nationalism and Communism, and it is this set of connections that *Underground* needs to reject. If the key years of neorealism corresponded in Italy to the time of leftist optimism, the same moment of film production in Yugoslavia was already tied to Tito's regime and the time after loss. While the textual logics of neorealism and the Yugoslav postwar films may be similar, the films cannot have the same nostalgic value from the point of view of the present, for the look back at them from any post-Communist perspective must be double-edged.

The ironic return that defines *Cinema Paradiso*'s and *Mediterraneo*'s references to the neorealist project demands at once a continued belief in its ideological stake and a realization of its failure. *Underground* is unable to sustain any such historical belief, for the time of *Slavica* is already the time of Communism and betrayal; neither is it able to reject it as a failure, for the melancholic object can never be completely overcome. *Underground* thus retains a nostalgic desire for the lost national past, while being unable to buy into any of its historical images. The partisan struggle remains the only possible location for a Yugoslav national identity, yet this moment was thoroughly coopted from the start. (Meanwhile, by the 1990s, the partisan film had become an ironic cliché of post-Yugoslav pop culture.) And so, instead of citing the rural landscape of *Slavica*, *Underground* revisits the partisan narrative only in parody. Blacky and Marko are supposedly Communist partisans in Belgrade, but their actions are represented as resolutely selfish, without a trace of political motivation. The opening sequences of the film cannot help but cite this defining moment of invasion, but even within this overdetermined space, there is an absolute refusal of landscape. If *Slavica* and the other films of the 1940s are defined by the visual production of nation, then *Underground*'s return to the inception of the state evidences an attempt to reach that kind of emotional and ideological claim but an inability to do so. There was, in the 1990s, no national space to return to. From this point of view, we can relate *Underground* to Goulding's schematic of *Slavica*'s narrative stages. In these terms, *Underground* is unable to take the crucial last step of connecting specific diegetic spaces to national space. Regional specificity in *Underground* cannot underwrite the federal nation, and so it sticks, repeating the trope of the imagined nation, but this time in miniature, as the island that breaks off from the mainland. This scene repeats the final step of *Slavica*, but overtly as a failure to become national.

And yet *Underground* cannot ignore altogether the discourse of the affective national landscape that it cannot include. The image that is not there holds a defining place in the film's visual rhetoric: it is the content of the crypt, the lost object of melancholic desire, and the historical space whose absence forces the text to speak from a position of abjection and irony. We can triangulate the location of this structuring absence through the kinds of space the film *does* map, for the fetishistic truth of national landscape is its constant reference point. The constrictive underground spaces imply a nation elsewhere, aboveground, but this space is never seen directly. National space is seen in found footage, but the status of these shots as partial, distorted, even propagandistic prevents any cathexis onto their national truths and deflects the historical real elsewhere. The final scene comes closest to showing what is not there, constructing an affective landscape that lays bare the logic of fantasy. *Slavica*'s landscape image functions as the absent cause of this visual system, for its affective truths are, from the point of view of the post-Communist present, always already a fantasy. Among all the intertextual references to be found in *Underground*, the most powerful is this missing image that centers the film's historical logic in its own invisibility. It stands for what the film cannot believe in and yet cannot forget, and it demands that every image of the national past reflect the impossibility of this space.

## Awakenings

Benjamin describes the flash of the dialectical image as a kind of awakening, where the elements of a historical constellation produce a new relation both to history and to the present moment. To this analogy, however, he adds this aphorism: "The first tremors of awakening serve to deepen sleep."[78] In this somewhat gnomic formulation, we can specify the kind of dialectical image at work in *Underground*'s impossible spaces. In laying bare the structure of Balkanism, in reading of the past through the ruins of the present, and in spectacularizing the historical image, *Underground* short-circuits the conventional Western narrative of Yugoslav history, forcing a confrontation with why the space of Yugoslavia should be so impossible and why its history so painful. But in its obsessive return to the fantasmatic image of the lost nation, the film gets stuck in its own logic and ends with the dream image of the floating landscape. This melancholic ending presages a deeper sleep, and it is perhaps this uncomfortable fantasy that leads critics like Žižek to discern in the film the unconscious structure of the ethnic cleansers. While I share his discomfort with such politically charged ambiguity, I would rather propose that in this ambiguity itself, by dint of the ideological friction of this constant return to the impossible image, we can trace the beginnings of a more genuine awakening.

What is particularly compelling about *Underground* is the extent to which these tensions both structure and destabilize the text. At times, the film seems impossibly confused, and yet it is the contradictions that render the ideological makeup of postwar Yugoslav nationality so visible. *Underground* thus forms a particularly rich case study, but it is not isolated from other contemporary Balkan films. The idea of a doubled relation to the past is common in post-Yugoslav films, where nostalgia, national politics, and the difficulty of historical memory frequently form the narrative problematic. To take an example that is thematically similar to *Underground*, although not historical, *Pretty Village, Pretty Flame* (Dragojević, 1996) frames the war in Bosnia with historical references to the partisan struggle and to the federal discourse of brotherhood. The film begins with the opening in 1970 of a "brotherhood tunnel" representing the link between neighboring Bosnian and Serb peoples. The tunnel soon falls into disuse and disrepair, and local children believe it contains a monster who might, if angered, emerge to destroy their villages. The symbolic weight of this trope clearly has something in common with *Underground*'s uses of space, although in this case the terms of the metaphor are more insistently ironic and its meanings less nuanced. The tunnel becomes central to the narrative in 1992, when Bosnian Serb soldier Milan and his company are trapped inside it and besieged by Bosnian Muslims. Here, the monster has indeed emerged, and the film suggests a liberal narrative of regret at the separation of Bosnian and Serb friends.

The film's relation to history, however, not only is found in the collapse of the brotherhood tunnel but also centers on the character of the

*Pretty Village, Pretty Flame*    The derelict "brotherhood tunnel" connects Bosnia and Serbia.

Bosnian Serb company captain. He is played by Velimir "Bata" Živoji-nović, an actor famous in Yugoslavia for his roles in partisan films, where he invariably played a brave Communist soldier. In *Pretty Village*, he still stands for this partisan generation, but his character is now marginalized. He is the commandant of the Serb unit and sees himself as fighting once more for Yugoslavia, but the soldiers under him mock him by playing the "Internationale" ("his song") and speak bitterly of Communist failures and corruption. And as they trade taunts and gunfire with their Bosnian captors, the idea of fighting "for Yugoslavia" is stripped away to raw violence. During the film's violent finale, the old partisan nonetheless sacrifices himself for these comrades, driving the company's truck out in a suicidal blaze of flames, while the soundtrack plays a partisan song. This ironic relationship to Yugoslav film history doubles the (knowing) spectator's sympathies, as well as questioning the similarities between the two wars. The iconography of the partisan film and the trope of underground space again work to structure the ambiguous political stakes of both historical conflicts.

We might expect a similar thematic in another war film, but even in other genres, the question of history and space recurs. In the Slovenian thriller *When I Close My Eyes*, a daughter's memory of her father's political murder is reawakened when she is the victim of a robbery. The noir trope of the past returning intersects with a politics of long memories and with the dangers of knowledge in a post-Communist state. And while the action takes place in a small town, it may be relevant that the crucial memory is a nightmarish vision of rural space, in which a body hangs from a tree. Here, the landscape of the past is less ambiguously desirable, and yet it is still the affective space of family and of loss.

In Yugoslav comedies, knowledge and memory are often hitched to an ironic point of view. In both *When Father Was Away on Business* and *Tito and Me*, the point of view is that of a child who cannot entirely understand the political events around him. Thus, in *Tito and Me*, the protagonist recalls as an adult a camping trip he took as a child in the 1950s to Tito's birthplace. Nostalgia for the lost landscape of childhood coexists with an ironic awareness of an experience that was far from idyllic and of the work of indoctrination that the child was only partially able to appreciate. Once again, the national landscape—Tito's birthplace no less—forms an ambiguously desirable location for family origins. This structure is not confined to Balkan films, of course, and *Tito* can be compared with the Swedish film *My Life as a Dog* or the Soviet *My Friend Ivan Lapshin* (Gherman, 1985). However, in the context of Yugoslav histories, this narrative mode tellingly enables an affective relationship to a political past that is not easily thinkable in positive terms. The work of nostalgia in these films is to produce an ironic relationship to historical space, where there is ambivalence but never a lack of engagement.

The other side of this structure is a sequence of contemporary films, particularly from Serbia, that take place resolutely in the present and can be likened to the neorealist attempt to "shoot in the present tense." Examples include *The Powder Keg* (Paskaljević, 1998) and *The Wounds* (Dragojević, 1998), both of which depict the violence of contemporary Belgrade. *The Powder Keg* follows several interconnected characters around Belgrade for a long and tense night, during which incipient violence is the subtext to many disparate social interactions. Although it does not refer directly to national and international events at all, the film derives its political power exactly from this almost total lack of context: not only is there no historical perspective, but there is no outside to Serbian space. The spectator is allowed no wider European discourse with which to distance herself from the claustrophobic logic of nation; as a result, the film describes the danger of an impoverished and isolated post-Communist Serbia. With an entirely different form of narrative, the film reproduces the sense of spatial enclosure and political impossibilities found in *Underground*.

What is distinctive about *Underground*'s production of post-Communist time and space, however, is the imbrication of these gestures: there is both the outward move—the examination of the past and of Europe—and the inward turn by means of the myopic enclosure of the cellar. Only

*The Wounds*   The lives of the young protagonists exemplify urban decay and teenage disaffection in 1990s Belgrade.

by considering these tropes together can we read history in terms of both ironic knowledge and affective identification. There is at once a directly politicized comparison drawn between 1941 and 1995 and a confusion in which space is reduced to the cellar, time is blurred so that all wars look alike, and the nation exists outside history. The film describes the ideology of Balkanism and speaks from its abjected place. History is therefore articulated through timelessness, a paradox that the text circles without ever resolving. Historicity inevitably entails the timeless Balkanist primitivism, and ironic distance on the Yugoslav past leads to a nostalgic attempt to mourn a loss outside the Western-defined violence of this space. The melancholic impossibility of any real "before" doubles back on the dubious pleasures of the deject, while even a rejection of the postwar nation cannot help but return endlessly to its founding image. This bind suggests an incomplete awakening—a historical gambit that seems to lead to a deeper sleep. Unable to resolve into any singular enunciative position, this dialectical image performs the space of its own historical limitation: what is revealed in *Underground*'s spectacular historicity is not a productive tension but a vicious circle.

# 5 Back-Projecting Germany

"I'm obsessed with Germany. For Denmark, it's a very big neighbor. Germany is a symbol. It is Europe."[1] With this formulation, or perhaps we should call it a confession, director Lars von Trier describes his film *Zentropa* in terms of an individual and a perceived national relationship to the spaces of Denmark, Germany, and Europe. What is striking about this avowedly personal commentary is how unself-consciously it lays bare the tensions involved in the "European film." That there are national positions to be taken up can be seen from the response of the French critic who quotes this interview: he takes immediate issue with what he calls von Trier's "provincial timidity" and points out that Germany is not, after all, coextensive with Europe. At one level, this exchange provides a humorous microcosm of European stereotypes, pitting the Dane, whose independent stance toward Europe belies a fear of German domination, against the French sense of national preeminence. More seriously, though, the series of elisions that structure von Trier's remark illustrate the difficulty of reading *Zentropa* in terms of nation. For while *Underground* described an impossible national space, and while it worked on the difficult connection of that national space to the larger space of Europe, the concept of nation was nonetheless a central point of reference. In *Zentropa*, by contrast, there is no simple relationship to nation. As von Trier's words suggest in their uneasy movement from *discours* to *histoire* and from Germany through Denmark to Europe, the meanings of national and supranational spaces can become slippery.

*Zentropa* was released internationally in 1991, a year after the reunification of Germany, and a year before the Maastricht Treaty was signed by the nations of the European Union. At first sight, the film seems distant from these contemporary concerns: its story is set in 1945, and its art-cinematic emphasis on style and form deny any obvious social engagement. The story, moreover, is not overtly about Europe but about Germany specifically. Leopold Kessler is a young German-American who comes to Germany in 1945 in a naïve attempt to help the country rebuild. Through family connections, he gets a civilian job working on the railways, where he meets and falls in love with Katharina Hartmann, the daughter of the owner of the rail company Zentropa. But Kate turns out to be a Nazi sympathizer, a former member of the Werewolf terrorist group, and through her, Leo becomes unwillingly embroiled in a terrorist plot. He ends up trapped on a train he has helped to blow up, and the film ends as he drowns, swallowed by the dangerous space of postwar Germany. However, the murky spaces of Germany in 1945 are not unconnected to the concerns of the "new Europe," and we can read *Zentropa*'s historical image in terms of European space. This chapter examines how the film stages European-ness as a textual problem, constructing a relationship between the spectacular and the geopolitical. This relationship, I argue, works to overlay 1945 with 1991 and to map cinematographic space onto or into the psychic space of Europe.

## The European Film

As I argued in chapter 3, the coproduction centers an inherent tension between the discourses of national art cinemas and those of international cooperation. Most coproduced films resolve this dilemma both textually and extratextually in much the same way—by associating both the subject of the film and its makers with one country. Usually, this involves an auteur-based claim on nationality, although sometimes it may be the star actor, location, or literary source that bases the film's claim on a national culture.[2] *Zentropa*, though, makes none of these claims, or at least not with any clarity. Lars von Trier is Danish, but the film is set in Germany and does not pay any obvious attention to Danish national culture. Dialogue is in English and German. The actors are variously Canadian, Swedish, and German, and the producers are just as diverse. In his industrial analysis of the film, Terry Illot characterizes its potential audience as "European art-house" and concludes that "*Zentropa* is that rare thing, a genuinely European film. Although Danish in origin, the film was made by Swedish, Danish, German, and French partners, filmed in English and German and shot partly in Poland."[3]

Leaving aside the popular connotations of the Europudding, this international production history suggests problems of both enunciation and address: Whose stories can a European film tell, and to whom should it speak? An apparently simple answer to the second question is offered by the film's producers, who claim that "the film was meant to appeal to the European audience: the Scandinavians, the Germans and the French."[4] Here we find precisely the kind of definition of Europe that the film in fact works to problematize, but has become politically and culturally dominant in the years since 1945. Europe in this rhetoric is northern and western Europe, just as, for von Trier, Germany is Europe. The broad notion of a "European audience" telescopes before our eyes. As this ideologically loaded example shows, the location of "Europe" is not simply an economic problem for a film with no clearly defined domestic market. I shall return to the implications of this western view of the continent, but for the moment the slippages we can already trace between Europe and western Europe, and between Germany and Europe, are most important. This telescoping effect—precisely the one by which von Trier is able to come to the conclusion that Germany is Europe—leads us to the second question raised by the film's internationality: How does it textualize national and international space?

Pierre Sorlin has argued that while there was an upsurge in historical films in Europe in the 1980s, very few of those films treat the history of a country other than their own.[5] (And this argument need not be limited to the 1980s, for historical films as a genre have at all periods tended to stick with nationally constituted histories.)[6] Thus, for example, French films such as *Une affaire de femmes* (Chabrol, 1988) and *Chocolat* deal with French wartime and colonial history, and the Yugoslav partisan films endlessly retread stories of the emergent nation. This logic presents a problem for a "genuinely European film." The question becomes: Which country's history should an international film recount? *Zentropa* does not base its narrative on the Danish history that an auteurist approach would suggest, nor does it construct a transnational European object.[7] Instead, in Sorlin's terms, it takes place in a foreign country and structures its narrative around that country's specific history. It is a film about a nation, but not a national film. This structure already suggests questions about ownership: Whose history is this? But this historical and geographical location is not merely a foreign one (as far as the coproduced film goes) but is a space as overdetermined in international film history as in European politics: Germany, 1945. Year Zero.

This choice of location immediately complicates any claim on nationality: although postwar occupied Germany is a unique and complex case, its influence refracts across much of the postwar European order. World War II and the battle against Nazism provided the foundation for the many ideological struggles of the second half of the twentieth century, and issues from the defeats of the West European Left to the beginnings of the Cold War and the movement for European union can be traced back to the immediate postwar German question. The fate of Germany's occupied space formed the nascent order's most pressing challenge, and the political debate over how to punish the Nazi past was rapidly overtaken by the fresh problem of the country's de facto partition. The crucial period from 1945 to 1948—which in Italy covers the time from the end of the war to the decisive victory of the Christian Democrats and which in Yugoslavia marks the new nation's construction and then expulsion from the Cominform—in Germany describes a time of suspension: between Nazism and partition, and between war and Cold War. During this time, Germany was a nation only by default, with no government other than that imposed by the various Allied authorities and an entirely uncertain future. Thus, the narrative space of *Zentropa* is already not-quite-national. In *Zentropa*, German space is not legible as national and does not primarily evoke a traditional national history; rather, Germany stands in a metonymic relation to the troubled political and historical spaces of something called "Europe."

## "Go Deeper into Europa"

The first site of metonymy the film creates is a gap between the voice-over and the image—more accurately, the voice-over and the diegesis. *Zentropa* opens with a lengthy sequence in which a traveling shot moves rapidly along a train track at night, while in voice-over we hear the monotonous countdown of a hypnotist (played by Max von Sydow), instructing an unseen subject that on the count of ten, he will be in "Europa." Since the next scene depicts Leo's arrival in Germany, the spectator quickly realizes that Leo is the hypnotized subject and "Europa" is the narrative's location. But there is an immediate ambiguity here. The hypnotist exhorts Leo to go "deeper into Europa," and his words do not take Europe merely as object but connote internationality in their form. He speaks English, yet says "Europa," which is Italian or Spanish, and his voice carries a Scandinavian accent. By contrast, the narrative is not taking place in some vague Europa but in a specific Germany, and the image that matches this voice-over is a concrete one of train tracks. Leo, the addressee, is located in a material place on a route between specifically listed German towns. Further, the relationship between the voice-over and the diegesis in which Leo's narrative takes place is temporally irresolvable. Since Leo dies at the end of the film, there is no future time in which he could be hypnotized to recall his time in Germany. Thus, the space of the voice-over (in which Leo is in "Europa") and the space of the diegesis (in which Leo is in "Germany") are contiguous but irreconcilable. Germany cannot simply signify as part of Europe in a naturalistic manner, and the two terms are brought into a tense proximity.

This example makes clear the cinematic distinction between a national space—which can be represented visually, as in the idea of the national landscape—and the international space of Europe, which cannot be. "Germany" appears to exist at the level of the image (seen in rail yards, houses, fields), but "Europa" is possible only through the disembodied voice. European space is invisible, existing as a political idea but not as a coherent location. While there are engrained histories of representation that underwrite the cinematic conjuration of Italy, of Yugoslavia, or of Germany, there is no image that, on a purely visual level, can claim to transcend those national signifiers to represent the continent directly. Any possible image would in the first place be national, and the connotation of European-ness could be of only a second order.[8] Thus, for *Zentropa* to speak as a European film, it must go through the national but at the same time must unhinge cinematic space from its national connotations and refigure it as European. For Germany to become Europa, German space must be denationalized. And this cinematic imperative to denationalize German space dovetails with the narrative location of the film in zoned and occupied—that is, denationalized—postwar Germany. It is in this brief period of national incoherence that the problem of European space can come into view.

*Zentropa* tropes the relationship of national to European space insistently, circling the problem of a terrain that is historically precise and yet not visibly marked and in which one element slides into the other, refusing clear and proper boundaries. The clearest textual condensation of this problem is the train, which should be a machine for the rational mapping of space but which instead works to destabilize any coherent narrative space. Thus, while Leo spends a good deal of time traveling across Germany, he mostly remains on the train, never able to enter the space of the country directly. Within the discourse of train travel, the film schematizes German space both visually and aurally: through the list of destinations heard in voice-over while Leo travels, through the rail map of Germany that he stands in front of in an early scene, and through the model train set we see in Max Hartmann's attic. Indirect representations of German

*Zentropa*   German space is mapped graphically.

space multiply, but the thing itself becomes more and more attenuated. Just as Leo is a hypnotized subject and not a direct participant, so the figure of the train allows only a mediated relationship to a European landscape that is never actually reached. Like Leopold, the film is never really there.

Furthermore, the objectivity of the train itself is brought into question. Leo's uncle, the railway worker, confesses his fear that sometimes the train changes direction and finds itself going backward instead of forward. Leo rejects this fear as irrational and offers a scientific explanation for what he interprets as an optical illusion. However, the climactic scene—following Leo's defusing of the bomb that he himself had set on the train—appears to prove his uncle right after all. Throughout the time that the bomb has been aboard, there has been a series of cutaways showing both the train and its relationship to the Neuwied bridge. First, we see the bridge in the distance, from Leo's point of view on the train, and then several shots (not point of view) showing the train approaching and then crossing the bridge. These shots, we can presume, provide a metadiscursive view of where the train really is. But after the train has crossed the bridge and Leo has defused the bomb, and after some intervening sequences dealing with Leo's examination and Katharina's arrest, Leo looks out the window and sees, once again, the same bridge approach. Immediately after his realization, there is a cutaway to a long shot of the train, which is, irrationally, once again crossing the same bridge, and from the same direction. Space is repeating itself, and with

*Zentropa*    The model railway repeats German space in miniature.

this objective proof of impossibility, the train blows up, demonstrating a narrative as well as a spatial disjuncture.

That an impossible German space should be figured by a train also has a historical precedent. Timothy Garton Ash writes that the concept of Mitteleuropa, a middle Europe rather than an eastern or a western Europe, became an impossibility during the postwar years. Not only did the splitting of Europe into two rigid spheres preclude any cultural sense of middle Europe, but in Germany the term was tainted by associations with its previous use by the Nazis. The word, he writes, lived on "only as a ghostly Mitropa on the dining cars of the Deutsche Reichsbahn."[9] Thus, the concept of a middle Europe existed only on trains, in an impossible space that had no political reality in a Germany split into East and West, but only, in Garton Ash's apt formulation, a spectral reality in the non-place of the train. In the wake of reunification, he argues that the idea of central Europe began to return as a political and cultural discourse, and it is this ghost, I think, that *Zentropa* projects onto its postwar trains. Mitropa is, after all, very close to Zentropa, and like the real-life railway's trace of a lost Mitteleuropa, the film's trains map a space that does not really exist.

The idea of German space as a void resonates with the *trou noir* (black hole) that Thierry Jousse finds structural to *Zentropa*.[10] In his article "The Voids of Berlin," Andreas Huyssen relates a discussion of the post-Wall Berlin architecture debate to what he sees as an entire history of voids. If Berlin in the early 1990s was famous mostly as a non-space, literally centered on a hole in the ground, Huyssen contends that "the notion of Berlin as a void is more than a metaphor, and not just a transitory condition."[11] He traces the twentieth-century history of the concept, citing Ernst Bloch, who in 1935 described Berlin as a place that "functions in the void," and touching on the architectural voids left by Hitler's grand projects, as well as by Allied bombings. Thus, he says:

> When the wall came down, Berlin added another chapter to its narrative of voids, a chapter that brought back shadows of the past and spooky revenants. For a couple of years, the very center of Berlin, the threshold between the Eastern and Western parts of the city, was a seventeen-acre wasteland that extended from the Brandenburg Gate down to Potsdamer Platz and Leipziger Platz, a wide stretch of dirt, grass, and remnants of pavement under a big sky that seemed even bigger given the absence of a high-rises skyline that is so characteristic of the city.[12]

For Berlin, as for Germany, the center that formed the border of East and West is the biggest void of all, and it is this uncanny space between places that *Zentropa* works to bring to light.

The difficulty of seeing such a non-space is voiced textually, where the void of German space resolves into a relationship between nothing to see and too much to see. The claim that there is nothing to see is first made by Leo's uncle, when Leo tries to look out the window in the dormitory

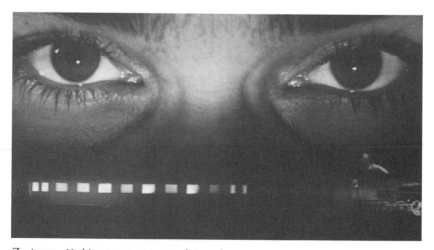

*Zentropa*   Nothing to see, or too much to see?

room in which he is staying. Angrily pulling back the curtains, Herr Kessler accuses Leo of waking those workers on night shifts and tells him that there is, in any case, nothing to see from the window. The phrase recurs on the train, where once again Leo is attempting to look out a window. This time, as the train leaves the platform, he pulls aside the blind and sees a mass of people running alongside the departing train, begging for money. Again his uncle pulls down the blind, claiming angrily that there is nothing to see and asking, "Have you no decency? The blinds must be closed, that is the rule." The visual consequence of this rule is to prevent the train windows from becoming screens to depict the landscape, and so the space of the train appears to be entirely separate from the country around it. As far as the landscape goes, there may or may not be nothing to see, but there is certainly nothing seen.

The claim of nothing to see is also made by the hypnotist in voice-over. Addressing Leo during his first journey as a sleeping car attendant, he intones, "You have traveled through the German night . . . you have met the German girl . . . but as you go on with your job in car 2306 there is little to see." The image that accompanies this speech is an extreme close-up of Leo's eyes at the top of the frame, and superimposed at the bottom is the train itself moving across the screen. As the juxtaposition of this voice-over with the image of huge eyes begins to suggest, however, the repeated claim that there is nothing to see implies an anxiety that the reverse might be true. And Leo does see out the train window in one scene, when Katharina opens the blinds to reveal the horrific sight of two hanged terrorists. If the discourse of "nothing to see" speaks of the fear of what might be seen, then this momentary image of dead bodies confirms that the view from the train is, indeed, too much. These dead bodies, like the starving men glimpsed later on the train, exemplify the European history that is too horrific to be seen, where "too much to see" refers explicitly to a politics of representability. But this notion of excessive vision is not just a political metaphor but a function of spectacle, where the tension between what can and what cannot be seen structures the film's historicity and enables a complex engagement with the image of the German and European past.

## Intertextuality, Postwar Film, and the Ruin Image

We can see a key elaboration of this structure in *Zentropa*'s intertextual references to another group of films set in immediate postwar Germany. In the wake of occupation, a number of films were shot in the ruins of Berlin and Frankfurt, and, like *Zentropa*, most of them were not German. In films such as *Germany Year Zero*, *A Foreign Affair*, and *Berlin Express* (Tourneur, 1948), the country was imagined not from a national but from an international perspective. These 1940s films—made, respectively, by an Italian and by expatriate Europeans in the United States—provide some of film history's most iconic images of post–World War II Germany, and yet they are not products of a German national cinema. In them, the nature and status of Germany become not national truths to be represented but the object of visual inquiry. To refer to these films is to invoke this history, in which the image of Germany becomes a projection by others onto a divided and uncertain space. *Zentropa* repeats this work of projection by dint of its status as another non-German film representing Germany in 1945, but it also textualizes the repetition through visual and narrative reference.

The narrative similarities are plentiful: from *Germany Year Zero*, *Zentropa* takes the fraught process of denazification, a question that also figures prominently in *Berlin Express*. Both films question the process's efficacy but nonetheless depict somewhat idealistic characters who are determined to make a difference in the new Germany. *A Foreign Affair* centers on a romance between an American man and a German woman who may or may not have been a Nazi. Like Max Hartmann in *Zentropa*, Marlene Dietrich's character, Erika von Schlütow, has the questionnaire

*Murderers Among Us*    Christmas Mass takes place in a bombed-out cathedral, with snow falling on the congregation.

*Zentropa*    The scene in the cathedral echoes that in *Murderers Among Us*, with a reverse shot of Leo entering the ruined church.

designed to assess past Nazi involvement falsified by an American offi-cer. And like von Schlütow, Katharina Hartmann turns out, indeed, to have had a Nazi past. Also quoted is the German postwar film *Murderers Among Us*, which, along with the foreign films, narrates the problems of national reconstruction in terms of guilt or innocence. *Zentropa* takes the noirish cast of its investigation from *Murderers Among Us*, and it cites, almost shot for shot, a scene in a bombed-out cathedral.

The most extensive structure of intertextuality, though, is that be-tween *Zentropa* and *Berlin Express*, which, as its title suggests, is also a film about trains.[13] Both films feature an American protagonist in Ger-many, with Lindley, like Leo, something of an innocent caught up in political intrigue beyond his grasp. Both films center on the dangers of terrorism from remaining Nazi sympathizers. *Berlin Express* contains an assassination plot against a good German on a train, a narrative device that is echoed directly in *Zentropa*'s sequence of the assassination of Mayor Ravenstein on Leo's first overnight assignment. Most strikingly, *Berlin Express* also uses a second-person narration, in which a disem-bodied voice-over narrates the American protagonist's actions as they happen on-screen. Thus, as Lindley walks toward the American military headquarters in Frankfurt, the voice-over says: "You approach the en-trance to the U.S. Army base." This unusual narrative strategy comes closest to that of *Zentropa* in a scene in which Lindley travels on the tit-ular train. He is looking out the train window, uneasily, as the voice-over says: "You're in his territory now . . . you're still not so sure you've got the upper hand . . . then you find yourself rolling over the former enemy border." The image is a point-of-view shot out the train window at night, showing a forest and a deserted road. The mysterious quality of the German landscape in relation to the known but perhaps still dangerous space of the train is made explicit when the voice-over comments: "Then back comes the doubt . . . you're in his territory now. The trees look the same, the sky's the same, the air doesn't smell any different." Like Leo, Lindley experiences German space by means of the train, and both films question what you can tell by looking out the window and whether the space of Germany is, after all, safe for foreigners.

But if *Zentropa* reminds us of a history in which German space was imagined from an international perspective, it also opens up a temporal and formal gap between the conditions of visual possibility in 1945 and those in 1991. For what makes the films of Jacques Tourneur, Billy Wilder, and Roberto Rossellini historically significant is not merely their timely narratives but their location shooting. These films were shot among the ruins of German cities, and they show an extremity of destruction that was historically unique.[14] *A Foreign Affair* opens with the American con-

*A Foreign Affair*    Ruins are emphasized in the background of shots.

*Germany Year Zero*   Ruins are emphasized in sequences of journeys that would classically be elided.

tingent flying into Berlin, and the aerial point-of-view shot from the window of their plane makes visually clear the vast extent of the city's destruction. Entire streets are missing, and most buildings are empty shells with only a few jagged walls left standing. Later in the film, in a shot construction also used in *Germany Year Zero*, characters walk or drive through the streets in sequences barely motivated by journeys that would classically be elided. In these narratively excessive tracking shots, the characters in the foreground signify less than the rubble that is constantly behind them. Here it is the documentary force of the ruin image—familiar to the contemporary audience from newsreels—that anchors the films' claim on the real. Although the films variously involve romantic, political, and mystery narratives, their power to represent the stakes of the postwar German problem comes as an effect of the evidentiary quality of their ruined mise-en-scènes.

That this concern for the indexical truth of the ruin image is part of the averred work of the films can be seen in the opening credits of *A Foreign Affair* and *Berlin Express*, both of which refer explicitly to their location shooting. *A Foreign Affair* begins with the intertitle, "A large part of this picture was photographed in Berlin." This assurance does not enable a better understanding of the narrative, which is largely generic and could have easily been shot in a studio; what it does is authenticate the film's relationship to Berlin's impossible space. Even more clearly, *Berlin Express* opens with the credit, "Actual scenes in Frankfurt and Berlin were photographed by authorization of the United States Army of Occupation, the British Army of Occupation, the Soviet Army of Occupation." The opening shot—as with all these films—is of rubble, and the title ensures that this space is read not as a set but as an index of the film's spatial and hence political authenticity.

Of course, the image of the German ruin is not confined to these films, and, indeed, within Germany, in what remained of a national film industry, a genre only half-ironically called the *Trümmerfilm* (ruin film) grew up. In addition to the well-known *Murderers Among Us* are films like *Marriage in the Shadows* (Maetzig, 1947) and *Between Yesterday and Tomorrow* (Braun, 1947), which use established genres such as the family melodrama and the thriller to address the recent past.[15] The relation of these films to discourses of indexicality is complex and can by no means be reduced to a univocal realism. For example, Thomas Elsaesser has emphasized the nonnaturalistic generic forebears of the German films, describing them as "halfway between Weimar's sordid realism and Hollywood's film noir."[16] And politically, too, these films run the gamut from critical social engagement to flagrant apologism and self-pity. Nonetheless, what binds these disparate films to one another and to the American and Italian ruin films is not reducible to a coincidence of location but pertains to the Benjaminian aura and to the effect of indexicality that we find in certain spatial images.

As I suggested with regard to *Underground*, two radically different images stood in the moment of 1945 as guarantees of indexicality and, as a consequence, as fetishistic promises of the visible truth of various postwar nations: the beautiful national landscape and the impossible space of the ruin. In regard to Germany, more than anywhere else, the ruin became in 1945 the key signifier of postwar truths. *Germany Year Zero* demonstrates the extent to which these spatial tropes are intertwined: in this film, the neorealist logic of the Italian national landscape is replaced with German destroyed space, for these images are two sides of the same coin. As Jousse argues, "Through a process asymptotically approaching documentary, [Rossellini] again delineates a quite concrete territory where the question of real space is determinant (especially in *Germany Year Zero*)."[17] The idea of real space, of the materiality of the postwar nation, became central at the historical moment when the future of many European nations was uncertain, and their physical destruction by war rendered visible a cost in human lives that was less easily representable—hence the ability of certain images of national space to produce an emotional effect of indexicality, wherein these cinematic images could offer to stand both within and beyond realism as the punctual truth of the postwar nation.

But there are no true ruin shots in *Zentropa*, and this absence as much as any of the intertextual references determines the film's relationship to the time and space of postwar Germany. The only views of wartime destruction in the film are the few establishing shots of the exterior of the Hartmann residence in Frankfurt, a brief exterior shot of a street, and the scene that echoes *Murderers Among Us* in a bombed-out cathedral. For example, we see Leo and his uncle arrive at the Hartmann house in long shot, with the house taking up most of the background and some rubble on the street in between. Although the rubble clearly connotes ruined buildings, the house in the background is intact and, indeed, somewhat palatial. The cathedral scene also undercuts its ruin status: while there is logically a ruin, for snow is falling inside the church, the establishing shot of the cathedral's facade does not reveal this destruction, and once inside it is impossible to see the walls. Editing produces the meaning of a ruined cathedral, but there is no individual image of destruction. In none of these scenes is ruination either clear or foregrounded. Aside from these few and inconclusive shots, the film takes place almost entirely indoors: on trains, inside the train station, in offices, and in the Hartmann house. The few exterior shots that exist either are in the countryside or are so tightly framed that no setting can be discerned.

Of course, there could be no actual ruins in a film made in 1990: unlike *Underground*, *Zentropa* was not filmed in a new battleground that could stand in, visually, for a historical one. And as a result of this difference, any ruin shots that might exist in *Zentropa* could not produce the affective shock of those in the 1940s films, for they would code only as set design rather than as momentary flashes of the real. Nonetheless, given the extent to which the film quotes these earlier ruin films, it is striking that the destroyed urban landscape of its German city settings is virtually absent from the mise-en-scène. *Zentropa*'s omission of ruin shots—and, indeed, its virtual omission of exterior long shots of any kind—is a structuring absence, a void that works against any mobilization of nation, effectively bracketing the mise-en-scène as a spectacle that refuses authenticity, a cinematic space outside the discourse of place.

This de-realization of space separates German space from the discourse of the nation. Without reference to the image that claims to be an index of postwar Germany, the film's space becomes both nonnational and unreal. But the absence of the ruin image is more than a refusal to represent a concrete national space: it is also a refusal of the ideological implications of the postwar German ruin. For if the Italian films used the indexical landscape image as part of a leftist claim on the new republic, the films set in Germany took the ruin as a liberal, rather than a radical, signifier of political redemption. In the conflation of liberation with ruination, images of rubble became signifiers of a cleansing of Germany, in which the Third Reich was physically swept away and the pain of destruction formed a catharsis for the German people. The ruin spoke as the fresh start made material. Thus, Michel Celemenski can argue that "at degree zero, humanity cannot but find its redemption. This is the principal message of Tourneur, Staudte, and Rossellini."[18] Here, the real landscape has a redemptive power that the narratives of the films, to a greater or lesser degree, can endorse.

But although the idea of the year zero caught on in public discourse, it holds little water as a serious political category. Elsaesser asks pointedly: "Was May 1945 the famous 'Zero Hour' and the chance for a new beginning or, rather, already the return of a period of political restoration, the creeping and scarcely clandestine rehabilitation of former Nazis in positions of power: industry at first, then government, administration, the judiciary, press and education?"[19] Clearly, he thinks the latter, and this interpretation of the postwar years is the dominant one in contemporary historiography.[20] And if the concept of a year zero is problematic, then so, too, is the ruin film, which became its visual correlative. The ruin image proposes a fictional break, which preempts any need to engage with the recent past. It enables the reassuring idea that Nazism is firmly consigned to the past, producing a discourse of new beginnings, at once optimistic and self-indulgent. For any claim on German national subjectivity, it is a sign of guilt and a sign of penance. It implies a new "we"—the we who regret—and this new subject cancels out the old Nazi one, articulating a non-Nazi German subject that precludes any possibility of Nazis remaining in the rubble. Thus the notion of a redemptive year zero can be seen as papering over the recent past.

The humanistic use of the ruin as redemption is put under scrutiny by Elsaesser with regard to the German-made films. Far from enabling a liberal politics of reconstruction, he suspects, the narratives of "middle-of-the-road protagonists, ordinary people, caught up and implicated through cowardice and misguidedness ... offered a [German] audience prepared to be contrite the comfort of fatalism and self-pity."[21] While he does credit such films as *Murderers Among Us* with critical social engagement, he is also suspicious both of that film's noirish mise-en-scène and of the various attempts at a neorealist engagement with everyday life among the ruins. He argues: "Thus the thriller format made it seem as if Nazism had been a conspiracy perpetrated by a clique of fanatics, lunatics and underworld criminals. The neo-realist mode, however, was always in danger of becoming frankly apologetic, suggesting that moral decency and individual courage had prevailed throughout and that the war when it came was the universal human tragedy it has always been in the popular mind, like a natural disaster such as a flood or a drought."[22] Naturally, these two impulses are not identical, and I do not want to conflate the politics of the postwar German film industry with the texts of Rossellini and Tourneur. But across their variously debated ideological imperatives, these films all share a logic of trauma in which the image of the ruined city promises both access to the real and a more or less overt stake in a liberal definition of that reality. The disruptive trauma of the real, along with the bombing of Germany, is defined as happening before the "now" of the indexical image. By locating the horror of German space in the image of the ruined city, the ruin film places the dislocation of Nazism firmly in the past and offers the need for reconstruction as a visual correlative of the political need to look forward and begin anew.

In omitting the ruin image, then, *Zentropa* refuses this logic and, with it, the liberal discourse on German identity and postwar history. If the year zero is a lie, the film refuses the contemporary image of that lie and, in so doing, suggests a different articulation of postwar history. The film's narrative directly thematizes a rejection of year zero optimism, both generally in the idealistic Leo's failure to help Germany and specifically in the focus on Nazi sympathizers from the Werewolves to the Hartmann family. The logic of the German ruin is one of temporal breaks, wherein the past is fundamentally distinct. It is the time before ruins. The future, equally, is distinguished as the time after ruins, when reconstruction will enable a new beginning predicated on complete change. Although this logic considers loss, basically it works to separate the present from both past and future, presenting Germany in 1945 as a blank slate. By contrast, *Zentropa*'s refusal to use the ruin image means that it can neither engage a rhetoric of a separate before nor look forward to a different future. Like *Underground* in this respect, the time that would seem to form a before is actually already in the history it seems to precede. For Germany, as for Yugoslavia, the end of the war is not a simple break. The supposed year zero was a fake, and in 1945 there was both still the legacy of Nazism, which has not disappeared, and already the divisiveness, zoning, and international expedience that would form the basis of the Cold War.

In its intertextual construction, then, *Zentropa* performs a doubled movement: on the one hand, it refers to the films of the immediate postwar years in Germany, but, on the other, it works to remove those textual elements that function as signs of a material space and time. As a result, place becomes unsettled, with German space being overlaid with the uncanny space of "Europa." But this troubling of the cinematic year zero discourse is not only spatial but temporal. It is temporal first in that by refusing the year zero concept, the film also refuses to locate Germany in a historical limbo. Instead, time spreads outward, bleeding back into Nazism and forward into the Cold War. But the ideological weight of these references is also historically contingent. To cite the aftermath of World War II takes on new meanings also in the wake of German reunification, when the relationship of Germany to Europe and the history of war and Cold War became once again politically central. It is in this context that *Zentropa* was released, and it is therefore necessary to read the stakes of its history through the politics of its present. We return once more to the question of 1945 from the perspective of 1991.

The historical moment of *Zentropa*'s release was much on the minds of its critics: as with *Underground*, current events conspired to ensure that the film was easily read as topical. *Zentropa* was released in Europe in 1991, just over a year after the reunification of Germany and less than two years after the fall of the Berlin Wall. And although the film is set entirely in the past, with none of the narrative codas that tie *Cinema Paradiso*'s and *Mediterraneo*'s historical situations to the present day, many critics saw the film as a direct commentary on post-Wall Europe. *Cahiers du Cinéma* read the film as a metaphor, in which postwar fascism and colonization of Europe by America made points about the same forces at work in the 1990s. And Jousse makes the case that "this country in ruins, plunged into a dark night . . . in a tunnel we can't see the end of . . . makes us think irresistibly of Eastern Europe (or Central Europe) today. The same confusion of values, the same sense of nihilism, the same chaos, the same hegemonic force of capitalism."[23]

That critical response to *Zentropa* should have focused on this metaphoric substitution of present for past is not surprising. While *Underground* makes plain its spatial tropes (the underground tunnel or the broken landscape), *Zentropa* makes plain a work of historical projection: from postwar to post-Wall. But while most critics saw this projection as a straightforward replacement, I would argue that the two historical spaces must be read together, with this temporal layering producing as much disjuncture as comparison. Just as the space of "Europa" and the space of "Germany" prove irreconcilable in the gap between voice-over and diegesis, so the relationship of past and present is one of proximity rather than substitution. Rather than pursue a metaphoric reading, in which 1945 is a veil covering over the truth of 1991, I suggest a metonymic relation in which the spaces of Germany and Europe, 1945 and 1991, must be seen as contiguous and mutually determining.

For Lars von Trier, Germany is what haunts Europe, exceeding its borders to stand for the continent. In *Zentropa*, German space can become European space because it is dematerialized and denationalized. Refracted through the lens of 1945 film references, and shorn of the indexical images of the ruined city, "Germany" is conjured not as a national landscape but as a haunting presence for postwar European history. The claim that *Zentropa* is a film of reunification is correct to the extent that its historical space does imply the unseen space of its contemporary location. The confusing landscapes through which Zentropa's trains carry Leo are not identical to those of the post-unification nation, but its denationalized space echoes the geography of 1990, in which both Germany and Europe became once again contested concepts. The two spaces are overlaid, without ever touching, like a ghost image on doubly exposed film. In order to map *Zentropa*'s disjunctive logic of European space and time, we must follow the appearances of this ghost and interrogate just how the film frames European space as horrific.

## Dark Continents

Of course, it is not hard to imagine Germany in 1945 as a place of horror. In addition to the vast material destruction documented by the ruin films, postwar German space resonated both with the recent atrocities of the Nazi regime and with the social and political turmoil that came with reconstruction. Widespread displacement and homelessness, a rise in looting and violent crime, and the possibility of violence from Allied soldiers and Nazi terrorists alike produced an atmosphere of, if not horror, certainly uncertainty and menace. And while the zoning of Germany by the Allied occupying forces enabled the construction of new government and social structures, these changes coincided both with the wider shift to a Cold War relationship among the Allies themselves and with the intensely controversial processes of denazification and reeducation of the German populace.[24] The remapping of German space that took place as the four zones gradually morphed into two states also entailed a remapping of German national identity, a question that was, after reunification, once more in process.

*Zentropa*'s narrative deals quite directly with a number of these historical issues, most centrally the problems surrounding the denazification questionnaires. Politics is not relegated to the margins of the narrative, as in the Italian films but, as in *Underground*, forms a major part of the plot. Max Hartmann's problem is the tension between his high-level links to the Nazis and the economic desire of the American authorities to see that his rail company remains in business. The questionnaire that Colonel Harris delivers to him becomes a dramatic turning point in the scene in which Max is obliged to agree that he saved a Jew. In this scene, the corruption of the process is precisely the point, as the Jew—who has clearly never met Max before in his life—unhappily performs a charade of recognition in front of the American soldiers who have blackmailed him into appearing. In one shot, a close-up of Max has a background of windows that dissolves into a back projection of the questionnaire itself. The document, whose briefly legible lines deny membership in the Nazi Party or paramilitary organizations, fills the frame in extreme close-up, its disproportion emphasizing its narrative significance. In the following sequence, Max is overwhelmed by his lies and commits suicide.

As with the Italian melodramas, however, the substance of *Zentropa*'s political engagement is not located in such overt narrative references. Rather, politics is again subject to a work of projection, in which generic codes structure the visual and narrative possibilities of the historical

*Zentropa*   A denazification questionnaire is projected behind Max Hartmann.

look back. The form of *Zentropa*'s look back is conditioned by the nature of its dark history: since mourning is not the obvious reaction to the German year zero, then it is clear that melodrama will not be the mode in which the period is reimagined.[25] Instead, the film appears to evoke dark genres such as the thriller, film noir, and horror. The space of Germany is shadowy and menacing, and in it lurk Nazi guerrillas called Werewolves, a reminder of primitive fears of supernatural beasts. That Nazism should be represented in terms of such a pre-modern discourse of terror might seem simplistic, but this space is repeatedly located in voice-over as "Europa." It is not that fascism is primitive but that Europe itself must rethink its claim on civilization.

In this construction of a horrific and nightmarish space, *Zentropa* takes up a philosophical rhetoric that reverses claims to European civilization and presents the continent's history of imperialism and genocide as the true locus of "primitive" barbarism.[26] Historian Mark Mazower elaborates this position in his book *Dark Continent: Europe's Twentieth Century*, in which he argues that Europe, not Africa, should be given the epithet "dark continent." For Mazower, Nazism is not an aberration but the defining ideology of the twentieth century in Europe. Moreover, Mazower sees Nazism's policy of spatial expansion as primary rather than simply practical: it took the logic of imperialism but transferred its North/South structure into an East/West one in which eastern Europe replaced the primitive colonies. Thus, Nazism brings the imperial dark continent to Europe and, in so doing, inadvertently reveals the true nature of European barbarism. Like Mazower, *Zentropa* reverses the terms of primitivist discourse, invoking the binary of civilization versus primitivism in order to question the place of Europe in this structure.

Within the field of film theory, the phrase "dark continent" is probably more familiar in the context of its use by Freud to refer to women than in its original, geographic meaning. In her article "Dark Continents: Epistemologies of Racial and Sexual Difference in Psychoanalysis and the Cinema," Mary Ann Doane points out that "Freud's use of the term 'dark continent' to signify female sexuality is a recurrent theme in feminist theory." And, she continues, not only do many feminists forget that the phrase is a Victorian one about Africa, but "in its textual travels from the colonialist image of Africa to Freud's description of female sexuality as enigma to feminist theorists' critique of psychoanalysis . . . the phrase has been largely stripped of its historicity."[27] Doane's article mostly considers the role of the white woman in articulating race and sexuality in American cinema, a topic that might seem distant to the historical questions posed by *Zentropa*.

And yet both Mazower and feminist theory share a desire to debunk an ideologically problematic attribution of "darkness," and Mazower's usage shares with Doane's rereading of feminist theory a concern for historicity. Freud's use of the term is metaphoric—the woman is like Africa in her unknowability, her mystery, her need to be mapped by man— whereas Mazower's dark continent is a literal attempt to rewrite the history of Europe so that it becomes the object of its own description. He is, as it were, returning the gaze. *Zentropa* also reverses the terms of civilization and primitivism, so that the space of Europe is dark, mysterious, and dangerous. As with Mazower—and, indeed, with *Underground*'s mobilization of Balkanism—this reinscription of primitivism in relation to European history brings into question the discourse's structuring assumptions. But in *Zentropa*, the trope of European space as horrific operates less through a realist representation or narrative engagement with the politics of the war than through a projection of those political questions onto two generic paradigms in which darkness, mystery, and violence are visually and narratively central: film noir and horror.

While Mazower's use of the dark continent trope is underwritten by a reappropriation of its historicity, he is not concerned with the subject of gender. But film noir and horror frequently center on issues of gender and sexuality and, indeed, have been key areas of analysis for exactly the kinds of feminist psychoanalytic theory with which Doane is engaged. The figures of the femme fatale and the feminized/sexualized monster have been widely theorized by feminists as laying bare the workings of a patriarchal visual economy, and Laura Mulvey's model of bodily display and narrative investigation corresponds neatly to the colonialist/Freudian metaphor of mapping the mysterious space of Africa/ woman. Certainly for Doane, the relevance of Freud's comparison for feminist film theory is the way it clarifies, inadvertently, the interdependence of notions of the feminine and the primitive, particularly in cinema, where the image of the white woman takes on a crucial role in articulating a racial and gendered ideology of desire.[28]

The femme fatale, standing for the dangers of femininity yet visually coded in terms of her whiteness (albeit sometimes a pale-skinned, dark-featured type), provides an example of how Doane's argument complicates previous feminist psychoanalytic theory. But *Zentropa* forces yet another turn of the screw, explicitly returning the mysterious femme fatale to the history of European expansion and racial politics. Katharina's uncertain morality derives from her potential connection to Nazism and its policy of, in Mazower's words, "treating Europeans as Africans."[29] The racial and ethnic politics of Europe in the 1940s underlie, and not only thematically, the mise-en-scène of the 1940s film noir. In *Zentropa*, the question of gcnre subtends both a spatial logic (here the dark continent instead of the political landscape) and a gendered one. The discourse of mysterious and primitive space, which encodes an ethnic and geopolitical logic of Europe, cannot be fully exhausted by the spaces of a spectacular mise-en-scène but must be diverted through the body of the woman. Within the intricate layering of these ideological and historical figures, the femme fatale forms a vector through which the logics of primitivism, historicity, and the dangerous space of Europe can be mapped in cinematic terms. By projecting politics onto film noir and horror, *Zentropa* forms a locus for all these meanings, connecting a critique of the European history of primitivism with a psychoanalytic and cinematic reinscription of the gendered questions of seeing and knowing, desire and memory.

## Noir and Fatality

Of course, in analyzing *Zentropa* in terms of horror and, especially, of film noir, it is necessary to recall that the film is not, really, either. *Zentropa* must be considered in the context of the contemporary art film rather than as a genre film per se. But it is one of the qualities of the postclassical art film to refer extensively to popular genres: as Amina Danton has argued, while the art cinema of the 1960s often transformed genre conventions, contemporary art films use them directly.[30] In addition to the issue of art-cinematic intertextuality, we must consider the generic specificity of film noir. Whereas the Italian films are melodramas, *Zentropa* is not a film noir but a set of references to noir. Noir, unlike melodrama, is generally thought of as historically and nationally specific. Certainly, there are arguments for various national noirs (for example, in the United Kingdom, France, and Denmark),[31] and it has become commonplace to speak of "neo-noirs," such as *The Usual Suspects* (Singer, 1995) and *The Last Seduction* (Dahl, 1994). But there is no need to invent terms such as "neo-comedy" and "neo-melodrama," and we do not have to make arguments for most genres existing in different countries. Noir is by definition American and postwar, and thus for a contemporary film to be considered noir is inevitably a question of reference. Through this doubling, this distance from the genre's original status, *Zentropa* invokes the historical and spectacular codes of film noir.

*Zentropa*'s most evident reference to film noir is its use of black-and-white cinematography. While some of the film is in color, or colorized, it is mostly shot on a shiny black-and-white stock that implies classical cinema in general and film noir in particular. In the opening scene, for example, Leo stands in a railway yard in the rain. Here, the mise-en-scène adds to the black-and-white film to produce a typically noirish effect: low-key lighting emphasizes dark shadows, with areas of bright light where the rain reflects on the bricks. In addition, other aspects of the mise-en-scène refer to noir conventions (or, indeed, clichés). Leo is wearing a raincoat and fedora, smoke is rising from the building, and he stands in a seedy urban milieu. The only dissonant element is the graffiti on the wall that he begins by facing, which gradually becomes legible as written in German. Within the first scene, the mise-en-scène of American films is recapitulated and then shifted into a European context.

*Zentropa*'s reiteration of film noir conventions is not limited to the mise-en-scène. The politics of postwar Germany also resonates with the noir narrative of mystery, crime, and moral uncertainty. As Janey Place describes it: "The dominant world view expressed in film noir is paranoid, claustrophobic, hopeless, doomed, predetermined by the past, without clear moral or personal identity. Man has been inexplicably uprooted from those values, beliefs and endeavours that offer him meaning and stability, and in the almost exclusively urban landscape of film noir (in pointed contrast to the pastoral, idealised, remembered past) he is struggling for a foothold in a maze of right and wrong."[32] Almost all these paradigmatic noir elements can be found in *Zentropa*: Leo is the center of a paranoid structure in which he is observed by everyone, from the terrorists to the American colonel and the railway company adjudicators, and the mise-en-scène of the trains is highly claustrophobic. Leo is a hero uprooted from his stable life as a conscientious objector in the United States and thrown into the amoral and dangerous universe of Germany in 1945. And the setting is indeed mostly urban, for the impossibility of landscape returns as a defining feature of *Zentropa*. The distance of *Zentropa*'s version of Europe in 1945 from that of the Italian films can be described as the distance from the political landscape to the impossible space or from the 1945 of neorealism to that of film noir.

The relationship of present to past is also, as Place makes clear, one of the key narrative tropes of noir. Pam Cook takes up this discussion in her reading of *Mildred Pierce* (Curtiz, 1945), in which she argues that noir as a genre works on the historical anxieties of the postwar period. For her (and for much feminist work on the genre), noir expresses both the repression of women and the reestablishment of a failing patriarchy after the war, where "this re-construction work . . . rests uneasily on this repression, aware of the continual possibility of the eruption into the present of the submerged past."[33] Place's version of the lost idyllic past—represented, for example, in *Out of the Past* (Tourneur, 1947)—is not taken up directly by *Zentropa*, where there is no image of a time before the chaos and mystery of the narrative present. Neither does *Zentropa*'s version of the postwar situation so easily fit Cook's gendered reading, which is, of course, specific to American films and politics. But the notion of a barely repressed past that might at any moment erupt into the present is uniquely relevant to the notion of postwar Germany as dark continent. The idea of a past crime that haunts the present is quite obviously political in *Zentropa*'s Germany and only shallowly submerged.

Of course, film noir already has a European past: while the genre is by definition American, its roots in interwar Europe are well known. Its aesthetic forebears include German Expressionism and French poetic realism. Even more important in this context is the mode of transmission of these influences to Hollywood, largely in the shape of European filmmakers (including actors, cinematographers, and other technical crew, as well as directors) who emigrated to the United States to escape from Nazism. Directors such as Fritz Lang and Billy Wilder helped influence American film of the 1940s, and thus we can read film noir, even at an industrial level, as a palimpsest of the history of Nazism. While only a few noir films refer directly to Nazism (for instance, the British noir *The Third Man*), the bad past is central to the historical evolution of the genre.

But *Zentropa* includes the investigation of an explicitly wartime past: Leo must discover whether Katharina was a Werewolf, if her father was a Nazi, and what was the history of the Zentropa railway company. The weighty question of what happened in the German past appears at various points in the narrative, most obviously in the scene with the Jew who tells the lie that Max Hartmann saved him. This sequence opens up the past in terms of German guilt or innocence and, of course, implies that the past is being falsified and covered up. Not only is there a bad past in noir, but the present does not always bring truth to light. There is also a sequence of emaciated Jewish prisoners on the train, which forms a brief visual trace of the railway's past of transportation. (The figure of the Jew appears in *Zentropa* only in terms of what cannot be seen within the text. Either it is the unrepresented past—where the first Jew narrates a false past to cover over the implied real one, and the Jews on the train appear as hallucinations from a past that the film cannot represent—or it is the extratextual future, for the Jew who exonerates Hartmann is played by Lars von Trier, in a cameo role that reminds the spectator of the present-day origins of the film.) In both cases, the difficulty of exca-vating the German past underwrites the noir investigation.[34]

Moreover, *Zentropa* adds another level of temporality to the noir rela-tionship to the past, for Leo's experiences in postwar Germany are them-selves the subject of a historical excavation. The noir plot is framed by a narrative structure of hypnosis, in which the entire diegesis is suppos-edly being remembered by Leo as an analysand at some time in the future. The film opens with a shot of railway tracks in the dark, and as the camera penetrates farther into this almost abstracted space, the voice-over intones "you go deeper and deeper and deeper." Falling into the psychic depth of a hypnotic trance is figured visually as moving for-ward into space, and this depth of field thematically sets up the dark, mysterious space of Europe as the landscape traversed by the German train. The voice-over continues, "on the count of ten you will be in Europa," placing European space as the end point of an unknown etiol-ogy and suggesting psychoanalysis as the mechanism for investigating the traumatic past. Shifting noir conventions slightly, the voice-over comes not from the protagonist but from his apparently omniscient ana-lyst. Read in these terms, the entire narrative is an attempt to bring the past to light, a psychoanalytic return to the scene of the crime.[35]

It is telling that the form in which the present exists within the film is so marginal. We never see the present: it is entirely absent from the image track and heard only at the edges of the soundtrack. The hypno-tist's voice is the only trace of the present within the text, and his second-person monologue serves to emphasize the empty or invisible space of the present-day European subject. We can see Leo, the conjuration of hypnotic suggestion, who dies in 1945, but what remains unseen is the subject who looks back. Equally, we can see the Europa of 1945, with its noirish mise-en-scène and its primitive and horrific spaces, but there is no image of the Europe of the present from which this historical space is projected. The horrific nature of this past inheres for the spectator, much as it does for the hypnotized Leo, in the fact that there is no out-side to it. The hypnotic voice-over is a framing device, but there is no access to the frame. It exists only to demand a position of knowledge, to locate the spectator as a subject who looks back to the historical moment of the narrative, but it does not allow the present to rescue either spec-tator or protagonist from the exigencies of the past.

Thus, *Zentropa* takes up the temporality of noir to figure the impos-sibility of a certain kind of historical narrative: the past does not neces-sarily shed light on the present. If the Italian films offer the experience of mourning, and *Underground* the uncertainty of melancholia, *Zentropa* textualizes the failure of psychoanalytic mechanisms to excavate the past. As Leo overcathects to the past, he loses the present, dying inside his hypnosis. The narrative of psychoanalysis promises to uncover the root of neurosis, just as the film noir promises to reveal the truth of past crimes. In each case, there must be an originary scene that will, as in Pascal Bonitzer's theory of the filmic labyrinth,[36] explain all that has come before in the narrative and all that comes after temporally. But, like many film noirs, *Zentropa* provides no primal scene at the center of its labyrinth: all that Leo's analytic inquiry leads to is death, and the film's investigative structure disappears into a void. Within the historical narrative, Leo is unable to help Germany or Katharina and is instead killed by the forces competing for Germany's future. In the framing narrative, there is even less resolution, for Leo's death inside his hypnosis illogically precludes any return to the narrative present. In either case, the look back is neither nostalgic nor melancholic, but fatal.

And the concept of fatality leads us inexorably to the figure who is, in 1940s films noir, the locus of moral uncertainty and possible past crimes: the femme fatale. Place's description of "man" as the subject uprooted from his moral values and stability is deliberate, for noir films conventionally center on the tension between a simple, upright male protagonist and a dangerous urban landscape, which is, quite directly, personified in the morally dubious but sexually alluring woman. Katharina is coded as a femme fatale first by her appearance: she dresses in glamorous 1940s fashions and is frequently framed in close-up. In the

*Zentropa*    The femme fatale is framed as an erotic spectacle of bodily display.

scene where Leo meets her for the first time in her father's private train compartment, she is initially seen in a full-color close-up, while the surrounding shots—including a reverse shot of Leo—are in black and white. This emphasis on her image as spectacular goes hand in hand with a conventional noir narrative of ambiguous morality. In the train scene, Katharina explains to Leo the existence of the so-called Werewolves: Nazi guerrillas who are being executed by the Allies. Later in the narrative, Leo has fallen in love with Katharina, and as she undresses, she confesses that she used to be a Werewolf. As she makes this confession, Katharina is framed in a moment of classical to-be-looked-at-ness, lying down and wearing a sheer slip, her hair fanned behind her. The femme fatale as erotic spectacle and as narrative threat are momentarily identical.

Where *Zentropa* alters, or rather augments, the traditional noir narrative is in the overt and self-conscious emergence of history into this scenario. While film noir has been theorized as a reaction to the politics of postwar America, *Zentropa* textualizes this process, making the recent history of the continent central to the plot. Thus, the dangerous urban landscape that Katharina personifies is not merely criminal but specifically Nazi. Elizabeth Cowie describes noir in terms of "a masculine scenario, that is, the film noir hero is a man struggling with other men, who suffers alienation and despair, and is lured by fatal and deceptive women."[37] Here, the men with whom Leo struggles are the mysterious forces of Nazism, who do not form an individual threat as much as a constantly unknowable and alienating landscape. Marc Vernet has mapped this relationship spatially, arguing that "the 'triangle' has often been pointed out as a principal form of relation among the characters: the young hero desires and conquers a rich woman who is quite often tied to an older man or some other representative of patriarchal authority."[38] In *Zentropa*, Nazism forms the third point of the triangle, to which Katharina is tied through the figure of her father. As the owner of the Nazi-era rail company Zentropa, as well as Leo's father-in-law, Max Hartmann represents patriarchal authority as inescapably linked to the Nazi past.

According to Doane, the femme fatale represents, above all, a problem of knowledge: "She harbors a threat which is not entirely legible."[39] And it is this mystery that the film noir narrative works to uncover. Her illegibility goes hand in hand with her spectacularity, so the question of knowledge is tied to vision. Excessively visible and yet narratively ambiguous, the femme fatale disturbs the relationship between what can be seen and what can be known. Katharina centers the question of what we can see of Nazism: the spectator cannot be sure if she is still a Werewolf, and the narrative works to close up this disjuncture between sight and knowledge. But this problem of knowledge—that we cannot tell who is guilty just by looking—not only is the case with regard to Katharina but describes the key problematic of *Zentropa*'s postwar German landscape. The space of *Zentropa*'s narrative is determined by this "epistemological trauma," where, as in *Berlin Express*, Leo's point of view is based on doubt about the status of the landscape around him. ("Then back comes the doubt . . . you're in his territory now. The trees look the same, the sky's the same, the air doesn't smell any different.") This is where the femme fatale focuses the political logic of the dark continent, defining European space as that which is dangerous, uncertain, and, most of all, duplicitous.

## Werewolves, Cats, and Women

"Duplicity" is a defining term of the femme fatale, but Katharina's duplicity is not limited to this generic figure. The narrative source of her guilt is her membership in a Nazi terrorist group, the Werewolves, and the idea of the werewolf also connects *Zentropa* to the horror genre. The doubled body of the werewolf is another figure of duplicity, seemingly human by day, but transforming into a monstrous creature by night. Of course, Katharina is not literally a werewolf, unlike the protagonists of classical "monster films" such as *The Wolf Man* (Waggner, 1941), supernatural beings who morph from human to wolf. Her change is not physical but ideological, from the "good German" during the day to the Nazi terrorist by night. This day/night logic is underscored when Katharina tells Leo how she worked with her father by day and then at night wrote the threatening letters that he received from the Werewolves. But the generic conventions of the werewolf (and of the hybrid human-animal in general) nonetheless underpin *Zentropa*'s construction of the dark continent and the discursive place of the woman within it.[40]

The first characteristic of the werewolf, as of the femme fatale, is a question of visibility. Because he or she seems human during the day, we cannot be sure who is a werewolf. In a generic horror film, this uncertainty becomes the site of suspense—either about the existence of a monster or about the time and place it might strike.[41] In Bonitzer's terms, the werewolf exists in blind space: the off-screen space that produces suspense. The monster, like the femme fatale, is a spectacular object, but its spectacularity depends on its being invisible for most of the horror film. In *Zentropa*, the invisibility of the monster is figured in terms of the thriller narrative, where the terrorist Werewolves operate clandestinely and are rarely seen. Moreover, when they are seen, they are hard to see as werewolves, for their bodily duplicity means they look just like everyone else. Thus, on two occasions, werewolves are labeled in writing to ensure visibility. The first example comes when Kate raises the blind and looks out the train window, only to see the bodies of two hanged men, with signs around their necks reading "werewolf" in German and Russian. Here, the writing serves narratively as a sign of guilt, but it also initiates a structure whereby the werewolf's body is deceptive and must be made to speak visually.

This structure repeats later in a train sequence, when Leo is sitting alone in the train corridor. He is in the lower-left-hand corner of the frame, and projected behind him is the word *Werwolf* in disproportionately large letters. At this point, the image works mainly to reinforce the idea of the werewolf being visible only through the written word, where the identities of the terrorists are mysterious and their plans unknown. Much later in the film, however, Leo is once again on the same train, on his honeymoon with Katharina. Again, he sits alone and is framed in the corner of the screen, and once more a giant image is projected behind him, representing his thoughts and anxieties. This time, the image is of Katharina's face. The effect is unusual, and its repetition inevitably recalls its previous use, so that Leo's projected image of Katharina is itself superimposed, for the spectator, onto the earlier image of the word *Werwolf*. This doubt about Katharina's status follows the moral ambiguity of the femme fatale: while she is repeatedly connected to the Werewolves—in mise-en-scène, as here, and in narrative—she is never seen to be one, and the spectator can therefore never be entirely sure of her guilt.

The second defining term of the werewolf proceeds also from its doubled body: the binary of day and night, human and animal, entails a logic of civilization and the primitive. In the horror film, it is frequently a modern, scientific milieu that is threatened by the supernatural, inexplicable, and animalistic. And the werewolf, with its human and animal elements, is able to trope a specifically modern fear of the primitive lurking within civilization. Thus, Walter Benjamin, writing about Poe's "Man of the Crowd," describes the story as "the case in which the flâneur completely distances himself from the type of the philosophical promenader, and takes on the features of the werewolf restlessly roaming a social wilderness."[42] Here, the werewolf represents the frightening aspect of modern life, which includes the possibility of evil existing within the city crowd,

precisely because the city is also a wilderness. Modern space is also primitive space in the werewolf metaphor: the modern man may also be a
beast, and the problem is that you cannot see the difference. Thus, by presenting postwar Germany in terms of hidden werewolves, *Zentropa*
works on both the overt iconography of the horror genre and its historical underpinnings. Europe becomes a primitive place where beneath the
veneer of civilization lies the dark continent.

There is one notable difference between Katharina and the conventional horror film werewolf, however, and that difference is gender. As a
femme fatale, Katharina is structured as a gendered spectacle, but the
werewolf figure in most horror films is male and rarely seen as a site of
sexual threat. The threat of the werewolf is primitive violence, but the
primitivism is that of excessive masculinity, viewed as unrefined by the
morality of civilized society. The beastliness of the werewolf contrasts in
this respect with the feminization of many other horror film monsters,
such as the vampire and the alien. However, *Zentropa*'s shape-shifting
femme fatale does have a cinematic predecessor: the protagonist of
*Cat People* (Tourneur, 1942), who may turn into a more conventionally
feminine feline monster. *Cat People*, I think, functions as another art-
cinematic intertext for *Zentropa*,[43] but, more important, its interconnection of the femme fatale and the monster subtends a discourse of primitivism that enables a clearer analysis of exactly how these generic figures
produce, in *Zentropa*, a somewhat different historical and spatial system.

*Cat People* ties monstrosity quite explicitly to both female sexuality
and a dark European history. Irena is a Serbian woman who believes that
is she is under an ancient village curse, whereby she will turn into a pan-
ther if she is sexually aroused and attack her partner. Her all-American
husband rejects this belief as mere superstition, but he is finally attacked
by Irena, who kills herself in remorse. The film has been analyzed frequently, mainly in terms of its sexual logics (although not always from a
feminist or psychoanalytic perspective), with Irena's excessive and animalistic sexuality forming the central term of debate.[44] Doane's reading
ties a feminist reading to a historical one, pointing out that "this opposition [between rational and irrational, science and poetry] is mapped
onto what in 1942 was necessarily another heavily loaded opposition—
that between the native and the foreign, the 'good old Americano' and
the Serbian, the familiar (Alice) and the strange (Irena)."[45]

This nexus of terms is part of a wider analysis, and Doane's interest
in Irena's national identity is only that "Serbian" connotes a general
sense of sinister exoticism. In the context of my argument, though, it
becomes telling that, in World War II, Serbia was on the American side

*Cat People*    Framing, costume, and mise-en-scène associate Irena with the animalistic, the dark, and the exotic.

and not, therefore, an obvious historical choice for demonization.[46] A wartime suspicion of the foreign undoubtedly plays a role in the narrative's general opposition of American to exotic, but the specificity of Irena's Serb background returns to a familiar structure. Serbia, as I argued in the previous chapter, signifies as primitive and exotic within the twentieth-century Western discourse of Balkanism, the same logic of abjection that *Underground* works on. And so *Cat People*, too, places its fatal woman within the logic of the dark continent. None of the readings of the film take up this ideological structure of primitivism, other than implicitly in the chain of associations—woman/irrational/primitive/sexual—that operates in the various feminist analyses. As with the trope of the dark continent in feminist theory, the primitive and exotic space is a secondary marker of the strangeness of female sexuality. That Irena is Serbian functions analytically as a symptom of her excessive sexuality, even though narratively it is presented as a cause.[47]

But in *Zentropa*, the elements of this structure are reversed, and the sexuality of the monster/femme fatale is no longer primary but symptomatic of the primitive nature of postwar European space. The political duplicity of 1940s Europe, which is unable to be expressed fully in the historical narrative, recurs in the mise-en-scène of film noir and horror, and, as with the Italian melodramas, the body of the woman is the site of this projection. Katharina, like Irena, is figured as both femme fatale and monster, although her duplicity does not imply an excess of female sexuality; rather, like that of the romantic objects in *Il Postino* and *Mediterraneo*, her duplicity operates as a fetish, standing in for what cannot be seen. And what cannot be seen, in *Zentropa*, is the impossible space of the continent: the barely submerged history papered over with a discourse of civilization and a western definition of "Europe." As politics is displaced onto romance in the Italian films, here it is displaced onto the *amour fou* of the fatal woman, which stands in not for the optimism of the young nation but for the seduction of the dark continent.

Gender is the discursive space in which this historical logic becomes visible. The figure of the dark and mysterious woman is a placeholder for political and historical traumas that are textually unspeakable. And this is exactly Doane's argument about the cinematic dark continent, where the white woman figures the unspeakable difference of race. In *Cat People*, we have the Serbian woman, in whom Balkanism returns in a gendered economy in which primitivism and darkness operate not in the usual Balkanist discourse of masculinity and savagery, but hitched to the Hollywood visual economy of excessive female sexuality and the visible/invisible monster of the horror film. These disparate versions of otherness have a cinematic history of interconnection: the foreign, the un-European, the feminine, the primitive, the sexual, the thing that you cannot quite see or cannot quite know, the epistemological problem of the femme fatale. What changes in *Zentropa* is that Katharina is not locatable as un-European. She is German and, in terms of the film's geographic slippage, stands as an exemplar of Europe as a whole. Germany in 1945 is, for *Zentropa*, the center of and not the exception to the continent's dark history. Thus, the space of excessive femininity and geographic abjection moves west and north, becomes "whiter." In *Underground*, the space of Yugoslavia is abjected, precisely unable to be located within Europe. In *Zentropa*, the excessive part is not only in Europe but also at its center. It is too European. And in locating an excess not within Europe but *of* Europe, the film begins to reimagine the continent's visual geographies.

This shift in the structure of abjection is bound up with the discourse of the werewolf figure itself, which, as a signifier of that which is primitive in European space, has its own geopolitical history. While the werewolf is an enduring character in the horror film, the genre borrows from a specifically European mythology. Folklorist Adam Douglas traces the idea of the werewolf as both ancient and overwhelmingly European, and he describes the frequent occurrence of the figure in Scandinavia, Denmark, and Germany. And if the werewolf has symbolized the dangerous and the pre-modern throughout northern Europe, it has also been overlaid in Germany with more political meanings. In the seventeenth century, a guerrilla group called itself Wehrwolf (a pun on the words "werewolf" and "war"), and in the 1920s, a book about the group proved immensely popular with the nascent German nationalist movement, selling almost as many copies as *Mein Kampf.* A paramilitary group sprang up at around this time, calling itself Operation Werwolf, and it, in turn, influenced the Nazi group depicted in *Zentropa*, so that by the mid-twentieth century the werewolf had become a political figure, connected to ideologies of land and nationalism.[48]

According to Douglas, "The Nazis recognised the value of the group spirit engendered by these hunting societies: in the 1920s a secret right-wing terrorist group in Germany called 'Operation Werwolf' prosecuted political murders. . . . Goebbels revived the organization in the last days of the Second World War as an underground resistance movement, and Himmler gave a peptalk urging them to harass Allied lines of communication 'like werewolves.'"[49] Like the political landscape, the idea of the terrorist werewolf proves to have been given its contemporary meaning by a Nazi. Opinion has been divided among historians as to the extent to which these Werewolves really existed, but Perry Biddescombe argues the case in favor:

> A careful examination of surviving evidence shows that, contrary to conventional wisdom, there was in 1944–5 a string of guerrilla attacks aimed at both the enemy powers and the German "collaborators" who worked with the occupiers in maintaining civil government. The number of such incidents probably peaked in the spring of 1945, when bridges were destroyed by saboteurs, Allied and Soviet soldiers murdered and their vehicles ambushed, public buildings mined or bombed, and underground leaflets widely used to threaten domestic opponents of the defeated Nazi regime.[50]

Moreover, the political logic of the Nazi werewolf did not end in 1945 but returned to haunt the new Europe of the 1990s. In Russia, a neo-Nazi group calling itself the Werewolf Legion perpetrated various terrorist attacks throughout the decade and claimed to be opposed to "Jews, Communists and democrats."[51] The 1990s haunt the image of the 1940s, and *Zentropa*'s political Werewolf conjures both histories.

## Bloodsuckers

The terroristic adoptions of the werewolf name are not the whole story, for horror has a cultural history in which the werewolf, along with other European monsters, developed along geopolitical and ethnic lines. In horror, the monster is frequently abjected in bodily terms, disturbing the boundaries of human and inhuman. In addition to the cat woman and wolf man, there is the category of the undead—the zombie, vampire, or mummy—which offers perhaps the best-known type of monstrous abjection. As with the work on *Cat People*, these monsters have been theorized in feminist terms, by which the abject is connected to the feminine.[52] But, as *Cat People* demonstrates, there is also a geographic component to this logic, in which monsters such as the werewolf and the vampire have been coded in modern texts as ethnic outsiders, who come from distant countries and whose unhuman nature derives from their primitive origins, which disturb the boundaries of European-ness.[53]

To clarify the stakes of this generic history for *Zentropa*, it may be productive to compare it with another west European art film that rewrites the ideological history of a horror figure and also does so in relation to Nazism. *Dr. Petiot* (de Chalonge, 1990) is set during and after World War II in Paris and is loosely based on the true story of a wartime serial killer who murdered Jews. In the film, Petiot is a doctor who poses as a Resistance agent in order to acquire his victims. He seeks out east European Jews hidden in France, and, by promising to smuggle them to South America, he persuades them to come in secret to his house, where he kills and incinerates them. Like *Zentropa*, the film is predominantly an art film but also draws on the conventions of both the thriller and the horror film. The serial killer plot offers a crime narrative, in which the Nazi occupation allows Petiot free rein for his killing, and he is threatened with capture only after the liberation of Paris. While the crime narrative follows a more realist historical structure, however, *Petiot* is also a horror film in which the doctor is constructed visually and ideologically through the generic codes of the vampire.

The film connects the figure of the vampire to the politics of ethnicity in its opening sequence, in which Petiot watches a film program that begins with a newsreel. After a bland story about a Parisian bike race, the newsreel turns to an anti-Semitic story on "how to tell a Jew from a Frenchman." This propagandistic sequence establishes that the film takes place under Nazi occupation, but it also prefigures two central questions: the meaning of the opposition between Jew and Frenchman (foreigner and European), and the question of what you can see by looking. After the newsreel, the feature begins, a horror film called *Hangman's Castle*, about a Nosferatu-like vampire. At this point, Dr. Petiot stands up, and his shadow falls onto the screen, where it coexists in an uneasy two-shot with the image of the vampire. He then steps through the screen and reappears in the black-and-white diegesis of the vampire movie. He exits the castle, but what is found outside is not a generic horror landscape but a Parisian arcade and the doctor's own office. A shift back at the end of the sequence from black and white to color implies a return to the real world of Paris, but Petiot's seamless transition from vampire's castle to arcade implies that the whole film takes place in the fictional space of the movie, in a diegesis that includes vampires.

The connection of Dr. Petiot with the figure of the vampire continues visually. As he cycles to see his patients, he wears a black cloak that billows behind him in a style reminiscent of horror films. His skin is excessively white in a manner that suggests the undead and references a history of screen Draculas. And as he travels to see his patients at night, Petiot is frequently shot in dark streets and tunnels, where smoke, fog, and shadows imply a horror setting. Aurally, too, Petiot is connected to the vampire seen in the film within the film. In a scene in which he is arranging with a Jewish couple their "journey" to Argentina, the sound effect of sharpening knifes, last heard during the horror film, recurs on

*Dr. Petiot*    Petiot looks like a vampire bat in a shadowy nighttime Paris.

the soundtrack. And, of course, this effect points to the root of the film's narrative conflation of Petiot with Dracula: like Dracula, he is a charming and powerful figure who preys on those he can entice into his home, consuming them in ritual fashion.

But there is more at stake here ideologically than the horrific nature of the serial killer or a metaphoric comparison of vampire with Nazi.[54] In locating Petiot as a French vampire and his victims as east European Jews, *Dr. Petiot* opens up a critique, both of the generic history of the vampire figure and of the historical location of that figure in relation to the politics of ethnicity in twentieth-century Europe. If the European monster exists as a dark and primitive contrast to white European civilization, then nowhere is this more evident than in Petiot's primary intertext, *Dracula*. The vampire was, of course, not invented in Bram Stoker's novel, and like the werewolf it has a long history in various European countries. However, it is in the novel that the modern cultural discourse of the vampire was codified, a structure that has been more or less repeated in the many filmed versions. In the novel, Dracula is ethnicized first of all as Slovakian. There is a strong discourse of Balkanism in the descriptions of Transylvania as primitive and full of feudal peasants, guttural speech, and pre-modern superstitions. However, Count Dracula is also described in terms that were, in the nineteenth century, typically coded as Jewish. Thus, "his face was a strong—a very strong—aquiline, with high bridge of the thin nose and peculiarly arched nostrils; with lofty domed forehead, and hair growing scantily around the temples, but profusely elsewhere. His eyebrows were very massive, almost meeting over the nose, and with bushy hair that seemed to curl in its own profusion."[55] The count's Semitic features, like his east European origin, prove symptomatic of his bodily monstrosity. He looks human but is actually unhuman.

This logic of corporeal uncertainty, in which ethnicity can only be hinted at and the count's body is rendered abject while appearing human, rewrites an already existing ethnic discourse in terms of the horror genre. The European outsider, an abject figure who is part of Europe but yet not really part of it, is a central discourse in European anti-Semitism, which focuses on the uncanny quality of the Jew. Unlike a more clearly defined racial category, the Jew has been perceived as slippery: he or she does not provide a spatial boundary but appears within "civilization." And the Jew is not necessarily visibly distinctive; the obsession of the Nazis with mapping Semitic features or heritage resulted from the impossibility of recognizing Jewishness visually. (Hence the prominence in *Dr. Petiot* of the newsreel story on how to tell the difference between a Jew and a Frenchman. Such films have a historical basis in Nazi propaganda and are often cited in films about the Holocaust.) Thus, the Jew provides the central template in the late nineteenth and early twentieth centuries for the monster who looks like everyone else but may underneath be sinister and foreign. And this is not only a question of cultural or literary history, for the same social forces that enabled the Jew to turn into the vampire also produced the extremist ethnic ideologies and Western policies on "Europe" that led to the rise of Nazism.

So for *Petiot*, the connection of the vampire and the Nazi is not only metaphoric but historical. However, the film reverses the ethnic and geographic structure of *Dracula*, so the vampire is west European—Parisian, no less—and the innocent victims are east European Jews. While *Dracula* works to abject the Eastern and the less-than-European, Petiot makes explicit the historical stakes of this structure and renders excessive and horrifying a figure of the West. And a comparable strategy is in play in *Zentropa*, where the figure of the werewolf undergoes a reversal from primitivism to "civilization" and from abject outsider to the position from which such abjection takes place: while Petiot's vampire is narratively aligned with the Nazis, *Zentropa*'s werewolves literally *are* Nazis.[56] In both films, the center of Europe (according to the Western discourse of postwar European civilization) becomes the origin of horrific monsters, and in both this horror returns explicitly to its origins in the ethnic politics of European space.

But *Zentropa* produces a more complex and, indeed, contradictory logic than *Dr. Petiot*, where the figure of the werewolf, unlike that of the vampire, comes doubly politicized by the various nationalist groups in Germany. Thus, what is in *Petiot* a neat reversal of white European and Jew, monster and victim, becomes in *Zentropa* a messier narrative, less susceptible to allegorical resolution. In part, this difference arises because the werewolf is a less obviously ethnicized figure than the vampire and can, as the existence of the Nazi Werewolves demonstrates, be construed more easily in positive terms than can the vampire. But more important than these factors is the question of historicity, for while *Petiot*'s narrative remains bounded by the war and by its symbolism of the Holocaust, *Zentropa* demands that the postwar past be read in relation to the present.

The film insists on the pastness of the narrative, and from Leo's hypnosis to the intertextuality of the film noir style, it frames the image of postwar Europe in terms of the look back. The reversed abjection, in which Europe and not its others must be seen as monstrous and primitive, is also implicated in this temporal structure. The horrific image of 1945 is haunted not only by its immediate past but also by its close future, in which the fifty-year splitting of Europe reiterated the logic of abjection. The East again became the site of difference, and in the West the ideological production of "European-ness" in the postwar years relied implicitly on abjecting discourses of civilization, Western-ness, and whiteness. In the context of German reunification, from which point *Zentropa* looks back, these logics began to take on new forms. For this reason, in the new Europe, neo-Nazi Werewolves recur in the former East, and fears of contamination in the European Union led to the politics of "fortress Europe." For *Zentropa*, the postwar doubles back fatally on the post-Wall.

## Surimpression

I have been arguing that *Zentropa*'s version of 1945 is textured by many levels of historicity: the contemporaneous history of genres, the past of war and of ethnic discourse, and the future of East and West, splitting and unification. But this density of reference, in which the film's Germany comes to center Europe and its troubled history, does not produce narrative space as a locus of historical origin, nor does it render the relationship of present to past fully legible. In all these instances, historical truth is defined as that which is hard to see. I would like to turn, now, to this question of vision and to think about history in relation to the cinematic image. For *Zentropa*, the relationship of past to present is figured primarily as a problem of vision: How do you see 1945 from the point of view of 1991? If 1945 in Germany is not a year zero, not a point of origin, but rather an in-between moment, fatally compromised by both its past and its future, then there can be no single image that could stand, indexically, as the truth of postwar Europe. Thus, *Zentropa* forces a radical engagement with the continent's impossible space, and it does so both narratively and visually. The problem of geopolitical space becomes a problem of cinematic space.

What is most striking in *Zentropa*'s art-cinematic form is its layering of discrete images, where a technologically sophisticated form of matte effect combines several superimposed and/or back-projected images in a single frame. This layering takes place in almost every shot in the film, combining color film with black and white, 16 mm with 35 mm, and wide angle with telephoto lenses. Thus, the foreground image usually has a different quality from the background; for example, in a scene by the river, Kate is in color, while the river behind her is filmed in black and white and shot at an entirely different angle from the straight-on image of Kate. Furthermore, image layers are frequently manipulated: in addition to the difference between black-and-white and color film, there is colorization, where part of the image may be sepia toned or highlighted in red. (The shot of the train's communication cord is an example.) The layers are also frequently projections, the quality of the back-projected image made visible by the flickering and degradation of the film. And it is not only a question of foreground versus background: von Trier describes adding up to seven layers of images, each shot with a different lens and different kind of film.[57]

The material differences among these layers preclude the production of a single, stable diegesis, and, instead, there is a proliferation of narrative spaces. Most obviously, there is a visible gap between foreground and background where color, film stock, and perspective do not match. All of the film's exteriors were shot without actors, so in these scenes there is always this disjuncture in which the characters and their locations never share the same actual space. Even within the shot/reverse shot structure, layering prevents the construction of a seamless space. In the sequence of Ravenstein's assassination, for example, there is a shot through a train compartment window, from behind the victim's shoulder, showing a medium frontal angle of the boy shooting at him. The image is monochrome, but the compartment window is a color

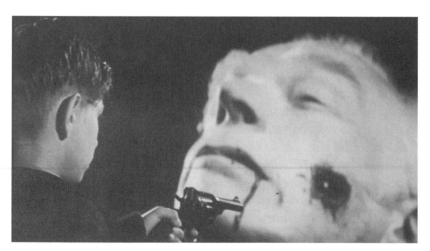

*Zentropa*    The boy in the foreground is in color, while the assassination victim in the background layer is back projected in black and white.

layer that becomes visible as blood spatters against it. We cut to a reverse angle shot, from over the boy's shoulder. Here he is in color, but Ravenstein is now a back-projected black-and-white image, in extreme close-up and disproportionately large. While the shot structure implies a coherent narrative space, the layers of the image work against it. These multiplied narrative spaces, which are readable in relation to one another but remain apart, provide a visual correlative of the voice-over, which stands in proximity to, but is never part of, the diegesis. It, too, implies another space, one that is related to that of Germany in 1945, but is never fully integrated into it. Like the voice-over, the image layers produce a non-space that is narratively meaningful and yet unlocatable, refusing to cohere into a singular form.

The proliferation of spaces finds its obverse in moments of transition between sequences, which often work to conflate spaces that are not, according to the narrative, the same. For example, the scene in which Kate and Leo stand by a riverbank ends with a two-shot of the couple, with the river projected in the background. Rather than cutting to the next scene, the two-shot remains and the background image dissolves from water to another back projection, that of a minister conducting a marriage ceremony. Leo and Kate appear not to have moved, but the new scene takes place in a different space, that of the church. Thus, transitions become graphic, and superimposition becomes a form of editing. Here, the classical logic of space is undermined not only by too many spaces but by too few, where the same image apparently represents two different spaces.

In *Figures de l'absence*, Vernet analyzes superimposition in both historical and semiotic terms, honing in on the specificity of its formal effects.[58] He distinguishes between two forms of *surimpression*: one corresponding to the English word "superimposition," and the other to back projection. In superimposition, he argues, there is a disproportion between the two elements in the frame, which works against the production of a coherent diegetic space. This effect could be disruptive but is usually classically contained—for example, in a psychological superimposition, where one of the images represents the thoughts of the character seen in the other image. There are examples of this form of classical superimposition in *Zentropa*, such as the scene discussed earlier in which Leo sits in the train corridor, worrying about Katharina. There, the background dissolves into the word *Werwolf*, which is precisely what Leo is thinking about at that moment. Or, to take another of Vernet's examples of classical containment, there is the slow dissolve, in which two images are briefly visible simultaneously without any undermining of realism. *Zentropa* uses this technique, too—for example, in a dissolve from the front of the train moving through a tunnel to Kate's face as she sleeps inside it. In both cases, the disproportion is "explained" by the two images not actually representing a single space.

Vernet describes back projection as distinct from superimposition because in it there is no disproportion between the two layers of image, and the effect is supposed to remain invisible. In a classical use of back projection, the two images represent the same space, and the identity of perspective and scale enables the effect to place objects together that could not be filmed together. The most common example of this kind of projection is the view from the car window, in which characters appear to be driving in an exterior location that is, in fact, a separate image projected onto the internal frame of the windshield. *Zentropa* contains one of these conventional shots: when Leo sits in the car of the Werewolf leader after Max Hartmann's funeral, the view from the rear window is a back projection. However, the effect is made obvious because the projected image is grainy and degraded, and the lengthy static shot emphasizes the appearance of an internally framed movie. This visibility points to the difference between *Zentropa*'s uses of superimposition and the classical logic outlined by Vernet. For while in classical cinema, back projection seeks to remain invisible and superimposition is visible only because it does not threaten the coherence of realist space, *Zentropa* renders both effects visible and uses both to fracture the integrity of its narrative spaces.

*Zentropa*    A classical use of back projection is rendered visible, as the composition emphasizes the internal screen.

In *Zentropa*, superimpositions are not contained as momentary evocations of two spaces at once but represent the same space through layers of image with different scales, perspectives, film stocks, or colors.[59] There is not the motivated break in diegetic space that Vernet's examples produce but, instead, a demand that narrative space be read as singular despite the disjunctive effects of superimposition. And the opposite takes place with back projection, which already represents a single space but is made to do so visibly, exchanging a special effect that was designed to efface itself with a formal effect that emphasizes the internal screen. This shift recapitulates the tension between what can and what cannot be seen—or, perhaps, what should and what should not be seen. Back projection, like the view from the train windows, should not be seen, yet here it is made spectacular. Ultimately, the distinction between back projection and superimposition disappears, at least as far as their narrative use goes, and both become part of a visually spectacular yet semiotically troubling multiplication of space.

As a result of this distinctive use of superimposition, not all of Vernet's analysis can be applied to *Zentropa*. His consideration of layering as a psychological metaphor, for example, is unhelpful in regard to *Zentropa*'s more radical restructuring of the image. What is important is his placement of *surimpression* as a textual figure that, while often a part of classical realism, alters the mechanisms of representation. For Vernet, it is part of a cinema-specific discourse of absence, which undermines representation even as it produces certain narrative meanings. Thus, he claims that "the flattening effect of superimposition is paradoxical since more representation (two or more spaces in one frame) gives less representation by the supression of visual depth perceived and by the projection on a single plane of two perspectival images at least."[60] More representation is always and at the same time less representation, and this idea begins to define the doubling process by which *Zentropa*'s layers can produce both too much to see and nothing to see.

Vernet attributes a certain radicalness to the *surimpression*, arguing that this push and pull of more and yet less representation necessarily makes the spectator aware of the apparatus. This claim may be overly general, and while *Zentropa*'s superimpositions can more easily be argued to foreground the apparatus than a more classical text could, it does not necessarily follow that any ideological conclusions can be drawn from this effect. Stephen Heath describes style as an area of "controlled excess,"[61] and in the context of art cinema, this caveat is especially significant. We cannot consider this self-conscious spectacularity to be radical when it is exactly this kind of visual excess that defines art cinema as a genre. Nonetheless, while it is not enough simply to claim that the film's mise-en-scène is excessive, it is crucial to examine the specific textual work done by its style.

Like the spectacular effects discussed in the preceding chapters, *Zentropa*'s projected layers "fall out" of the narrative, breaking with verisimilitude and producing a fetishistic relationship to the spectacular image. But unlike the landscape or the underground tunnel, their effect is primarily located not in mise-en-scène per se but in the formal manipulation of the image. Here, Andrew Higson's idea of spectacle "falling out" becomes almost literal, as layers of image are separated from the body of the text. In Mulvey's terms, spectacle momentarily breaks with Renaissance perspective, producing a flat space in which surface replaces narrative depth.[62] *Zentropa*'s superimpositions do this almost constantly, emphasizing the surface quality of each layer. To take one example, during the scene of Leo in the car of the Werewolf leader, there is a shot/reverse shot in which no single layer is able to stand unmarked as a direct representation of three-dimensional space. We first see Kate, outside, from Leo's point of view: she is in color, against a background that is back-projected black-and-white film. We then cut back to a two-shot of Leo and the Werewolf in the car, in which Leo is now in color and the other man is back projected, in a grainy and degraded black and white. While the spectator can and must read narrative across these disparate layers, each codes primarily as a surface, in which the materiality of the film preempts any sense of depth.

One of the results of this texturing is a difficulty in producing identification, so the spectator is distanced from the mechanisms of classical narrative absorption. Certainly, there is some identification with Leo, from whose point of view the narrative takes place, at least in terms of knowledge. (And in the previous example of layering, it is Leo's color, 35-mm, unprojected image that comes closest to being formally unmarked.) But identification with Leo as an optical and narrative point of view is weak, and the constant emphasis on the spectacular surfaces of each projected image prevents a full effect of suture. Heath, reading Jean-Pierre Oudart on suture, claims that "cinema as discourse, that is, is seen as implicated in loss, the loss of the totality of the image, the loss of the extreme pleasure of absorption in the image as the spectator is set as the subject of the film: 'the cinema is characterised by an antinomy of reading and pleasure.'"[63] Thus, suture regulates the relation of spectacle and narrative, Imaginary and Symbolic, with, for Oudart at least, spectacle and pleasure slipping into one structure. What happens with *Zentropa*'s superimposition, then, is that the undermining of suture does not operate to disorient the spectator in regard to narrative—the plot is still quite clear—but, rather, to reorient the spectator toward spectacle.

## Spectacle, Historicity, and Absence

Privileging spectacle has both a spatial and a temporal significance. For Heath, the key operation of suture is the changing of space into place that classical cinema performs. But *Zentropa* does not let this happen, and the back-projected images remain in separate spaces, never entirely stitched into a singular diegetic place. And this question of place, for *Zentropa*, is always also a question of location, where the ideological vectors of the term have both a cinematic and a geopolitical inflection. To the extent that *Zentropa* prevents the production of cinematic place, it also unbalances its representation of geographic place. Where there is no single narrative space, there also can be no geographic specificity, and the disjunctures involved in layers of superimpositions prevent the articulation of a coherent location for Europe.

Thus, we can read the layers of projection in *Zentropa* as a formal replication of the cellar/surface structure in *Underground*: both imagine impossibly split spaces in which a singular image of nation is precisely what is impossible. Like *Underground*, *Zentropa* refuses the national landscape image of neorealism, but the two films make international as well as national claims on these spaces. Just as *Underground*'s cryptic cellar cannot be imagined as part of a Western concept of Europe, so *Zentropa*'s projected spaces are, in the supposed center of the continent, insurmountably fractured. The image layers that touch but cannot be merged refract the divisions and impossibilities of postwar Europe—suggesting a history that runs from the zoning of occupied Germany, through the splitting of Eastern and Western Europe, to the imperfect present of unification (German) and union (European). And the ghostly spectacle of projection, the uncanny doubling in which one image is always an absent presence, reinscribes the splitting of Europe in terms of the circuits of desire that the "real" West projects onto (and receives from) its insubstantial other. In both films, Europe is defined by the spaces that cannot meet. However, in *Zentropa*, what Vernet calls the vertiginous space of the *surimpression* effects a more radical deconstruction of European unity, in which the ambivalent identifications and impossible location of "Europe" seep into the very form of the image.

And there is also a temporal element to this mode of spectacle that, in *Zentropa*, in turn, makes a claim on the historical. The pressure of the spectacular, which is for Heath a complex play of imaginary pleasures within the symbolic discourse of narrative, is affective to the extent that it stages an outside to the discursive logic of costumes, mise-en-scène, story, and so on. It is always a "field of absence,"[64] the space that classical narrative sutures. Insofar as *Zentropa* incompletely sutures the spectator, that absence takes on a greater presence. Moreover, it is not only the imperfection of suture as a general category that produces an effect of absence but the particular nature of *surimpression*. For Christian Metz, superimposition performs a unique doubling, combining fusion and separation, metaphor and metonymy, and, most important, enunciative and evocative markers.[65] Vernet takes up this idea of grafting evocation onto representation—in other words, turning signification into affect—as a way of thinking: superimposition as a figure of absence. The doubling of the superimposed or projected image redoubles also the gap between photograph and reality: like the photocopy, the projected image is another step removed from the profilmic, and it is the sudden visibility of this gap that is evocative.[66]

Vernet suggests a temporality to this effect, not in the structure of absence itself but in the history of cinema. Superimposition, he argues, has become such a cliché that it inevitably signifies a nostalgic historicizing of a lost classical form. For him, it is, above all, this encrustation of reference that proves evocative, as a signifier of film history as much as any specific content.[67] This element of referentiality is undoubtedly at work in *Zentropa*, where formal and textual references to films of the 1940s abound, and where classical uses of superimposition and back projection are revisited. The film has little to be nostalgic about, but there is, nonetheless, an emotional investment in the forms and images of the past, whereby spectacle negotiates between immersion in the past and knowledge of the present's difference. *Zentropa*'s superimposition produces exactly this oscillation in the pleasure *of* the historical effect and yet also the more distanced and more ambivalent pleasure *in* the effect.

Sean Cubitt also analyzes special visual effects in terms of the history of cinema, arguing that most media theorists read digital spectacle nostalgically, as evidence of postmodern loss. Citing Jean Baudrillard, Fredric Jameson, and Paul Virilio, he identifies a narrative of "previously . . . but now,"[68] which in cinematic terms refers to a previous investment in the real and the human, to be contrasted with the current vogue for the digital and the spectacular. While he clearly does not buy into these readings entirely, Cubitt uses them to trace a broad context for contemporary special effects, historicizing postmodern theories rather than applying them directly. He links the theoretical narrative of nostalgia to the claim that postclassical cinema has turned away from narrative and performance and toward special effects as an attempt to regain a sense of awe. Thus, spectacle is connected intimately with loss as a symptom of postclassical cinema's relationship to the history of the medium. This idea is a useful one, because it historicizes postmodern media theories, enabling a less pessimistic reading of the simulacral image. By interrogating films like *Independence Day* (Emmerich, 1996), Cubitt suggests that contemporary effects also have a textual temporality, which he thinks of in terms of the sublime. For him, however, this effect is a temporality out of time, with no access that he can see to history. His analysis is compelling, but I would contend that in different uses of effects technology we can discover the relationship to history that Cubitt leaves open but undiscovered in the blockbuster. *Zentropa* explores this temporality of loss, for it uses effects within the context of a historical narrative, so the contemporary impetus to recapture the awe of early cinema is coarticulated with the direct representation of an earlier historical moment. Effects in the history film take on even more keenly the attempt to make real what is not real: the hypercathexis involved in bringing an image of what has been lost to light.

Thus, alongside the narrative history of Europe, *Zentropa* thematizes the postmodern narrative of cinematic loss, in which it becomes difficult to conceive of the real and the indexical in relation to a digital age of spectacular effects. The difference between the 1940s and the 1990s is the historical gap at issue narratively, and this difference is also coded as a problem of the image. If 1945 is a central moment of European political history, it is also the moment of neorealism and the ruin film, when the truth-claim of the cinematic index exerted its greatest ideological pressure. Correspondingly, if 1990 involves the loss of cinematic certainty in the digitally altered image, then it also implies the ambivalent politics attending the collapse of European Communism, the reunification of Germany, and, indeed, postmodern theories themselves. And what is significant is that *Zentropa* not only textualizes but problematizes this narrative of before and after. There is no year zero, and the ruin film cannot show the unmediated truth of Germany. As a consequence, the image of 1990 is no less true for its spectacular manipulations, and it becomes necessary to read historical difference through rather than against the nostalgic investment in a cinematic or a political "before."

This work of textualization accounts for the way in which the *Zentropa* uses effects technology, as compared with a film like *Independence Day*. While *Independence Day* works best if you do not think about the digital (even as you take extratextual pleasure in its technological splendor), *Zentropa* works at all only to the extent that the effect problematizes the status of the image. While you cannot film alien spaceships without effects, you can film a man standing on a train, and to create such an everyday image out of back projections is to destabilize rather than to extend representation. In other words, *Zentropa*'s effects do not work to make the impossible look real but to render the everyday less real. This is different from the use of effects in Hollywood blockbusters because while we know that the alien spaceships in *Independence Day* are effects, we do so because we know that there are no aliens, not because we can see a visual gap. Content excepted, they look real. Or if they do not, then this is a failure of effects technology, the criticism of the spectator who found the film unconvincing because the effects looked like effects. In *Zentropa*, seeing the cracks is precisely the point; in fact, it is in these cracks, in the interstices of superimposition, that historicity takes place.

The way that *Zentropa*'s effects draw attention to their distance from the real shows how the temporal break produced in the back-projected image not only is contingent on the cinematic history of the trope but also derives from its textual production. While the classical use of the figure minimizes its disjunctive effects, in *Zentropa* the back-projected image draws attention to its manipulation, its reprojection, its distance from the profilmic. And yet, in the moment of this distance, it simultaneously reminds us of that which is absent, drawing attention to the indexical precisely by pointing out its attenuation. There is a shot of Katharina standing in front of a river, where the "wrongness" of the superimposition produces a momentary impression of indexicality in regard to the background image. The water running behind Kate is seen from a "wrong" perspective, in a close-up rather than a medium shot, and from a straighter angle than that of the foreground. But this disjuncture forces the spectator to see the water in detail, to focus on the materiality of its movement, on the small twig that directs the stream into a V shape. In noticing the "wrongness" of the water, we take note of something we would otherwise have passed over as background: we direct our attention to the exact location and physical presence of the water. And this effect of indexicality depends on the doubled gap between projected image and the profilmic: it becomes a fragment of the real precisely because of its compelling absence.

Like the auratic image of the tree and the branch, these moments of indexicality cross the pleasure of the spectacular with the shiver of loss. The projected images are a constant reminder of the apparatus, of the

*Zentropa*    A fragment of the real: the background image of the river is shown in disjunctive close-up.

temporality of cinema by which that which is represented is absent. And absence defines the historical image. As with the Italian films, a temporal effect of spectacle overlays and complicates the historical discourse of narrative. This is clear in a shot of Leo's uncle talking to another railway worker in the station. The two men are framed in a medium shot, in black-and-white, bright film, while the background, showing people working and a building partly obscured by smoke, is projected, also in black and white, but in a grainier, old-looking film stock. Proportion is kept between the two layers, and yet the image is haunted by its temporal and historical gaps. The background image looks like old film, degraded and scratchy as a document of the past. Its immediate effect is to make the characters in the foreground appear stagy, their claim on history new and inauthentic. This effect is reminiscent of Siegfried Kracauer's "real trees," as the indexical pull of the background usurps the costume-based realism of the narrative's historicity. But what disrupts the narrative in this case is not the materiality of nature but that of film itself. A pastness based on signification is momentarily supplanted by a pastness based on affect, on the temporal loss implied by the doubly inaccessible space of the projected "old" film.

In this instance, the footage itself is not actually old, and its content is not historically punctual: its effect is purely a function of the image. In these moments,[69] the doubled and projected image produces historicity formally. Thus, in the railway scene, even within the diegesis of 1945, the background image connotes age. This is not because of its con-

tent, which is only an appropriately atmospheric setting, with no historically significant details, but because the projected image itself implies
pastness. Seen as a piece of film, it compels in its indexicality: this comes
from the past. Emplaced within the narrative space of 1945, it suggests
a *mise-en-abyme* of temporal distance: we look at an image of the past,
within which there is an image of the past, and so on. We can never
reach the truth of historical space, only multiplying markers of historicity, and the moment of this realization produces a sense of the impossibility of the past. The constant refusal of symbolic cohesion textualizes
historical absence, the impossibility of seeing a place and time of European postwar origin. Just as Leo cannot quite reach the real space of Germany, so the spectator cannot quite reach the real space of a historical
diegesis. History becomes not only a question of representation but also
one of haunting.

Jousse describes the subject of the film as *trucage*,[70] which in French
means both "cinematic special effects" and, more generally, "conning"
or "duplicity." These visible superimpositions are examples of *trucage* as
effects, but they also suggest a work of duplicity, understood as a discourse on doubling and impossibility. The layers of back projection in
which there can be no single diegetic truth follow the same logic as the
split body of the werewolf and the duplicitous one of the femme fatale.
And haunting is another kind of splitting, where past and present, or
East and West, come into proximity without ever quite touching. The
relationship of Europe in 1945 to Europe in 1990 is a similarity but also
a disturbance: there is no comfort in this proximity.

## Conjuring the European Subject

To some degree, the look back in *Zentropa* is of the same nature
as that in the Italian films and in *Underground*: the period from 1945 to
1948 in Germany was once again a time of great political upheaval, with
the optimism that comes with the institution of a new republic. And in
this instance, the slide from the moment of possibility into a Cold War
stagnation could not be clearer, with the breakup of Germany into East
and West. Soviet control in the East mirrored conservative hegemony in
the West: like Italy, West Germany's postwar governments were dominated by the Right, and despite various resurgences of opposition
throughout the 1960s and particularly the 1970s, it was not until reunification that the political landscape was subject to radical change. Thus,
as in Italy and Yugoslavia, *Zentropa*'s production was contemporary with

the collapse of the postwar order. In the wake of its end, the film returns to the historical moment that led to its inception.

Further, the nature of the change in Germany invited widespread meditation on the nation's relation to the past. While the wars in the former Yugoslavia demanded a response that left little immediate space for analysis, and the "clean hands" scandals in Italy were not necessarily viewed in their historical context, the fall of the Berlin Wall was first and foremost experienced as a historical shift, prompting an intellectual and cultural reexamination of Germany's place in Europe. This reviewing was also a form of haunting, in which the new Germany was compelled to return to the specters of its shared Nazi past, as well as those of Communism in the East.[71] But perhaps most significant in this context is the debate over the past and future of the Left, in which the lost moment of potential in 1989 to 1990 recapitulated a similar missed opportunity in 1945 to 1949. The lost cause that was the postwar hope for a neutral Germany, aligned neither with the United States nor with the Communist bloc, was briefly resuscitated in the discourse of the Third Way.

Before reunification, there had been support, particularly in the German Democratic Republic (GDR) and among leftists in the West, for a new German constitution and a system that would be "neither capitalism nor Stalinism but genuine and democratic socialism."[72] With reunification, the space of Germany returned closely to its postwar borders, but this expansion was also a loss for the Left, since, of course, the former GDR was simply incorporated into the West, and the Third Way degenerated into a watered-down form of postsocialist party politics. There proved to be little space for engagement with the politics of the anti-Communist Left. Thus, while the events of November 1989 could be regarded as only a positive change, the discourse of reunification inevitably entailed an experience of loss and ambivalence for the European Left. As Peter Schneider wrote in 1991: "Doesn't it look as if developments have proved our worst enemies right?"[73] The fear of appearing to be on the wrong side, to having been consigned to obsolescence alongside Soviet Communism, stymied the west European Left in the early 1990s, and it was in Germany that this discourse was most overtly articulated.

Andreas Huyssen describes the mood of the post-unification East in terms of melancholia and nostalgia, while Matthias Greffrath argues that the loss of a leftist utopia had occurred fifty years before and that German melancholia was thus misplaced.[74] In both cases, the national-political discourse of 1990 is contingent on a relationship to the postwar past and a relationship defined in terms of loss. And for Greffrath, the experience of 1990 is basically a misreading, a projection of the past onto the present in which the proximity of these images allows for a political slippage. It would be more accurate, I think, to say that while the political losses of the postwar order had their origin in the 1940s, only in the wake of the collapse of that order can they be felt and understood as such. And the proximity of these two historical spaces—their sudden geographical and ideological closeness, and yet the disjuncture of their essential historical distance—is what *Zentropa*'s structure of projections and splittings makes visible.

*Zentropa*'s textual work inscribes the ambivalent relationship between Germany now and Germany then, but it also maps a fractured and recursive form of historical engagement for Europe in general, along with a no-less-fractured European space from which to look. There is the disjuncture between East and West Germany and that between Eastern and Western Europe: the "painful border" of Emir Kusturica, in which two geopolitical spaces are proximate but structurally unable to meet.[75] Further, as the reunification debate suggests, the question about the future of Germany was also, both in 1945 and in 1990, a question about the future of Europe. The years following the fall of the Wall were also those leading up to the Maastricht Treaty, which inaugurated the European Union. And this is not so coincidental. As Ron Pryce points out, the uncertain status of postwar Germany led to the defensive formation of the European Coal and Steel Community,[76] while the crisis of reunification spurred moves toward economic and political union. Thus, German space is historically central to the formation of Europeanness, and there is another proximity between the image of Germany and the uncertain self-image of Europe.

Moreover, for a coproduced film, there are other national identities at play. There is a relationship between Germany and Europe, but there are also relationships between France, Sweden, Poland, and, most strikingly, Denmark and Europe. As its producers inadvertently say, *Zentropa* is primarily a northwest European film, and the structure of splittings and impossible spaces also refers to the disjuncture between Denmark and Germany or that between the smaller west European countries and Europe as a whole. Denmark became somewhat notorious within Europe in 1992, when its populace voted against the Maastricht Treaty— Desmond Dinan describes a national "ambivalence toward European integration."[77] The final agreement gave Denmark "opt-outs" from many of the treaty's clauses, and jokes circulating in the early 1990s described the new Europe as incorporating a footnote that read "except Denmark." Thus, the main location of the film's coproduction also implies an ambivalent proximity to Europe, a discourse on inside and outside, European and not-European.

The result of these spatial and temporal doublings is a very different form of historical engagement, in which the coproduced film maps a European rather than a national subject position.[78] The film does not speak as a German film; it does not address a national subject; and, most important, it does not engage a specifically German relationship to history. Instead, it attempts to address a European subject and to articulate both the horrors and the losses of a European history. Of course, this European subject does not actually exist: it is another void, another of the impossible spaces around which *Zentropa*'s non-space coheres.[79] To project the precise spectator position whose impossibility the film simultaneously narrates demands a constantly shifting relationship to historical desire and spectacular affect. This is what makes *Zentropa* such a compelling case study for the question of a European cinema at the moment of inception of the so-called new Europe. The film hails a European subject while calling attention to the textual and ideological pitfalls of doing so. Moreover, it stages the historical exigencies of such an identity for all Europeans.

Here we can pin down *Zentropa*'s relationship to the discourse of mourning, for without a coherent subject position, there can be neither an affective historical image nor a place from which to cathect to such a lost object. Thus, there is no beautiful landscape, no image that could stand in for the losses of the European past. In mapping the terrain of splits and projections, the film at once acknowledges this impossibility and yet attempts to construct a European space, like Frankenstein's monster, out of disparate scraps of image. There is still a historical look back from a position of loss, insofar as the film reiterates the failures of the postwar order. However, this look produces neither the melodrama of mourning nor the stuckness of melancholia, because it cannot envisage a subject who mourns. It has no apparatus of nostalgia with which to look back and no lost object to mourn. As the monster analogy suggests, history in *Zentropa* inevitably entails horror.

But instead of refusing the discourse of loss altogether, *Zentropa* constructs history as a double loss, looking back on a history that it also needs to debunk. There is no single Europe at the moment of reunification, and there was no single Europe before partition. What centers the historical image is exactly this knowledge—that it is necessary to return to the postwar past despite its feet of clay. *Zentropa* structures the impossibility of creating a truly European image, but in staging the collocation of the continent's disjunctive historical spaces, it begins to imagine the stakes in an idea of Europe outside the dominant Western discourse. And if there is none of the emotional charge of mourning, neither is the film's historicity simply ironic or affectless. Like the Italian films, *Zentropa* was released at the moment when change became imaginable, and its production of European space in terms of impossibility speaks to the "where now?" moment of the European Left, in which the fall of Communism and the collapse of the German Third Way exerted a troubling pressure on any ability to conceive of a future. Any engagement with Europe as a point of identification is, at this moment, necessarily ambivalent. Thus, the film does not invoke historical affect—it is not a claim on "our" history—but, rather, it stages the problem of affect for the yet-to-be-produced European subject.

Spectacular images in *Zentropa* entail loss despite themselves, producing a haunted relationship to the image of a past in which the film nonetheless refuses to believe. Thus, the film textualizes the impossibility of this historical relation, splitting the diegesis with disjunctive layers of film. Along with the other films I have been considering, then, *Zentropa*'s historical image at once speaks of the ideological impact of the past and of its contemporary status as beautiful image. It circles the spectator from the historical moment to the moment in the present from which history can be experienced as such. In *Zentropa*, this constant circling articulates an ambivalent spectator position, at once invested in the losses of the past and yet critically distanced from any form of identification with its image. The impossibility of reaching a singular image of historical truth reflects back on the impossibility of representing the European present.

This circling structure connects Metz's reading of superimposition to the dialectical image. The layered and projected image in *Zentropa* is at once enunciative and expressive, producing specific historical meanings, short-circuiting representation altogether, and creating a dialectical relationship between history as signification and history as the affective pull of spectacular loss. What remains affective is the missed opportunity in which things could have been different: Leo's brief and quickly fatal period of optimism in the moment before Europe was split. But there is no longer any belief in such optimism, either with regard to understanding that past or, for the European Left in 1990, about the future. It is this moment—of desire for political desire—that the impossible spaces and half-structured mournings of *Zentropa* describe.

The idea of the dialectical image describes this imbrication of past and present, which goes beyond a nostalgic or a horrified relation to the past, and beyond the political melancholy of the present, to demand that the spaces, histories, and identities of postwar Europe be thought anew. Benjamin argues that "while the relation of the present to the past is purely temporal, the relation of what-has-been to the now is dialectical: not temporal in nature but figural,"[80] and in *Zentropa*, the figuration of spectacular space subtends a historical tension. For Benjamin, a dialectical approach to history transforms the present as much as the past, and, indeed, he describes Konvolut K of *The Arcades Project* as "an attempt to become aware of the dialectical . . . turn of remembrance" and as "an experiment in the technique of awakening."[81] The collocation of memory-work and the reemergence of consciousness is familiar in *Zentropa*'s context: a frequent trope of the fall of the Wall was a "return to history" or an "awakening" for Eastern Europe. But temporality, like space, is open to reversals. In its spectacular projections, its reiteration of the stakes of splitting at the moment of unification, and its historical return to a nightmare landscape from which there is no awakening, *Zentropa* suggests that such radical changes are no less necessary for the European West.

# 6 Toward a Theory of European Space

The post-Wall moment in European history is transitory: as the events of 1989 grow more distant, politics and culture develop in new directions. However, the historical films that emerged at this time not only are significant as reflections of European identity in a particular place and time, but also bring into focus what Walter Benjamin calls a constellation—a pattern of historical, aesthetic, and critical discourses—that enables us to read history alongside the present. The particular constellation illuminated by post-Wall history films not only allows us to see European postwar histories otherwise, but, just as important, provokes new readings of contemporary cinema, of film theories, and of the politics of representation.

First, we find in these films the obverse of what is usually assumed about heritage film, or the postclassical art film. Against critiques that such films have abandoned political and aesthetic radicalism, this approach locates in them a post-Wall politics of space and time. Such a politics cannot be read along the old models of countercinematic modernisms: just as new theories of location emerged in the 1990s, so did new cinematic practices. Some of these practices have been examined in detail in the preceding chapters: the staging of nostalgia, the remapping of space, the coarticulation of the indexical and the spectacular. Taken cumulatively, these emergent forms suggest another heading for European cinema and a framework within which such a heading might be analyzed. In place of a binary of popular cinema and art cinema (or related pairs such as memory/history and nostalgic/political), we find an interpenetration of these terms that opens up a more nuanced relationship to place, space, and history. In the European context, this approach enables connections to be drawn across previously discrete categories—not only between nostalgic heritage films and difficult art films, but also between the former East and West European cinematic traditions. This work is crucial to developing an understanding of contemporary European cinema, since the old models prove decreasingly useful as Europe's political and cultural spaces merge and transform. If we are to escape from the various hierarchies of "Europe," we must reimagine space and history beyond West European art cinema.

This is why the articulation of cinematic space with geopolitical space is so important. We do not locate the new European cinema only in films that thematize continental politics or in those that illustrate new modes of production. Instead, we begin from the image, moving from the space of the frame to that of geography. Only by taking seriously contemporary textual practice can we unpick the post-Wall discourses of homelessness and belonging. In contrast to the vaguely symbolic images of the Euro currency, we must discern Europe in the specific, the concrete, the detail. The political question, of course, as with the money, is which detail or, rather, whose detail. But we do not need to restrict ourselves to this essentially nationalistic form of ownership discourse. Instead, we may map diverse textual cartographies, following the traces of East and West, North and South across cinematic landscapes that will frequently exceed the spaces of Europe.

In redrawing this map, we find a way out of a theoretical impasse: how to read cinematic spectacle politically today. The question of spectacle has recurred throughout this book—from the pretty pictures of the heritage film to the controversial linkage of visual excess to Serbian war crimes. But "spectacle" is a slippery term, at once foundational to many theories of cinema and yet surprisingly rarely defined or directly theorized. Laura Mulvey contends that the figure of the woman is central to visual pleasure,[1] but where else does cinematic spectacle inhere? How is spectacle itself to be defined? To analyze contemporary European film is to address this question, for both heritage film and art cinemas are largely defined in terms of a visual aesthetic. Easily categorized as spectacular (neo-gaudy, *la belle image*), these films demand that we consider the location of spectacle in national as well as gendered images.

One of the main disincentives to thinking anew about spectacle in contemporary cinema is the way in which, post-1970s and -1980s feminist theory, the dominant critical context for understanding spectacle has been overwhelmingly negative. While some studies have thought spectacle productive in relation to genre (horror, the musical, porn, costume drama), this line of approach has been superseded in recent years. Instead, spectacle has been understood, explicitly or implicitly, within a particular Marxist model that derives from debates on modernity and mass culture, but has been mobilized as part of the discourse on post-modernity. Thus, Fredric Jameson calls the cinematic image porno-graphic on the opening page of *Signatures of the Visible*. And thus Paul Virilio, even while criticizing Marxism, makes a strikingly similar case when he claims that the photographic image is pornographic. He goes on to chart the rise of "parasitic images" in Europe, "phatic images" like advertising, that force the subject to look and command attention without being legible. In this discourse, spectacle in film is a part of Guy Debord's famous "society of the spectacle," in which the oversaturation of images materializes capitalist ideology, preventing any engagement with social meaning.[2]

There are endless examples of this notion of spectacle in recent film studies. Michael Rogin claims that "spectacle is the cultural form for amnesiac representation, for spectacular displays are superficial and sensately intensified, short lived and repeatable."[3] In a more extended analysis, Wheeler Winston Dixon's book *The Transparency of Spectacle* explicitly updates Debord in a polemic against spectacular film of all kinds and in favor of computer images and the "directness" of Third World cinemas. Of European cinema, he says, "The few foreign films that attain moderately wide release in the United States are lavish cos-tume spectacles," going on to say that these kinds of viewing experi-ences enable people not to think but to be "coddled" and "tranquilized."[4] And it is not only recent films that are critiqued: in a discussion of 1950s German war films, Anton Kaes argues that despite the films' claim to be antiwar, "the images [of battle] overpower any critical intentions; moral messages evaporate when up against visual pleasure and spectacle."[5] So dominant, so taken for granted, is this understanding of spectacle, that few critics question its use.

But there is a problem here, and it lies in a slippage between the Marxist concept of spectacle and the specifically cinematic one implied by the term "visual pleasure." For the spectacle criticized by Debord, or, indeed, circulated in earlier debates around mass culture and moder-nity, is not specifically cinematic—not even necessarily visual. Debord uses the image as a trope that allows him to identify a much broader social regime, and the debates of the Frankfurt School around mass cul-ture are by no means simply condemnatory. It is not that these theorists are useless for film studies but that the concept of spectacle employed by them is not the same as cinematic spectacle, and the differences are important. Moreover, ignoring the differences will produce an implicitly gendered theory, for what gets elided in these critiques of spectacle is exactly the feminist insistence on the meaningfulness of visual pleasure.

Thus, while spectacle for Mulvey does remove distance, it no more tranquilizes than does narrative. As a central mode of spectatorial engagement with the film text, what it differs from is narrative identification, not disengaged critique. Hence, within feminist theory, spectacle cannot be a bad object in this simple manner and may, in fact, be positive insofar as it breaks down, or temporarily suspends, the patriarchal sadistic narrative. The power of the image for feminist theory is, after all, the power of the woman in the image. It is suggestive that while Mulvey is fairly even-handed in her dissection of both narrative's and spectacle's patriarchal functions, more recent critics have reverted to a knee-jerk opposition to spectacle that recalls the anti-imagistic strain in Marxism even when it does not come from a Marxist perspective. It is somewhat depressing for feminism that even when a topic other than gender is under discussion, ideological value must be couched in the gendered terms of spectacle = bad, narrative = good.

The gap between these theoretical models opens up a space for critique. A feminist method can read spectacle as productive of meaning and can interrogate its ideological valences without falling prey to the implicit sexism of antispectacular approaches. For this theoretical heading, contemporary European cinema forms a revealing case study. It is only within the current field of cinematic possibility (where spectacle connotes at once art-cinematic merit, Hollywood emptiness, and postmodern style) that national cinemas could mobilize the spectacular in quite the ways that they do. Films like *Mediterraneo* connect women's bodies to the national landscape in a way familiar from many national cinemas, but they also reinscribe this figure in the landscapes of postclassical global cinema and post–Cold War politics. When we consider the textual strategies at play in European films, it becomes clear that spectacle, far from being empty, structures complex negotiations of space, place, and history. To reevaluate theories of spectacle is also to rethink conventional wisdom about much contemporary cinema. But, equally, the practices of post-Wall films enable a new assessment of spectacle and its theoretical significance.

And this theoretical mapping is a historical work in itself: film theory's engagement with spectacle, with the relationship of aesthetics to politics, forms part of the same historical map of Europe that the films engage. Benjamin's influential account of the aestheticization of politics derives from his experience of Nazism, of course. Equally, postwar European critical engagements with the politics of the image can be read through the histories of the Cold War, West European Marxisms, and a primarily British and French relationship to capitalist film culture. That new theoretical models should emerge in relation to the end of the Cold War and the invention of the "new Europe" should not surprise us. Such intellectual developments are part of the same historical process that produced new cinematic movements and new political groupings.

Thus, the ways in which post-Wall films renegotiate European history and cinematic spectacle are not separable. When Benjamin discusses the dialectical image, his point is to reimagine the work of historiography and the political necessity of thinking about both past and present. In a letter to Theodor Adorno, he writes that he hopes he will have a firm position in the Marxist debate, "if only because the decisive question of the historical image will here be fully developed for the first time."[6] The constellation illuminated by these films compels us to rethink the historical image after Cold War Marxism. It makes clear that the recurrence of a relationship between 1945 and 1989 is not coincidental but articulates significant changes in the construction of European history, politics, and the image. We must reflect on the meaning of these changes for European film theory as much as for film history.

Stephen Barber argues that contemporary European cinemas tend to move beyond Europe, citing such postcolonial narratives as Claire Denis's *Beau Travail* as exemplary.[7] Encounters with the postcolonial Other are certainly a common theme, but we can also interpret this impetus as a critical warning: we must read for European and cinematic specificity, and yet we must always look outward, resisting essentializing logics. In this spirit, then, I would like to end with two examples that in some way stand outside the limits of "European cinema." One is a non-European film, and the other is European, but not a film. These texts might point to pathways among disparate histories and cultural forms, or they might demand other headings entirely, unassimilable by the institutions of "Europe" or "cinema." In either case, they will signal borders to this map of European cinema, leaving open to question the border's value.

The first example is a Taiwanese film, *The Hole*, directed by Tsai Ming-Liang in 1999. The film is typical of a certain kind of postclassical transnationalism: it was made as part of French distributor Haut et Court and German-French television network Arte's "2000 as seen by . . ." series of films, in which well-known filmmakers from around the world were asked to make films about the impending millennium. Thus, the film was a coproduction (Taiwan and France) and was made with global distribution in mind. The series included films by Abder-rahmane Sissako, Walter Salles, and Hal Hartley, placing Tsaï's film squarely within a commercial logic of international art house auteurs. But the "2000 as seen by . . ." series was also a work of mapping, an attempt to limn its own constellation of cinematic geography: New York, Rio de Janeiro, Mali, Belgium, Taipei. The global system in fragments, frozen in time.

If the film series reminds us of Jameson's geopolitical aesthetic, com-pulsively aping the late capitalist global system through its alienated spaces and transnational flow, then *The Hole* condenses these paranoid networks into one building in Taipei. The film takes place on the eve of the millennium, in an apocalyptic Taipei that has been evacuated because of a mystery contagion that, we are told, makes people scuttle and hide like cockroaches. Few inhabitants remain in the rain-soaked housing projects, but the unnamed protagonists are among the strag-glers. The man lives in one apartment; the woman, in the flat directly downstairs. Because of the constant rain, water begins to leak into the downstairs apartment. A botched plumbing job leaves a hole in the floor. Soon, the man expands the hole and begins penetrating the space below with eyes, legs, and umbrellas. Like *Underground*, *The Hole* turns everyday spaces into uncanny and fantasmatic ones, with the trope of the hole simultaneously staging alienation and the disturbing scene of its rupture.

There are other suggestive points of comparison. Unable to be fully national, combining Chinese Communism with an industrial center of global capitalism, Taiwan in the 1990s also troubles regional and national spaces. The film's spatial logic seems at first to describe the labyrinthine impossibility of postmodern Taiwan. Like the films of Edward Yang, or indeed Tsaï's earlier works, *The Hole* presents Taipei's space as incoherent, desolate, and bleakly commodified.[8] The man visits his old store in a deserted mall, leaving out accumulating tins of food for a solitary cat. Back in the apartment, commercials for noodles mix with news stories about the millennial disease. The hole in the floor seems to reiterate this economic breakdown at the domestic level. The man makes misguided attempts at bodily connection through the hole, while the woman begins to demonstrate disturbing symptoms of infection.

The film surprises, however: into this dark and crumbling diegesis emerges the spectacular and utopian space of the musical. While the man's fantasy involves penetrating the hole to his neighbor's flat, this narrative is interspersed with musical numbers that represent the wo-man's fantasy. In these scenes, bright lighting and colorful costumes transform the building into the stage of a glamorous 1950s romantic musical. As with the traditional musical, these spectacular production numbers "fall out" of the narrative, creating a striking contrast with the dramatic storyline. But they also use spectacle in a way similar to that of the European films: to map geopolitical space differently and to rework a dominant politics of representation. The inclusion of the musical scenes creates a series of binaries that complicate the logic of urban alienation: upstairs/downstairs, male/female, reality/fantasy, narrative/production number, apocalypse/utopia. In juxtaposing the apocalyptic space of the abandoned city with the utopian space of the musical romance, the film suggests another form of dialectical image.

And, like the European films, this staging of spectacle is also historical. *The Hole*'s musical scenes feature songs by Grace Chang (also called Ge Lan), a popular Chinese film star of the 1950s and 1960s. Chang's films, including *Mambo Girl* (Yi, 1957) and *Air Hostess* (Yi, 1959), speak of a significant moment of transnational influence in Chinese modernity. For example, *The Wild, Wild Rose* (Wang, 1959) features Chang singing Bizet's *Carmen* in Mandarin, and both the film's musical numbers and its modernist production design combine Chinese, European, and South American styles. *Air Hostess* thematizes the glamour of air travel in the 1950s, with Chang playing the eponymous heroine. Set in various Asian tourist locations (Hong Kong, Thailand, Singapore), the film uses the travel narrative to connect transnational musical styles (for example, the song "Oh Calypso") to touristic film spectacle (for example, sequences of Chang visiting temples and waterfalls). Chang's career peaked in the late 1950s and early 1960s, and her star persona draws heavily from this moment of cross-cultural pollination. Her vocal style and dancing seamlessly mesh Chinese and Western popular song. In addition, she almost always played the good girl, domesticating foreign culture within a traditional model of Chinese womanhood. Thus, for *The Hole* to refer to her films is to look back at a period of emergent globalization and to recall that period's most optimistic self-image.

Thus, although *The Hole* is far removed from the histories of European film, we can trace connections across the global networks of contemporary film culture. Both industrially and aesthetically, the film makes us question the ways that disparate places engage with their national, regional, and global histories. While we cannot simply transpose European structures to Asia, we must be aware of how film histories, no less than capital, ebb and flow beyond the borders of Europe.

The second example returns to Europe but is a television program rather than a film. In 1996, British television screened a nine-part miniseries called *Our Friends in the North* (Jones, James, and Urban), a drama narrating the history of the British Left from the 1960s to the present through the travails of a group of friends from the northern English city of Newcastle. Each episode takes place a few years after the previous one, and most are set in the year of a general election. The episodic structure of televisual narrative presents a significant difference between this text and European films of the same period; for one thing, the program's nine seventy-minute episodes enabled a level of political and historical detail that would be hard to fit into a feature-length film. We could compare *Our Friends* with *Underground*, but without the breakneck pace, or with *Cinema Paradiso*, but filling in the historical blanks. One result of its televisual form, then, is a more gradual narrative of political decline, as week by week, national politics intersects with the lives of the four protagonists.

British television has a long history of this kind of political drama, and the debates it has engendered are not unrelated to the European history film. The 1970s Ken Loach and Tony Garnett series *Days of Hope* opened up popular memory debates in the United Kingdom, and the television film *The Ploughman's Lunch* (Eyre, 1983) became a canonical text for discussions of postmodern history films. Similar issues of realism, memory, and political engagement have influenced filmic and televisual histories; moreover, there is a great deal of overlap in the industries. Loach, who wrote *Days of Hope*, went on to make political history films like *Land and Freedom*, while television companies like the BBC and FilmFour produced many of the most influential British films of the 1980s and 1990s. Like *The Hole*, though, *Our Friends* is interesting not only for its production context. In its textual processes, too, the series suggests a relationship to the spatial and historical concerns of European cinema.

First, there is the strange rhetorical slippage of its title. While the reference to "the north" at first seems to denote Newcastle, the northern English hometown of the protagonists, it is in fact a reference to political corruption in Africa. The quotation is from a secret memo sent from Shell to British Petroleum in the 1960s, discussing the need to protect the oil industry against the effects of decolonization: the "friends in the north" are here the colonial Rhodesian government. This context is never referred to within the program's narrative, which takes place during the time period of African decolonization, but which focuses almost entirely on domestic political corruption. This slippage offers at once an analogy of British and colonial power relations and a neat doubling of the terms of geopolitical advantage. The British North, like the colonial

South, is historically peripheral, its working-class protagonists making their way to the metropolis in order to advance. Thus, the title maps a colonial space onto a national one, overwriting a British history of working-class realism with a postcolonial logic.

Second, *Our Friends* structures history through a narrative of mourning. Along with the European heritage film, it contends that political histories and national spaces exert an emotional pressure that can be textualized only through the temporality of loss. The political mood of the United Kingdom in the mid-1990s was similar to that in many other European countries, where the end of state Communism had produced confusion for the Left and the promise of the "new Europe" seemed uncertain. As with the Italian films, *Our Friends* looks back to a moment when change seemed genuinely possible—in this case, through the radicalization of party politics in the 1960s. By gradually outlining the corruption and decline of this movement, the program's serial narrative stages this history differently from films about the period, using viewers' memories of the previous episodes as a central temporal mechanism rather than flashbacks or temporal elisions. Nonetheless, the final episode concludes with a demand on the nostalgic memories of the spectator, as all four characters meet again for the first time since the first episode, forcing spectatorial awareness of all that has changed in the intervening years. Political losses are compressed into the melodramatic structure of personal losses, and a moving effect occurs as the end credit music begins.

Each episode had ended with a song that was in the charts the year in which the episode takes place—already a powerful index of popular memory and nostalgic investment in the recent past—and the final episode ends with the Oasis song "Don't Look Back in Anger." While this sentiment more or less matches the half-reconciliation of the protagonists, it stands as a direct counterpoint to the apparent logic of the historical narrative, in which the failure of the leftist project seems to demand precisely a reaction of anger. But, of course, the song itself is a historical reference, citing John Osborne's play *Look Back in Anger* (also filmed by Tony Richardson in 1958), the ur-text of postwar British working-class culture. And the cultural shift from *Look Back in Anger* to "Don't Look Back in Anger" describes the political losses incurred between the 1960s and the 1990s. In negating the title, the song performs the impossibility of Osborne-esque indignation in the cultural climate of the 1990s. And yet, insofar as it mourns that loss, it undermines it, producing at the very least a melancholic desire for political anger. The impossibility of the song's demand, alongside its narrative necessity, is what provokes the viewer to tears, collapsing melodramatic affect with political mourning.

*Our Friends*, then, implies that the logic of post-Wall European cinema finds echoes in other cultural forms. Among television, theater, and popular music there are also textual flows, and in mapping the cultural spaces of the new Europe, it may be necessary to negotiate between cinematic specificity and interdisciplinary passages.

This concatenation of textual effects characterizes post-Wall European cinema—a desire for history, tinged with a double-edged nostalgia for the political losses of that same history, and an investment in the spectacular image as the place where an ambivalent relationship to the past can be expressed. European cinema in the 1990s may be negotiating a form of historiophilia, a somewhat masochistic pleasure in the distance of the historical other, of that which has been lost. But this pleasure is never solely nostalgic, for its investment in history is always at the same time an engagement in the present, and its use of spectacle is a simultaneous mapping of political space. Textual reiterations of post-war history form a central strand in a cinematic reworking of the location and meaning of "Europe," at the time of its political transformation.

For Europe, the early 1990s provided a unique moment of potential for change, even as they demanded mourning for the losses of the previous fifty years. It is in the particular form of this in-between moment, what *Berlin.killer.doc* calls "the interim," that we can trace a thread among these diverse films. Speaking of the post–Cold War chasm between east and west Europeans, Slavoj Žižek suggests that "perhaps, however, this double disappointment, this double failed encounter between the ex-communist dissidents and Western liberal democrats is crucial for the identity of Europe; perhaps what transpires in the gap that separates the two perspectives is a glimpse of a Europe worth fighting for."[9] In constructing relationships between past and present in terms of spectacle, space, and history, European cinema crystallizes the potential of this moment, forming a constellation that enables us to think both backward and forward to a different Europe.

# Notes

## 1. Mapping European Cinema in the 1990s

1. Duncan Petrie, ed., *Screening Europe: Image and Identity in Contemporary European Cinema* (London: British Film Institute, 1992).

2. Jacques Derrida, *The Other Heading: Reflections on Today's Europe*, trans. Pascale-Anne Brault and Michael B. Naas (Bloomington: Indiana University Press, 1992), 44.

3. Mark Betz, "The Name Above the (Sub)Title: Internationalism, Coproduction, and Polyglot European Art Cinema," *Camera Obscura* 16:1, no. 46 (2001): 1–44. Betz surveys a range of often conflicting historiographic work on the coproduction. Despite the difficulty of finding exact figures, he discerns trends in his statistics: coproduction is found in Italy from 1943 and in France from 1946. What is a trickle in the immediate postwar years becomes a major mode of production by the 1950s and a dominant form in the early 1960s. In France, for example, forty-seven national films were made in 1962, along with forty-one coproductions. In Italy, 13 coproductions in 1952 rose to 155 in 1964.

4. Examples could include *Bhaji on the Beach* (Chadha, 1993), *Welcome to Sarajevo* (Winterbottom, 1997), and *La Haine* (Kassovitz, 1995). Similar issues were discussed in sociology and politics. See, for example, Brian Jenkins and Spyros A. Sofos, eds., *Nation and Identity in Contemporary Europe* (London: Routledge, 1996).

5. Well-known *beur* films are *Cheb* (Bouchareb, 1991) and *Salut Cousin!* (Allouache, 1996). Turkish German films include *Head-On* (Akin, 2004) and *Berlin in Berlin* (Çetin, 1994). Critical work that touches on these topics includes Leslie Adelson, "Touching Tales of Turks, Germans, and Jews: Cultural Alterity, Historical Narrative, and Literary Riddles for the 1990s," *New German Critique* 80 (2000): 93–124; Hamid Naficy, *An Accented Cinema: Exilic and Diasporic Film-*

*making* (Princeton, N.J.: Princeton University Press, 2001); and Christian Bosséno, "Immigrant Cinema: National Cinema—The Case of Beur Film," in *Popular European Cinema,* ed. Richard Dyer and Ginette Vincendeau (New York: Routledge, 1992), 47–57.

6. Derrida, *Other Heading,* 12–13.

7. Paul Gilroy, *The Black Atlantic: Modernity and Double Consciousness* (Cambridge, Mass.: Harvard University Press, 1993). In an argument that has been highly influential, Gilroy posits that while blackness is not essential, anti-essentialism leaves little room for theorizing the experience of race. His proposal of anti-anti-essentialism is not a refutation of the critique of essence, but, like Gayatri Spivak's "strategic essentialism," is an attempt to move beyond the stale and limiting essentialist/anti-essentialist debate. See also Gayatri Chakravorty Spivak, "Subaltern Studies: Deconstructing Historiography," in *In Other Worlds: Essays in Cultural Politics* (New York: Routledge, 1987), 197–221.

8. Slavoj Žižek, "A Leftist Plea for 'Eurocentrism,'" *Critical Inquiry* 24 (1998): 988, and "Multiculturalism, or the Cultural Logic of Multinational Capitalism," *New Left Review* 225 (1997): 49.

9. Etienne Balibar, *Politics and the Other Scene* (London: Verso, 2002), and *We, the People of Europe? Reflections on Transnational Citizenship,* trans. James Swenson (Princeton, N.J.: Princeton University Press, 2004).

10. The category of space is too broad to reference exhaustively, but key works include André Bazin, *What Is Cinema?* trans. Hugh Gray, 2 vols. (Berkeley: University of California Press, 1967, 1971), and Stephen Heath, *Questions of Cinema* (Bloomington: Indiana University Press, 1981).

11. Thomas Elsaesser, "Cinema—The Irresponsible Signifier or 'The Gamble with History': Film Theory or Cinema Theory," *New German Critique* 40 (1987): 71.

12. It is open to debate whether the heritage film can be considered a genre proper or, rather, a category of film that exists across several genres. It is often discussed as if it were a genre, and my use of the term reflects this common categorization.

13. Andrew Higson, "Re-presenting the National Past: Nostalgia and Pastiche in the Heritage Film," in *Fires Were Started: British Cinema and Thatcherism,* ed. Lester Friedman (London: University College London Press, 1993), 109–29; Antoine de Baecque, "Le Cinéma d'Europe à la recherche d'une forme," *Cahiers du Cinéma* 455–456 (1992): 78–79.

14. Richard Dyer, "Feeling English," *Sight and Sound,* March 1994, 17–19.

15. See the debates on popular memory in *Cahiers du Cinéma* 251–252, 268–269, 275, 278, particularly Michel Foucault, "Film and Popular Memory," *Cahiers du Cinéma* 251–252 (1974): 25.

16. Michel Foucault, "Entretien avec Michel Foucault," *Cahiers du Cinéma* 251–252 (1974): 8 (my translation).

17. Ibid., 13.

18. This historical look back was particularly fraught in France, as revisions of the "myth of the Resistance" ruffled feathers on both the Gaullist Right and the Communist Left. The commissioning and then practical abandonment by the tele-

vision network Office de Radiodiffusion Télévision Française (ORTF) of Marcel Ophüls's epic documentary of collaboration, *The Sorrow and the Pity* (1969), is a key turning point in this history. See, for instance, Naomi Greene, *Landscapes of Loss: The National Past in Post-War French Cinema* (Princeton, N.J.: Princeton University Press, 1999), and Keith Reader, "Reconstructing the Past Through Cinema: The Occupation of France," in *Reconstructing the Past: Representations of the Fascist Era in Post-War European Culture*, ed. Graham Bartram, Maureen Slawinski, and David Steel (Keele, Eng.: Keele University Press, 1996), 177–85.

19. See, for instance, John Caughie, "Progressive Television and Documentary Drama," *Screen* 21, no. 3 (1980): 9–35.

20. John Caughie, "Halfway to Paradise," *Sight and Sound*, May 1992, 10–13.

21. Terence Davies has continued to address historical topics that emphasize class issues and the lives of women, albeit in an American context. *The House of Mirth* (2000) adapts Edith Wharton's novel in which a middle-class woman has little to fall back on without the support of wealthy men. Less art cinematic in style, it nonetheless ends on a painterly reference, with the suicidal protagonist posed in a tableau reminiscent of a painting by John Singer Sargent.

22. While the original sense of the word "nostalgia," coined in Switzerland in the seventeenth century from the Greek *nostos* (return home) plus the Latin *-algia* (pain, longing, or suffering), was a painful desire to return home, it is the term's more popular usage that has dominated discourses on European history films. Nostalgia is popularly perceived to be a pleasurable look back, in which the emotional engagement in the past overrides any friction evoked by historical loss. The older meaning still has force, however, as we see in examples like Davies's films, where the look back to the past is always caught up in pain.

23. See, for instance, Sander Gilman, "Is Life Beautiful? Can the Shoah Be Funny? Some Thoughts on Recent and Older Films," *Critical Inquiry* 26 (2000): 279–308; Imre Kertesz, "Who Owns Auschwitz?" *Yale Journal of Criticism* 14, no. 1 (2001): 267–72; and Maurizio Viano, "*Life Is Beautiful*: Reception, Allegory, and Holocaust Laughter," *Jewish Social Studies* 5, no. 3 (1999): 47–66.

24. Michel Chion, "Quiet Revolution . . . and Rigid Stagnation," *October* 58 (1991): 69–80.

25. Dogme itself continues to produce significant European films, including *Mifune* (Kragh-Jacobsen, 1999) and *Italian for Beginners* (Scherfig, 2000). It is also influential as a loose production center, with Lars von Trier's Zentropa coproducing non-Dogme films in various countries, the Trollhattan studio bringing productions into Denmark, and Dogme as a movement spreading across the globe. Outside of Dogme, there have been many other significant variants on European new realisms, including the brothers Luc and Jean-Pierre Dardenne in Belgium and Erick Zonca in France.

26. Dogme manifesto (available at: http://www.dogme95.dk/menu/menuset .htm).

27. Fredric Jameson, *Postmodernism; or, The Cultural Logic of Late Capitalism* (Durham, N.C.: Duke University Press, 1995); Miriam Hansen, "Early Cinema, Late Cinema: Transformations of the Public Sphere," in *Viewing Positions: Ways of*

*Seeing Film*, ed. Linda Williams (New Brunswick, N.J.: Rutgers University Press, 1994), 134–52.

28. As Priya Jaikumar argues with regard to Michael Powell and Emeric Pressburger's *Black Narcissus* (1947), however, even the European colonial narrative can stage the breakdown of this system ("'Place' and the Modernist Redemption of Empire in *Black Narcissus*," *Cinema Journal* 40, no. 2 [2001]: 57–77). Moreover, in this film the historical crisis of colonial space is staged through the spectacular mise-en-scène of Himalayan Mopu, with excessively detailed costume and production design, as well as colorful (gaudy) sets, embodying the madness that sweeps the pristine white nuns.

29. Homi Bhabha, *The Location of Culture* (New York: Routledge, 1994).

30. Ackbar Abbas, *Hong Kong: Culture and the Politics of Disappearance* (Minneapolis: University of Minnesota Press, 1997).

31. Pam Cook, *Screening the Past: Memory and Nostalgia in Cinema* (New York: Routledge, 2005), which includes an essay on *In the Mood for Love*.

32. Franco Moretti, "Kindergarten," in *Signs Taken for Wonders: Essays in the Sociology of Literary Forms*, trans. Susan Fischer, David Forgacs, and David Miller (London: Verso, 1997), 157–81.

33. Bhabha, *Location of Culture*, 154.

34. Ibid., 152–53.

35. Mark Mazower, *Dark Continent: Europe's Twentieth Century* (New York: Knopf, 1999), 398.

36. Cited in Stephen Brockmann, "The Reunification Debate," *New German Critique* 52 (1991): 4.

## 2. The Dialectic of Landscape in Italian Popular Melodrama

1. Martin Warnke, *Political Landscape: The Art History of Nature*, trans. David McLintock (London: Reaktion Books, 1994), 1–2.

2. Walter Benjamin, "The Work of Art in the Age of Mechanical Reproduction," in *Illuminations*, trans. Harry Zohn, ed. Hannah Arendt (New York: Schocken Books, 1969), 241.

3. A typical example is John Lyttle's review: "'The English Patient' Has 12 Oscar and 13 BAFTA Nominations. But, Asks John Lyttle, Why All This Fuss over a Dressed-up Costume Drama with Nowhere to Go?" *Independent*, February 27, 1997, 10.

4. Other examples could be *Belle Epoque* (Trueba, 1992), *La Reine Margot* (Chéreau, 1994), *Hedd Wyn* (Turner, 1992), and *Europa Europa* (Holland, 1990).

5. Andrew Higson, "The Heritage Film and British Cinema," in *Dissolving Views: Key Writings on British Cinema*, ed. Andrew Higson (London: Cassell, 1996), 233.

6. Andrew Higson, "Re-presenting the National Past: Nostalgia and Pastiche in the Heritage Film," in *Fires Were Started: British Cinema and Thatcherism*, ed. Lester Friedman (London: University College London Press, 1993), 109–29.

7. Sue Harper, *Picturing the Past: The Rise and Fall of the British Costume Film* (London: British Film Institute, 1994).

8. Peter Aspden, "Nuovo Cinema Paradiso," *Sight and Sound*, February 1994, 62.

9. Julian Graffy, "Il Postino," *Sight and Sound*, November 1995, 49.

10. Peter Aspden, "Mediterraneo," *Sight and Sound*, April 1991, 50.

11. Vincent Canby, "'Cinema Paradiso': Memories of Movies in a Movie," *New York Times*, February 2, 1990, 15, and "Roundelay of Love on an Isle in Wartime," *New York Times*, March 22, 1992, 48; Jean A Gili, "Le Facteur: Un poète amateur contre l'injustice du monde," *Positif* 423 (1996): 58.

12. I am interested in the closeness of scholarly to journalistic criticisms, because it seems that their similarity speaks of the apparent obviousness of this genre, and of the perception that the accusations of melodrama and unhistorical- ity do not require any further interrogation. Perhaps because these films are not exactly melodramas in the sense of women's pictures, the body of feminist theory that has insisted on a more ideologically complex reading of melodramatic struc- tures is rarely brought to bear on these films, which can be safely dismissed as reactionary to the extent that they are sentimental or nonrealist.

13. Susannah Radstone, "Cinema/Memory/History," *Screen* 36, no. 1 (1995): 34–47.

14. Quoted in ibid., 34. See also Fredric Jameson, *Postmodernism; or, The Cul- tural Logic of Late Capitalism* (Durham, N.C.: Duke University Press, 1995).

15. Radstone, "Cinema/Memory/History," 41.

16. Ibid., 37. A different interpretation is offered in Millicent Marcus, *After Fellini: National Cinema in the Postmodern Age* (Baltimore: Johns Hopkins Univer- sity Press, 2002), 201. She argues that the film's use of old movie clips does indeed contain political friction, whereas *La terra trema* fails to raise the social conscious- ness of the Giancaldo audience.

17. Radstone, "Cinema/Memory/History," 43. For Benjamin, experience could be categorized as either *Erlebnis* or *Erfahrung*. *Erlebnis* is typical of experience in modernity and consists of fragmentary sensations that never form a coherent whole. Examples might be the mass media, the shocks and jolts of the crowd, and factory labor. *Erlebnis* is simply lived through, without meaningful interaction. *Erfahrung*, by contrast, names a more authentic process of experience, in which meaning is transmitted and maintained. An example would be the tradition of sto- rytelling. Radstone's connection of *Erfahrung* and storytelling to *discours* and *Erlebn- is* and the novel to *histoire* is certainly neat, but within the context of cinema this linkage seems to leave room for only the most unclassical texts to be progressive; any text that does not eschew realism altogether will inevitably produce a historical metadiscourse and so, by her standards, slide into *histoire* and preclude *Erfahrung*.

18. Richard Dyer, "Feeling English," *Sight and Sound*, March 1994, 17–19; Hig- son, "Re-presenting the National Past."

19. Higson, "Re-presenting the National Past," 109.

20. While connecting heritage films to the rise of a right-wing version of national heritage in the 1980s undeniably has a good measure of truth to it (at least

in the United Kingdom), Higson's next step is inadequate. Criticizing nonrealist films for not being realist is as unhelpful as the claim that realism is the only way to produce a more politically engaged film culture. A counterexample might be Dogme '95, which is concerned with realism and authenticity but does not appear to tie them to any political radicalism.

21. Higson, "Re-presenting the National Past," 119.

22. Dyer, "Feeling English," 18.

23. Higson, "Re-presenting the National Past," 113.

24. Ibid., 120.

25. Aspden, "Nuovo Cinema Paradiso," 62.

26. It is instructive in this regard to compare Italian cinema and its reception with German films. While much New German Cinema dealt directly with Nazism, German films have also dealt with the aftermath of Hitler and have considered German history and identity in the postwar years. Perhaps because German history is better known, or is always already politicized, it would be rare for a German historical film to be criticized as apolitical purely for dealing with the postwar years. It is also telling that Aspden feels a British film would inevitably carry the baggage of colonialism while an Italian film could claim no such weight.

27. Palmiro Togliatti's famous *svolta di Salerno* (Salerno turn) generated a great deal of discussion among those on the Left as to whether it was too great a compromise to work with the discredited government of Pietro Badoglio, which had collaborated with the Fascists, or whether it was more important to push for a republic or to compromise and concentrate on forming a government. Certainly, though, the creation of the Partito Nuovo enabled the Communist Party to become the major left-wing opposition party in Italy in the postwar years, comparable less to other Communist Parties than to the Socialist, Social Democratic, and Labour Parties in the rest of Western Europe. See Lawrence Gray, "From Gramsci to Togliatti: The Partito Nuovo and the Mass Basis of Italian Communism," in *The Italian Communist Party: Yesterday, Today, and Tomorrow*, ed. Simon Serfaty and Lawrence Gray (Westport, Conn.: Greenwood Press, 1980), 21–36.

28. Elizabeth Wiskemann, *Italy Since 1945* (London: Macmillan, 1971), 136.

29. Spencer M. Di Scala, *Italy: From Revolution to Republic, 1700 to the Present* (Boulder, Colo.: Westview Press, 1998); Gray, "From Gramsci to Togliatti"; Muriel Grindrod, *Italy* (New York: Praeger, 1968); Norman Kogan, *A Political History of Postwar Italy* (New York: Praeger, 1981); S. J. Woolf, ed., *The Rebirth of Italy, 1943–50* (New York: Humanities Press, 1972).

30. Di Scala, *Italy*, 273.

31. Quoted in P. Adams Sitney, *Vital Crises in Italian Cinema: Iconography, Stylistics, Politics* (Austin: University of Texas Press, 1995), 2. This summary is not quite as paranoid as it may appear: recently released government documents have revealed the extent of U.S. covert operations in Italy, which because of its geographic position and strong Communist Party was felt to be a particular danger during the Cold War. Anti-PCI propaganda was paid for by the Central Intelligence Agency (CIA), and during the 1970s, terrorist acts were engineered in order to destroy support for the radical Left. See Vittorio Bufacchi and Simon Burgess, *Italy*

*Since 1989: Events and Interpretations* (New York: St. Martin's Press, 1998). For a sophisticated interpretation of the relationship between Pasolini's films and the political structures of postwar Italy, see Angelo Restivo, *The Cinema of Economic Miracles: Visuality and Modernization in the Italian Art Film* (Durham, N.C.: Duke University Press, 2002).

32. Mark Gilbert, *The Italian Revolution: The End of Politics, Italian Style?* (Boulder, Colo.: Westview Press, 1995), 6.

33. Volodia Teitelboim, *Neruda: An Intimate Biography*, trans. Beverly J. DeLong-Tonelli (Austin: University of Texas Press, 1991), 332.

34. *Cinema Paradiso* was released in 1989, *Mediterraneo* in 1991, and *Il Postino* in 1994. The fact that two of these films were released before the emergence of the *mani pulite* crisis prevents them from being read simply as a displaced reaction to political events. Rather, their narrativization of a need to look back to the postwar years functions as part of the cultural shift that led up to the collapse of the First Republic and, indeed, set the conditions within which the breakdown could become possible.

35. Sarah Waters, "'Tangentopoli' and the Emergence of a New Political Order in Italy," *West European Politics* 17, no. 1 (1994): 169–82.

36. The PCI was far from following Moscow policy directives, and for much of this period it was closer to the French Socialists than to the Eastern bloc.

37. A good example of the way in which *partitocrazia* was quite naturalized in Italian culture is the structure of the RAI television network, in which the three state channels were allocated to a party each, according to relative importance. In this *lottizazione* (allocation), RAI Uno, the main entertainment and news channel, was controlled by the DC; RAI Due, a similar but less popular channel, was controlled by the PSI; and the PCI was given the consolation prize of RAI Tre, the arts and education channel, which, of course, had substantially lower ratings. This system affected budget, editorial, and programming decisions, as well as employment, because only those with the correct party membership could expect to be hired at each channel.

38. Bufacchi and Burgess, *Italy Since 1989*; Martin Bull and Martin Rhodes, "Between Crisis and Transition: Italian Politics in the 1990s," *West European Politics* 20, no. 1 (1997): 1–13; Donald Sassoon, "Tangentopoli or the Democratization of Corruption: Considerations on the End of Italy's First Republic," *Journal of Modern Italian Studies* 1, no. 1 (1995): 124–43; Alexander Stille, "Badfellas," *New Republic*, August 10, 1992, 12–13.

39. *Tangenti* are common bribes or kickbacks, and as Milan was uncovered to run on a system of corruption, it was nicknamed Tangentopoli, or Kickback City.

40. Stille, "Badfellas," 12.

41. "'Clean Hands': Who's Next?" *Business Week*, March 8, 1993, 57.

42. Andrew Phillips, "Decline and Fall," *Maclean's*, March 22, 1993, 22–24.

43. Bettino Craxi was convicted in absentia and died in exile in Tunisia, while Giulio Andreotti was acquitted of both sets of charges after two lengthy trials in Milan and Palermo.

44. Giuseppe Turani and Cinzia Sasso, quoted in Stille, "Badfellas," 12.

45. Sassoon, "Tangentopoli," 126.

46. Pier Paolo Giglioni, "Political Corruption and the Media: The Tangentopoli Affair," *International Social Science Journal* 48, no. 3 (1996): 381–94; Patrick McCarthy, "Italy at a Turning Point," *Current History* 96, no. 608 (1997): 111–15; Carol Mershon and Gianfranco Pasquino, eds., *Italian Politics: Ending the First Republic* (Boulder, Colo.: Westview Press, 1995).

47. Phillips, "Decline and Fall," 22.

48. Stille, for instance, makes this case in "Badfellas."

49. Bull and Rhodes, "Between Crisis and Transition." See also Michael Braun, *L'Italia da Andreotti a Berlusconi: Rivolgimenti e prospettive politiche in un paese a rischio*, trans. from German by Carlo Mainoldi (Milan: Feltrinelli, 1995).

50. Stille, "Badfellas," 12.

51. Quoted in Bufacchi and Burgess, *Italy Since 1989*, 1 n.12.

52. Quoted in Michael Sheridan, "Revolution Italian-Style," *Vanity Fair*, July 1993, 48.

53. Thomas Elsaesser, "Tales of Sound and Fury: Observations on the Family Melodrama," in *Home Is Where the Heart Is: Studies in Melodrama and the Woman's Film*, ed. Christine Gledhill (London: British Film Institute, 1987), 43–69. See also, in the same anthology, Geoffrey Nowell-Smith, "Minnelli and Melodrama," 70–74, and Laura Mulvey, "Notes on Sirk and Melodrama," 75–79, who discuss the genre in both psychoanalytic and ideological terms.

54. Elsaesser, "Tales of Sound and Fury," 64.

55. Steve Neale, "Melodrama and Tears," *Screen* 27, no. 6 (1986): 6–22.

56. Franco Moretti, "Kindergarten," in *Signs Taken for Wonders: Essays in the Sociology of Literary Forms*, trans. Susan Fischer, David Forgacs, and David Miller (London: Verso, 1997), 157–81.

57. Ibid., 160.

58. Neale, "Melodrama and Tears," 12.

59. Ibid., 9–12.

60. Moretti, "Kindergarten," 160.

61. Peter Brooks, *The Melodramatic Imagination* (New Haven, Conn.: Yale University Press, 1976), 56–80.

62. Neale, "Melodrama and Tears," 19.

63. Ibid., 21.

64. Radstone, "Cinema/Memory/History," 45.

65. Higson, "Heritage Film," 238.

66. Quoted in Pierre Sorlin, *Italian National Cinema, 1896–1996* (London: Routledge, 1996), 75.

67. Higson, "Re-presenting the National Past," 115.

68. Sigmund Freud, "Mourning and Melancholia," in *The Standard Edition of the Complete Psychological Works of Sigmund Freud*, trans. and ed. James Strachey (London: Hogarth Press, 1957), 14:235–58.

69. Ibid., 245. For Freud, hypercathexis describes the process by which the mourning subject reviews each memory of the lost object and withdraws the psychic charge or link, the cathexis, that connects them. Successful mourning requires a painful process of hypercathexis, and melancholia will occur without it.

70. And, to a lesser extent, those involving familial patterns: Totò and Alfredo, Mario and Neruda, and Farina and the lieutenant.

71. Freud, "Mourning and Melancholia," 249.

72. Mary Ann Doane, *The Desire to Desire: The Woman's Film of the 1940s* (Bloomington: Indiana University Press, 1987); Christine Gledhill, ed., *Home Is Where the Heart Is: Studies in Melodrama and the Woman's Film* (London: British Film Institute, 1987).

73. Linda Williams, "'Something Else Besides a Mother': *Stella Dallas* and the Maternal Melodrama," in *Home Is Where the Heart Is*, ed. Gledhill, 299–325.

74. Indeed, one of Radstone's more convincing readings relates to the family romance in which Alfredo stands in as a father for Totò. While I might disagree that this structure is as reactionary as Radstone's analysis claims, it is certainly the case that this narrative model can be found in all the films I am discussing. In *Il Postino*, Pablo Neruda becomes a surrogate father for Mario (and, indeed, is played by the same actor who plays Alfredo), and in *Mediterraneo* the captain can be seen as a kind of father to the orphaned Farina.

75. Higson, "Re-presenting the National Past," 117.

76. Laura Mulvey, "Visual Pleasure and Narrative Cinema," *Screen* 16, no. 3 (1975): 6–18.

77. Rosalind Krauss, "Photography's Discursive Spaces: Landscape/View," *Art Journal* 42, no. 4 (1982): 311–19.

78. Wheeler Winston Dixon, *The Transparency of Spectacle: Meditations on the Moving Image* (Albany: State University of New York Press, 1998).

79. See, for example, Ellen Strain, "Exotic Bodies, Distant Landscapes: Touristic Viewing and Popularized Anthropology in the Nineteenth Century," *Wide Angle* 18, no. 2 (1996): 70–100.

80. Mira Liehm, *Passion and Defiance: Film in Italy from 1942 to the Present* (Berkeley: University of California Press, 1984), 78.

81. Giuseppe De Santis, "Per un paesaggio italiano," *Cinema* 116 (1941): 71–75.

82. Quoted in David Overbey, ed., *Springtime in Italy: A Reader in Neorealism* (Hamden, Conn.: Archon Books, 1979), 78.

83. Mario Cannella, "Ideology and Aesthetic Hypotheses in the Criticism of Neo-Realism," *Screen* 14, no. 4 (1974): 5–60.

84. Linda Williams, *Hard Core: Power, Pleasure, and the "Frenzy of the Visible"* (Berkeley: University of California Press, 1989).

85. Of course, the landscape image is *indirectly* gendered as feminine—both by the well-worn connection of woman to nature and by the opposition of horizontal landscape to vertical, phallic cityscape.

86. André Bazin, *What Is Cinema?* vol. 2, trans. Hugh Gray (Berkeley: University of California Press, 1971).

87. An important exception here is the work of Krauss, who uses Bazin's theory of cinematic specificity to theorize the photographic index in terms of the chemical trace.

88. Roland Barthes, *Camera Lucida: Reflections on Photography*, trans. Richard Howard (New York: Hill and Wang, 1981).

89. Hal Foster, *The Return of the Real: The Avant-Garde at the End of the Century* (Cambridge, Mass.: MIT Press, 1996).

90. André Bazin, *What Is Cinema?* vol. 1, trans. Hugh Gray (Berkeley: University of California Press, 1967).

91. Siegfried Kracauer, *Theory of Film: The Redemption of Physical Reality* (Princeton, N.J.: Princeton University Press, 1997).

92. Ibid., 35.

93. Ibid., 77.

94. Ibid., 81.

95. Ibid., 71.

96. Miriam Hansen, introduction to Kracauer, *Theory of Film*, xxv.

97. Radstone refers briefly to the aura in her reading of *Cinema Paradiso*, where she mobilizes Benjamin's terms *Erfahrung* and *Erlebnis* to characterize the difference between those historical films that engage in memory work and those that fall into a narcissistic nostalgia ("Cinema/Memory/History," 43–44). Given that her ultimate aim is to critique *Cinema Paradiso*'s lack of engagement with history and lived culture, it is not surprising that she cites the aura only in terms of its absence, as an instance of how the film structures experience not as *Erfahrung* but as *Erlebnis*. While I disagree with this reading, I think Radstone's turn to Benjamin to think about historically based films is a crucial move, and I believe that the notion of the aura presents a connection among history, temporality, and the image that needs to be teased out in relation to the issues at stake in these films.

98. Benjamin, "Work of Art in the Age of Mechanical Reproduction," 222.

99. Ibid., 221.

100. Miriam Hansen, "Benjamin, Cinema and Experience: 'The Blue Flower in the Land of Technology,'" *New German Critique* 40 (1987): 179–224.

101. Ibid., 186.

102. Walter Benjamin, "A Small History of Photography," in *One-Way Street and Other Writings*, trans. Edmund Jephcott and Kingsley Shorter (London: Verso, 1985), 240–57.

103. Ibid., 243.

104. Ibid., 250.

105. Hansen, "Benjamin, Cinema and Experience," 212.

106. Walter Benjamin, "Central Park," trans. Lloyd Spencer, *New German Critique* 34 (1985): 41.

107. Cited in Hansen, "Benjamin, Cinema and Experience," 212.

108. Walter Benjamin, "Theses on the Philosophy of History," in *Illuminations*, 257.

109. Thomas Elsaesser, "Cinema—The Irresponsible Signifier or 'The Gamble with History': Film Theory or Cinema Theory," *New German Critique* 40 (1987): 76.

110. Walter Benjamin, *The Arcades Project*, trans. Howard Eiland and Kevin McLaughlin (Cambridge, Mass.: Belknap Press of Harvard University Press, 1999), 462–63.

111. The term "image" in Benjamin is, of course, not specifically pictorial, but

neither is it actively antipictorial. He uses the term in its literary theoretical context, which is less weighted than its placement in a film-theoretical argument might suggest.

112. Walter Benjamin, "Konvolut N" [Theoretics of Knowledge; Theory of Progress], trans. Leigh Hafrey and Richard Sieburth, *Philosophical Forum* 15, nos. 1–2 (1983–1984): 18.

113. Benjamin, *Arcades Project*, 388.

114. Francesco Casetti, "Le Néoréalisme italien: Le cinéma comme reconquête de réel," *CinémAction* 60 (1991): 70–78; Liehm, *Passion and Defiance*; Millicent Marcus, *Italian Film in the Light of Neorealism* (Princeton, N.J.: Princeton University Press, 1986).

115. Liehm, *Passion and Defiance*, 80.

116. Giuseppe De Santis, "Italie: Ruralité et néoréalisme," *CinémAction* 36 (1986): 60–61.

117. Marcus, *Italian Film*.

118. An example would be Maurizio Nichetti's popular comedy *Icicle Thief* (1989), a pun on *The Bicycle Thief* (U.S. title; released as *Bicycle Thieves* in Great Britain; in Italian, *Ladri di saponette* and *Ladri di biciclette*).

119. Bazin, *What Is Cinema?* 2: 64–65.

120. We can trace the contours of this difference in the characters also. Mario's simple man refers clearly to 'Ntoni in *La terra trema*, but whereas 'Ntoni's simplicity stands for a humanity and political idealism, Mario's innocence seems unusual, even within the narrative.

121. Angela Dalle Vacche, *The Body in the Mirror: Shapes of History in Italian Cinema* (Princeton, N.J.: Princeton University Press, 1992), 103.

122. Quoted in ibid., 98.

123. Roland Schneider, "1944–1951: Le néoréalisme italien," *CinémAction* 55 (1989): 48 (my translation).

124. Marcus, *Italian Film*, xiv.

125. Peter Bondanella, *Italian Cinema: From Neorealism to the Present* (New York: Ungar, 1983).

126. See, for example, Bull and Rhodes, "Between Crisis and Transition," and Grindrod, *Italy*.

127. Bernard Wall, *Italian Art, Life and Landscape* (Melbourne: Heinemann, 1956), 202–3.

128. Quoted in Bufacchi and Burgess, *Italy Since 1989*, 21.

129. Sassoon, "Tangentopoli," 130–32.

130. Bull and Rhodes, "Between Crisis and Transition."

131. Gilbert, *Italian Revolution*; Paul Ginsborg, "Explaining Italy's Crisis," in *The New Italian Republic: From the Fall of the Berlin Wall to Berlusconi*, ed. Stephen Gundle and Simon Parker (London: Routledge, 1996), 19–39.

132. Quoted in Ginsborg, "Explaining Italy's Crisis," 22.

133. Sorlin, *Italian National Cinema*, 87.

134. Bondanella, *Italian Cinema*, 36.

135. Stille, "Badfellas," 13.

## 3. A Conspiracy of Cartographers?

1. J. B. Harley, "Deconstructing the Map," *Cartographica* 26, no. 2 (1989): 1–20. Harley is the major figure in critical cartography. Barbara Belyea compares him with Jacques Derrida and Michel Foucault in developing a theory of maps as discursive texts that are inextricably linked to systems of power ("Images of Power: Derrida/ Foucault/ Harley," *Cartographica* 29, no. 2 [1992]: 1–9). Although Belyea criticizes Harley's work for retaining an underlying positivism, his importance in articulating the imbrications of power and textuality in maps cannot be overstated.

2. The film is also a literary adaptation in the sense that *Rosencrantz and Guildenstern Are Dead* was a play before it was a film. And it is quite possible to read playwright and director Tom Stoppard in terms of cultural capital, where an authorial discourse could place him as part of Britain's contemporary literary heritage.

3. Jean Baudrillard, "The Precession of Simulacra," in *Simulacra and Simulation*, trans. Sheila Faria Glaser (Ann Arbor: University of Michigan Press, 1994), 1–42.

4. Fredric Jameson, *Postmodernism; or, The Cultural Logic of Late Capitalism* (Durham, N.C.: Duke University Press, 1995).

5. Ibid., 50–51.

6. We may note here the discrepancy between England and the United Kingdom: while heritage films are typically concerned with a culturally exportable version of a narrowly English history, *Rosencrantz and Guildenstern* suggests a broader Britishness by dint of casting the Scottish actor Iain Glen as Hamlet.

7. Jameson, *Postmodernism*, 52.

8. Anthony Vidler, "Agoraphobia: Spatial Estrangement in Georg Simmel and Siegfried Kracauer," *New German Critique* 54 (1991): 32–33.

9. Henri Lefebvre, *The Production of Space*, trans. Donald Nicholson-Smith (Oxford: Blackwell, 1991); David Harvey, *The Condition of Postmodernity: An Enquiry into the Origins of Cultural Change* (London: Blackwell, 1989); Edward Soja, *Postmodern Geographies: The Reassertion of Space in Critical Social Theory* (New York: Verso, 1989); Charles Jencks, *The New Paradigm in Architecture: The Language of Postmodernism* (New Haven, Conn.: Yale University Press, 2002).

10. Victor Burgin, *In/different Spaces: Place and Memory in Visual Culture* (Berkeley: University of California Press, 1996); Rosalyn Deutsche, *Evictions: Art and Spatial Politics* (Cambridge, Mass.: MIT Press, 1997).

11. Irit Rogoff, *Terra Infirma: Geography's Visual Culture* (London: Routledge, 2000), 8.

12. Ibid., 3.

13. Andreas Huyssen, "The Voids of Berlin," *Critical Inquiry* 24, no. 1 (1997): 57–81.

14. We may read here a hint of Fritz Lang's *M* (1931), another film about the nature of a killer in Berlin, and one that represents maps frequently.

15. Giuliana Bruno, *Atlas of Emotion: Journeys in Art, Architecture and Film* (New York: Verso, 2002). See also Bruno, "Ramble City: Postmodernism and *Blade Runner*," *October* 41 (1987): 61–74.

16. Stephen Barber, *Projected Cities: Cinema and Urban Space* (London: Reaktion Books, 2002). See also Linda Krause and Patrice Petro, eds., *Global Cities: Cinema, Architecture, and Urbanism in a Digital Age* (New Brunswick, N.J.: Rutgers University Press, 2002).

17. Bruno, *Atlas of Emotion*, 3.

18. The film has also been read in terms of South Asian diasporic cinema, as in Jigna Desai, *Beyond Bollywood: The Cultural Politics of South Asian Diasporic Film* (London: Routledge, 2004). While it is undoubtedly important to place the film in a diasporic context, this categorization does not detract from the necessity of reading Black British film as part of European cinema.

19. Paul Julian Smith, *The Moderns: Space, Time and Subjectivity in Contemporary Spanish Culture* (Oxford: Oxford University Press, 2000). See also Dimitris Eleftheriotis, *Popular Cinemas of Europe: Studies of Texts, Concepts and Frameworks* (London: Continuum, 2001).

20. Burgin, *In/different Spaces*.

21. Franco Moretti, *Atlas of the European Novel, 1800–1900* (New York: Verso, 1999).

22. Rogoff, *Terra Infirma*, 108.

23. Hamid Naficy, *An Accented Cinema: Exilic and Diasporic Filmmaking* (Princeton, N.J.: Princeton University Press, 2001). For examples of how the idea of national cinema has been reexamined and expanded in the post-Wall age, see Mette Hjort and Scott Mackenzie, eds., *Cinema and Nation* (New York: Routledge, 2000).

24. Paul Hainsworth, "Politics, Culture and Cinema in the New Europe," in *Border Crossing: Film in Ireland, Britain and Europe*, ed. John Hill, Martin McLoone, and Paul Hainsworth (Belfast: University of Ulster/British Film Institute, 1994), 8–33.

25. An example of this kind of coproduction would be *Calendar* (Egoyan, 1993; Canada/Armenia/Germany). Solely within Asia, see, for example, *Autumn Moon* (Law, 1992; Hong Kong/Japan).

26. Steve Neale, "Melodrama and Tears," *Screen* 27, no. 6 (1986): 30.

27. John Hill, "The Future of European Cinema: The Economics and Culture of Pan-European Strategies," in *Border Crossing*, ed. Hill, McLoone, and Hainsworth, 53–80.

28. Angus Finney, *The State of European Cinema: A New Dose of Reality* (London: Cassell, 1996), 92.

29. Terry Ilott, *Budgets and Markets: A Study of the Budgeting of European Film* (London: Routledge, 1996), 137.

30. Hill, "Future of European Cinema," 54, 68.

31. Antoine de Baecque, "Le Cinéma d'Europe à la recherche d'une forme," *Cahiers du Cinéma* 455–456 (1992): 78–79.

32. I suspect the Europudding of being more of a sound bite than a helpful descriptive term, and research reveals many more discussions of the concept than examples of its application.

33. Serge Toubiana, "L'Europe! l'europe! l'europe!" *Cahiers du Cinéma* 455–456 (1992): 38.

34. Quoted in Duncan Petrie, ed., *Screening Europe: Image and Identity in Contemporary European Cinema* (London: British Film Institute, 1992), 67.

35. Examples of national identities abound in European politics, from rightwing nationalisms in France, Germany, and Russia, to the sometimes more liberal rhetoric of Scottish and Catalan nationalism, and, of course, to ethnonationalisms in the Balkans. The increase of European identities, or attempts to produce them, is evidenced in television programming such as MTV (Music Television) Europe, or in the increased media interest in cultural events such as European cities of culture and international festivals. Tellingly, I was surveyed in 1992 by a national polling organization, which wanted to know if I felt more Scottish, more British, or more European.

36. Philip Rosen, "The Concept of National Cinema in the 'New' Media Era," in *Historia general del cine: El cine en la era del audiovisual*, ed. Manuel Palacio and Santos Zonzunegui (Madrid: Catedra, 1995), 12:25.

37. See, for example, Harlan Kennedy, "Go Deeper," *Film Comment* 27, no. 4 (1991): 68–71. Kennedy argues that "*Europa* is a film so extravagantly playful that it seems like a fire-sale of postmodernist tropes." He reads this play as productive not of meaning but only of self-referential in-jokes, citing Orson Welles, Alfred Hitchcock, Richard Wagner, and Franz Kafka.

38. A similar excavation could be done on *Underground*'s references, although, as later sections will expand, its relationship to European cultural history is more strained.

39. Steve Neale, "Art Cinema as Institution," *Screen* 22, no. 1 (1981): 13.

40. Thomas Elsaesser, "Putting on a Show: The European Art Movie," *Sight and Sound*, April 1994, 26.

41. Michael Chion, "Quiet Revolution . . . and Rigid Stagnation," *October*, no. 58 (1991): 75.

42. Andrew Higson, "Re-presenting the National Past: Nostalgia and Pastiche in the Heritage Film," in *Fires Were Started: British Cinema and Thatcherism*, ed. Lester Friedman (London: University College London Press, 1993), 109–29.

43. Stanko Cerović, "Canned Lies," 1995, *Bosnia Report* (available at: http://www.barnsdle.demon.co.uk/bosnia/caned.html [accessed April 6, 2000]).

44. This was undoubtedly a fair point, as many critics discussed *Underground* as though it were a Bosnian film, and one British newspaper referred to the film's setting as Slavonia, a geographic term that, in this context, sounds willfully archaic.

45. See various issues of *Libération* and *Le Monde* during the summer and fall of 1995, especially Alain Finkielkraut, "L'Imposture Kusturica," *Le Monde*, June 2, 1995, 28.

46. Serge Regourd, "Alain Finkielkraut et Jdanov," *Le Monde*, June 9, 1995, 16 (my translation). For a lengthier defense of Kusturica, see Goran Gocić, *Notes from the Underground: The Cinema of Emir Kusturica* (London: Wallflower Press, 2001).

47. Dina Iordanova, "'Underground': Historical Allegory or Propaganda?" *Historical Journal of Film, Radio and Television* 19, no. 1 (1999): 69–86. Iordanova has also written on the topic in her books *Cinema of Flames: Balkan Film, Culture*

*and the Media* (London: British Film Institute, 2001) and *Emir Kusturica* (London: British Film Institute, 2002)

48. Iordanova, "Underground," 69.

49. Slavoj Žižek, "Multiculturalism, or the Cultural Logic of Multinational Capitalism," *New Left Review* 225 (1997): 37.

50. Žižek claims that "[Kusturica] thereby unknowingly provides the libidinal economy of the ethnic slaughter in Bosnia: the pseudo-Bataillean trance of excessive expenditure, the continuous and mad rhythm of drinking-eating-singing-fornicating. And, *therein consists the 'dream' of the ethinic cleansers, therein resides the answer to the question 'How were they able to do it?'*" (ibid., 39–40).

51. Although Jameson would probably agree with him on principle, he might not thank me for the comparison with Finkielkraut's hyperbolic rhetoric.

52. Finkielkraut, "L'Imposture Kusturica," 28 (my translation).

53. Cerović, "Canned Lies."

54. Iordanova, "Underground," 76–77.

55. Quoted in Regourd, "Alain Finkielkraut et Jdanov," 16.

56. Ackbar Abbas, *Hong Kong: Culture and the Politics of Disappearance* (Minneapolis: University of Minnesota Press, 1997).

57. A similar rhetorical move, although on the surface it might seem to contradict the idea of an end to history, was the trope of a return to history that attended the fall of state Communism across Eastern Europe. In this discourse, Western Europe became equated with history itself, and the years of Communism were seen as a suspension out of time. For East European countries, the space of "Europe" itself is here defined as being in history, and the return to some conceptual space of "Europe" becomes the same thing as a return to historical time.

58. André Bazin, *What Is Cinema?* trans. Hugh Gray (Berkeley: University of California Press, 1967), 1:160–61.

59. For a discussion of Svankmejer's Czech surrealism and the histories involved in his aesthetics, see Michael O'Pray, "Jan Svankmejer: A Mannerist Surrealist," in *Dark Alchemy: The Films of Jan Svankmejer*, ed. Peter Hames (Westport, Conn.: Praeger, 1995), 48–77.

60. For the sake of conciseness, I will refer simply to Yugoslavia, unless it is necessary to specify the years after 1992, when I will indicate either the former Yugoslav republics that I am referring to or the region as a whole. Likewise, I will refer simply to Germany unless it is clearly important to specify the German Democratic Republic (GDR, East Germany) or the Federal Republic of Germany (FRG, West Germany).

61. Quoted in Iordanova, "Underground," 81.

62. John B. Allcock, "Borders, States, Citizenship: Unscrambling Yugoslavia," in *The Changing Shape of the Balkans*, ed. F. W. Carter and H. T. Norris (Boulder, Colo.: Westview Press, 1986), 63–80; William Carr, *A History of Germany, 1815–1990* (London: Arnold, 1991); Slavoj Žižek, "A Leftist Plea for 'Eurocentrism,'" *Critical Inquiry* 24 (1998): 988–1009.

63. Joseph Rothschild and Nancy M. Wingfield contend that a logic of spatial expansion constantly underwrote Nazi racial rhetoric: "Indeed, the capacity for . . . spatial expansion was defined as the test and measure of racial vitality"

(*Return to Diversity: A Political History of East Central Europe Since World War II*, 3d ed. [New York: Oxford University Press, 2000], 3).

64. V. R. Berghahn, *Modern Germany: Society, Economy and Politics in the Twentieth Century* (Cambridge: Cambridge University Press, 1987); Carr, *History of Germany*.

65. Allcock, "Borders, States, Citizenship," 67.

66. Ibid., 66.

## 4. Yugoslavia's Impossible Spaces

1. Joseph Rothschild and Nancy M. Wingfield, *Return to Diversity: A Political History of Eastern Central Europe Since World War II*, 3d ed. (New York: Oxford University Press, 2000), 263.

2. See, for example, Phyllis Auty, "Yugoslavia," in *Central and South East Europe, 1945–1948*, ed. R. R. Betts (London: Royal Institute of International Affairs, 1950), 52–94; L. S. Stavrianos, *The Balkans Since 1453* (New York: Holt, Rinehart and Winston, 1958); and Rothschild and Wingfield, *Return to Diversity*.

3. Auty, "Yugoslavia," 55.

4. Sigmund Freud, "Mourning and Melancholia," in *Collected Papers*, vol. 4, *Papers on Metapsychology*, trans. Joan Rivière (New York: Basic Books, 1962), 154.

5. Ivo Banac, "Political Change and National Diversity," *Daedalus* 119, no. 1 (1990): 141–59.

6. Freud, "Mourning and Melancholia," 155 (my emphasis).

7. Susannah Radstone, "Cinema/Memory/History," *Screen* 36, no. 1 (1995): 34–47. While Radstone's equation of mourning with the social and melancholia with a refusal of the social is perfectly plausible, I read Freud somewhat differently. I argue that while melancholia demonstrates a certain stoppage or problematization of the structure of mourning, it also presumes a relationship with the social. This relationship may be difficult, indirect, or illogical, but it is nonetheless an engagement with the social realm— and one that is crucial to *Underground*.

8. Dina Iordanova, "'Underground': Historical Allegory or Propaganda?" *Historical Journal of Film, Radio and Television* 19, no. 1 (1999): 76. For Iordanova, "Yugo-nostalgia" is a problem endemic to intellectuals who live in the West and have the luxury of claiming not to take sides. She sees this position as tenable only in the West, for, as in Northern Ireland, it becomes impossible not to take up an ethnic identity when one returns. This seems to be a plausible reading, especially given the historical relationship between nostalgia and geographic distance. However, in reading *Underground*'s textual logic, I am less convinced that this nostalgia can be simply dismissed as politically reactionary. The film displays a nostalgia not for Communism but for a more psychically complex notion of a "before."

9. Nicolas Abraham and Maria Torok, *The Wolf Man's Magic Word*, trans. Nicholas Rand (Minneapolis: University of Minnesota Press, 1986).

10. Jacques Derrida, "Fors: The Anglish Words of Nicolas Abraham and Maria Torok," trans. Barbara Johnson, in ibid., xvi.

11. Ibid., xvii.

12. Ibid. It is important to note that Derrida ultimately complicates this argument, claiming that there is no difference between introjection and incorporation.

13. Ibid., xiv.

14. Iordanova, "Underground," 75.

15. Mark Wheeler, "Not so Black as It's Painted: The Balkan Political Heritage," in *The Changing Shape of the Balkans*, ed. F. W. Carter and H. T. Norris (Boulder, Colo.: Westview Press, 1996), 8.

16. David A. Norris, *In the Wake of the Balkan Myth: Questions of Identity and Modernity* (New York: St. Martin's Press, 1999).

17. Slavoj Žižek, "Multiculturalism, or the Cultural Logic of Multinational Capitalism," *New Left Review* 225 (1997): 28–51.

18. Mark Mazower, *Dark Continent: Europe's Twentieth Century* (New York: Knopf, 1999), xiii.

19. Timothy Garton Ash, *The Uses of Adversity: Essays on the Fate of Central Europe* (New York: Random House, 1989), 179.

20. Leslie H. Gelb, quoted in Renata Salecl, *The Spoils of Freedom: Psychoanalysis and Feminism After the Fall of Socialism* (London: Routledge, 1994), 13.

21. Iordanova, "Underground," 80.

22. Edward W. Said, *Orientalism* (New York: Random House, 1979).

23. Žižek, "Multiculturalism," 38.

24. Norris, *In the Wake of the Balkan Myth*, 7.

25. Milica Bakić-Hayden and Robert M. Hayden, "Orientalist Variations on the Theme 'Balkans': Symbolic Geography in Recent Yugoslav Cultural Politics," *Slavic Review* 51, no. 1 (1992): 2.

26. Maria Todorova, "The Balkans: From Discovery to Invention," *Slavic Review* 53, no. 2 (1994): 453. In an appropriation of postcolonial language, Bosnian writer Dzevad Karahesan speaks as an "Indian," comparing Bosnians and Yugoslavs in general with colonized peoples in their relationship with western Europe ("Europe's Wild East, or What Europe's Failure to Understand Bosnia Says About Europe" [available at: http://www.barnsdle.demon.uk/bosnia/wildes.html]). In addition to the East/West logics of Orientalism and of the Cold War, Balkanism involves a North/South binary that echoes both that of the postcolonial order and that of an earlier organization of European cultural space. As Robert Bideleux argues in relation to eastern Europe in the 1990s: "The almost universal demise of highly centralized communist rule and command economies has cleared the way for a simpler North-South division of the world into 'haves' and 'have-nots,' as the more successful East European and East Asian states are gradually joining the rank of the rich North, while the poorer or less successful post-communist states are becoming part of the impoverished South" ("In Lieu of a Conclusion: East Meets West?" in *European Integration and Disintegration*, ed. Robert Bideleux and Richard Taylor [London: Routledge, 1996], 294). Bakić-Hayden and Hayden add: "This modern economic geography of the world reflects and continues an older European political geography in which 'undisciplined' 'passionate' peoples of southern Europe (e.g. Italy, Spain, Greece) were contrasted to the industrious, rational cul-

tures of the north" ("Orientalist Variations on the Theme 'Balkans,'" 4). As with Orientalism, so with the post-Communist order, the Balkans fit into a cultural space that can be adduced as less civilized, less truly European.

27. Todorova, "The Balkans," 455. Todorova expands this argument in her book-length study of Balkanism, *Imagining the Balkans* (London: Oxford University Press, 1997).

28. Norris, *In the Wake of the Balkan Myth*, 5.

29. Todorova, "The Balkans," 476.

30. Bideleux, "In Lieu of a Conclusion," 290.

31. Wheeler, "Not so Black as It's Painted," 3.

32. Rothschild and Wingfield, *Return to Diversity*, 184.

33. Bakić-Hayden and Hayden, "Orientalist Variations on the Theme 'Balkans,'" 1.

34. Ibid., 5.

35. Taras Kermauner, quoted in ibid., 8.

36. Marko Barisić, quoted in ibid., 9.

37. Ibid., 12.

38. Quoted in Todorova, "The Balkans," 478.

39. Iordanova, "Underground," 80.

40. Žižek, "Multiculturalism," 39.

41. Ibid., 38.

42. Said, *Orientalism*, 325.

43. Julia Kristeva, *Powers of Horror: An Essay on Abjection*, trans. Leon S. Roudiez (New York: Columbia University Press, 1982).

44. Irit Rogoff, *Terra Infirma: Geography's Visual Culture* (London: Routledge, 2000); Giuliana Bruno, *Atlas of Emotion: Journeys in Art, Architecture and Film* (New York: Verso, 2002).

45. Kristeva, *Powers of Horror*, 8.

46. To a lesser extent, this structure mirrors that of the Italian films, in which the south of Italy also signifies a less modern, less progressive space and is, for that exact reason, more able to confront and dislodge the national stereotypes with which the films play.

47. Žižek, "Multiculturalism," 40–44. Not to mention the Western liberalism that first applauded the breakup of Yugoslavia and then wrung its hands and did nothing while Sarajevo was destroyed.

48. Salecl, *Spoils of Freedom*, 134. Salecl claims that most of the Western news pictures showing Bosnian Muslim women in headscarves were set up and that the women wear the scarves only on religious occasions or when asked to by Western journalists. The journalists, in Salecl's analysis, wanted to produce the image of exotic and primitive difference, which would reassure viewers at home that the people of the Balkans were not like them.

49. Todorova, "The Balkans," 460.

50. Žižek, "Multiculturalism," 38.

51. This is the sequence that Stanko Cerović particularly objects to, on the grounds that Kusturica singled out Slovene and Croat towns as welcoming to the Nazis ("Canned Lies," 1995, *Bosnia Report* [available at: http://www.barnsdle

.demon.co.uk/bosnia/caned.html (accessed April 6, 2000)]). Alain Finkielkraut also cites it as evidence of Kusturica's anti-Slovene bias ("L'Imposture Kusturica," *Le Monde*, June 2, 1995, 28).

52. These sequences also point to the practice, particularly in Soviet photographs, of doctoring images to remove those who had been edited out of official history. The mendacity of official Communist Party media is also parodied in the film within the film.

53. Norris, *In the Wake of the Balkan Myth*, 165.

54. This sequence mocks Communist Party revisionism, as well as any notion of historical realism: when Blacky kills the actor playing Frantz, the confused director applauds his belated expression of realism.

55. Pascal Bonitzer, "Partial Vision, Film and the Labyrinth," *Wide Angle* 4, no. 4 (1981): 56–63.

56. Ibid., 63.

57. Norris, *In the Wake of the Balkan Myth*, 155.

58. Walter Benjamin, "Theses on the Philosophy of History," in *Illuminations*, trans. Harry Zohn, ed. Hannah Arendt (New York: Schocken Books, 1968), 253–64.

59. Walter Benjamin, *The Arcades Project*, trans. Howard Eiland and Kevin McLaughlin (Cambridge, Mass.: Belknap Press of Harvard University Press, 1999), 463.

60. Ibid., 475.

61. Quoted in Derrida, "Fors," xxi n.13.

62. Charles Najman, "Surimpressions," *Cinématographe* 89 (1983): 34–35 (my translation).

63. Daniel J. Goulding, *Liberated Cinema: The Yugoslav Experience* (Bloomington: Indiana University Press, 1985), 3.

64. In this context, it is instructive to recall Timothy Garton Ash's description of his conversations with Croats and Serbs in the mid-1990s (*History of the Present: Essays, Sketches and Despatches from Europe in the 1990s* [London: Penguin, 2000], 192). He realized that the phrase "before the war" meant something entirely different to former Yugoslavs than it does to west Europeans. "The War," meaning the important war, the one that does not require a specific name, remains World War II for those in the West, but in Yugoslavia it now denotes the war of the 1990s.

65. Benjamin, *Arcades Project*, 474.

66. Here it is useful to distinguish what remains of Yugoslavia—that is, Serbia and Montenegro—from former Yugoslav republics such as Slovenia and Croatia, which by the late 1990s had a stable postwar order.

67. Miriam Hansen, introduction to Siegfried Kracauer, *Theory of Film: The Redemption of Physical Reality* (Princeton, N.J.: Princeton University Press, 1997), xxv.

68. Only *Besmrtna mladost* [*Immortal Youth*] (Nanović, 1948) takes place in occupied Belgrade.

69. Quoted in Goulding, *Liberated Cinema*, 8.

70. Ibid., xiv.

71. Ibid., 8.

72. Mira Liehm and Antonin J. Liehm, *The Most Important Art: Soviet and East-ern European Film After 1945* (Berkeley: University of California Press, 1977), 126.

73. Goulding, *Liberated Cinema*, 21.

74. Ibid., 19.

75. Liehm and Liehm, *Most Important Art*, 125.

76. This entwining of the national landscape with the figure of the woman was clearly effective: not only was *Slavica* enormously successful on its release, but in the years that followed, Slavica became a popular girls' name in the country.

77. Goulding, *Liberated Cinema*, 19–20.

78. Benjamin, *Arcades Project*, 391.

## 5. Back-Projecting Germany

1. Quoted in Françoise Audé, "Le Point de vue du noyé," *Positif* 369 (1991): 40.

2. *Il Postino*, to take one example, was directed by a British director, Michael Radford, but it is easily considered an Italian film because of its Italian location, narrative, and star (Massimo Troisi).

3. Terry Ilott, *Budgets and Markets: A Study of the Budgeting of European Film* (London: Routledge, 1996), 108.

4. Bo Christensen, quoted in ibid., 112.

5. Pierre Sorlin, *European Cinemas, European Societies, 1939–1990* (London: Routledge, 1991).

6. There are exceptions, of course. In recent years, *Land and Freedom* deals with the Spanish Civil War, albeit from the narrative perspective of a British vol-unteer. And many Hollywood films have depicted non-American histories, although some of these would be better thought of as biopics or epics than as his-tory films proper.

7. A series of transnational-themed films in Europe in the 1990s have addressed questions of immigration, ethnicity, and nation. Examples include *Beautiful People* (Dizdar, 1999) and *Steam: The Turkish Bath* (Ozpetek, 1997). How-ever, these films are overwhelmingly contemporary in setting and narrative, seek-ing to document recent cultural change rather than to reread the past.

8. A politically delicate version of this problem beset the designers of the Euro banknotes. They discovered that the original plan of using drawings of actual European landmarks on the notes was controversial, for whichever country's buildings were represented on the lower denominations would be sure to feel slighted. The solution was to abandon the use of actual places and, rather, design generic castles and public buildings that could connote European styles of archi-tecture without referring to specific countries.

9. Timothy Garton Ash, *The Uses of Adversity: Essays on the Fate of Central Europe* (New York: Random House, 1989), 179.

10. Thierry Jousse, "Zentropa," *Cahiers du Cinéma* 445 (1991): 35.

11. Andreas Huyssen, "The Voids of Berlin," *Critical Inquiry* 24, no. 1 (1997): 62. In *Present Pasts: Urban Palimpsests and the Politics of Memory* (Stanford, Calif.:

Stanford University Press, 2003), Huyssen traces connections among many sites of cultural memory, locating Berlin's voids as part of a contemporary Western crisis of memory and city space that includes the Jewish Museum in Berlin and the Memory Park in Buenos Aires, as well as the site of the World Trade Center in New York.

12. Huyssen, "Voids of Berlin," 64–65.

13. There is even a minor character in the film named Kessler.

14. Wolfgang Schivelbusch, *In a Cold Crater: Cultural and Intellectual Life in Berlin, 1945–1948*, trans. Kelly Barry (Berkeley: University of California Press, 1998). Schivelbusch argues that while there are other examples of the total destruction of cities—Guernica, Hiroshima—none of those were important big cities beforehand. Berlin was the first annihilation of a previously well known city. *Zentropa* does not concentrate on Berlin, but the idea of impossible spaces, gaps, and losses connects postwar Germany with the argument I have been making about European spaces more generally.

15. This genre became a frequent reference point in postwar German cinema, especially when New German Cinema began to disinter the legacy of war and to return to the questions of guilt and innocence. Many New German Cinema films repeated the gesture of the ruin film, but in a more politicized fashion: *Germany, Pale Mother* (Sanders-Brahms, 1980) and *The Marriage of Maria Braun* (Fassbinder, 1979) are examples of this move.

16. Thomas Elsaesser, "The German Cinema as Image and Idea," in *Encyclopedia of European Cinema*, ed. Ginette Vincendeau (London: British Film Institute, 1995), 174.

17. Thierry Jousse, "Europe: L'autre état," *Cahiers du Cinéma* 455–456 (1992): 58 (my translation).

18. Michel Celemenski, "Le Mur des lamentations," *Cinématographe* 89 (1983): 9–10 (my translation). Celemenski does see disparities in the extent to which the films' narratives endorse the redemptive power of destruction—he adds that Billy Wilder and Robert Siodmak do not believe in it but more cynically see Berlin returning as soon as possible to how it was before. Nonetheless, the basic structure of his argument places the real spaces of destruction as the locus of this ideology of redemption.

19. Thomas Elsaesser, *New German Cinema: A History* (New Brunswick, N.J.: Rutgers University Press, 1989), 247.

20. See, for example, V. R. Berghahn, *Modern Germany: Society, Economy and Politics in the Twentieth Century* (Cambridge: Cambridge University Press, 1987); William Carr, *A History of Germany, 1815–1990* (London: Arnold, 1991); and A. J. Ryder, *Twentieth-Century Germany: From Bismarck to Brandt* (New York: Columbia University Press, 1973). For a broad view of modern German political history, see Gordon Craig, *Germany, 1866–1945* (New York: Oxford University Press, 1978).

21. Elsaesser, *New German Cinema*, 250.

22. Ibid., 253. It is interesting to compare this criticism with those made against Kusturica that he also depicted the wars in former Yugoslavia to be natural disasters rather than political acts.

23. Jousse, "Zentropa," 35–36 (my translation).

24. Nicholas Pronay, "'To Stamp Out the Whole Tradition . . . ,'" in *The Political Re-education of Germany and Her Allies After World War II*, ed. Nicholas Pronay and Keith Wilson (Totowa, N.J.: Barnes and Noble Books, 1985), 1–36. The questionnaires are also discussed in Berghahn, *Modern Germany*; Carr, *History of Germany*; and Mark Mazower, *Dark Continent: Europe's Twentieth Century* (New York: Knopf, 1999).

25. For a canonical consideration of mourning in postwar Germany, see Alexander Mitscherlich and Margarete Mitscherlich, *The Inability to Mourn: Principles of Collective Behavior*, trans. Beverley R. Placzek (New York: Grove Press, 1975). The topic has also been addressed in relation to film in Eric Santner, *Stranded Objects: Mourning, Memory, and Film in Postwar Germany* (Ithaca, N.Y.: Cornell University Press, 1993), and has been important to histories of German cinema and to critical discourse on trauma. See, for instance, Cathy Caruth, *Unclaimed Experience: Trauma, Narrative, and History* (Baltimore: Johns Hopkins University Press, 1996).

26. For the best-known version of this argument, see Theodor Adorno and Max Horkheimer, *Dialectic of Enlightenment*, trans. John Cumming (London: Verso, 1997).

27. Mary Ann Doane, "Dark Continents: Epistemologies of Racial and Sexual Difference in Psychoanalysis and the Cinema," in *Femmes Fatales: Feminism, Film Theory, Psychoanalysis*, ed. Mary Ann Doane (New York: Routledge, 1991), 209.

28. In American cinema history, this logic is one predominantly of black and white, an economy in which, as Doane argues in "Dark Continents," visible racial difference is both a problem and a necessity. In terms of *Zentropa*, this discourse must be rethought to involve an embodiment of ethnic difference, where the lack of visible difference is exactly the issue.

29. Mazower, *Dark Continent*, xiii.

30. Amina Danton, "Léo et les loups," *Cahiers du Cinéma* 449 (1991): 33–35.

31. For discussions of film noir in Denmark, see Peter Cowie, Françoise Buquet, Risto-Mikael Pitkänen, and Godfried Talboom, *Le Cinema des pays nordiques*, trans. Giovanna Minelli (Paris: Editions du Centre Pompidou, 1990); Uffe Stormgaard and Sören Dyssegaard, eds., *Danish Films* (Copenhagen: Danish Film Institute, 1973); Forsyth Hardy, *Scandinavian Film* (London: Falcon Press, 1952); Ebbe Neergaard, *The Story of Danish Film*, trans. Elsa Gress (Copenhagen: Det Danske Selskab, 1962); Morten Piil, "Warmth and Irony, Solidarity and Satire," trans. David Hohnen, in *Danish Films*, ed. Stormgaard and Dyssegaard, 2–29; and Astrid Søderbergh Widding, "Denmark," in *Nordic National Cinemas*, ed. Tytti Soila, Astrid Søderbergh Widding, and Gunnar Iversen (London: Routledge, 1998), 7–30. While I do not have space to analyze the Danish postwar films in detail, it is clear that the postwar dramas form another set of intertexts for *Zentropa*.

32. Janey Place, "Women in Film Noir," in *Women in Film Noir*, ed. E. Ann Kaplan (London: British Film Institute, 1980), 35–67.

33. Pam Cook, "Duplicity in *Mildred Pierce*," in *Women in Film Noir*, ed. Kaplan, 68–69.

34. This unrepresented past can be thought also in terms of the psychoanalytic structure of the return of the repressed, a trope frequent in the gothic horror nar-

rative that *Zentropa* also uses. Here, the figure of the Jew stands in for what is repressed by the historical parameters of the narrative and, moreover, what is repressed unsuccessfully by the text. The film does not thematize the Holocaust explicitly—or, indeed, any of the historical realities of Nazism—and it is only in these momentary eruptions of the past into the body of the film that this absence can become a textual presence.

35. Psychoanalysis is a common narrative trope in American film noir, and we often find psychoanalysts working on protagonists in an attempt to bring the past to light. Examples from the 1940s include *Spellbound* (Hitchcock, 1945) and *Whirlpool* (Preminger, 1949).

36. Pascal Bonitzer, "Partial Vision, Film and the Labyrinth," *Wide Angle* 4, no. 4 (1981): 56–63.

37. Elizabeth Cowie, "Film Noir and Women," in *Shades of Noir: A Reader*, ed. Joan Copjec (London: Verso, 1996), 122.

38. Marc Vernet, "The Filmic Transaction: On the Openings of Films Noirs," *Velvet Light Trap* 20 (1983): 8. This neat structure is precisely a part of *Zentropa*'s referential relationship to the history of noir: the clarity of the correspondence is what signifies in this mannered redoubling of history.

39. Doane, "Dark Continents," 1.

40. In the East, the spectator fills in her own primitivism, seeing the East as automatically primitive, and thus *Underground* can make its point without special effort, but in the West, the idea of primitive space must be produced—hence werewolves and vampires, signifiers of the archaic, the gothic, the dangerous.

41. Bonitzer, "Partial Vision," 56–63. Bonitzer discusses *Jaws* (Spielberg, 1975), in which the spectator knows there is a shark but for much of the film is unable to see it. The other use of off-screen space is in a film like *Cat People*, where we are uncertain as to whether Irena is a monster or whether there is some other, rational explanation for the disturbing events of the narrative.

42. Walter Benjamin, *The Arcades Project*, trans. Howard Eiland and Kevin McLaughlin (Cambridge, Mass.: Belknap Press of Harvard University Press, 1999), 417–18.

43. On this point, it is useful to note that Jacques Tourneur directed *Cat People* and *Berlin Express*, both of which find repeated reference in *Zentropa*.

44. John Berks, "What Alice Does: Looking Otherwise at *The Cat People*," *Cinema Journal* 32, no. 1 (1992): 26–42; Robin Wood, "The Shadow Worlds of Jacques Tourneur," *Film Comment* 8, no. 2 (1972): 64–70; Tom Gunning, "'Like unto a Leopard': Figurative Discourse in *Cat People* and Todorov's *The Fantastic*," *Wide Angle* 10, no 3 (1988): 30–39. The relationship of this sexuality to a discourse of foreignness is taken up in several readings. Wood, for example, describes the film in terms of "honest, upright, uncomplicated Americans . . . who are impinged upon by outside 'foreign' forces at once sinister, mysterious and fascinating" ("Shadow Worlds," 65–66). And in "What Alice Does," Berks makes a case for historical analysis, reading the film, like film noir, in the context of postwar anxieties about women in the workplace.

45. Mary Ann Doane, *The Desire to Desire: The Woman's Film of the 1940s* (Bloomington: Indiana University Press, 1987), 49.

46. Or, more correctly, the Kingdom of the Serbs, Croats, and Slovenes.

47. *Cat People* is another film to narrate the failure of psychoanalysis: the analyst attempts to cure Irena's sexual neurosis but is thwarted by the reality of her monstrosity.

48. Sabine Baring-Gould, *The Book of Werewolves: Being an Account of a Terrible Superstition* (New York: Causeway Books, 1973); Perry Biddiscombe, *Werwolf! The History of the National Socialist Guerrilla Movement, 1944–1946* (Toronto: University of Toronto Press, 1998); Adam Douglas, *The Beast Within* (London: Chapmans, 1992).

49. Douglas, *Beast Within*, 26.

50. Biddescombe, *Werwolf!* 6.

51. "Two Neo-Nazis in Russia Receive Prison Terms," *St. Louis Post-Dispatch*, March 31, 1996, 6E.

52. See, for example, Barbara Creed, *The Monstrous Feminine: Film, Feminism, Psychoanalysis* (New York: Routledge, 1993).

53. In addition to these monsters that are un-European within Europe, there are also those that situate horror elsewhere, such as the Orientalist mummy.

54. Petiot himself is not a Nazi, and he appears to select Jews merely because they are easy targets. But there is an obvious metaphor at work in his mass murders: this is clearest in the scene where the furnace in which he burns his victims' bodies is discovered at work. This element of the text seems less interesting than the uses of the vampire, and it is certainly more direct.

55. Bram Stoker, *Dracula* (New York: Penguin, 1993), 28. For context on Dracula's colonial logic, see Stephen D. Arata, "The Occidental Tourist: Dracula and the Anxiety of Reverse Colonization," *Victorian Studies* 33, no. 4 (1990): 621–45.

56. Outside Europe, we can find related examples of films that use the horror genre to trope a racialized ideological reversal. In the South African film *Pure Blood* (Kaplan, 2000), the white racists of South Africa's apartheid regime are vampires, whose desire for racial purity manifests itself in a literal blood lust. This film is also an art film, although it more extensively takes on the forms of the splatter horror picture.

57. Quoted in Harlan Kennedy, "Go Deeper," *Film Comment* 27, no. 4 (1991): 69.

58. Marc Vernet, *Figures de l'absence* (Paris: Editions de l'Etoile, 1988). Vernet takes the concept of superimposition at its most broad to mean a doubled layering of the image, covering a variety of technological effects. The French word *surimpression* gives a slightly different meaning than the English "superimposition," a distinction that does not alter our understanding of Vernet's argument but does allow for a more inclusive sense of the doubled image.

59. This nonmatching of scale, where two different-size objects coexist within the frame, also appears in the mise-en-scène in the manner of a visual joke. One example of this is the train set, where Katharina and Leo lying among the tiny trains repeats the visual logic of superimposition. Another is the scene in which Leo is weighed on giant, out-of-proportion scales, a choice of object that is itself a visual pun.

60. Vernet, *Figures de l'absence*, 63 (my translation).

61. Stephen Heath, "Narrative Space," *Screen* 17, no. 3 (1976): 52.

62. Andrew Higson, "Re-presenting the National Past: Nostalgia and Pastiche in the Heritage Film," in *Fires Were Started: British Cinema and Thatcherism*, ed. Lester Friedman (London: University College London Press, 1993), 109–29; Laura Mulvey, "Visual Pleasure and Narrative Cinema," *Screen* 16, no. 3 (1975): 6–18.

63. Stephen Heath, *Questions of Cinema* (Bloomington: Indiana University Press, 1981), 89.

64. Ibid., 88.

65. Christian Metz, *L'Énonciation impersonelle, ou, le site du film* (Paris: Méridiens Klincksieck, 1991).

66. Vernet, *Figures de l'absence*, 64.

67. Ibid., 60.

68. Sean Cubitt, "Le réel, c'est l'impossible: The Sublime Time of Special Effects," *Screen* 40, no. 2 (1999): 123.

69. There are many examples of this effect: another is when Leo stands outside the church, where the projected background is extremely distorted.

70. Jousse, "Zentropa," 35.

71. Stephen Brockmann, "The Reunification Debate," *New German Critique* 52 (1991): 3–30.

72. Gareth Pritchard, "National Identity in a United and Divided Germany," in *European Integration and Disintegration*, ed. Robert Bideleux and Richard Taylor (London: Routledge, 1996), 166.

73. Quoted in Brockmann, "Reunification Debate," 4.

74. Andreas Huyssen, "After the Wall: The Failure of German Intellectuals," *New German Critique* 52 (1991): 109–43; quoted in Brockmann, "Reunification Debate," 27.

75. For another expression of this idea, see Sander Gilman, "German Reunification and the Jews," *New German Critique* 52 (1991): 173–91. For Gilman, the Berlin Wall appeared as a scar on the German body politic, signifying not the Cold War but guilt and punishment for the Holocaust. What is particularly interesting is the repetition of this discourse of borders as traumatic and the way in which spatial signifiers double back on historical ones.

76. Ron Pryce, "The Maastricht Treaty and the New Europe," in *Maastricht and Beyond: Building the European Union*, ed. John Pinder, Andrew Duff, and Roy Pryce (London: Routledge, 1994), 3–18. The European Coal and Steel Community (ECSC) was the first stage toward building European economic cooperation and is widely seen as the beginnings of what would become the European Economic Community. See also Desmond Dinan, *Ever Closer Union? An Introduction to the European Community* (Boulder, Colo.: Rienner, 1994).

77. Dinan, *Ever Closer Union?* 184.

78. We can constrast *Zentropa* with another film that uses back projections to stage German history: *Hitler: A Film from Germany* (Syberberg, 1978). Here projection is used as part of an explicitly national discourse on the experience of German identity and engagement with the past. For readings on this question, see Timothy Corrigan, *New German Film: The Displaced Image* (Austin: University of

Texas Press, 1983), 154; Elsaesser, *New German Cinema*, 264–67; and Corey K. Creekmur, "The Cinematic Photograph and the Possibility of Mourning," *Wide Angle* 9, no. 1 (1987): 41–49.

79. The European subject may not exist, but the ability to propose such a thing meaningfully is readable as a specifically west European point of view. While *Underground*'s attempt to include an eastern country within Europe meets with the impossibility of abjection, a west European film has more access to the discourses of international unity.

80. Benjamin, *Arcades Project*, 462–63.

81. Ibid., 388.


# 6. Toward a Theory of European Space

1. Laura Mulvey, "Visual Pleasure and Narrative Cinema," *Screen* 16, no. 3 (1975): 6–18.

2. Fredric Jameson, *Signatures of the Visible* (New York: Routledge, 1990); Paul Virilio, *The Vision Machine* (London: British Film Institute, 1994); Guy Debord, *Society of the Spectacle* (Detroit: Black and Red, 1983).

3. Michael Rogin, "'Make My Day!': Spectacle as Amnesia in Imperial Politics," *Representations* 29 (1990): 106.

4. Wheeler Winston Dixon, *The Transparency of Spectacle: Meditations on the Moving Image* (Albany: State University of New York Press, 1998), 5.

5. Anton Kaes, *From Hitler to "Heimat": The Return of History as Film* (Cambridge, Mass.: Harvard University Press, 1989), 16.

6. Quoted in Walter Benjamin and Theodor W. Adorno, *The Complete Correspondence, 1928–1940* (Cambridge, Mass.: Harvard University Press, 2001), 202.

7. Stephen Barber, *Projected Cities: Cinema and Urban Space* (London: Reaktion Books, 2002).

8. Edward Yang's films include *Taipei Story* (1985), *The Terrorizer* (1986), and *A Brighter Summer Day* (1991). Tsai Ming-Liang's earlier films include *Rebels of the Neon God* (1992) and *Vive l'amour* (1994), both of which outline an alienated, bleakly spectacular Taipei.

9. Slavoj Žižek, "A Leftist Plea for 'Eurocentrism,'" *Critical Inquiry* 24 (1998): 1004.

# Bibliography

Abbas, Ackbar. *Hong Kong: Culture and the Politics of Disappearance*. Minneapolis: University of Minnesota Press, 1997.

Abraham, Nicolas, and Maria Torok. *The Wolf Man's Magic Word*. Translated by Nicholas Rand. Minneapolis: University of Minnesota Press, 1986.

Adelson, Leslie. "Touching Tales of Turks, Germans, and Jews: Cultural Alterity, Historical Narrative, and Literary Riddles for the 1990s." *New German Critique* 80 (2000): 93–124.

Adorno, Theodor, and Max Horkheimer. *Dialectic of Enlightenment*. Translated by John Cumming. London: Verso, 1997.

Allock, John B. "Borders, States, Citizenship: Unscrambling Yugoslavia." In *The Changing Shape of the Balkans*, edited by F. W. Carter and H. T. Norris, 63–80. Boulder, Colo.: Westview Press, 1986.

Arata, Stephen D. "The Occidental Tourist: Dracula and the Anxiety of Reverse Colonization." *Victorian Studies* 33, no. 4 (1990): 621–45.

Aspden, Peter. "Mediterraneo." *Sight and Sound*, April 1991, 50.

Aspden, Peter. "Nuovo Cinema Paradiso." *Sight and Sound*, February 1994, 62.

Audé, Françoise. "Le Point de vue du noyé." *Positif* 369 (1991): 39–40.

Auty, Phyllis. "Yugoslavia." In *Central and South East Europe, 1945–1948*, edited by R. R. Betts, 52–94. London: Royal Institute of International Affairs, 1950.

Bakić-Hayden, Milica, and Robert M. Hayden. "Orientalist Variations on the Theme 'Balkans': Symbolic Geography in Recent Yugoslav Cultural Politics." *Slavic Review* 51, no. 1 (1992): 1–15.

Balibar, Etienne. *Politics and the Other Scene*. London: Verso, 2002.

Balibar, Etienne. *We, the People of Europe? Reflections on Transnational Citizenship*. Translated by James Swenson. Princeton, N.J.: Princeton University Press, 2004.

Banac, Ivo. "Political Change and National Diversity." *Daedalus* 119, no. 1 (1990): 141–59.

Barber, Stephen. *Projected Cities: Cinema and Urban Space.* London: Reaktion Books, 2002.

Baring-Gould, Sabine. *The Book of Werewolves: Being an Account of a Terrible Superstition.* New York: Causeway Books, 1973.

Barthes, Roland. *Camera Lucida: Reflections on Photography.* Translated by Richard Howard. New York: Hill and Wang, 1981.

Baudrillard, Jean. "The Precession of Simulacra." In *Simulacra and Simulation,* translated by Sheila Faria Glaser, 1–42. Ann Arbor: University of Michigan Press, 1994.

Bazin, André. *What Is Cinema?* Vol. 1. Translated by Hugh Gray. Berkeley: University of California Press, 1967.

Bazin, André. *What Is Cinema?* Vol. 2. Translated by Hugh Gray. Berkeley: University of California Press, 1971.

Belyea, Barbara. "Images of Power: Derrida/Foucault/Harley." *Cartographica* 29, no. 2 (1992): 1–9.

Benjamin, Walter. *The Arcades Project.* Translated by Howard Eiland and Kevin McLaughlin. Cambridge, Mass.: Belknap Press of Harvard University Press, 1999.

Benjamin, Walter. "Central Park." Translated by Lloyd Spencer. *New German Critique* 34 (1985): 32–58.

Benjamin, Walter. "Konvolut N" [Theoretics of Knowledge; Theory of Progress]. Translated by Leigh Hafrey and Richard Sieburth. *Philosophical Forum* 15, nos. 1–2 (1983–1984): 1–40.

Benjamin, Walter. "A Small History of Photography." In *One-Way Street and Other Writings,* translated by Edmund Jephcott and Kingsley Shorter, 240–57. London: Verso, 1985.

Benjamin, Walter. "Theses on the Philosophy of History." In *Illuminations,* translated by Harry Zohn, edited by Hannah Arendt, 253–64. New York: Schocken Books, 1968.

Benjamin, Walter. "The Work of Art in the Age of Mechanical Reproduction." In *Illuminations,* translated by Harry Zohn, edited by Hannah Arendt, 217–52. New York: Schocken Books, 1968.

Benjamin, Walter, and Theodor W. Adorno. *The Complete Correspondence, 1928–1940.* Cambridge, Mass.: Harvard University Press, 2001.

Berghahn, V. R. *Modern Germany: Society, Economy and Politics in the Twentieth Century.* Cambridge: Cambridge University Press, 1987.

Berks, John. "What Alice Does: Looking Otherwise at *The Cat People.*" *Cinema Journal* 32, no. 1 (1992): 26–42.

Betz, Mark. "The Name Above the (Sub)Title: Internationalism, Coproduction, and Polyglot European Art Cinema." *Camera Obscura* 16:1, no. 46 (2001): 1–44.

Bhabha, Homi. *The Location of Culture.* New York: Routledge, 1994.

Biddiscombe, Perry. *Werwolf! The History of the National Socialist Guerrilla Movement, 1944–1946.* Toronto: University of Toronto Press, 1998.

Bideleux, Robert. "In Lieu of a Conclusion: East Meets West?" In *European Integration and Disintegration,* edited by Robert Bideleux and Richard Taylor, 281–95. London: Routledge, 1996.

Bondanella, Peter. *Italian Cinema: From Neorealism to the Present.* New York: Ungar, 1983.

Bonitzer, Pascal. "Partial Vision, Film and the Labyrinth." *Wide Angle* 4, no. 4 (1981): 56–63.

Bordwell, David. "The Art Cinema as a Mode of Film Practice." *Film Criticism* 4, no. 1 (1979): 56–63.

Bosséno, Christian. "Immigrant Cinema: National Cinema—The Case of Beur Film." In *Popular European Cinema,* edited by Richard Dyer and Ginette Vincendeau, 47–57. New York: Routledge, 1992.

Braun, Michael. *L'Italia da Andreotti a Berlusconi: Rivolgimenti e prospettive politiche in un paese a rischio.* Translated from German by Carlo Mainoldi. Milan: Feltrinelli, 1995.

Brockmann, Stephen. "The Reunification Debate." *New German Critique* 52 (1991): 3–30.

Brooks, Peter. *The Melodramatic Imagination.* New Haven, Conn.: Yale University Press, 1976.

Bruno, Giuliana. *Atlas of Emotion: Journeys in Art, Architecture and Film.* New York: Verso, 2002.

Bruno, Giuliana. "Ramble City: Postmodernism and *Blade Runner.*" *October* 41 (1987): 61–74.

Bufacchi, Vittorio, and Simon Burgess. *Italy Since 1989: Events and Interpretations.* New York: St. Martin's Press, 1998.

Bull, Martin, and Martin Rhodes. "Between Crisis and Transition: Italian Politics in the 1990s." *West European Politics* 20, no. 1 (1997): 1–13.

Burgin, Victor. *In/different Spaces: Place and Memory in Visual Culture.* Berkeley: University of California Press, 1996.

Canby, Vincent. "'Cinema Paradiso': Memories of Movies in a Movie." *New York Times,* February 2, 1990, 15.

Canby, Vincent. "Roundelay of Love on an Isle in Wartime." *New York Times,* March 22, 1992, 48.

Cannella, Mario. "Ideology and Aesthetic Hypotheses in the Criticism of Neo-Realism." *Screen* 14, no. 4 (1974): 5–60.

Carr, William. *A History of Germany, 1815–1990.* London: Arnold, 1991.

Caruth, Cathy. *Unclaimed Experience: Trauma, Narrative, and History.* Baltimore: Johns Hopkins University Press, 1996.

Casetti, Francesco. "Le Néoréalisme italien: Le cinéma comme reconquête de réel." *CinémAction* 60 (1991): 70–78.

Caughie, John. "Halfway to Paradise." *Sight and Sound,* May 1992, 10–13.

Caughie, John. "Progressive Television and Documentary Drama." *Screen* 21, no. 3 (1980): 9–35.

Celemenski, Michel. "Le Mur des lamentations." *Cinématographe* 89 (1983): 9–10.

Cerović, Stanko. "Canned Lies." 1995. *Bosnia Report.* Available at: http://www.barnsdle.demon.co.uk/bosnia/caned.html (accessed April 6, 2000).

Chion, Michel. "Quiet Revolution . . . and Rigid Stagnation." *October* 58 (1991): 69–80.

"'Clean Hands': Who's Next?" *Business Week,* March 8, 1993, 57.

Cook, Pam. "Duplicity in *Mildred Pierce*." In *Women in Film Noir*, edited by E. Ann Kaplan, 68–82. London: British Film Institute, 1980.

Cook, Pam. *Screening the Past: Memory and Nostalgia in Cinema*. New York: Routledge, 2005.

Corrigan, Timothy. *New German Film: The Displaced Image*. Austin: University of Texas Press, 1983.

Cowie, Elizabeth. "Film Noir and Women." In *Shades of Noir: A Reader*, edited by Joan Copjec, 121–66. London: Verso, 1996.

Cowie, Peter, Françoise Buquet, Risto-Mikael Pitkänen, and Godfried Talboom. *Le Cinema des pays nordiques*. Paris: Editions du Centre Pompidou, 1990.

Craig, Gordon. *Germany, 1866–1945*. New York: Oxford University Press, 1978.

Creed, Barbara. *The Monstrous Feminine: Film, Feminism, Psychoanalysis*. New York: Routledge, 1993.

Creekmur, Corey K. "The Cinematic Photograph and the Possibility of Mourning." *Wide Angle* 9, no. 1 (1987): 41–49.

Cubitt, Sean. "Le réel, c'est l'impossible: The Sublime Time of Special Effects." *Screen* 40, no. 2 (1999): 123–30.

Dalle Vacche, Angela. *The Body in the Mirror: Shapes of History in Italian Cinema*. Princeton, N.J.: Princeton University Press, 1992.

Danton, Amina. "Léo et les loups." *Cahiers du Cinéma* 449 (1991): 33–35.

de Baecque, Antoine. "Le Cinéma d'Europe à la recherche d'une forme." *Cahiers du Cinéma* 455–456 (1992): 78–79.

Debord, Guy. *Society of the Spectacle*. Detroit: Black and Red, 1983.

Derrida, Jacques. "Fors: The Anglish Words of Nicholas Abraham and Maria Torok." Translated by Barbara Johnson. In Nicholas Abraham and Maria Torok, *The Wolf Man's Magic Word*, translated by Nicholas Rand, xi–xlviii. Minneapolis: University of Minnesota Press, 1986.

Derrida, Jacques. *The Other Heading: Reflections on Today's Europe*. Translated by Pascale-Anne Brault and Michael B. Naas. Bloomington: Indiana University Press, 1992.

Desai, Jigna. *Beyond Bollywood: The Cultural Politics of South Asian Diasporic Film*. London: Routledge, 2004.

De Santis, Giuseppe. "Italie: Ruralité et néoréalisme." *CinémAction* 36 (1986): 60–61.

De Santis, Giuseppe. "Per un paesaggio italiano." *Cinema* 116 (1941): 71–75.

Deutsche, Rosalyn. *Evictions: Art and Spatial Politics*. Cambridge: MIT Press, 1997.

Dinan, Desmond. *Ever Closer Union? An Introduction to the European Community*. Boulder, Colo.: Rienner, 1994.

Di Scala, Spencer M. *Italy: From Revolution to Republic, 1700 to the Present*. Boulder, Colo.: Westview Press, 1998.

Dixon, Wheeler Winston. *The Transparency of Spectacle: Meditations on the Moving Image*. Albany: State University of New York Press, 1998.

Doane, Mary Ann. "Dark Continents: Epistemologies of Racial and Sexual Difference in Psychoanalysis and the Cinema." In *Femmes Fatales: Feminism, Film Theory, Psychoanalysis*, edited by Mary Ann Doane, 209–48. New York: Routledge, 1991.

Doane, Mary Ann. *The Desire to Desire: The Woman's Film of the 1940s.* Bloomington: Indiana University Press, 1987.

Douglas, Adam. *The Beast Within.* London: Chapmans, 1992.

Dyer, Richard. "Feeling English." *Sight and Sound,* March 1994, 17–19.

Eleftheriotis, Dimitris. *Popular Cinemas of Europe: Studies of Texts, Concepts and
Frameworks.* London: Continuum, 2001.

Elsaesser, Thomas. "Cinema—The Irresponsible Signifier or 'The Gamble with History': Film Theory or Cinema Theory." *New German Critique* 40 (1987): 40–87.

Elsaesser, Thomas. *New German Cinema: A History.* New Brunswick, N.J.: Rutgers
University Press, 1989.

Elsaesser, Thomas. "Putting on a Show: The European Art Movie." *Sight and
Sound,* April 1994, 22–27.

Elsaesser, Thomas. "Tales of Sound and Fury: Observations on the Family Melodrama." In *Home Is Where the Heart Is: Studies in Melodrama and the Woman's
Film,* edited by Christine Gledhill, 43–69. London: British Film Institute, 1987.

Elsaesser, Thomas. "The German Cinema as Image and Idea." In *Encyclopedia of
European Cinema,* edited by Ginette Vincendeau, 172–75. London: British Film
Institute, 1995.

Finkielkraut, Alain. "L'Imposture Kusturica." *Le Monde,* June 2, 1995, 28.

Finney, Angus. *The State of European Cinema: A New Dose of Reality.* London: Cassell, 1996.

Foster, Hal. *The Return of the Real: The Avant-Garde at the End of the Century.* Cambridge, Mass.: MIT Press, 1996.

Foucault, Michel. "Entretien avec Michel Foucault." *Cahiers du Cinéma* 251–252
(1974): 8.

Foucault, Michel. "Film and Popular Memory." *Cahiers du Cinéma* 251–252 (1974):
25.

Freud, Sigmund. "Mourning and Melancholia." In *Collected Papers.* Vol. 4, *Papers
on Metapsychology,* 152–70. Translated by Joan Rivière. New York: Basic Books,
1962.

Garton Ash, Timothy. *History of the Present: Essays, Sketches and Despatches from
Europe in the 1990s.* London: Penguin, 2000.

Garton Ash, Timothy. *The Uses of Adversity: Essays on the Fate of Central Europe.* New
York: Random House, 1989.

Giglioni, Pier Paolo. "Political Corruption and the Media: The Tangentopoli
Affair." *International Social Science Journal* 48, no. 3 (1996): 381–94.

Gilbert, Mark. *The Italian Revolution: The End of Politics, Italian Style?* Boulder,
Colo.: Westview Press, 1995.

Gili, Jean A. "Le Facteur: Un poète amateur contre l'injustice du monde." *Positif*
423 (1996): 58.

Gilman, Sander. "German Reunification and the Jews." *New German Critique* 52
(1991): 173–91.

Gilman, Sander. "Is Life Beautiful? Can the Shoah Be Funny? Some Thoughts on
Recent and Older Films." *Critical Inquiry* 26 (2000): 279–308.

Gilroy, Paul. *The Black Atlantic: Modernity and Double Consciousness.* Cambridge,
Mass.: Harvard University Press, 1993.

Ginsborg, Paul. "Explaining Italy's Crisis." In *The New Italian Republic: From the Fall of the Berlin Wall to Berlusconi*, edited by Stephen Gundle and Simon Parker, 19–39. New York: Routledge, 1996.

Gledhill, Christine, ed. *Home Is Where the Heart Is: Studies in Melodrama and the Woman's Film*. London: British Film Institute, 1987.

Gocić, Goran. *Notes from the Underground: The Cinema of Emir Kusturica*. London: Wallflower Press, 2001.

Goulding, Daniel J. *Liberated Cinema: The Yugoslav Experience*. Bloomington: Indiana University Press, 1985.

Graffy, Julian. "Il Postino." *Sight and Sound*, November 1995, 49.

Gray, Lawrence. "From Gramsci to Togliatti: The Partito Nuovo and the Mass Basis of Italian Communism." In *The Italian Communist Party: Yesterday, Today, and Tomorrow*, edited by Simon Serfaty and Lawrence Gray, 21–36. Westport, Conn.: Greenwood Press, 1980.

Greene, Naomi. *Landscapes of Loss: The National Past in Post-War French Cinema*. Princeton, N.J.: Princeton University Press, 1999.

Grindrod, Muriel. *Italy*. New York: Praeger, 1968.

Gunning, Tom. "'Like unto a Leopard': Figurative Discourse in *Cat People* (1942) and Todorov's *The Fantastic*." *Wide Angle* 10, no. 3 (1988): 30–39.

Hainsworth, Paul. "Politics, Culture and Cinema in the New Europe." In *Border Crossing: Film in Ireland, Britain and Europe*, edited by John Hill, Martin McLoone, and Paul Hainsworth, 8–33. Belfast: University of Ulster / British Film Institute, 1994.

Hansen, Miriam. "Benjamin, Cinema and Experience: 'The Blue Flower in the Land of Technology.'" *New German Critique* 40 (1987): 179–224.

Hansen, Miriam. "Early Cinema, Late Cinema: Transformations of the Public Sphere." In *Viewing Positions: Ways of Seeing Film*, edited by Linda Williams, 134–52. New Brunswick, N.J.: Rutgers University Press, 1994.

Hansen, Miriam. Introduction to Siegfried Kracauer, *Theory of Film: The Redemption of Physical Reality*, vii–xlv. Princeton, N.J.: Princeton University Press, 1997.

Hardy, Forsyth. *Scandinavian Film*. London: Falcon Press, 1952.

Harley, J. B. "Deconstructing the Map." *Cartographica* 26, no. 2 (1989): 1–20.

Harper, Sue. *Picturing the Past: The Rise and Fall of the British Costume Film*. London: British Film Institute, 1994.

Harvey, David. *The Condition of Postmodernity: An Enquiry into the Origins of Cultural Change*. London: Blackwell, 1989.

Heath, Stephen. "Narrative Space." *Screen* 17, no. 3 (1976): 19–75.

Heath, Stephen. *Questions of Cinema*. Bloomington: Indiana University Press, 1981.

Higson, Andrew. "The Heritage Film and British Cinema." In *Dissolving Views: Key Writings on British Cinema*, edited by Andrew Higson, 232–48. London: Cassell, 1996.

Higson, Andrew. "Re-presenting the National Past: Nostalgia and Pastiche in the Heritage Film." In *Fires Were Started: British Cinema and Thatcherism*, edited by Lester Friedman, 109–29. London: University College London Press, 1993.

Hill, John. "The Future of European Cinema: The Economics and Culture of Pan-European Strategies." In *Border Crossing: Film in Ireland, Britain and Europe*, edited by John Hill, Martin McLoone, and Paul Hainsworth, 53–80. Belfast: University of Ulster/British Film Institute, 1994.

Hjort, Mette, and Scott Mackenzie, eds. *Cinema and Nation*. New York: Routledge, 2000.

Huyssen, Andreas. "After the Wall: The Failure of German Intellectuals." *New German Critique* 52 (1991): 109–43.

Huyssen, Andreas. *Present Pasts: Urban Palimpsests and the Politics of Memory*. Stanford, Calif.: Stanford University Press, 2003.

Huyssen, Andreas. "The Voids of Berlin." *Critical Inquiry* 24, no. 1 (1997): 57–81.

Ilott, Terry. *Budgets and Markets: A Study of the Budgeting of European Film*. London: Routledge, 1996.

Iordanova, Dina. *Cinema of Flames: Balkan Film, Culture and the Media*. London: British Film Institute, 2001.

Iordanova, Dina. *Emir Kusturica*. London: British Film Institute, 2002.

Iordanova, Dina. "'Underground': Historical Allegory or Propaganda?" *Historical Journal of Film, Radio and Television* 19, no. 1 (1999): 69–86.

Jaikumar, Priya. "'Place' and the Modernist Redemption of Empire in *Black Narcissus*." *Cinema Journal* 40, no. 2 (2001): 57–77.

Jameson, Fredric. *Postmodernism; or, The Cultural Logic of Late Capitalism*. Durham, N.C.: Duke University Press, 1995.

Jameson, Fredric. *Signatures of the Visible*. New York: Routledge, 1990.

Jencks, Charles. *The New Paradigm in Architecture: The Language of Postmodernism*. New Haven, Conn.: Yale University Press, 2002.

Jenkins, Brian, and Spyros A. Sofos, eds. *Nation and Identity in Contemporary Europe*. London: Routledge, 1996.

Jousse, Thierry. "Europe: L'autre état." *Cahiers du Cinéma* 455–456 (1992): 56–59.

Jousse, Thierry. "Zentropa." *Cahiers du Cinéma* 445 (1991): 35–36.

Kaes, Anton. *From Hitler to "Heimat": The Return of History as Film*. Cambridge, Mass.: Harvard University Press, 1989.

Karahesan, Dzevad. "Europe's Wild East, or What Europe's Failure to Understand Bosnia Says About Europe." Available at: http://www.barnsdle.demon.co.uk/bosnia/wildes.html (accessed April 6, 2000).

Kennedy, Harlan. "Go Deeper." *Film Comment* 27, no. 4 (1991): 68–71.

Kertesz, Imre. "Who Owns Auschwitz?" *Yale Journal of Criticism* 14, no. 1 (2001): 267–72.

Kogan, Norman. *A Political History of Postwar Italy*. New York: Praeger, 1981.

Kracauer, Siegfried. *Theory of Film: The Redemption of Physical Reality*. Princeton, N.J.: Princeton University Press, 1997.

Krause, Linda, and Patrice Petro, eds. *Global Cities: Cinema, Architecture, and Urbanism in a Digital Age*. New Brunswick, N.J.: Rutgers University Press, 2002.

Krauss, Rosalind. "Photography's Discursive Spaces: Landscape/View." *Art Journal* 42, no. 4 (1982): 311–19.

Kristeva, Julia. *Powers of Horror: An Essay on Abjection*. Translated by Leon S. Roudiez. New York: Columbia University Press, 1982.

Lefebvre, Henri. *The Production of Space*. Translated by Donald Nicholson-Smith. Oxford: Blackwell, 1991.

Liehm, Mira. *Passion and Defiance: Film in Italy from 1942 to the Present.* Berkeley: University of California Press, 1984.

Liehm, Mira, and Antonin J. Liehm. *The Most Important Art: Soviet and Eastern European Film After 1945.* Berkeley: University of California Press, 1977.

Lyttle, John. "'The English Patient' Has 12 Oscar and 13 BAFTA Nominations. But, Asks John Lyttle, Why All This Fuss over a Dressed-up Costume Drama with Nowhere to Go?" *Independent,* February 27, 1997, 10.

Marcus, Millicent. *After Fellini: National Cinema in the Postmodern Age.* Baltimore: Johns Hopkins University Press, 2002.

Marcus, Millicent. *Italian Film in the Light of Neorealism.* Princeton, N.J.: Princeton University Press, 1986.

Mazower, Mark. *Dark Continent: Europe's Twentieth Century.* New York: Knopf, 1999.

McCarthy, Patrick. "Italy at a Turning Point." *Current History* 96, no. 608 (1997): 111–15.

Mershon, Carol, and Gianfranco Pasquino, eds. *Italian Politics: Ending the First Republic.* Boulder, Colo.: Westview Press, 1995.

Metz, Christian. *L'Énonciation impersonelle, ou, le site du film.* Paris: Méridiens Klincksieck, 1991.

Mitscherlich, Alexander, and Margarete Mitscherlich. *The Inability to Mourn: Principles of Collective Behavior.* Translated by Beverley R. Placzek. New York: Grove Press, 1975.

Moretti, Franco. *Atlas of the European Novel, 1800–1900.* New York: Verso, 1999.

Moretti, Franco. "Kindergarten." In *Signs Taken for Wonders: Essays in the Sociology of Literary Forms,* translated by Susan Fischer, David Forgacs, and David Miller, 157–81. London: Verso, 1997.

Mulvey, Laura. "Notes on Sirk and Melodrama." In *Home Is Where the Heart Is: Studies in Melodrama and the Woman's Film,* edited by Christine Gledhill, 75–79. London: British Film Institute, 1987.

Mulvey, Laura. "Visual Pleasure and Narrative Cinema." *Screen* 16, no. 3 (1975): 6–18.

Naficy, Hamid. *An Accented Cinema: Exilic and Diasporic Filmmaking.* Princeton, N.J.: Princeton University Press, 2001.

Najman, Charles. "Surimpressions." *Cinématographe* 89 (1983): 34–35.

Neale, Steve. "Art Cinema as Institution." *Screen* 22, no. 1 (1981): 11–39.

Neale, Steve. "Melodrama and Tears." *Screen* 27, no. 6 (1986): 6–22.

Neergaard, Ebbe. *The Story of Danish Film.* Translated by Elsa Gress. Copenhagen: Det Danske Selskab, 1962.

Norris, David A. *In the Wake of the Balkan Myth: Questions of Identity and Modernity.* New York: St. Martin's Press, 1999.

Nowell-Smith, Geoffrey. "Minelli and Melodrama." In *Home Is Where the Heart Is: Studies in Melodrama and the Woman's Film,* edited by Christine Gledhill, 70–74. London: British Film Institute, 1987.

O'Pray, Michael. "Jan Svankmejer: A Mannerist Surrealist." In *Dark Alchemy: The Films of Jan Svankmejer,* edited by Peter Hames, 48–77. Westport, Conn.: Praeger, 1995.

Overbey, David, ed. *Springtime in Italy: A Reader in Neorealism.* Hamden, Conn.: Archon Books, 1979.

Petric, Duncan, ed. *Screening Europe: Image and Identity in Contemporary European Cinema.* London: British Film Institute, 1992.

Phillips, Andrew. "Decline and Fall." *Maclean's*, March 22, 1993, 22–24.

Piil, Morten. "Warmth and Irony, Solidarity and Satire." Translated by David Hohnen. In *Danish Films*, edited by Uffe Stormgaard and Sören Dyssegaard, 2–29. Copenhagen: Danish Film Institute, 1973.

Place, Janey. "Women in Film Noir." In *Women in Film Noir*, edited by E. Ann Kaplan, 35–67. London: British Film Institute, 1980.

Pritchard, Gareth. "National Identity in a United and Divided Germany." In *European Integration and Disintegration*, edited by Robert Bideleux and Richard Taylor, 154–73. London: Routledge, 1996.

Pronay, Nicholas. "'To Stamp Out the Whole Tradition . . .'" In *The Political Re-education of Germany and Her Allies After World War II*, edited by Nicholas Pronay and Keith Wilson, 1–36. Totowa, N.J.: Barnes and Noble Books, 1985.

Pryce, Ron. "The Maastricht Treaty and the New Europe." In *Maastricht and Beyond: Building the European Union*, edited by John Pinder, Andrew Duff, and Roy Pryce, 3–18. London: Routledge, 1994.

Radstone, Susannah. "Cinema/Memory/History." *Screen* 36, no. 1 (1995): 34–47.

Reader, Keith. "Reconstructing the Past Through Cinema: The Occupation of France." In *Reconstructing the Past: Representations of the Fascist Era in Post-War European Culture*, edited by Graham Bartram, Maureen Slawinski, and David Steel, 177–85. Keele, Eng.: Keele University Press, 1996.

Regourd, Serge. "Alain Finkielkraut et Jdanov." *Le Monde*, June 9, 1995, 16.

Restivo, Angelo. *The Cinema of Economic Miracles: Visuality and Modernization in the Italian Art Film.* Durham, N.C.: Duke University Press, 2002.

Rhodes, Martin, and Martin Bull. "Between Crisis and Transition: Italian Politics in the 1990s." *West European Politics* 20, no. 1 (1997): 1–13.

Rogin, Michael. "'Make My Day!': Spectacle as Amnesia in Imperial Politics." *Representations* 29 (1990): 99–123.

Rogoff, Irit. *Terra Infirma: Geography's Visual Culture.* London: Routledge, 2000.

Rosen, Philip. "The Concept of National Cinema in the 'New' Media Era." In *Historia general del cine: El cine en la era del audiovisual.* Vol. 12, edited by Manuel Palacio and Santos Zonzunegui. Madrid: Catedra, 1995.

Rothschild, Joseph, and Nancy M. Wingfield. *Return to Diversity: A Political History of East Central Europe Since World War II.* 3d ed. New York: Oxford University Press, 2000.

Ryder, A.J. *Twentieth-Century Germany: From Bismarck to Brandt.* New York: Columbia University Press, 1973.

Said, Edward W. *Orientalism.* New York: Random House, 1979.

Salecl, Renata. *The Spoils of Freedom: Psychoanalysis and Feminism After the Fall of Socialism.* London: Routledge, 1994.

Santner, Eric. *Stranded Objects: Mourning, Memory, and Film in Postwar Germany.* Ithaca, N.Y.: Cornell University Press, 1993.

Sassoon, Donald. "Tangentopoli or the Democratization of Corruption: Considerations on the End of Italy's First Republic." *Journal of Modern Italian Studies* 1, no. 1 (1995): 124–43.

Schivelbusch, Wolfgang. *In a Cold Crater: Cultural and Intellectual Life in Berlin, 1945–1948.* Translated by Kelly Barry. Berkeley: University of California Press, 1998.

Schneider, Roland. "1944–1951: Le néoréalisme italien." *CinémAction* 55 (1989): 47–57.

Sheridan, Michael. "Revolution Italian-Style." *Vanity Fair*, July 1993, 46–53.

Sitney, P. Adams. *Vital Crises in Italian Cinema: Iconography, Stylistics, Politics.* Austin: University of Texas Press, 1995.

Smith, Paul Julian. *The Moderns: Space, Time and Subjectivity in Contemporary Spanish Culture.* Oxford: Oxford University Press, 2000.

Søderbergh Widding, Astrid. "Denmark." In *Nordic National Cinemas*, edited by Tytti Soila, Astrid Søderbergh Widding, and Gunnar Iversen, 7–30. London: Routledge, 1998.

Soja, Edward. *Postmodern Geographies: The Reassertion of Space in Critical Social Theory.* New York: Verso, 1989.

Sorlin, Pierre. *European Cinemas, European Societies, 1939–1990.* London: Routledge, 1991.

Sorlin, Pierre. *Italian National Cinema, 1896–1996.* London: Routledge, 1996.

Spivak, Gayatri Chakravorty. "Subaltern Studies: Deconstructing Historiography." In *In Other Worlds: Essays in Cultural Politics*, 197–221. New York: Routledge, 1987.

Stavrianos, L. S. *The Balkans Since 1453.* New York: Holt, Rinehart and Winston, 1958.

Stille, Alexander. "Badfellas." *New Republic*, August 10, 1992, 12–13.

Stoker, Bram. *Dracula.* New York: Penguin, 1993.

Stormgaard, Uffe, and Sören Dyssegaard, eds. *Danish Films.* Copenhagen: Danish Film Institute, 1973.

Strain, Ellen. "Exotic Bodies, Distant Landscapes: Touristic Viewing and Popularized Anthropology in the Nineteenth Century." *Wide Angle* 18, no. 2 (1996): 70–100.

Teitelboim, Volodia. *Neruda: An Intimate Biography.* Translated by Beverly J. DeLong-Tonelli. Austin: University of Texas Press, 1991.

Todorova, Maria. "The Balkans: From Discovery to Invention." *Slavic Review* 53, no. 2 (1994): 453–82.

Todorova, Maria. *Imagining the Balkans.* London: Oxford University Press, 1997.

Toubiana, Serge. "L'Europe! l'europe! l'europe." *Cahiers du Cinéma* 455–456 (1992): 38.

Vernet, Marc. *Figures de l'absence.* Paris: Editions de l'Etoile, 1988.

Vernet, Marc. "The Filmic Transaction: On the Openings of Films Noirs." *Velvet Light Trap* 20 (1983): 2–9.

Viano, Maurizio. "*Life Is Beautiful*: Reception, Allegory, and Holocaust Laughter." *Jewish Social Studies* 5, no. 3 (1999): 47–66.

Vidler, Anthony. "Agoraphobia: Spatial Estrangement in Georg Simmel and Siegfried Kracauer." *New German Critique* 54 (1991): 31-46.

Vincendeau, Ginette, ed. *Encyclopedia of European Cinema*. London: British Film Institute, 1995.

Virilio, Paul. *The Vision Machine*. London: British Film Institute, 1994.

Wall, Bernard. *Italian Art, Life and Landscape*. Melbourne: Heinemann, 1956.

Warnke, Martin. *Political Landscape: The Art History of Nature*. Translated by David McLintock. London: Reaktion Books, 1994.

Waters, Sarah. "'Tangentopoli' and the Emergence of a New Political Order in Italy." *West European Politics* 17, no. 1 (1994): 169–82.

Wheeler, Mark. "Not so Black as It's Painted: The Balkan Political Heritage." In *The Changing Shape of the Balkans*, edited by F. W. Carter and H. T. Norris, 1–8. Boulder, Colo.: Westview Press, 1996.

Williams, Linda. "'Something Else Besides a Mother': *Stella Dallas* and the Maternal Melodrama." In *Home Is Where the Heart Is: Studies in Melodrama and the Woman's Film*, edited by Christine Gledhill, 299–325. London: British Film Institute, 1987.

Williams, Linda. *Hard Core: Power, Pleasure, and the "Frenzy of the Visible."* Berkeley: University of California Press, 1989.

Wiskemann, Elizabeth. *Italy Since 1945*. London: Macmillan, 1971.

Wood, Robin. "The Shadow Worlds of Jacques Tourneur." *Film Comment* 8, no. 2 (1972): 64–70.

Woolf, S .J., ed. *The Rebirth of Italy, 1943–50*. New York: Humanities Press, 1972.

Žižek, Slavoj. "A Leftist Plea for 'Eurocentrism.'" *Critical Inquiry* 24 (1998): 988–1009.

Žižek, Slavoj. "Multiculturalism, or the Cultural Logic of Multinational Capitalism." *New Left Review* 225 (1997): 28–51.

# Filmography

Published sources may offer disparate titles and years for foreign films. This filmography uses the following format:

*U.S. release title or, where none, standard English translation/domestic release title or titles* (director or directors, country or countries of production, year of first theatrical release)

*The Adventures of Felix/Drôle de Félix* (Olivier Ducastel and Jacques Martineau, France, 2000)
*The Age of Innocence* (Martin Scorsese, United States, 1993)
*Aimée and Jaguar* (Max Färberböck, Germany, 1999)
*Air Hostess/Kong zhong xiao jie* (Yi Wen, Hong Kong, 1959)
*Alone/Sam* (Vladimir Pogacić, Yugoslavia, 1959)
*Alphaville, a Strange Adventure of Lemmy Caution/Alphaville, une étrange adventure de Lemmy Caution* (Jean-Luc Godard, France/Italy, 1965)
*Amarcord* (Federico Fellini, Italy/France, 1973)
*Autumn Moon/Qiuyue* (Clara Law, Hong Kong/Japan, 1992)
*¡Ay, Carmela!* (Carlos Saura, Spain/Italy, 1990)
*Backbeat* (Iain Softley, United Kingdom/Germany, 1994)
*The Basque Ball: Skin Against Stone/Pelota vasca: La piel contra la piedra* (Julio Medem, Spain, 2003)
*Beau Travail* (Claire Denis, France, 2000)
*Beautiful People* (Jasmin Dizdar, United Kingdom, 1999)
*Before the Rain/Pred dozhdot* (Milcho Manchevski, Republic of Macedonia/ France/United Kingdom, 1994)
*Belle Epoque/Belle Époque* (Fernando Trueba, Spain/Portugal/France, 1992)
*Berlin Express* (Jacques Tourneur, United States, 1948)
*Berlin in Berlin* (Sinan Çetin, Turkey/Germany, 1994)

*Berlin.killer.doc* (Bettina Ellerkamp and Jörg Heitman, Germany, 1999)

*Between Yesterday and Tomorrow/Zwischen Gestern und Morgen* (Harald Braun, Germany, 1947)

*Bhaji on the Beach* (Gurinder Chadha, United Kingdom, 1993)

*The Bicycle Thief/Ladri di biciclette* (Vittorio De Sica, Italy, 1948)

*Bitter Rice/Riso amaro* (Giuseppe De Santis, Italy, 1949)

*Black Narcissus* (Michael Powell and Emeric Pressburger, United Kingdom, 1947)

*Blue/Trois couleurs: Bleu/Trzy kolory: Niebieski* (Krzysztof Kieślowski, France/Poland/Switzerland/United Kingdom, 1993)

*A Brighter Summer Day/Guling jie shaonian sharen shijian* (Edward Yang, Taiwan, 1991)

*Buttoners/Knoflíkári* (Petr Zelenka, Czech Republic, 1997)

*The Cabinet of Doctor Caligari/Das Kabinett des Doktor Caligari* (Robert Weine, Germany, 1920)

*Calendar* (Atom Egoyan, Canada/Armenia/Germany, 1993)

*Camille Claudel* (Bruno Nuytten, France, 1988)

*Caravaggio* (Derek Jarman, United Kingdom, 1986)

*Cat People* (Jacques Tourneur, United States, 1942)

*The Celebration/Festen/Dogme #1—Festen* (Thomas Vinterberg, Denmark/Sweden, 1998)

*Cheb* (Rachid Bouchareb, Algeria/France, 1991)

*Chico* (Ibolya Fekete, Germany/Croatia/Hungary/Chile, 2002)

*Chocolat* (Claire Denis, France/West Germany/Cameroon, 1988)

*Christ Stopped at Eboli/Cristo si è fermato a Eboli* (Francesco Rosi, Italy/France, 1979)

*Cinema Paradiso/Nuovo cinema Paradiso* (Giuseppe Tornatore, Italy/France, 1988)

*The Conformist/Il conformista* (Bernardo Bertolucci, Italy/France/West Germany, 1970)

*Dark Blue World/Tmavomodrý svet* (Jan Sverák, Czech Republic/United Kingdom/Germany/Denmark/Italy, 2001)

*Day of Wrath/Vredens dag* (Carl Theodor Dreyer, Denmark, 1943)

*Days of Hope* (Ken Loach, United Kingdom television, 1975)

*Delicatessen* (Jean-Pierre Jeunet and Marc Caro, France, 1991)

*Difficult Years/Anni difficili* (Luigi Zampa, Italy, 1948)

*Distant Voices, Still Lives* (Terence Davies, United Kingdom, 1988)

*Divided We Fall/Musíme si pomáhat* (Jan Hrebejk, Czech Republic, 2000)

*La dolce vita* (Federico Fellini, Italy/France, 1960)

*Dr. Petiot/Docteur Petiot* (Christian de Chalonge, France, 1990)

*The Earth Trembles/La terra trema/La terra trema: La episodio del mare* (Luchino Visconti, Italy, 1948)

*Edward II* (Derek Jarman, United Kingdom, 1991)

*Enchanted April* (Mike Newell, United Kingdom, 1992)

*The English Patient* (Anthony Minghella, United States, 1996)

*Europa Europa/Hitlerjunge Salomon* (Agnieszka Holland, Germany/France/Poland, 1990)

*A Foreign Affair* (Billy Wilder, United States, 1948)

*Forrest Gump* (Robert Zemeckis, United States, 1994)

*From the East/D'Est* (Chantal Akerman, Belgium/France/Portugal, 1993)

*Germany, Pale Mother/Deutschland bleiche Mutter* (Helma Sanders-Brahms, West Germany, 1980)

*Germany Year Zero/Germania anno zero* (Roberto Rossellini, Italy/Germany/France, 1948)

*Gertrud* (Carl Theodor Dreyer, Denmark, 1964)

*Golden Balls/Huevos de oro* (J. J. Bigas Luna, Spain/Italy/France, 1993)

*Gone with the Wind* (Victor Fleming, United States, 1939)

*Hate/La Haine* (Mathieu Kassovitz, France, 1995)

*Hawks and Sparrows/Uccellacci e uccellini* (Pier Paolo Pasolini, Italy, 1966)

*Head-On/Gegen die Wand/Duvara karsi* (Fatih Akin, Germany/Turkey, 2004)

*Hedd Wyn* (Paul Turner, United Kingdom, 1992)

*Hey Cousin!/Salut Cousin!* (Merzak Allouache, France/Algeria/Belgium/Luxembourg, 1996)

*Hitler: A Film from Germany/Hitler—ein Film aus Deutschland* (Hans-Jürgen Syberberg, West Germany, 1978)

*The Hole/Dong* (Tsai Ming-Liang, Taiwan/France, 1999)

*The House of Mirth* (Terence Davies, United Kingdom/France/Germany/United States, 2000)

*Howards End* (James Ivory, United Kingdom/Japan, 1992)

*Icicle Thief/Ladri di saponette* (Maurizio Nichetti, Italy, 1989)

*Immortal Youth/Besmrtna mladost* (Vojislav Nanović, Yugoslavia, 1948)

*In the Mood for Love/Fa yeung nin wa* (Wong Kar-wai, Hong Kong/France/Thailand, 2000)

*In the Name of the Law/In nome della legge* (Pietro Germi, Italy, 1949)

*Independence Day* (Roland Emmerich, United States, 1996)

*Italian for Beginners/Dogme #12—Italiensk for begyndere* (Lone Scherfig, Denmark/Sweden, 2000)

*Jamón, jamón* (J. J. Bigas Luna, Spain, 1992)

*Jaws* (Steven Spielberg, United States, 1975)

*Jean de Florette* (Claude Berri, France/Switzerland/Italy, 1986)

*JFK* (Oliver Stone, United States, 1991)

*Khrustalyov, My Car!/Khrustalyov, mashinu!* (Aleksei Gherman, Russia/France, 1999)

*Kon-Tiki* (Thor Heyerdahl, Norway/Sweden, 1950)

*Kozara* (Veljko Bulajić, Yugoslavia, 1963)

*The Krays* (Peter Medak, United Kingdom, 1990)

*Lacombe, Lucien/Lacombe Lucien* (Louis Malle, France/West Germany/Italy, 1974)

*Land and Freedom/Tierra y libertad* (Ken Loach, United Kingdom/Spain/Germany/Italy, 1995)

*The Last Metro/Le Dernier Métro* (François Truffaut, France, 1980)

*The Last Seduction* (John Dahl, United States, 1994)

*Letter from an Unknown Woman* (Max Ophüls, United States, 1948)

*Life Is Beautiful/La vita è bella* (Roberto Benigni, Italy, 1997)

*Lilya 4-ever/Lilja 4-ever* (Lukas Moodysson, Sweden/Denmark, 2002)

*The Long Day Closes* (Terence Davies, United Kingdom, 1992)

*Look Back in Anger* (Tony Richardson, United Kingdom, 1958)

*Lovers of the Arctic Circle/Los amantes del Círculo Polar* (Julio Medem, Spain/France, 1998)

*The Lovers on the Bridge/Les Amants du Pont-Neuf* (Leos Carax, France, 1991)

*The Lower Depths/Les Bas-fonds* (Jean Renoir, France, 1936)

*M/M—Eine Stadt sucht einen Mörder* (Fritz Lang, Germany, 1931)

*Mambo Girl/Man bo nu lang* (Yi Wen, Hong Kong, 1957)

*Manon of the Spring/Manon des sources* (Claude Berri, France/Italy/Switzerland, 1986)

*Marriage in the Shadows/Ehe im Schatten* (Kurt Maetzig, Germany, 1947)

*The Marriage of Maria Braun/Die Ehe der Maria Braun* (Rainer Werner Fassbinder, West Germany, 1979)

*Maurice* (James Ivory, United Kingdom, 1987)

*Mediterraneo* (Gabriele Salvatores, Italy, 1991)

*Mifune/Dogme #3—Mifunes sidste sang* (Søren Kragh-Jacobsen, Denmark/Sweden, 1999)

*Mildred Pierce* (Michael Curtiz, United States, 1945)

*Miller's Crossing* (Joel Coen, United States, 1990)

*Miracle in Milan/Miracolo a Milano* (Vittorio De Sica, Italy, 1951)

*The Morning/Jutro* (Mladomir "Puriša" Đorđević, Yugoslavia, 1967)

*Murderers Among Us/Die Mörder sind unter uns* (Wolfgang Staudte, Germany, 1946)

*My Friend Ivan Lapshin/Moy drug Ivan Lapshin* (Aleksei Gherman, Soviet Union, 1985 [completed in 1982 but shelved for three years])

*My Life as a Dog/Mitt liv som hund* (Lasse Hallström, Sweden, 1985)

*The Night Porter/Il portiere di notte* (Liliana Cavani, Italy/United States, 1974)

*On Their Own Ground/Na svoji zemlji* (France Štiglić, Yugoslavia, 1948)

*Ordet* (Carl Theodor Dreyer, Denmark, 1955)

*Orlando* (Sally Potter, United Kingdom/Russia/France/Italy/Netherlands, 1992)

*Our Friends in the North* (Simon Cellan Jones, Pedr James, and Stuart Urban, United Kingdom television, 1996)

*Out of the Past* (Jacques Tourneur, United States, 1947)

*Paisan/Paisà* (Roberto Rossellini, Italy, 1946)

*Partisan Stories/Partizanske priče* (Stole Janković, Yugoslavia, 1960)

*A Passage to India* (David Lean, United Kingdom/United States, 1984)

*Passion* (Jean-Luc Godard, France/Switzerland, 1982)

*The Patriotic Woman/Die Patriotin* (Alexander Kluge, West Germany, 1979)

*The Pillow Book* (Peter Greenaway, United Kingdom/France/Netherlands, 1996)

*The Ploughman's Lunch* (Richard Eyre, United Kingdom, 1983)

*The Postman/Il Postino* (Michael Radford, Italy/France/Belgium, 1994)

*The Powder Keg/Cabaret Balkan/Bure Baruta* (Goran Paskaljević, Yugoslavia/Macedonia/France/Greece/Turkey, 1998)

*Pretty Village, Pretty Flame/Lepa sela lepo gore* (Srđan Dragojević, Yugoslavia, 1996)

*Prospero's Books* (Peter Greenaway, United Kingdom/France/Netherlands/Italy/Japan, 1991)

*Pure Blood* (Ken Kaplan, South Africa, 2000)

*¡Que Viva Mexico!/Da zdravstvuyet Meksika!* (Sergei Eisenstein, Soviet Union/ United States/Mexico, 1932 [unfinished])

*Queen Margot/La Reine Margot* (Patrice Chéreau, France/Italy/Germany, 1994)

*Reassemblage* (Trinh T. Minh Ha, United States, 1982)

*Rebels of the Neon God/Ching shao nien nacha* (Tsai Ming-Liang, Taiwan, 1992)

*Red/Trois couleurs: Rouge/Trzy kolory: Czerwony* (Krzysztof Kieślowski, Poland/ France/Switzerland, 1994)

*Rome, Open City/Roma, città aperta* (Roberto Rossellini, Italy, 1945)

*A Room with a View* (James Ivory, United Kingdom, 1985)

*Rosencrantz and Guildenstern Are Dead* (Tom Stoppard, United Kingdom/United States, 1990)

*Saving Private Ryan* (Steven Spielberg, United States, 1998)

*Schindler's List* (Steven Spielberg, United States, 1993)

*Shakespeare in Love* (John Madden, United Kingdom/United States, 1998)

*Slavica* (Vjekoslav Afrić, Yugoslavia, 1947)

*Spellbound* (Alfred Hitchcock, United States, 1945)

*Stavisky* (Alain Resnais, France/Italy, 1974)

*Steam: The Turkish Bath/Hamam* (Ferzan Ozpetek, Italy/Turkey/Spain, 1997)

*Storm over Asia/Potomok Chingis-Khana* (Vsevolod Pudovkin, Soviet Union, 1928)

*Story of Women/Une affaire de femmes* (Claude Chabrol, France, 1988)

*The Sun Is Far Away/Daleko je sunce* (Rados Novaković, Yugoslavia, 1953)

*The Superfluous Girl/Prekobrojna* (Branko Bauer, Yugoslavia, 1962)

*Tabu* (F. W. Murnau, United States, 1931)

*Taipei Story/Qingmei zhuma* (Edward Yang, Taiwan, 1985)

*The Terrorizer/Kongbu fenzi* (Edward Yang, Taiwan/Hong Kong, 1986)

*The Third Man* (Carol Reed, United Kingdom, 1949)

*This People Must Live/Živjeće ovaj narod* (Nikola Popović, Yugoslavia, 1947)

*Three/Tri* (Aleksandar Petrović, Yugoslavia, 1965)

*The Tit and the Moon/La teta i la lluna* (J. J. Bigas Luna, Spain/France, 1994)

*Tito and Me/Tito i ja* (Goran Marković, Yugoslavia, 1992)

*Toto the Hero/Toto le héros* (Jaco Van Dormael, France/Belgium/Germany, 1991)

*The Town Is Quiet/La Ville est tranquille* (Robert Guédiguian, France, 2001)

*Tragic Hunt/Caccia tragica* (Giuseppe De Santis, Italy, 1947)

*Ulysses' Gaze/To Vlemma tou Odyssea* (Theo Angelopolous, Greece/France/ Italy, 1995)

*Umberto D.* (Vittorio De Sica, Italy, 1952)

*Underground/Bila jednom jedna zemlja* (Emir Kusturica, Yugoslavia/France/ Germany/Hungary, 1995)

*The Usual Suspects* (Bryan Singer, United States, 1995)

*Videograms of a Revolution/Videogramme einer Revolution* (Harun Farocki and Andrei Ujica, Germany, 1992)

*La Vie de Bohème/Boheemielämää* (Aki Kaurismäki, Finland/France/Italy/Sweden, 1992)

*Vive l'amour/Aiqing wansui* (Tsai Ming-Liang, Taiwan, 1994)

*Welcome to Sarajevo* (Michael Winterbottom, United Kingdom/United States, 1997)

*What Have I Done to Deserve This?*/*¿Qué he hecho yo para merecer esto?!!* (Pedro Almodóvar, Spain, 1984)

*When Father Was Away on Business*/*Otac na službenom putu* (Emir Kusturica, Yugoslavia, 1985)

*When I Close My Eyes*/*Lo zaprem oči* (Franci Slak, Slovenia, 1993)

*When You Hear the Bells*/*Kad čuješ zvona* (Antun Vrdoljak, Yugoslavia, 1969)

*Whirlpool* (Otto Preminger, United States, 1949)

*White*/*Trois couleurs: Blanc*/*Trzy kolory: Biały* (Krzysztof Kieślowski, France/Poland/Switzerland/United Kingdom, 1994)

*White Shadows in the South Seas* (W. S. Van Dyke, United States, 1928)

*The Wild, Wild Rose*/*Ye mei gui zhi lian* (Wang Tian-lin, Hong Kong, 1959)

*The Wolf Man* (George Waggner, United States, 1941)

*The Wounds*/*Rane* (Srđjan Dragojević, Yugoslavia/Germany, 1998)

*Zelig* (Woody Allen, United States, 1983)

*Zentropa*/*Europa* (Lars von Trier, Denmark/Sweden/France/Germany/Switzerland, 1991)

# Index